Exploring World History
Part 2

The Renaissance to the Present

*For all those who have in any way shared the sacred and imperishable gospel
with those from every tribe and tongue and people and nation (Revelation 5:9).
You have helped to fulfill God's plan for mankind and have offered hope where there was none.*

Exploring World History Part 2
Ray Notgrass with Charlene Notgrass and John Notgrass

ISBN 978-1-60999-062-6

Copyright © 2014 Notgrass Company. All rights reserved.
No part of this material may be reproduced without permission from the publisher.

This book is licensed for sale only in the United States of America.

Previous Page: Seoul, South Korea, 2011

Front Cover Images: London (Gabriel Vallina / Flickr / CC-BY-2.0), Johannes Gutenberg, Chinese Boy (Bertha Boynton Lum / Library of Congress), Napoleon (N. Currier / Library of Congress), Queen Victoria (George Hayter), Crown Prince of Thailand, c. 1900 (Library of Congress). *Back Cover Image:* Pagoda in Bukit Panjang New Town, Singapore (kewl / Flickr / CC-BY-2.0). *Author Photo:* Mary Evelyn McCurdy.

All product names, brands, and other trademarks mentioned or pictured
in this book are used for educational purposes only.
No association with or endorsement by the owners of the trademarks is intended.
Each trademark remains the property of its respective owner.

Unless otherwise noted, scripture quotations taken from the New American Standard Bible,
Copyright 1960, 1962, 1963, 1971, 1972, 1973, 1975, 1977, 1995
by the Lockman Foundation Used by permission.
See the Credits for other sources of Bible quotations.

Cover design by Mary Evelyn McCurdy
Interior design by John Notgrass

Printed in the United States of America

Notgrass Company
975 Roaring River Road
Gainesboro, TN 38562

1-800-211-8793
www.notgrass.com
books@notgrass.com

Detail from The Battle of San Romano, *Paolo Uccello (Italian, c. 1440)*

Table of Contents

16 The Renaissance 435

76 - A Different Focus 437
77 - Key Event: The Invention of the Printing Press 443
78 - Key Person: Leonardo da Vinci 449
79 - Everyday Life: A History of Western Music 454
80 - Bible Study: Worldliness vs. Godliness 461

17 The Age of Reformation 465

81 - Martin Luther and the Break with Rome 467
82 - Key Person: John Calvin 473
83 - Key Movement: The Anabaptists 477
84 - History of the English Bible 481
85 - Bible Study: Grace 488

18 The Age of Exploration 493

86 - Discovering New Worlds 495
87 - Key Person: Christopher Columbus 502
88 - Key Event: The English Defeat of the Spanish Armada 507
89 - Everyday Life: Homes and Household Furnishings 511
90 - Bible Study: Exploring the Promised Land 515

17th-Century World Map

Johannes Kepler, German Scientist (1571-1630)

19 The Scientific Revolution 519

- 91 - A New View 521
- 92 - Key Event: The Heresy Trial of Galileo Galilei 527
- 93 - Key Person: Isaac Newton 531
- 94 - Everyday Life: Clothing Through the Centuries 535
- 95 - Bible Study: The Value of Life 541

20 The Age of Revolution 545

- 96 - Revolutions in England and America 547
- 97 - Key Event: The French Revolution 553
- 98 - Key Person: John Locke 561
- 99 - Everyday Life: Eating Through the Centuries 566
- 100 - Bible Study: Freedom and Responsibility 573

21 The Making of Modern Europe 577

- 101 - Key Person: Napoleon 579
- 102 - Revolution, Reaction, and Reorganization 584
- 103 - Key Event: Unification in Italy and Germany 591
- 104 - Everyday Life: A Short History of Western Art 599
- 105 - Bible Study: Honesty 605

22 Britain: Industry and Empire 609

- 106 - Britain in the 19th Century 611
- 107 - Key Issue: The Irish Question 619
- 108 - Key Person: George Müller 623
- 109 - Everyday Life: A History of Transportation 629
- 110 - Bible Study: Kindness 637

23 A Revolution in Thought 641

- 111 - Karl Marx 643
- 112 - Charles Darwin 649
- 113 - Sigmund Freud 656
- 114 - Everyday Life: Education and the Work of John Dewey 661
- 115 - Bible Study: Higher Criticism 667

Russian Revolution, 1917

Table of Contents

24 The World at War 671

116 - The Great War 673
117 - World War II 681
118 - Key Person: Winston Churchill 689
119 - Everyday Life: The Cultural History of Japan 693
120 - Bible Study: Peace 699

25 The Cold War 705

121 - Freedom vs. Communism 707
122 - Key Event: The Space Race 713
123 - Key Person: Ronald Reagan 719
124 - Everyday Life: The U.S. and the U.S.S.R. 723
125 - Bible Study: Fighting the Good Fight 731

26 The Making of Modern Asia 735

126 - China: From Dynasties to Communism 737
127 - India: A Clash of Cultures 743
128 - Japan, Korea, and Southeast Asia 749
129 - Christian Missionaries to Asia 755
130 - Bible Study: Helping the Poor 759

27 The Making of Modern Latin America 763

131 - Many Countries, One Goal 765
132 - Mexico's Story 772
133 - Key Person: Simón Bolívar 777
134 - Everyday Life: Indigenous Peoples of Latin America 781
135 - Bible Study: Justice 786

Plaza de la Independencia, Granada, Nicaragua

A man in South Sudan captures the day's festivities as his country becomes officially independent on July 9, 2011.

28 The Making of Modern Africa 791

- 136 - European Colonization 793
- 137 - Ethiopia 799
- 138 - Everyday Life: The Culture of the Maasai 803
- 139 - South Africa 807
- 140 - Bible Study: Africa in the Bible 813

29 Into the 21st Century 817

- 141 - Technology and Trade 819
- 142 - The Making of the Modern Middle East 824
- 143 - Key Persons: The Homeschooling Family 831
- 144 - Everyday Life: A History of Keeping Time 835
- 145 - Bible Study: Modern Church History 841

30 Looking Backward, Looking Forward 847

- 146 - How Christianity Changed the World 849
- 147 - Lessons from World History 855
- 148 - Living in the Modern World 861
- 149 - Becoming a World Christian 866
- 150 - Bible Study: Eternity After This World 871

Credits 875

Index 881

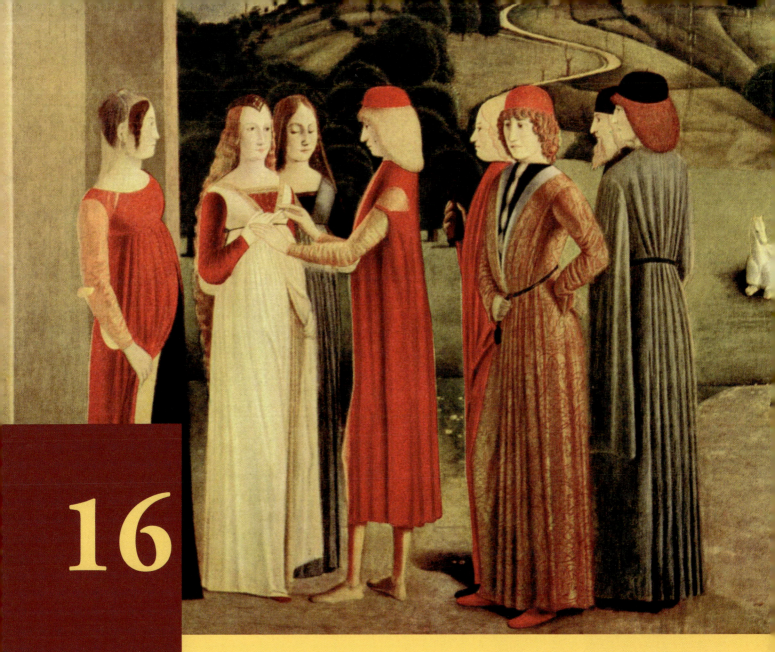

16

The Renaissance

Summary — The Renaissance saw significant scientific investigation of the world and a blossoming of artistic expression. New ways of thinking challenged the traditional perspective that saw God at the center of life. The invention of printing opened up new possibilities for widespread learning and sharing of ideas. Leonardo da Vinci was the classic Renaissance man, with interests and abilities in many areas. Also in this unit, we give an overview of music. In the Bible study, we contrast worldliness and godliness.

Lessons
76 - A Different Focus
77 - Key Event: The Invention of the Printing Press
78 - Key Person: Leonardo da Vinci
79 - Everyday Life: A History of Western Music
80 - Bible Study: Worldliness vs. Godliness

The Betrothal *(Italian, c. 1470)*

Memory Work

Learn Psalm 150 by the end of the unit.

Books Used

The Bible
In Their Words
Here I Stand

Project (choose one)

1) Write 300 to 500 words on one of the following topics:
   - Analyze a painting by one of the well-known Renaissance artists, such as the *Mona Lisa* or *The Last Supper*. Tell what you think is effective in the painting and why it is still admired.
   - Tell what both science and art contribute to a culture, why we need both, and how they work together and compliment each other. See Lesson 76.
2) Attend a concert with music by one of the composers mentioned in Lesson 79. If this is not possible, listen to recordings of the work of four of them, at least fifteen minutes per composer. Your local library should have a collection of recordings.
3) Conduct further research on Leonardo da Vinci's skill and achievement and create a poster that celebrates his life and includes examples of his achievements, experiments, and ideas. See Lesson 78.

Optional Research Paper: If you plan to write a longer research paper as part of this course, plan with a parent when you will work on it. See pages xii-xv of Part 1.

Literature

For the next three units, you will read Roland Bainton's classic biography of Martin Luther, *Here I Stand*. This is history as it should be written: a well-trained scholar who loves the Lord, the church, and his subject. You will gain insights into Luther and his times, and you will derive an understanding of the swirl of people and events that surrounded Luther's historic break with the Roman Catholic Church. We will discuss the Protestant Reformation in Unit 17.

A word of encouragement: You might feel a bit lost with all of the names and the various doctrinal positions that Bainton gives in this book. You might have a hard time keeping up with who agreed with whom and who opposed whom. Try not to worry about that level of detail; instead, get the big picture of what the key issues were and who the main players were. At this Bainton does an excellent job.

Bainton was born in England in 1894 but lived in the United States from the age of eight. For over forty years he was professor of church history at Yale University. Bainton wrote several other books on church history, many of them on the Reformation period. He died in 1984.

Hans and Margarethe Luther, Martin's Parents

Ceiling of the Sistine Chapel

Lesson 76

A Different Focus

The European Renaissance (French for rebirth), generally dated from about 1300 to 1650, saw many changes and new ways of looking at the world. The nature and rapidity of change made it appear as though the very underpinnings of society were coming loose, even though the trends leading to these changes had been developing for some time.

Causes of the Renaissance

Several factors contributed to these changes. Contact with the Byzantine and Islamic cultures, brought on by increased trade and by the Crusades, opened up a new world of thinking and re-introduced the old world of the Greeks and Romans to Europe. Increased trade made more wealth available to Europeans, wealth which could be used for many different purposes. The growth of cities created centers of learning and artistic activity.

The European economy was changing. Europe had long had an agricultural economy in which nobles oversaw their individual manors where serfs worked the fields. Europeans became more involved in international trade in which merchants bought and sold many items, including spices, jewels, and silk and wool fabrics.

Social Upheaval

Changes in climate in the early 1300s led to poor harvests, which caused widespread famine. In 1320 peasants in France declared a revolution to throw down the nobility and establish a Christian commonwealth. Agricultural serfs and the urban poor attacked castles and monasteries. The pope condemned the uprisings, and small armies of knights on horseback wiped out the desperate mobs. A similar French uprising in 1358 involved perhaps one hundred thousand working poor. English peasants revolted in 1381. None of these efforts bettered the lives of peasants.

The Ottoman Turks became a major power in 1299. They captured Constantinople in 1453 and made it the capital of their Muslim empire. This ended the last vestige of the Roman Empire. Turkish control extended into Eastern Europe and the Balkans. Conflict between Muslims and Orthodox Christians in the region has continued until today.

The most calamitous event of this period, however, was the Black Plague, which peaked in the mid-13th century. The Plague killed perhaps a third of the European population. Many people saw the disease as a punishment from God.

Miracle of the Relic of the Cross at the Ponte di Rialto, Vittore Carpaccio (Italian, c. 1496). *In the 14th century, a purported piece of the cross of Christ, thought to have miraculous powers, had been donated to a group in Venice, Italy. This painting illustrates a scene showing an attempted healing in the upper left, but it also depicts the bustling commercial activity of the city.*

An Economic Revolution

Italian merchants came to dominate trade in the Mediterranean during the 11th and 12th centuries. They invested much of their profit back into their businesses and made even more money. These were the first capitalists, who used investment capital to increase their profits. Merchants in the Hanseatic League of cities in northern Europe gained control of trade on the Baltic by pooling their resources. They built trading ships and made trade agreements with foreign nations. Dutch and Belgian traders profited from trade with Germany, Italy, and England.

Lesson 76 - A Different Focus

The increase in credit arrangements, business investments, and the use of bills of exchange all contributed to the rise of the banking industry. The Medici family in Italy became a powerful economic and political force through their banks. Jacob Fugger in Augsburg, Germany became the wealthiest European banker. He reaped profits from mining activities in his area and opened branch banks throughout Europe.

International trade spelled the end of the medieval trade guilds in Europe. The guilds had limited markets, limited power, and limited surplus capital. Merchant companies, often organized as family partnerships, developed a system whereby they bought raw materials such as wool directly from the growers, paid workers to make fabric and clothing, and then sold the products to foreign buyers. The merchants thus controlled the entire process of production from raw materials to finished goods. This made obsolete the apprentice-journeyman-master system of local markets and small profits.

With the new money-based economy, nobles found it to their advantage to free the serfs and make them tenants who rented the land for cash instead of a portion of the crop. Tenants could sell their own portion at local markets for cash. This gave the former serfs greater freedom, but they risked being put off the land if the noble did not find their work as tenants profitable. The capitalist system thus extended even into rural areas. By 1500 serfdom was gone from England and rare in western Europe.

All of society seemed more fluid and subject to change. Some wealthy merchants bought manorial estates, and some nobles became urban businessmen. Children of the nobility and of merchants began to intermarry. Serfs were gaining their freedom. A sense of greater possibilities for peoples' lives grew in Europe.

Political Changes

Generally speaking, European countries developed into centralized nation states with more powerful kings. Such arrangements provided more social and political stability. This also made investment in trade and exploration more possible. However, Italy, the leading influence of the Renaissance, did not have a unified national government.

Italian unification was hindered by several factors. The pope and the Holy Roman Emperor repeatedly clashed over control of the peninsula. The papacy saw unification as a threat to the autonomy of the Papal States. In addition, Italy had a tradition of strong independent city-states that continued into the Renaissance. These city-states were the legacy of the estates of landowners during the late Roman Empire.

A Glass of Wine with Caesar Borgia, *John Collier (English, 1893). This painting illustrates the intrigues and immorality that plagued Renaissance Italy. Cesare Borgia (left) is shown pouring wine for the young man on the right. His sister Lucrezia stands beside him. The man seated in red is Pope Alexander VI. He fathered Cesare, Lucrezia, and two other children by one of his several mistresses before he became pope. The painting gives the impression that Cesare is poisoning the young man; such an act would not be out of character for members of the Borgia family.*

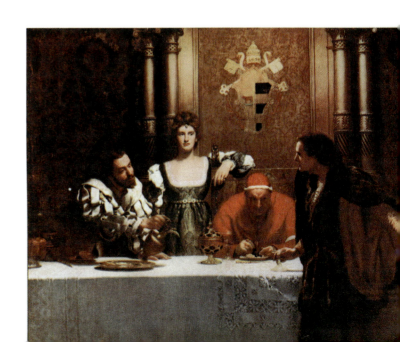

Pope Julius II called on Donato Bramante to design Saint Peter's Basilica in 1506. After Bramante's death and work by other architects, Michelangelo received the commission. He designed the impressive dome. The Basilica was finally consecrated in 1626.

The political leaders of Italy during the Renaissance were the powerful rulers of the city-states and wealthy, influential families such as the Medicis and the Borgias. Through their financial power, the Medicis exerted significant influence in politics even though few held any office. Pope Alexander VI, a member of the Borgia family, was known for his ruthlessness and immorality.

Conflicts among various factions in the city-states, usually led by rival bankers or wealthy families, led to instability. Strong men called despots gained control and established order. Professional soldiers known as *condottieri* hired out as mercenary police forces to whoever made the best offer. In this setting of uncertainty, many wanted to see an effective, unified government. Among these was Niccolo Machiavelli, whose book *The Prince*, published in 1513, was intended to be a manual for whatever despot might rise to rule all of Italy.

Machiavelli did not hold to the traditional belief that government was an agent of God. To him, rulers were simply concerned with peace and prosperity; and however they accomplished this was acceptable. Because he thought the people were unreliable, he argued that the ruler must be strong and maintain an effective army. Whatever enabled the ruler (whom Machiavelli called the Prince) to maintain his strength was the right thing to do; hence, in Machiavelli's thinking, the end justified the means. He thought it was especially effective for a leader to appear one way but actually be another, since the populace would often be fooled by this.

Humanism

The major change in thinking that took place in the Renaissance was the shift from a focus on God to a focus on man. The other-worldly thoughts of the Middle Ages were replaced by a strong focus on this world. Although many artists, scientists, and other cultural leaders were believers, an increasing number of them did not emphasize God in their work. Instead, they explored various aspects of human life and made it the center of their endeavors. Patrons of the arts did not sponsor individuals to study theology or to evangelize people. Instead, they tended to support artists who exercised their talents and pursued their interests without regard for their spiritual priorities.

Several reasons lay behind this change. Disappointing events such as the Crusades and the Inquisition as well as the worldliness of the Roman Catholic Church turned many against honoring the way of God. The medieval values of piety, prayer, and poverty held little appeal compared to the attraction of increasing wealth and the possibilities for material advancement through hard work and wise investment. The code of chivalry, with its emphasis on duty, honor, and family, was replaced by the middle class ethic of business, thriftiness, and profit. In addition, the rediscovery of ancient pagan writers such as Plato turned many away from the study of Scripture.

Growing interest in ancient civilizations and languages and the increasing availability of books led to changes in education. Schools were no longer just for the training of priests. Academies were established in many cities, and Latin and Greek were added to the curricula. Usually this formal education was for boys only; girls continued to be trained at home. The social ideal changed from the medieval knight to the refined and educated gentleman.

Lesson 76 - A Different Focus

Italians saw themselves as cultural descendants of the Roman Empire. Although it was the home of the papacy, Italy was more secular in its thinking than much of Europe. It had significant Muslim and Byzantine influences, and the peninsula enjoyed great wealth from its international commerce. We will look at literature, art, and music from the period in the next three lessons. In Unit 19 we will study scientific developments that began during the Renaissance.

The Role of the Church

During the Renaissance, the Roman Catholic Church lost its position as the dominant force in European society. Catholics continued to worship God and to serve their local communities in many positive ways. However, when some Church leaders acted in worldly ways, the ability of the Church to influence the world for the Lord diminished.

Thomas Aquinas built a bridge between reason and revelation when those two approaches seemed in conflict. In northern Europe, many Christian scholars wanted to find a way to be both Christians and humanists. Desiderius Erasmus encouraged this as much as or more than anyone.

Erasmus was born in 1466 in Rotterdam, the Netherlands, the illegitimate son of a priest. The school he attended was operated by an order of monks who emphasized living by the example of Jesus in service and love. This outlook, what Erasmus called the "philosophy of Jesus," became the guide for his entire life. He was ordained a priest but spent most of his life researching and writing.

The scholar Erasmus saw the value of studying both God and man. He thought that a broad education could help a person in his walk with God. Erasmus believed that Christians could benefit from knowing the lives of such ancients as Socrates, Plato, and Cicero.

At the same time, he studied Greek to know the New Testament better. He published a Greek New Testament in 1516 based on his studies of Greek manuscripts known at the time. He also produced a Latin translation of the New Testament because he believed that the Bible should be accessible to as many people as possible.

Erasmus appreciated the good he saw in the Church, but he did not just accept things as they were. He wanted to rid the Church of pride, hypocrisy, selfishness, and worldliness. His 1509 work *The Praise of Folly* ridiculed human failings and man's tendency to appreciate foolishness more than serious matters. He directed his sharpest attacks against folly that he saw in the Church. After the Protestant Reformation began, he remained a loyal Catholic and opposed Martin Luther in a desire to preserve the unity of the Church.

Dutch artist Hendrick de Keyser designed this statue of Erasmus. It was cast by Jan Cornelisz Ourderogge and put on display in Rotterdam in 1622 outside the Church of St. Lawrence.

The Passing of the Renaissance

The burst of creativity that characterized the Renaissance slowed during the 17th century. Spain, Portugal, France, England, and the Netherlands had established colonies in the New World of North and South America. This hurt Italian trade. Political instability and fewer financial resources prevented Italians from pursuing Renaissance endeavors as they once had.

The Renaissance was a mixture of good and bad. Education became more widely available, and many lives were enriched by broader educational opportunities. The loosening of the grip of feudalism enabled more individuals to use their God-given talents to honor Him and bless others. The power of the Roman Catholic Church began to weaken, and the stage was set for the dramatic changes of the Reformation. We are inspired and amazed by the accomplishments of talented Renaissance artists.

On the other hand, the exercising of human talent was not always kept under the Lordship of Christ. The way of secularism came to influence and sometimes dominate human life. International trade sought greater profits but did not always follow godly principles. As heirs of the Renaissance legacy, we must separate the good from the bad, appreciate what is worthy, and reject what is unholy.

*For wisdom is better than jewels;
and all desirable things cannot compare with her.
Proverbs 8:11*

Assignments for Lesson 76

In Their Words Read the excerpt from *The Praise of Folly* (pages 156-157).

Literature Begin reading *Here I Stand*. Plan to finish it by the end of Unit 18.

Student Review Optional: Answer the questions for Lesson 76.

Gutenberg Bible Photographed at the Library of Congress (1930)

Lesson 77 - Key Event

The Invention of the Printing Press

The book you have before you is a direct result of an event that occurred during the Renaissance. The copy of the Bible that you read is a direct result of that same event, as are your other books, newspapers and magazines, and all printed materials. The printing process used today is different from that which came into existence over five hundred years ago, but a direct line connects the two processes. In the mid-15th century, Johann Gutenberg developed a printing press with movable type. The full impact of this invention on our world is hard to calculate.

Background to the Invention

People have been writing at least since the time of ancient Sumer and Egypt. They have used many different surfaces and instruments: clay tablets and cylinders, papyrus sheets, and walls of stone. For thousands of years, the only way to make a copy of a written document was to write it over again. Writing at the time of the New Testament was done on sheets of papyrus using a technique developed in Egypt.

In the eighth century AD, the Chinese experimented with a printing technique that used raised characters carved on wooden blocks. Three hundred years later, the Chinese and the Koreans

The Gutenberg Bible was printed in three volumes, as seen in the photo above. Twenty-one complete copies are known to have survived to the present. The image of Gutenberg at left is a 16th-century engraving.

443

did some work with printing characters made from various materials, such as clay, wood, bronze, and iron. However, the complexity of the characters in their languages made the work impractical. The Chinese are also credited with making paper from wood pulp and rags about 100 AD. The process was kept secret for centuries but was eventually discovered by Arabs who had contact with the Chinese. Arab traders introduced the process to Europeans.

Westerners had been printing on paper with carved wooden blocks for some time before Gutenberg. Printers took large flat pieces of wood and carved out the wood to leave letters and pictures raised. These blocks were then covered with ink and paper was pressed down on them. The process was time consuming and expensive. Each block could only be used for that one page, and the wood eventually wore down. Books were more commonly copied by hand on parchment (animal skins), but again the process was slow and expensive.

The Life of Gutenberg

Johann Gensfleich zur Laden zum Gutenberg was born around 1400 in Mainz, Germany. His parents were apparently fairly wealthy. Johann was apprenticed to a goldsmith and also learned gem cutting.

While living in Strasbourg, France, Gutenberg began developing aspects of an improved printing process. He utilized wine presses and paper-making techniques to develop a method of making die-cast metal forms of individual letters that could be arranged by hand in a mold to form a page. The page was then put in a press and covered with ink (Gutenberg also had to develop a new kind of ink that would stay on metal letters). A sheet of paper was pressed down on the mold, and the images were transferred to the paper. Many copies of that page were made, then the type could be taken out and another page made up. When all of the printing was done, the pages were bound into a book.

Gutenberg left Strasbourg in 1438. Ten years later he was back in Mainz. Gutenberg borrowed heavily to finance his work. By 1455 he had completed his masterpiece printed book, a Bible in Latin that had forty-two lines per page. However, one of his creditors sued Gutenberg for failure to pay back a loan. Gutenberg had to hand over the type and press, but he did manage to print a Psalter (a copy of the Book of Psalms). Starting over, Gutenberg apparently printed other works in his later life. He received a pension and other benefits from the archbishop of Mainz. Gutenberg died in 1468.

This reproduction of a printing press like the one Gutenberg developed is located at St. Mary's Church, Lübeck, Germany.

Renaissance Literature

Francesco Petrarca (known as Petrarch, 1304-1374) is considered the founder of Renaissance humanism. As a law student, he read Cicero and became enamored with classic literature. He collected ancient manuscripts, amassed a large personal library, and encouraged other wealthy individuals to do the same. As a poet, Petrarch perfected the sonnet form. Because of his pursuit of learning, Petrarch was awarded a laurel wreath by the king of Naples in 1341, reminiscent of the crowns given to winners in the Pythian games in ancient Greece. Thus Petrarch became the first poet laureate of modern times. The portrait at left was drawn near the end of his life by the Italian artist Altichiero.

One of Petrarch's followers, Giovanni Boccaccio (1313-1375), was one of the first Westerners in modern times to study Greek. His tutor translated the works of Homer into Latin and made those classics available to Renaissance Europe. Boccaccio wrote several works of literature, including The Decameron, *a collection of stories told by people who had escaped Florence during the Black Plague.*

In France, Francois Rabelais (c. 1494-1553) was a former monk who wrote humorous works in which the Church and monasteries were often the target. Michel de Montaigne developed the form of the essay (from the French, meaning personal views). Montaigne was a relativist in his beliefs. Because we cannot know all truth with certainty, he said, holding to one's beliefs with dogmatic insistence and persecuting others for their differing views were both wrong. Sir Thomas More (1478-1535), an Englishman, published Utopia *in 1516. It described an imaginary society that was a planned and peaceful place (Utopia means no place). Spain's Miguel de Cervantes (pictured at right, 1547-1615) wrote* Don Quixote, *a satire on the medieval code of chivalry, which was published in two volumes in 1605 and 1615.*

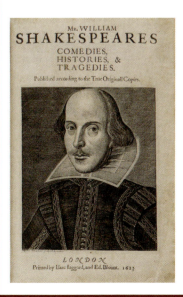

The greatest English writer of the Renaissance was the poet and playwright William Shakespeare (1564-1616). Shakespeare's writings reveal his knowledge of ancient literature. In contrast to the miracle and morality plays that preceded him, Shakespeare focused on the foibles and struggles of humans with little concern for eternity or Biblical themes. As brilliant as they are, Shakespeare's plays are full of the human-centered spirit of the times. The title page from a 1623 edition of his plays is shown at left.

These facts might sound tame to us today, but at the time they were revolutionary. Petrarch, Boccaccio, Rabelais, Montaigne, and others did not see God as the goal toward which they strove or the Scriptures as their standard of truth. Instead, they were moved by the writings of the ancient Greek and Roman pagans; and those works became their model.

This photo shows modern type in boxes of a type case, with some letters set in a composing stick. Before the 1800s, capital letters were commonly stored in a drawer above the other letters. They became known as upper case letters.

The author's father, Wesley Notgrass, operated a linotype machine for many years for The Daily Herald *newspaper in Columbia, Tennessee. He was able to enjoy some of the changes that computer technology brought to printing before he retired in 1981.*

The Impact of Printing

The effect of Gutenberg's work was felt quickly. By 1500 about one thousand print shops had been established in Europe. These printers had produced some ten million pamphlets and books. The first books were still expensive, but soon less costly materials were used. The quality of the product declined somewhat with this change, but many more copies were printed.

Gutenberg's invention impacted education, scholarship, communication, and almost every walk of life. The value of literacy increased significantly, and a growing body of knowledge was made available to more people. Newspapers soon appeared, and in the years to come lending libraries, magazines, and other advances developed that we now take for granted.

Lesson 77 - Key Event: The Invention of the Printing Press

Later Developments in Printing

The printing process remained about the same for over four hundred years. Books and newspapers were produced by a worker placing individual letters in a form (having to read the small letters backwards so they would print correctly!), covering the form with ink, pressing paper down, and then binding the finished product.

In 1887 the linotype machine was invented, so named because a typesetter could automatically produce one complete line-of-type at a time. The large machine held master letters that were put together into a line of type when the operator typed in the letters on a keyboard. The machine then made a hot metal mold of the line. The molds of the lines were put together to make a page, and the master letters were automatically returned to the machine to be used again. The type did not have to be set by hand any longer.

A replica of the Gutenberg-style press is on display at the Featherbed Alley Printshop Museum in St. George's, Bermuda. This press was in regular use for 300 years.

Many rapid changes in printing technology have occurred since the invention of the linotype. In the late 20th century, computer technology enabled printers to produce printed materials much more easily. Pages for national newspapers and magazines can be transmitted digitally to regional printers to enable printing and distribution more quickly.

Some documents today are never put in hard copy form (actual paper and ink); they are only available in digital form. Still, even with a computer, to generate a printed document someone has to put letters together to make words on a page. Then ink or toner has to be applied to paper.

What Printing Means to You

You have a copy of the Bible not because you had a couple of thousand dollars to buy a handmade copy, but because the printing press made the Bible available to you at a reasonable cost. Missionaries are able to distribute copies of the Bible in hundreds of languages around the world.

You are as well educated as you are not because your family could afford private tutors and rare books, but because educational materials are readily available. Your knowledge of the world has been enhanced by the books you have at home and can borrow from the library. News and opinions are circulated around the world through publications that help inform billions of people. Because of printing, everyday people, not just kings and priests, have access to information.

When you come bring the cloak which I left at Troas with Carpus, and the books, especially the parchments.
2 Timothy 4:13

Modern printing presses can generate hundreds of full-color pages every minute. The Lithrone S40 pictured above was developed by the Japanese company Komori. A similar press printed Exploring World History.

Assignments for Lesson 77

In Their Words   Read Sonnet XVIII by Shakespeare and the excerpt from *Don Quixote* (pages 158-163).

Literature   Continue reading *Here I Stand*.

Student Review   Optional: Answer the questions for Lesson 77.

The Last Supper, *Leonardo (c. 1498)*

Lesson 78 - Key Person

Leonardo da Vinci

Many talented individuals exhibited skill and developed new techniques in art during the Renaissance. Giotto di Bondone (c. 1266-1337) used the technique of foreshortening to give depth to his paintings. He also perfected the fresco (painting on fresh plaster). Jan Van Eyck (c. 1390-1441) from Flanders in Belgium emphasized realistic detail and improved the use of oil paints instead of powdered pigments or tempera.

The art of the Renaissance, while displaying amazing talent, gives a good example of the turn toward humanism. Prior to this period, almost all paintings portrayed Biblical scenes or Madonna and Child interpretations. Ideas from the Bible were seen as the only ones worthy of such effort. With the Renaissance, however, artists began portraying everyday people.

A Renaissance Man

Leonardo da Vinci (1452-1519) lived at the height of the Renaissance in Italy. With interests in a wide variety of fields, he was always exploring color, nature, anatomy, and other areas of human life.

Leonardo was born April 15, 1452 near Vinci, Italy. His father, Ser Piero, was a wealthy notary. His mother, Caterina, was a peasant woman. Leonardo's parents were not married, and his father married another woman, Alberia di Giovanni Amadori.

Leonardo evidently spent time in his early years exploring nature with his uncle Franceso around Vinci. His family moved to Florence in 1460. Since he was an illegitimate child, many professions were not open to Leonardo. About age fifteen, he became an apprentice to artist Andrea del Verrochio. He was trained in painting and sculpture and began producing major works of his own in the 1470s and 1480s.

About 1482 Ludovico Sforza, the duke of Milan, gave Leonardo employment. Leonardo brought a letter of recommendation, likely written by himself, that described his wonderful talents not only as an artist, but also as an engineer, architect, and musician. Ludovico might have given Leonardo a job as a musician initially, but Leonardo ended up serving the duke as a military engineer and architect. Leonardo also designed a spectacular celebration for the marriage of the duke's nephew.

In 1499 French soldiers drove the Sforza family out of Milan. Leonardo had been making a statue of Ludovico's father. French archers used Leonard's terra-cotta model of the statue for target practice. Leonardo returned to Florence in 1500.

In 1502 he began service under Cesare Borgia, duke of Romagna. Continuing work as an architect and engineer, he oversaw work on fortresses in the territories controlled by the pope. Leonardo helped to decide on the location for Michelangelo's statue of David. He met Niccolo Machiavelli, who later wrote *The Prince* and who helped Leonardo get another art commission.

After his time in Florence, he returned to Milan. He became a court painter for Louis XII of France. Between 1514 and 1516, Pope Leo X provided patronage for Leonardo at the Vatican. Leonardo entered the service of the French King Francis I in 1516.

Art

Leonardo spent a long time on his artwork. He left multiple works unfinished. He created fewer works than many other famous artists, but his work was still influential. Leonardo mastered the techniques of sfumato and chiaroscuro. Sfumato involves blending tones for a soft hazy effect. Chiaroscuro depicts forms with an emphasis on contrasts between light and shadow. Artists such as Raphael, Andrea del Sarto, and Fra Bartolomeo were among those who learned from him.

He painted *The Last Supper* off and on during the 1490s. For this gripping scene of Jesus and the Apostles, Leonardo used an oil-tempera mixture that did not stick well to the wall.

Mona Lisa *was stolen from the Louvre in 1911 and hidden for two years until the thief was caught. It is widely considered the most valuable painting in the world, valued for insurance purposes at $100 million in the 1960s (over $750 million in today's money).*

It began to deteriorate even in his lifetime. In the 1600s monks cut a door through the bottom of it, and Allied bombing nearly destroyed it during World War II. *The Last Supper* (shown on the previous page) has been restored multiple times by various artists over the centuries.

Mona Lisa (1503-1506) is Leonardo's only surviving portrait from that period in Florence. It is also known as *La Gioconda*. He kept it with him, even when he traveled. Now on display at the Louvre in Paris, it is one of the most recognized paintings in the world.

In addition to his paintings, Leonardo produced numerous sculptural, architectural, and scientific drawings. His artistic talent thus blended with his interest in science.

Lesson 78 - Key Person: Leonardo da Vinci

Michelangelo

Michelangelo di Lodovico Buonarroti Simoni (1475-1564) was a younger contemporary of Leonardo, but they had little contact with each other. Michelangelo excelled Leonardo as a painter, but he actually preferred being a sculptor. His seventeen-foot-tall David *as well as his tender* Pieta *(shown at right) are breathtaking works. Renaissance sculpture recaptured the free-standing technique of classical Greece and Rome. Medieval sculpture, by contrast, was usually in the form of reliefs on walls.*

Pope Julius II asked Michelangelo to carve statues for his elaborate tomb; but when that project ran aground, the pope asked him to paint the ceiling of his private chapel (built by Pope Sixtus IV, it was thus called the Sistine Chapel). Four years and many hours on the scaffolding later, Michelangelo had covered ten thousand square feet with paintings that included some three hundred figures. He also painted The Last Judgment *on the end wall of the chapel.*

Finally, Michelangelo turned to architecture. His many works included the dome of St. Peter's Basilica, which is as wide as the Pantheon but three hundred feet higher. The work was not finished before he died, and his original floor plans for the structure were altered after his death.

Science

Leonardo's scientific pursuits involved careful observation. He made hypotheses and performed experiments as he searched for logical natural principles. Many of his copious notes are written backward in a special shorthand, which made them difficult for others to decipher and implement. He likely wrote from right to left because he was left-handed.

He studied human and animal anatomy. He learned about blood circulation and eyesight. He understood that the moon affects tides, and he examined fossil shells. He also made designs and illustrations for inventions such as a diving suit, a flying machine, an air-cooling system, a device to project an enlarged image on a screen, and an assault chariot.

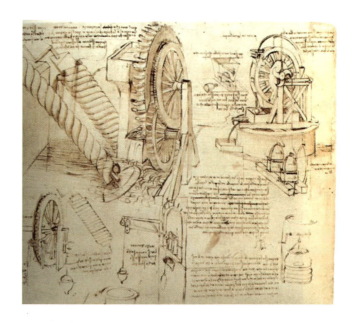

Leonardo had a great interest in water, as seen in his drawings above. He contributed to the science of hydraulics and likely created a hydrometer to measure liquid density. He was also involved with irrigation and canal design.

Art Around the World During the European Renaissance

1. The people of Easter Island carved hundreds of huge statues called moai, as seen at right. The largest are up to 30 feet tall and weigh over 80 tons. The statues were moved into position after carving.

2. The Chimú culture predated the Inca in modern-day Peru. The woven mantle shown at right depicts pelicans and tuna.

3. The Portuguese brought the Catholic faith to the Kingdom of the Kongo. It had a major influence on the culture, as seen in the bronze crucifix above left.

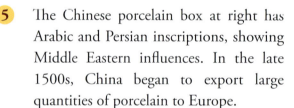

4. The statue of Buddha shown at left is from Angkor, Cambodia, capital of the Khmer Empire.

5. The Chinese porcelain box at right has Arabic and Persian inscriptions, showing Middle Eastern influences. In the late 1500s, China began to export large quantities of porcelain to Europe.

Lesson 78 - Key Person: Leonardo da Vinci

Legacy

Leonardo died on May 2, 1519, in France. In his will, he left his manuscripts, drawings, and various tools to his student Francesco Melzi. The drawing at left is widely considered to be a self-portrait by Leonardo. He left his remaining paintings, including the *Mona Lisa*, to another student, Salai.

Leonardo's research was not published during his lifetime, for reasons that remain unclear. Some portions of his manuscripts, later scattered around Europe, were published; but much of his work was forgotten for centuries. Ten separate collections of his manuscripts now exist (Microsoft's Bill Gates purchased one collection). Modern artisans in Florence, Italy, have used Leonardo's drawings and notes to create models of many of his inventions.

Leonardo da Vinci demonstrated a wide range of skills which humans, who are created in God's image, can perform. Through his interest and investigation, he achieved for himself a prominent place in the Renaissance of learning and expression.

*[Hiram] was filled with wisdom and understanding
and skill for doing any work in bronze.
1 Kings 7:14*

Assignments for Lesson 78

In Their Words   Read the excerpts from Leonardo's manuscripts (pages 164-166).

Literature   Continue reading *Here I Stand*.

Student Review   Optional: Answer the questions for Lesson 78.

Detail from Cherub Playing, *Rosso Fiorentino (Italian, 1518)*

Lesson 79 - Everyday Life

A History of Western Music

Scholars and artists of the Renaissance looked back to recover what they perceived as the glories of Greek civilization. In this lesson we will also look back, not just to the times of the Greeks, but to the dawn of Creation to explore the history of music.

Music in the Bible

The gift of music comes from God. When God created the earth, the morning stars sang together (Job 38:4-7). People have enjoyed music since earliest history. Shortly after the Creation, the Bible mentions Jubal, the father of all who play the lyre and pipe (Genesis 4:21). During the time of the patriarchs, there was music in Paddan-Aram in modern day Syria. Laban lived there and talked to Jacob about the timbrel and the lyre in Genesis 31:27. The first mention of people singing is in Exodus 15. After God parted the Red Sea and the Israelites walked through it on dry ground, Moses and the Israelites sang a song to the Lord.

Both men and women were involved in music in the Old Testament. After crossing the Red Sea, Aaron's sister Miriam led the women in dancing and playing timbrels (Exodus 15:20). In Judges, the judge Deborah, along with her military helper Barak, sang a song of praise to the Lord (Judges 5). Jephthah's daughter sang and played tambourines (Judges 11:34). After David and his army won a battle, women sang, danced, and played musical instruments (1 Samuel 18:6-7).

The book of Psalms teaches details about music during the time of the Old Testament. Verses in several psalms mention praising God with an instrument. David himself played the harp well (1 Samuel 16:16).

Many titles at the beginning of individual psalms include musical instructions. Some indicate the specific instrument to be used, including stringed instruments and the flute. Some mention the names of the leaders of the Levitical singers installed by David. They were Asaph, Jeduthun, and Heman. Many titles mention the choir or music director. Some seem to indicate a specific tune for the psalm. For example, the title for Psalm 22 mentions "Doe of the Morning," which might be a tune.

The musical instrument most associated with the Bible is the harp. The Bible also mentions a ten-string lyre in Psalms 33 and 92. King Solomon used almug wood brought in on ships to make harps and lyres (1 Kings 10:12).

Percussion instruments included tambourines (Psalm 68:25), timbrels (Psalm 81:2), castanets

454

(2 Samuel 6:5), and cymbals. The cymbals of 1 Chronicles 15:19 were made of bronze.

Wind instruments included pipes (Psalm 150:4), flutes (Job 21:12 and 30:31), and trumpets. Trumpets were blown by priests (2 Chronicles 29:26) and were used by soldiers (2 Samuel 2:28). The Bible mentions trumpets made of hammered silver (Numbers 10:1-10) and rams' horn trumpets, which the Lord commanded the priests to use when conquering Jericho (Joshua 6:1-6).

The New Testament mentions music often. When Jesus arrived at the home of Jairus to raise his daughter, flute players were there to mourn her death (Matthew 9:18-26). In Matthew 11:17 Jesus mentioned flute playing and dancing. Before Jesus and his disciples went to the Garden of Gethsemane, they sang a hymn (Mark 14:26). When Paul and Silas were in prison, they sang hymns to God. The other prisoners listened to them sing (Acts 16:25). Hebrews 2:12 tells of Jesus singing the Father's praise. In 1 Corinthians 15:52 we learn of the last trumpet sound, when the dead are raised and mortals become immortal.

The New Testament teaches the importance of music in a person's heart. In 1 Corinthians 14:15 Paul speaks of singing with the mind and the spirit. Paul wrote to Christians telling them to speak to one another in psalms, hymns, and spiritual songs. He said to sing and make melody with your heart to the Lord (Ephesians 5:19). In Colossians 3:16 he wrote that we must let the word of Christ dwell richly within us. With all wisdom we must teach and admonish one another with psalms, hymns, and spiritual songs, while we sing to God with thankfulness in our hearts. The music of the early church was evidently *a cappella*, singing without instruments.

Other Ancient Music

Singing has been important in many cultures throughout world history. Some cultures have used songs to tell stories. An ancient Sumerian song tells the story of a great flood. Another Sumerian song is about an argument between a pick-ax and a plow. The "Oxen Song" was an ancient Egyptian work song, which told oxen to thresh for themselves and to give themselves no rest.

By 700 BC Greeks were using music in many areas of life. Our word music comes from *mousike*, the Greek word for music, dance, and poetry. The words orchestra, harmony, and guitar are also based on Greek words. Schools for Greek boys included instruction in music. Events in the ancient Olympic games included a singing competition and a competition for musicians playing the aulos, a reed instrument like an oboe. The Greeks also used the kithara, a guitar-like instrument with four strings.

Harps from around the time of Abraham have been discovered in the Royal Tombs of Ur in modern Iraq. This Egyptian painting from around 1400 BC depicts a blind harpist. Lyrics from ancient Egyptian songs have also been found about subjects such as oxen threshing, worrying at night, and a love-sick man.

The Greek mathematician Pythagoras (c. 582-497 BC) discovered the pitches of the notes that are still used in western music. He proved that the octave is a natural part of sound. Clesibius, a Greek from Alexandria, Egypt, invented a piston pump around 30 BC. He used it to power a simple organ. About 150 AD the Greek astronomer Ptolemy wrote down the Greek theory of music.

The Romans borrowed musical ideas from the Greeks but added the sound of trumpets. In 284 AD a concert was held in the Colosseum in Rome which featured 100 trumpets, 100 horns, and 200 pipes.

Church Music

In the late 300s AD, Ambrose of Milan, Italy, collected hymns and chants used in services of the Roman Catholic Church. Much of the music was sung by a leader with one or two choruses answering each other, similar to the temple music of the Old Testament.

During the Middle Ages, minstrels entertained audiences with songs about epic events, some real and some imaginary. Troubadours generally wrote and performed songs about chivalry and romance. The manuscript below features an illustration of Perdigon, a French troubadour (d. 1212). There were several prominent female troubadours, called trobairitz.

Pope Gregory the Great served from 590 to 604. The musical style called Gregorian chants is named after him. Many singers sang in unison with the higher voices singing an octave higher. There was no harmony in these "plainsongs."

Around 1025 Guido D'Arezzo, a Benedictine monk, developed a four-line music staff (the five-line staff came into use in the 1200s). D'Arezzo also developed a method for teaching tunes to choirs. He discovered that tunes were easier to learn if the teacher used syllables. The modern *do, re, mi, fa, so, la, ti* scale of syllables is a result of his work. He developed the method based on a song about John the Baptist that was written in Latin. The music of that song was sung like a scale. His original scale of syllables was *ut, re, mi, fa, sol, la, sa*, the beginning sounds of each line in that song.

Music of the Middle Ages

Pilgrims sang as they walked to Rome or to other places considered holy by the Church. People of the Middle Ages watched traveling players as they acted out Bible stories in musical plays called masques or miracle plays. People also passed down folk songs from generation to generation. Traveling musicians carried their harps and lutes from town to town, singing for their dinner and a place to sleep. They sang love songs, story songs, and songs about nature. These traveling musicians were called minstrels in England, minnesingers in Germany, and troubadours in France. German musicians organized guilds and trained apprentices. The best German musicians came to be called master-singers.

Music of the Renaissance

Before the invention of Gutenberg's printing press, music was written by hand. In 1473 the first complete piece of music was printed. Printing made it possible for the general public to have music for their own enjoyment.

Lesson 79 - Everyday Life: A History of Western Music

For centuries, groups of singers had sung only one melody though they often sang those melodies at different octaves or at different intervals on the musical scale. Composers began to write music with different melodies for different groups of voices. These different melodies were sung at the same time.

Some composers began writing songs called madrigals designed to be sung in homes. Madrigal music became popular, especially in the upper classes of northern Italy and England. This vocal chamber music was written for two to nine singers. Each singer had his or her own part. With the printing press making music easier to own, wealthy gentlemen collected madrigal music. Well-educated ladies and gentlemen were expected to be able to sight read. Singing madrigals became a popular after-dinner pastime.

By the 1400s the nobility, religious leaders, towns, and ships had bands which played on special occasions. The bands were either loud with trumpets and harsh reed instruments or soft with instruments like strings, keyboards, and flutes.

Great composers began to write masterpieces for the Catholic and Lutheran Churches. Nobles supported musicians to play for the enjoyment of the court.

Classical Music

The Renaissance led to the development of classical music. Music scholars generally use the term classical to refer to music composed between the mid-18th and the early 19th centuries. In common usage, the Baroque music of the 17th to mid-18th centuries and Romantic music of the 19th and early 20th centuries is often described as classical music also.

Classical music is composed for trained performers rather than for amateur musicians. These compositions do not include much freedom for improvisation. This type of music is also known as art music.

Manuscript of a Composition by Josquin des Prez

Influential Composers

Renaissance

- Josquin des Prez (c. 1450-1521) was a Franco-Flemish composer. His music was deeply religious and emotional.

Baroque

- Henry Purcell (1659-1695) wrote the first famous English opera, *Dido and Aeneas*.

- Johann Sebastian Bach (1685-1750), a German, had a great musical family that included both his parents and his sons. He composed some of the world's best organ music. He also wrote *The Well-Tempered Clavier* and the *St. Matthew Passion*.

- Antonio Vivaldi (1678-1741), an Italian, published in 1725 a group of concertos that became known as *The Four Seasons*. He wrote about 350 concertos for a solo instrument with an orchestra.

- George Frédéric Handel (1685-1759) was a German composer working mainly in England. His *Water Music* suites were first performed in 1717, and his oratorio *Messiah* in 1742.

An opera is a dramatic play in which all or most of the words are sung, accompanied by an orchestra. An oratorio features solos, a chorus, and an orchestra; but it has no costumes, no set, and no dramatic action. George Frédéric Handel wrote both. The 19th-century painting above by French artist Edouard Jenan Conrad Hamman portrays Handel with King George I of England, who was also born in Germany.

Classical

- Austrian Joseph Haydn (1732-1809) composed 104 symphonies in his lifetime. He developed the string quartet. His most successful piece was his oratorio, *The Creation* (1798).

- Wolfgang Amadeus Mozart (1756-1791), an Austrian, was a child prodigy who began composing at age five. Among his numerous works are the operas *The Marriage of Figaro* and *The Magic Flute*. He used a wide range of instruments in the orchestra, including the wind section and Eastern instruments like the triangle, bass drum, and cymbals.

- Franz Schubert (1797-1828), an Austrian composer, wrote over 600 songs for singer and piano as well as many other works.

- Ludwig van Beethoven (1770-1827) composed many different types of musical pieces, even after he began to lose his hearing around age thirty. When he debuted his famous Ninth Symphony in 1824, he could not hear the audience's standing ovations.

Romantic

- Felix Mendelssohn (1809-1847) was a German composer, pianist, conductor, and teacher. He wrote concertos, symphonies, sonatas, songs, and the oratorios *St. Paul* and *Elijah*.

- Frédéric Chopin (1810-1849) was a Polish composer, who wrote almost exclusively for the piano. He wrote preludes, mazurkas, and waltzes.

- The German composer Robert Schumann (1810-1856) began a periodical for music criticism that encouraged open-mindedness

Beethoven, Joseph Karl Stieler (German, 1820)

for new music forms and introduced talented composers like Mendelssohn, Chopin, and Brahms. He wrote *Scenes from Childhood* in 1838, which included his famous "Reverie."

- Richard Wagner (1813-1883) was a German composer of thirteen operas, including *The Flying Dutchman*.

- Franz Liszt (1811-1886) was a remarkable pianist and composer. His *Hungarian Rhapsodies* were inspired by the folk music of his native Hungary.

- Russian Peter Ilyich Tchaikovsky (1840-1893) tried to compose music every day. Among his works are the ballets *Swan Lake*, *The Sleeping Beauty*, and *The Nutcracker*.

- Johannes Brahms (1833-1897) was a German composer and talented pianist. His work *A German Requiem* for solo voices, chorus, and orchestra used passages from the Bible in German.

- Antonin Dvořák (1841-1904) was a Czech composer who wrote symphonies, operas, and chamber music. He is best known for his Symphony No. 9 (titled *From the New World*), which includes melodies from American folk songs and spirituals. He wrote it while he lived in the United States for three years.

Twentieth Century

- American John Philip Sousa (1854-1932) wrote over one hundred marches. After serving with the U.S. Marine Band, Sousa created his own band that toured the world.

- German composer and conductor Richard Strauss (1864-1949) wrote a polka at age six. He is best known for his operas and symphonic poems.

Igor Stravinsky (c. 1930)

- Russian composer Igor Stravinsky (1882-1971) wrote music for the ballet, church, circus, dance band, opera, player piano, and symphony orchestra. Stravinsky believed that music praises God.

- American George Gershwin (1898-1937) wrote music played by symphony orchestras as well as popular hits. Gershwin favorites include *Rhapsody in Blue*, *An American in Paris*, and the opera *Porgy and Bess*.

- Leonard Bernstein (1918-1990), another American, was a composer, conductor, music director, and outstanding pianist. He wrote the music for the Broadway show *West Side Story* (1957) and was the first head of the New York Philharmonic who was born and trained in the United States.

Folk and Popular Music

Folk music is a term for informal musical traditions passed down from one generation to another. Lyrics and tunes are changed as the community participates in the development and performance of the music with simple, portable instruments. Immigrants from Europe, Africa, and Asia brought their folk music traditions to North America, where they continued to evolve and blend together.

Technological and social changes in the 19th and 20th centuries spurred the development of popular music. Cheaper printing allowed sheet music to spread more widely, and growing urban populations provided large audiences for traveling performers. The introduction of the gramophone (record player) and the radio allowed audiences in different cities and countries to hear exactly the same musical performance for the first time in world history. Access to larger audiences allowed for a greater proliferation of styles of music such as bluegrass, blues, jazz, and country. The electric guitar facilitated the rise of rock 'n' roll music in the 1950s, which brought together elements from blues, jazz, gospel, and country music. Musical experimentation has continued in more recent decades with styles such as reggae, disco, hip-hop, and electronica.

Susan Boyle (b. 1961) from Scotland is the youngest of ten children. She never married and cared for her mother until her mother's death in 2007. Boyle had received vocal training and won local singing competitions, and her mother had encouraged her to audition for the TV show Britain's Got Talent. Her performance in 2008 amazed the audience and judges, and she became a worldwide sensation. Despite her tremendous success, Boyle maintains a modest lifestyle and remains active in her church.

Serve the Lord with gladness;
Come before Him with joyful singing.
Psalm 100:2

Assignments for Lesson 79

In Their Words — Read the songs by Charles D'Orléans (page 167).

Literature — Continue reading *Here I Stand*.

Student Review — Optional: Answer the questions for Lesson 79.

St. Bernardino Preaching *(Italian, c. 1463)*

Lesson 80 - Bible Study

Worldliness vs. Godliness

The great spiritual struggle of our lives is the conflict between God's way and the world's way. If it were left up to us, we might want to have some of each; but that option is not open to us if we want to be faithful to God (Matthew 6:24). There can be no compromise with the world in this battle because the world is under the domination of Satan (Ephesians 2:2, John 12:31).

The Issue Is Your Soul

Dealing with worldliness does not just involve whether a movie or television program has "too many" bad words or how much wealth is too much wealth for one person or family to own. These and other specific questions are involved, but the main issue is your soul. Your soul is at stake in the battle with the world, and the specific questions are the points of conflict between God's way and the world's way. Make no mistake: the world's way is Satan's way.

Both sides want to control you, and the competition for your soul is fierce. Satan will stop at nothing to have you, even disguising himself as an angel of light (2 Corinthians 11:14). God loves you so much that He was willing for His Son to bear your sins and to die on your behalf (2 Corinthians 5:21). You are valuable and precious, and both sides see you as worth all that can be done to own you.

The battle is not with the created world and material things as such, though many teachers of heretical doctrine have misunderstood this through the years. The created world itself is not bad. God made it and declared it to be good (Genesis 1:31).

By our sin, however, the world has fallen under the dominion of Satan. The things of this world that we should use to glorify God often replace God in our hearts. People set up things of the world as their idols, but in reality such things do not make good gods. All of the idols we manufacture are powerless to help us; they actually harm us.

What Is Worldliness?

Almost every Christian agrees that worldliness is wrong, but almost every Christian has a different definition of what worldliness is. Most of us define it as the way that the world influences other people. In other words, we think that worldliness is the other guy's problem. Such self-deceptive thinking is itself an example of worldliness.

Unit 16 - The Renaissance

The so-called Arnolfini Portrait (an untitled 1434 work by Dutch painter Jan van Eyck) illustrates the material wealth that became available to more people during the Renaissance.

have it. God addressed this in the Tenth Commandment, the prohibition against coveting (Exodus 20:17). Our tendency is to want more and to be unsatisfied with what we have, especially if someone else has more.

The boastful pride of life refers to the arrogant, sinful pride that one can have with regard to what one possesses or accomplishes in worldly terms. The world tell us that we ought to be important in the eyes of others. The way of the world says that if someone accumulates wealth or status or the admiration of others, he is a success, regardless of his relationship with God.

It is not wrong to want a place for your family to live. It is wrong and worldly to want a house that is nicer or larger than someone else's or to try to find peace and happiness in a house. Clothes are good, but clothes that draw attention to oneself or that feed the lust of the flesh are not good. Movies are not inherently bad, but movies are of the world if they glamorize ungodliness and fleshly lusts or if they mock God.

Who Is Worldly?

Non-Christian people are not the only ones who are worldly. Christians can be worldly also. In the parable of the sower, Jesus describes those who have heard the word of God, but "as they go on their way they are choked with worries and riches and pleasures of this life, and bring no fruit to maturity" (Luke 8:14).

One of the great deceptions of Satan is to influence Christians to think that their level of worldliness is acceptable because they are

The most succinct definition in the Bible of worldly influences is in 1 John 2:16. "For all that is in the world, the lust of the flesh and the lust of the eyes and the boastful pride of life, is not from the Father, but is from the world." Notice that this does not say material things in themselves are wrong. Our attitudes toward them are what can be wrong.

The lust of the flesh refers to those desires that gratify self. It includes sensual desires but also involves anything that pleases the physical self. When we want physical pleasure at the expense of being faithful to God, we are giving in to worldliness. Paul said that things of the world are things "which God has created to be gratefully shared in by those who believe and know the truth" (1 Timothy 4:3). God has created a proper way for material things to be enjoyed, but they are not to rule us.

The lust of the eyes means the "I wants," the desire for more of what you see. Much in the world is attractive to us, and worldly thinking wants to

Lesson 80 - Bible Study: Worldliness vs. Godliness

Christians or because their degree of worldliness is less than that of the people to whom they compare themselves.

These examples reflect the influence of worldliness on Christians. A preacher overindulges his desire for food. A church leader wants a bigger building to impress the community. A teenager in the youth group calls attention to himself or herself by dressing to impress or entice. A church member equates church membership with social standing. A businessman compromises his integrity and honesty to get ahead in his work. A couple watches popular but raunchy movies and television shows.

The problem during the Renaissance was not that some people were worldly, but that people who claimed to be Christian were driven and motivated by the world. When the lives of church leaders look no different from the lives of those who make no claim to be Christians, that is worldliness. When the church pursues policies of power and the accumulation of wealth, that is worldliness. When Christians imitate the ways of the pagans without regard for how that impacts their faith or the faith of others, that is worldliness.

Christians are called to keep themselves unstained by the world (James 1:27). This, along with caring for widows and orphans, is what James says constitutes pure and undefiled religion. Christians do not have to leave the world to avoid becoming worldly (1 Corinthians 5:10). They are to be changed within by developing a godly way of thinking and by following God's standards while they live in the world (Romans 12:1-2).

This 1606 painting by Italian artist Federico Barocci depicts Michelina of Pesaro (1300-1356). Married into a noble family, she allowed pleasure and people to crowd out God. After the death of her husband and her son, she devoted herself to a life of charity and service.

Asking Basic Questions

The battle against the world involves asking yourself some basic questions, being honest with your answers, and doing whatever it takes to please God.

- What are you seeking (Matthew 6:33)? Does your life give evidence that you are seeking God's kingdom and righteousness? Do the things that you put before your eyes draw you closer to God or distract you from God?

- What brings you happiness (Matthew 5:3-12)? Are you excited about clothes and the opposite sex but bored with God?

- What answers do you give for what you do in your life? Do you make excuses to try to make the questionable things you do acceptable (Luke 14:18-20), or are you motivated by the love of God in your thoughts, words, and actions (Colossians 3:17)?

How Will You Fare in the Battle?

The way of the world is deceptive (1 Corinthians 6:9 and 15:33, Galatians 6:7). Satan will not come at you in a red suit with horns and a pitchfork and say, "Follow me to hell." Instead, his influence will be subtle. The way of the world will be attractive or appear to be easy or inconsequential. The individual choices you face will not appear to force you to choose between God and Satan. At some point, however, you might turn around and realize that you left the way of God a long way back and that it will be difficult to return to it—if you ever stop to think about it at all. It is better to go through life different from the world and be able to enter heaven than it is to get along fine in the world and lose your life in the end (Matthew 5:29-30).

Perhaps the ruler of this world fights so desperately for our souls because he knows that his is a lost cause and he wants to take as many down with him as he can. The ultimate outcome of the battle has already been decided. Jesus has overcome the world (John 16:33). You and I, however, live on a part of the battlefield where the conflict is still raging. The key to how you will fare in this great spiritual conflict is within your own heart.

"Therefore come out from their midst and be separate," says the Lord. "And do not touch what is unclean; and I will welcome you."
2 Corinthians 6:17

Assignments for Lesson 80

Bible — Recite or read Psalm 150 from memory.

In Their Words — Read the excerpt from "The Ascension of Christ" by Savonarola (pages 168-171).

Literature — Continue reading *Here I Stand*.

Project — Complete your project for the unit.

Student Review — Optional: Answer the questions for Lesson 80 and take the quiz for Unit 16.

17

The Age of Reformation

Summary   The Protestant Reformation was given great impetus by Martin Luther, supported by many other people, and repeated in many places. This unit also examines the influence of John Calvin and of the Anabaptist movement. The translation of the Bible into English is a fascinating story that has affected the lives of millions in a powerful way. The Bible study is on the meaning of grace.

Lessons
81 - Martin Luther and the Break with Rome
82 - Key Person: John Calvin
83 - Key Movement: The Anabaptists
84 - History of the English Bible
85 - Bible Study: Grace

Detail from Luther Before the Diet of Worms
Anton von Werner (German, 1877)

Memory Work Learn Ephesians 4:4-6 by the end of the unit.

Books Used The Bible
In Their Words
Here I Stand

Project (choose one)

1) Write 300 to 500 words on one of the following topics:

- Write an editorial for the *Wittenburg Times* newspaper either defending or criticizing Martin Luther. See Lesson 81.

- Write a report about a Christian group or denomination. Tell how it began, its distinctive doctrines, and any well-known members. Tell what you respect about the group.

2) Memorize Ephesians 2:1-10.

3) Write and illustrate a children's book about the life and accomplishments of Martin Luther. See Lesson 81. The book should be at least fifteen pages long.

Detail from Luther Burns the Papal Bull, *Karl Aspelin (Swedish, c. 1900)*

Lesson 81

Martin Luther and the Break with Rome

The slick-talking salesman—a monk—enters the marketplace, sets up a cross and a table, and begins making his pitch. "Your friends and relatives who have died are languishing in purgatory. By contributing to the construction of St. Peter's Church in Rome, you can free the soul of your loved one from torment. It is a good work that you do, and the surplus of good works built up by the apostles and saints will be applied to your loved one. You have the power to release them from their suffering. Remember: 'As soon as the coin in the coffer rings, the soul from purgatory springs.'" (The Roman Catholic Church teaches that, when a person dies, his soul goes to purgatory for a period of time. The length depends on his sinfulness in life. In purgatory, his soul must be purged or purified so that he can enter heaven.)

People in the crowd press forward to give their money, and they receive in exchange the letters of indulgence granting forgiveness. When the last seeker is finished, the salesman and his helpers move on to the next town. All of this is done in the name of God. Jesus had objected to the temple becoming a religious marketplace, but now the Church was operating a religious marketplace.

For the eager young priest Martin Luther, anguished both about his own soul and about the state of the Catholic Church, this was too much. His response to scenes such as this and to other abuses in the Catholic Church initiated the most far-reaching movement to occur since Christ and the early church. The world that came after him was different because of his protests against Catholic doctrine and practice and his call for reform.

Background to the Reformation

Several strands of history came together to produce the Protestant Reformation. First, the hierarchy of the Roman Catholic Church had become worldly and corrupt. Popes and bishops were not always godly men. Often they were men of political influence or the puppets of those who had influence. Church leaders spent much time in political maneuvers involving kings and nobles. In addition, the Church had amassed a tremendous amount of wealth and property.

Second, some Catholic practices had departed significantly from the Bible. The clergy held tight control on the members by the way they used confession, communion, and Church traditions.

The Catholic emphasis on good works made people think that they had to (and could) earn salvation. Doctrines such as papal authority and purgatory were used as clubs against people.

Third, the Renaissance had introduced a new way of looking at the world. Many were willing to think about, question, and criticize what had long been accepted practice. New ideas emerged about the nature of religion and the worth of the individual that challenged traditional Catholic teachings.

Other factors were involved as well. Growing nationalism caused many in Europe to feel less of a tie to Rome. The printing press helped spread more quickly new ideas that emerged. An increasing desire for meaningful faith caused people to wonder if other approaches to God besides traditional Catholic practices might provide a richer personal spiritual life.

This 16th-century woodcut shows people buying indulgences. The man in the upper left shows papal seals to demonstrate his authority from the Church, and the man in the lower right collects the money.

Luther's Early Life

Martin Luther, born in 1483, had a deep passion to serve God. When he was caught in a thunderstorm as a young man, he committed himself to becoming a monk. Visiting Rome in 1510, he was aghast at the wealth and corruption that characterized the center of Catholic faith. He earnestly wanted spiritual peace, but the methods of the Catholic Church did not bring it to him.

Luther was given the opportunity to teach at the University of Wittenberg in Saxony. In preparation for his work, Luther did an amazing thing. Since he was going to teach theology, he decided to read the Bible. As he did, his eyes were opened. He saw the difference between the Old and New Testaments.

In the New Testament, Luther saw an emphasis on grace and faith and a discrediting of the idea that works can earn salvation. He saw nothing to support the selling of indulgences and many other practices of the Catholic Church. Luther became convinced that salvation was based on one's faith in Christ, not on the performing of certain works declared to be meritorious by the Church.

The Selling of Indulgences

The immediate cause for Luther's protest was the selling of indulgences by the Catholic Church. The Church held that the good deeds and holy relics of the saints had created a surplus of good works which were available to other people (and even their loved ones in purgatory) by giving donations to the Church. Earlier popes had offered forgiveness for those who participated in the Crusades.

In 1517 the pope wanted to finance the remodeling of St. Peter's Basilica in Rome. At the same time, Bishop Albert Hohenzollern of Brandenburg wanted to become archbishop of Mainz, a position which could be his by the payment of a fee. The pope endorsed a plan by which half of the money

Lesson 81 - Martin Luther and the Break with Rome

raised by the sale of indulgences would go to his construction project and the other half would go to Albert.

The selling of these indulgences did not take place in Wittenberg itself since Frederick the Wise, the Elector of Saxony, did not want competition for another indulgence sale taking place there on All Saints Day, November 1. On that day Frederick would have his extensive collection of relics on display. Indulgences were being sold in a nearby town, however, so many people from Wittenberg made the trip to buy what the Church was selling.

Luther's Opposition

On the eve of All Saints Day, October 31, 1517, Martin Luther nailed a list of ninety-five theses or points for discussion on the front door of the Castle Church in Wittenberg. This was a common practice for those who wanted to generate a public discussion on some topic. What was different about Luther's list was its length and its direct challenge to Catholic practices. He denounced papal practices, including the selling of indulgences and the idea that the pope could forgive sins, as well as other doctrines and practices of the Church. He saw the trafficking in indulgences as only one symptom of a flawed system.

Reactions both for and against Luther were strong and swift. Strenuous debate swirled about Luther's stance, and Luther himself published tracts that helped spread his ideas. Three years later, Luther was condemned as a heretic. In response, Luther burned the decree against him. The next year, 1521, he was called to appear before Church and civic officials at the Diet (or Parliament) in the city of Worms. This was a political body handling Luther's challenge to Church authority because there was no line between church and state. Both institutions supported each other. There Luther gave a famous speech defending what he had done.

Luther was declared a heretic and banished from the empire, but he was "kidnapped" by the order of a friendly noble, Frederick, and kept in seclusion at

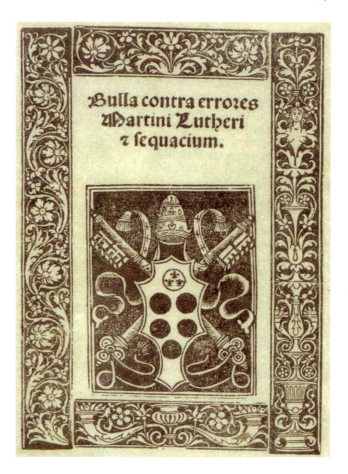

A printed copy of the 1520 papal "Bull Against the Errors of Martin Luther and Followers." The name comes from the metal seal (Latin, bulla*) that was placed on the document.*

Wartburg Castle for a time. He came out of seclusion about a year later and spent much of the rest of his life guiding the movement he had begun. The charge of heresy against him came from an authority that he did not recognize, was not supported in Scripture, and was heretical itself in his own eyes, so Luther was not concerned about it.

Luther was not the first person to question Catholic doctrines and practices. The Waldensians had done so several centuries before but had been wiped out. Wycliffe and Hus had spoken out against Catholic abuses but were discredited. Erasmus had critiqued some of the Church's practices. Girolamo Savonarola had preached against the immorality and worldliness of the Church in Florence, Italy in the 1490s; but he was condemned and executed.

Martin Luther, a former monk, married Katharina von Bora, a former nun, in 1525. He was forty-one, and she was twenty-six. Katharina managed a busy home that included six children born to the couple, four foster children, and numerous students who came to learn from her famous husband. The portrait at right was painted by a family friend, Lucas Cranach the Elder (c. 1530).

The difference with Luther was (1) the time had come and the tide of opposition had become so strong that it could not be held back, and (2) Luther had the backing of some of Germany's powerful political figures. The long-running conflict between the pope and German political leaders meant that the German leaders preferred supporting a renegade fellow countryman as opposed to the Roman pope.

Analyzing Luther's Ideas

Martin Luther was a profound and active thinker and teacher. His ideas did not come to him all at once; they developed over a period of years. He was not perfect, but he was willing to move beyond the status quo and point people back to God and the Scriptures. The core of his faith was his understanding that salvation was by faith in Christ alone because of God's mercy. Salvation did not come as the result of any works of merit that a person might perform. Luther reduced the seven sacraments of the Catholic Church to two: baptism and communion.

Another basic element of Luther's teaching was his acceptance of the Bible only as a guide for faith and practice. He rejected the authority of the pope, monasticism, the celibacy of priests, and many other Catholic doctrines because they are not found in the Bible.

A third foundation of his beliefs was the value of the individual believer before God. Each Christian could approach God himself, Luther said, without the intercession of a priest. Every believer had the right and the necessity to study the Bible on his own, so Luther translated the Bible into German for all to read. His translation had a profound effect on the faith (and the language) of the German people. His hymnal encouraged all to sing, not just the choir. Services in the churches that supported Luther were conducted in German, not Latin.

As we said above, Luther was not perfect. He was so sure about his ideas that he strongly opposed any who disagreed with him. He wanted the freedom to think anew, but he did not grant that freedom to others. Luther did not believe in the transubstantiation of communion, but he did believe that Christ was actually present in the elements (he took Christ's statement, "This is my body," literally);

and he had no tolerance for any other belief. He was harshly critical of poor people who rebelled against the heavy taxes of the German lords, even encouraging their being put to death by the authorities. Near the end of his life, he wrote strongly in favor of persecution against Jews.

Luther did not intend to break from the Catholic Church but only to reform it. To him, the church was simply the church and he wanted to reform its practices. When the Catholic Church did not accept his reforms and excommunicated those who followed him, Luther's fellow believers realized that they were a separate fellowship from that led by the pope.

The Impact of Luther

Congregations and German leaders decided whether they wanted to become Lutherans or remain Catholic. These were not decisions reached by popular vote or calm, rational discussion. Social unrest and even violence marked several cities. By the time of Luther's death in 1546, about half of the princes in the Holy Roman Empire had sided with Luther against the pope for the churches in their districts. The next year, the Catholic Emperor Charles V launched a military campaign to force Lutheran churches back into the Catholic fold.

After several years of bloody fighting, a council produced the Peace of Augsburg in 1555. Each prince could choose the Catholic or Protestant Church to be the state religion for his territory. Toleration for the group not chosen varied from district to district. Thus the division in Christendom was officially recognized by the German authorities. As it worked out, most of northern Germany was officially Lutheran while most of southern Germany was officially Catholic.

What Luther began spread throughout Europe. Lutheranism became the predominant religious expression in the Scandinavian countries. Ulrich Zwingli began preaching reform messages about the time of Luther. He became the political leader of Zurich, Switzerland; but he was killed in 1531 at the age of forty-seven in a battle between opposing religious forces. John Calvin was a Frenchman whose reforming ideas won him the opposition of the Catholic king of France. Calvin's strong ideas and forceful personality moved him to the forefront of reform (see next lesson).

Men from other countries in Europe studied with Calvin, and soon Reformed movements blossomed elsewhere: the Huguenots in France, the Presbyterians in Scotland, the Dutch Reformed in the Netherlands, and the Puritans in England. Puritans who settled in the English colonies of America had a profound influence on the shape of American life and faith. Protestant movements were much weaker in Spain and Italy, where papal influence was strong.

The English Reformation took a somewhat different course because the main issue there was political, not theological. Henry VIII desperately wanted a male child so that the relatively new Tudor dynasty could remain in power. When his first wife, Catherine of Aragon, did not bear a son who survived infancy, Henry sought from the pope an annulment of the marriage. When that did not happen, in 1533 the Archbishop of Canterbury annulled the marriage and Henry married Anne Boleyn.

The pope excommunicated Henry, but in 1534 Parliament declared the king to be the head of the Church of England. The English Church cut off contact with the pope, and the king dissolved all Catholic monasteries in England.

Henry gave lands formerly owned by the monasteries to his political friends to strengthen their support. When the Church of England began, its hierarchy, beliefs, and practices were quite similar to those of the Catholic Church.

Protestant Reformers were tired of the pope calling the shots. They wanted the freedom to believe differently. However, they often did not want to extend this freedom to those who might differ with them. They wanted to be rid of Catholic dominance so that they could call the shots. Luther, Calvin, Henry VIII, and other reformers could be just as intolerant as the Catholic Church had been.

Portrait of Henry VIII of England
Hans Holbein the Younger (German, c. 1537)

Thus says the Lord, "Stand by the ways and see and ask for the ancient paths, where the good way is, and walk in it; and you will find rest for your souls." But they said, "We will not walk in it."
Jeremiah 6:16

Assignments for Lesson 81

In Their Words — Read Luther's Ninety-Five Theses and "A Mighty Fortress Is Our God" (pages 172-178).

Literature — Continue reading *Here I Stand*.

Student Review — Optional: Answer the questions for Lesson 81.

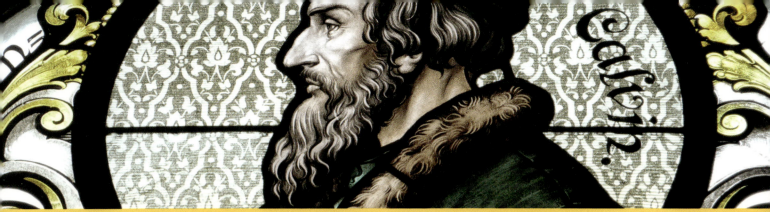

Stained Glass Portrait, Evangelical Church of Hockenheim, Germany

Lesson 82 - Key Person

John Calvin

John Calvin was born in France in 1509 to Gerard and Jeanne Calvin. He grew up as a Catholic and trained to become a priest. His father, a lawyer, encouraged him to study law instead. As a young man, Calvin was exposed to the ideas of church reformation and humanism. He developed his theological understanding through his study of the Bible, the writings of church leaders, and contemporaries such as Martin Luther.

Because of persecution against Protestants in France, Calvin moved to Switzerland. At the age of twenty-six, he published the initial version of *Institutes of the Christian Religion*. He revised it several times, with the final edition appearing in 1559. This was his comprehensive statement of faith that has directly and indirectly influenced generations of believers.

In Geneva

Calvin visited Geneva, Switzerland, in the 1530s as the citizens considered their response to Reformation ideas. He and fellow reformer Guillaume Farel were forced to leave in 1538, but Genevan officials invited Calvin back in 1541. Calvin returned with his new wife, Idelette de Bure. Their one child died in infancy, and Idelette died in 1549.

John Calvin did not hold an official government position in Geneva, but he became an influential leader in the community. He received a house and income from the city. He preached frequently and wrote voluminously.

Calvin helped develop laws that touched on civil and religious matters. He promoted a city school system and the development of Geneva Academy under Theodore Beza. He also encouraged community improvements such as good hospitals, a suitable sewage system, and commercial development. He thought churches should use the common language (in this case French), and his writings in French contributed to the development of that language.

Religious toleration was not common in that age. The government of Geneva integrated powers of church and state. The city government expelled religious dissenters. One such dissenter was Michael Servetus, whose religious views were considered radical. Servetus was convicted of heresy and condemned to be burned to death.

John Calvin approved of the conviction and the sentence, though he recommended beheading as less painful. Calvin even visited Servetus in prison in an attempt to persuade him to change his opinions. Servetus was burned at the stake on October 27, 1553.

Defenders of Calvin argue that since religious intolerance was common in Europe at this time, Calvin was no worse than his contemporaries. Since John Calvin put himself forward as a teacher and Bible interpreter, others have condemned his decision in this case. The affair of Michael Servetus does not mean that everything John Calvin did and taught was wrong, but it remains a stain on his life's work.

Calvin continued his work in Geneva for the rest of his life. He died in 1564 at the age of fifty-four and was buried in an unmarked grave.

His Influence

The teachings of John Calvin and his spiritual heirs have had a major effect on the world. Calvin's spiritual and social ideals contributed to the rise of republicanism and capitalism in the modern world. Presbyterian and Reformed Churches are the most direct descendants of Calvin's thought. Other religious communities such as some Congregationalists and Baptists adhere to similar

Calvin corresponded with religious and political figures across Europe. Below is a 1552 letter from Calvin to King Edward VI of England.

John Calvin preached daily at St. Pierre Cathedral in Geneva for many years. A wooden chair that he used is still on display.

tenets. Puritans were also influenced by Calvin's teaching. Puritans in New England, such as Jonathan Edwards, had a profound impact on religious and political thought in the United States.

Anyone who calls people back to God and His word does good. Calvin did good. He was one among many reformers who recognized ecclesiastical abuses and misunderstandings and called for renewal. Calvin believed that he taught a true interpretation of the Bible. He said of his *Institutes* that they were "God's work rather than mine." As with all men besides Christ and the inspired apostles, however, we should not accept his conclusions without question, nor should we acknowledge John Calvin as our supreme authority.

To paraphrase Paul's words, Calvin was not crucified for us, and we were not baptized in the name of Calvin (1 Corinthians 1:13). To identify ourselves proudly as "Calvinists" or with the name

Catholic Counter-Reformation

From the Catholic perspective, the Protestant movements were a tragedy that destroyed the unity of the one true church. Many Catholics struggled to admit the possibility of problems with Church teaching or practice. They saw it as the church of Jesus, regardless of whether individuals in it—even popes—were right or wrong. However, many Catholic leaders realized that some response was necessary. What came about were some mild changes and a reaffirmation of traditional Catholic doctrine and practices.

A reform movement within the Catholic Church in Spain began in the late 15th century under Francisco Jiménez de Cisneros, a cardinal in Toledo (portrait at left). He worked to improve the standard of morality among the clergy and to oppose infidels and heretics. The Society of Jesus (Jesuits), also begun by a Spaniard, Ignatius of Loyola, was a monastic movement dedicated to strengthening the commitment of Catholics to their traditional doctrines largely through educational efforts. The Jesuits also sent missionaries around the world. Notice the men in black in the illustration at right from India (artist Nar Singh, c. 1605).

After the Protestant movement spread like wildfire throughout Europe, even the papacy began to admit that changes needed to take place in the Catholic Church. Pope Paul III summoned the Council of Trent, which met on and off for eighteen years (1545-1563). The pope, the Jesuits, and others loyal to the Church controlled the proceedings. Bishops were instructed to make sure that priests did not engage in immorality and that those who kept concubines cease that practice. Each diocese was to open a seminary or school of theology for the training of priests. The selling of indulgences was outlawed, although the granting of indulgences by the pope was allowed to continue.

On the other hand, the council reaffirmed all Catholic doctrine and tradition as authoritative and condemned Protestant teachings. The Inquisition was revived in Spain, Italy, Belgium, and the Netherlands. An Index or list of books that questioned Catholicism was created, and Catholics were forbidden to read any books in the Index. The Index was not discontinued until 1965.

During the late 16th and early 17th centuries, religious disagreement led to multiple wars across Europe, though political and social factors also played a part. A 1602 naval battle between Dutch and Spanish ships is pictured at left (Hendrick Cornelisz Vroom, 1617). The areas of Catholic and Protestant strength in Europe have remained virtually unchanged since 1570. Catholicism is stronger in Italy, Spain, France, and Austria. Lutheranism is stronger in Germany and Scandinavia. The Reformed tradition is stronger in Switzerland and Scotland, and Anglicanism is still the official state religion of Great Britain.

of anyone besides Christ is exactly the problem Paul was addressing with the Corinthians. Labels and required creeds do not promote unity among followers of Christ. Instead, they drive wedges between those who should naturally be attached to one another.

We should honor and appreciate the noble work of men and women who have gone before us. We should learn from their wisdom, their successes, their struggles, and their faults how we can better serve God today. However, we must recognize Christ only as our supreme example and our supreme teacher. Consider in closing these words from John Calvin's *Commentary on Corinthians—Volume 1* (on verses 10-13 of chapter 1):

> [Paul's] object is to maintain Christ's exclusive authority in the Church, so that we may all exercise dependence upon him, that he alone may be recognized among us as Lord and Master, and that the name of no individual be set in opposition to his. Those, therefore, that draw away disciples after them (Acts 20:30), with the view of splitting the Church into parties, he condemns as most destructive enemies of our faith. Thus then he does not suffer men to have such pre-eminence in the Church as to usurp Christ's supremacy. He does not allow them to be held in such honor as to derogate even in the slightest degree from Christ's dignity. There is, it is true, a certain degree of honor that is due to Christ's ministers, and they are also themselves masters in their own place, but this exception must always be kept in view, that Christ must have without any infringement what belongs to him—that he shall nevertheless be the sole Master, and looked upon as such. Hence the aim of good ministers is this, that they may all in common serve Christ, and claim for him exclusively power, authority, and glory—fight under his banner—obey him alone, and bring others in subjection to his sway.

[Christ] is also head of the body, the church;
and He is the beginning, the first-born from the dead,
so that He Himself will come to have first place in everything.
Colossians 1:18

Assignments for Lesson 82

In Their Words Read John Calvin's Introduction to *Institutes of the Christian Religion* and the excerpt from *The Life of St. Teresa of Jesus* (pages 179-182).

Literature Continue reading *Here I Stand*.

Student Review Optional: Answer the questions for Lesson 82.

German-Speaking Mennonites in Belize, 2010

Lesson 83 - Key Movement

The Anabaptists

Martin Luther opened a door that could not be shut. Once the prevailing religious establishment was challenged, any religious tradition was fair game. Luther, Calvin, and other reformers made great strides in returning the practices and beliefs of those who were followers of Christ to the standards of the Bible.

However, their reforms were not perfect. Another movement that emerged about the same time was made up of people who wanted to press further along the road of restoring the church of the New Testament. They were not perfect either, but they were willing to question not only the Catholics but also the reformers. Members of this diverse movement were commonly known as Anabaptists.

Infant vs. Believer Baptism

One of the main Anabaptist teachings, and the one from which they derived their nickname, was on the subject of baptism. The Catholic Church had practiced infant baptism for centuries. It had become a way for the Catholic Church to claim for its own the children who were thus sprinkled and to encourage parents to rear their children as Catholics.

In his call for a return to Biblical authority, Luther accepted infant baptism and rationalized it as an expression of the child's inclusion into the Christian community. Calvin also retained infant baptism as a comfort to the parents of the child and an induction of the child into the church tradition.

A few teachers, mostly in Switzerland, denied that infant baptism could be a part of a return to New Testament Christianity. They held that infant baptism had no power or authority and that those who had been baptized as infants needed to be baptized again as believing adults. The term Anabaptist means baptized again. This is what critics called the group. Those in the group did not see what they were advocating as another baptism. To them, Scripture authorized only one baptism, and that was for adults who believed. They called themselves Baptists. Interestingly, although the word *baptizein* in Greek means to immerse, most Anabaptists did not insist on immersion as the correct form of baptism. Most often they practiced effusion or pouring of water on the candidate. The form was not as important to them as the meaning of what was done.

Church and State

A second major issue for Anabaptists was the relationship of the church to the government. Luther and Calvin never really questioned the close connection between church and state. They saw the church as playing an important role in influencing society for God, and they saw the government as ordained by God. The church and the government supported each other in the work that each had to do.

Here again the Anabaptists differed strongly with the reformers. When the Anabaptists read the New Testament, they saw the church being persecuted by the government, not partnering with it. Anabaptists believed in a strict and complete separation between the church and the government, so much so that they advocated having nothing to do with the government including the rendering of military service. To them, a union between the church and the government only resulted in a corrupted church that took on worldly ways.

Identity of the True Church

Another issue, related to the first two, involved the nature and identity of the true church. This was a subject that was hotly debated during the Reformation period. People wanted to know who was right, which group was right, and what minimum essentials were necessary to produce a church that was pleasing to God. The reformers believed that the Catholic Church was not the true church, but they differed over what needed to change and what needed to be included to produce the church of the New Testament.

For Luther, the true church involved faithful preaching of the Word and the observance of the two sacraments, baptism and communion. Calvin also stressed correct church organization. Anabaptists, however, emphasized the holy lifestyle of the members. Regardless of what errors or inconsistencies might be present in what the church did as a body, the members of that church needed to be pure and godly in their lives. All of the reformers were reacting against the failings of the Catholic Church. The Anabaptists reacted strongly to the ungodly and immoral lifestyles of some Catholic leaders and worldliness in the Catholic Church. For this reason, the practice of church discipline was always of great importance to Anabaptists. Sin, immorality, and worldliness could not be tolerated in the Lord's true church.

This is a major reason why the Anabaptists rejected infant baptism. To them, the true church did not consist of people who had been put through a religious ritual as an infant. Instead, the church was made up of people who had been born again, who had made a conscious decision to follow Christ, and who had expressed that commitment in baptism. This is also a reason why the Anabaptists opposed an interdependence between church and state. A church closely intertwined with the government (1) was doing what the New Testament did not authorize or exemplify and (2) would be worldly.

Dutch Anabaptists began moving to Poland in the 16th century, establishing successful farms and communities.

After declining to a few hundred members in the 19th century, the Hutterites began to grow again. By the early 2000s, there were over 40,000 Hutterites, primarily in Canada and the United States, with colonies also in Australia, Japan, and Nigeria. They live in cooperative communities, such as this one in Montana.

Anabaptist History

A congregation of Anabaptist believers was established in 1525 in Zurich, Switzerland. Other groups in Northern Europe were coming to similar conclusions around the same time, and the movement began to spread. Most Anabaptists were from the lower social classes. They hoped for a better life in this world, and some tried to set up utopian or equalitarian communities. Some of their more prominent leaders included Balthasar Hubmaier, Hans Denck, and Jacob Hutter (one group was called the Hutterites). In 1534 militant Anabaptists took control of Munster, Germany. They drove out all Protestants and Catholics and set up a theocratic government. Sixteen months later the Catholic bishop recaptured the city and executed the Anabaptists.

Menno Simons (c. 1496-1561) of the Netherlands was a Catholic priest who adopted the Anabaptist faith and became a respected moderate leader in the movement. His followers came to be called Mennonites. Because they refused to swear oaths or to serve in the military, they were often seen as subversives and were harshly persecuted. In 1683 many Mennonites began immigrating to the Pennsylvania colony in America where they were promised religious freedom. Other Mennonites settled in communities across the American Midwest.

The Anabaptists were never a movement that followed a single set of beliefs. They held to the autonomy of each individual congregation and thus did not have one leading spokesman or theologian. Because of their diversity and because they held their doctrines with great fervor, Anabaptists and Mennonites tended to split and splinter as time went on. A Swiss Mennonite bishop of the late 17th century, Jacob Amman, developed a following that came to be called the Amish. Many groups around the world trace their roots to the Anabaptists.

A group of Mennonites met with a group of British Separatists in Holland, who had gone there to escape the persecutions of King James I. One Briton, John Smyth, adopted the Anabaptist teachings, baptized himself and several others, and organized the first English Baptist Church in 1609 (remember that the Anabaptists called themselves Baptists). The group resisted Smyth's attempt to make them Mennonites, and Smyth was excommunicated. Some of the group returned to England as the persecution against Separatists lessened there, and they formed another Baptist congregation in London. As time went on, several Baptist groups were formed. The Baptist movement appealed to many in colonial America in part because of its simplicity of doctrine and congregational autonomy. Today Baptists make up the largest Protestant denomination in the United States.

Dirk Willems was a Dutch Anabaptist who was captured by Catholic authorities in the Netherlands for promoting the baptism of adults. He escaped from prison by tying rags together and letting himself out of a window. As a guard chased him across a frozen pond, the guard fell through the ice and called for help. Willems turned to rescue his pursuer, who then arrested him again. Willems was burned at the stake in 1569.

Legacy of the Anabaptists

The Anabaptists are sometimes called the Third Wing of the Reformation (after the Lutherans and the Calvinists). They took Luther's call for reform further and challenged more assumptions. In addition to the obvious heritage of Mennonite, Amish, and Baptist groups today, other believers have been influenced by the Anabaptist teachings on the importance of holy living, the necessity of a person coming to faith in order to be a candidate for baptism, and the need for the church to be distinct from the state and from the world.

*Therefore I, the prisoner of the Lord,
implore you to walk in a manner worthy of the calling
with which you have been called.
Ephesians 4:1*

Assignments for Lesson 83

In Their Words Read the excerpts from *Martyrs Mirror* (pages 183-185).

Literature Continue reading *Here I Stand*.

Student Review Optional: Answer the questions for Lesson 83.

The First Edition of the 1611 King James Bible

Lesson 84

History of the English Bible

The Bible was written in languages used by regular people. The Old Testament was written in Hebrew and Aramaic, the languages of the Israelites. The New Testament was written in koine Greek, the everyday language used in the first century Mediterranean world. Greek was a widely-used language when Rome conquered Western Europe and the Mediterranean Rim, which included southern Europe, Asia Minor, the Middle East, and northern Africa. The Romans spread Greek as a second language throughout much of the Roman Empire. God chose this common, everyday language for the New Testament to help spread the gospel.

As Christianity spread, the desire arose for translations of the Scriptures into other languages. The New Testament was quickly translated into Arabic, Armenian, Coptic, Ethiopic, Georgian, Gothic, Old Latin, and Syriac.

When Rome became the center of the Roman Catholic Church, Latin became its most commonly used language. In 382 AD Pope Damasus I commissioned Jerome to translate the Old and New Testaments into Latin. This translation is called the Vulgate or in Latin *vulgata editio*, meaning "popular edition." A short time later the Syriac Peshitta was completed. People were used to the older Latin and Syriac translations, so acceptance of the Vulgate and Syriac Peshitta took time.

For many centuries Latin was the official language of the Roman Catholic Church throughout Europe, including England. However, few people spoke or understood Latin. The Latin Vulgate Bibles were used almost exclusively by the clergy. The story of the translation of the Bible into English is really the story of the Bible moving from the hands of the clergy into the hands of the common people.

Early Translations

The first complete translation of Scripture into English was not finished until 1382, but portions were translated between the seventh and 14th centuries. Before Gutenberg's invention of the printing press, all Bible manuscripts were made by hand. A beautiful manuscript of the four Gospels was completed by monks on Lindisfarne Island, off the coast of Northumberland in England, about 700 AD. The manuscript was expertly illuminated with Celtic and Germanic designs. The first letters of each Gospel are especially beautiful. An Anglo-Saxon priest, Aldred, inserted a word-for-word Anglo-Saxon translation between the lines of the Latin text, probably in the mid- to late 900s.

Wycliffe and Tyndale

John Wycliffe taught philosophy at Oxford University in England and served as a parish priest. He believed that people could have a direct and personal relationship with God. If Christians closely followed the Scriptures, Wycliffe said, they could govern themselves without a pope. Wycliffe wanted to give the English-speaking people a Bible in their own language. He and his followers produced a handwritten English translation from the Latin Vulgate. After Wycliffe's death in 1384, this translation was distributed widely. Reformers Jan Hus of Bohemia and Martin Luther of Germany were influenced by the teachings of Wycliffe. The Catholic Church reviewed what Church leaders called Wycliffe's heresies and had his body exhumed and burned.

First Page of the Gospel of John from the Tyndale Bible

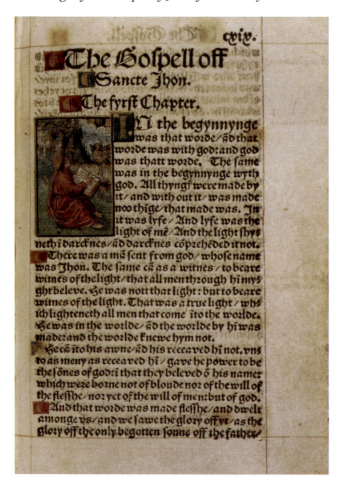

William Tyndale studied at the universities of Oxford and Cambridge. He became committed to translating the Bible from the original Greek and Hebrew into English. He once told an opponent, "If God spare my life, ere many years I will cause a boy that driveth the plow shall know more of the Scripture than thou doest." In translating the Bible, Tyndale used the first printed New Testament in Greek, which had been issued by Erasmus in 1516. After problems in England, Tyndale went to Germany and completed his translation in 1525. He had copies printed in Worms, Germany, and the first copies were smuggled into England the next year. Catholic Church officials spoke out against it, and copies were burned in public.

Tyndale published the Pentateuch (Genesis-Deuteronomy) in 1530 and Jonah in 1531. In 1534 he was betrayed and imprisoned by Catholic authorities who suspected him of having Lutheran sympathies. Two years later, he was strangled and burned at the stake by officers of the Catholic Church. As Tyndale died, he cried out, "Lord, open the king of England's eyes."

Great Bible, Geneva Bible, Bishops' Bible, Douay-Rheims Bible

Miles Coverdale also studied at Cambridge and entered the Augustine monastery there. He was deeply influenced by Robert Barnes, prior of the monastery, who shared many of Martin Luther's beliefs. Coverdale left the monastery in 1526 to preach against confession, image worship, and other Church practices. Following the start of the English Reformation, in 1538 the vicar-general of the Church of England commissioned Coverdale to oversee an authorized translation of the Scriptures.

Published in 1539, it was known as the Great Bible because of its large size. It was dedicated to King Henry VIII and was the first English Bible authorized to be read in churches. King Henry VIII encouraged its distribution. A copy was placed in every church in England, where people flocked to see it. Preachers complained that some people were more interested in reading the Bible than in hearing their sermons. The king of England's eyes were finally opened.

The Geneva Bible was an English translation published in 1560. It was called the Geneva Bible because it was first printed in Geneva, Switzerland, by a group of English dissenters who differed with the Anglican Church. The Bible was small, legible, and had commentary and illustrations throughout the text. It was the first Bible to have each verse as a separate paragraph with a verse number. The commentary reflected the Reformed views of John Calvin and his followers.

The English clergy undertook a revision of the Great Bible. Published in 1568, it was called the Bishops' Bible. It was not as scholarly and did not become as popular as the Geneva Bible. Generally speaking, the Bishops' Bible was used in churches and the Geneva Bible was used in homes.

English Catholics who were exiles in Europe formed an English College at the University of Douai in Flanders. Some of them began a new English translation, not translated from the original Greek and Hebrew but from the Latin Vulgate. The New Testament was published in 1582 in Rheims, France. In 1609-10 the Old Testament was published in two volumes. The complete Douay-Rheims Bible was revised and published in 1749-1752 by Richard Challoner, an English Catholic Bishop.

King James Bible

As the 17th century began, England was coping with the political and religious upheavals of the previous decades. Henry VIII had broken with Rome, his successor Mary had tried to realign her realm with Rome, and finally Elizabeth had restored the Protestants to supremacy. Then came the end of

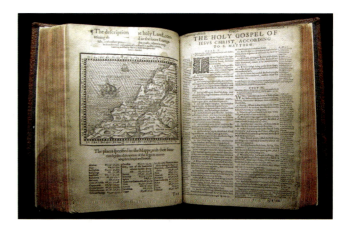

The Geneva Bible was issued in many different sizes and formats. Even many people with low incomes could afford at least a copy of the New Testament. Some editions had illustrations and maps, as shown in the example at right.

the Tudor line and the start of the Stuart dynasty with James of Scotland. Meanwhile, English versions of the Bible were proliferating. Many wanted a resolution to the confusing situation.

In 1604 King James I summoned representatives of diverse religious groups to a meeting to discuss religious toleration. At this meeting Dr. John Reynolds of Oxford University brought up the idea of a new translation. James welcomed the idea and began to work toward that goal. It seems that James himself decided that there would be no notes of comment except what was necessary to translate the text. One purpose of the effort was to produce a translation that all believers could use, one not slanted toward a particular set of beliefs.

The work began in 1607. The goal was to revise the 1602 edition of the Bishop's Bible. Forty-eight scholars who were experts in Greek and Hebrew worked on the project. The scholars were divided into six groups. Two worked at Westminster (London), two at Oxford, and two at Cambridge. Each group worked on specific books and sent their work to the other groups for review. The translators worked for two years and nine months to revise the Bishop's Bible and then sent the revision to the printers.

Comparison of Bible Versions (John 1:1)

Greek	εν αρχη ην ο λογος και ο λογος ην προς τον θεον και θεος ην ο λογος
Latin Vulgate	In principio erat Verbum et Verbum erat apud Deum et Deus erat Verbum
Wycliffe	In the bigynnyng was the word, and the word was at God, and God was the word.
Tyndale	In the beginning was the Word, and the Word was with God, and the Word was God.
KJV/RSV/NASB/NIV	In the beginning was the Word, and the Word was with God, and the Word was God.
The Living Bible (TLB)	Before anything else existed, there was Christ, with God. He has always been alive and is himself God.

The first copies were printed in 1611. The new translation was dedicated to King James. The title page stated, "Appointed to be read in Churches." The King James Bible is an excellent translation because its purpose was to be true to the original Greek and Hebrew. The translators relied heavily on the work of William Tyndale, who ironically had been killed as a heretic just seventy-seven years earlier.

Revisions of the KJV

The King James Version (KJV) eventually became the most widely-used English translation, even though it did have its critics. The KJV was not a perfect translation. The printing process was plagued with errors. Correcting these mistakes and revisiting the translation of certain phrases brought about several editions of the KJV after 1611. In addition, the 1611 edition printed the Apocrypha between the Old and New Testaments, a fact which concerned many Protestants since the Apocrypha is accepted as Scripture by the Roman Catholic Church but not by most Protestants. Moreover, the 1611 edition used then-current spellings for many words, which were changed in later editions.

The 1769 Oxford edition of the KJV became the standard edition most frequently printed since that time. Listed below are several major translations that have been made based on the King James.

English Revised Version (1885). In February 1870 the Church of England initiated a revision of the King James translation. Two British committees were formed, one for the Old Testament and one for the New. Later, two American committees were formed; they reviewed the work and communicated their suggestions. Committee members represented various denominations.

American Standard Version (1901). The American committees associated with the English Revised Version (ERV) published their edition of the revision. The main variations from the ERV involve differences in American and British English.

Revised Standard Version (1952). This was a revision of the American Standard Version. The revision was completed by a committee of scholars and was published by the International Council of Religious Education. A New Revised Standard Version was published in 1989.

New King James Version (1982). The NKJV uses contemporary American vocabulary while trying to retain the structure and basic language of the King James Version.

The English Standard Version (2001). Using the Revised Standard Version text as a starting point, a team of over one hundred members from twelve countries and twenty denominations worked to create a new translation using modern English and recent scholarship.

Lesson 84 - History of the English Bible

Other Recent Translations

The best way to produce an accurate Biblical translation is to do what the King James translators did: translate directly from the Greek and Hebrew texts. Since the 1960s, various teams of translators have worked to produce original translations that are not based directly on the work of William Tyndale and the scholars who prepared the King James translation. The following are a few popular ones:

Jerusalem Bible (1966). This version by Catholic scholars was translated from the original languages but influenced by a French translation produced in Jerusalem. Author J.R.R. Tolkein translated the book of Jonah.

New English Bible (1970). Initiated by the Church of Scotland, the committee of translators included members of several denominations. A revision, the Revised English Bible, was published in 1989.

New American Standard Bible (1971). Published by the Lockman Foundation, this has been considered the most literal word-for-word modern translation. An updated edition was released in 1995.

New International Version (1978). Produced by conservative American Protestants and evangelicals, it quickly became the most popular translation besides the KJV. The NIV aimed for dynamic equivalency rather than structural equivalency; that is, the translators worked phrase by phrase rather than word by word in an attempt to render original sentence structure in modern English style. This approach necessarily includes some degree of interpretation in the translation process. Updated versions appeared in 1984 and 2011.

New Living Translation (1996). *The Living Bible* (1971) by Kenneth Taylor, loosely based on the American Standard Version of 1901, became the best-known Bible paraphrase. The New Living Translation (NLT) was originally planned as a revision of *The Living Bible*. Instead, a team of ninety scholars produced an entirely new translation, following the example of the NIV in translating more thought-for-thought than word-for-word. A revision of the NLT was released in 2004.

***The Message* (2002).** Eugene Peterson, an American writer and pastor, spent ten years working from the original languages to create this translation. *The Message* uses informal, idiomatic English in a free-flowing style.

Holman Christian Standard Bible (2004). One hundred scholars from seventeen denominations created this version in an effort to communicate the Biblical message with clear, modern English.

Common English Bible (2011). This version was sponsored by the publishing houses of several mainline denominations (the Disciples of Christ, Presbyterian Church USA, Episcopal Church, United Church of Christ, and United Methodist Church). It includes the apocryphal books along with the Old and New Testaments.

Many specialty Bibles have been published that include notes and commentary alongside the Biblical text. These include the Kids Bible, Teen Bible, Prophecy Bible, Men's Devotional Bible, and Homeschool Mom's Bible. The notes in these Bibles are helpful, but they are written by human beings. When we study the Scriptures, we should make sure that we first look at what God says in His inspired Word. This photo shows Bibles for sale in Johannesburg, South Africa.

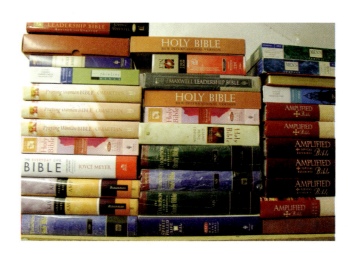

What Else Was Happening? (1500-1650)

1. Juan Diego told the Archbishop of Mexico City in 1531 that he had seen a vision of Mary, who requested that a church be built there. A shrine to Our Lady of Guadalupe featuring an iconic painting of Mary (detail at right) began drawing pilgrims immediately.

2. In the mid-1500s, traditional African religious beliefs were brought to Brazil as the Portuguese imported African slaves. Elements of these beliefs, such as the worship of ancestral spirits, have survived in independent religious systems and in mixture with Christian practices.

3. Suleiman I (1494-1566) was the Sultan of the Ottoman Empire and Caliph of Islam at the dawn of the Reformation. A variety of people facing religious persecution fled Europe to find toleration in his Muslim realm. The Protestants and Muslims shared opposition to the Catholics.

4. The Kalmyk people descended from migrants from western Mongolia. Their independent khanate, the first and only nation in Europe with a majority Buddhist population, was founded in 1630. It lasted about one hundred years until it was absorbed by Russia. The girl at center right is Annushka, a Kalmyk serf and pupil of a Russian Countess (1767).

5. Guru Nanak (1469-1539) was the founder of Sikhism. Leadership of the religion passed down through ten gurus (pictured at right). The collected writings of these teachers, known as Guru Granth Sahib, are acknowledged by Sikhs as their final, "living" guru.

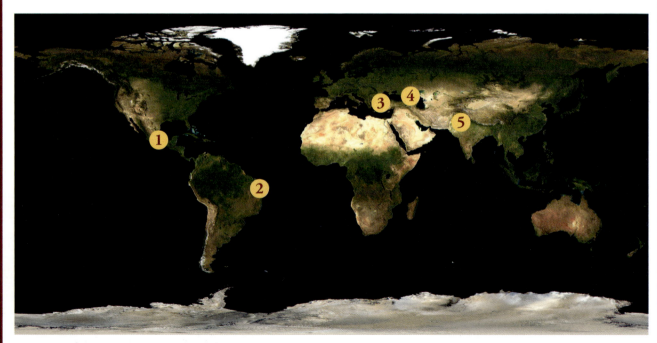

Lesson 84 - History of the English Bible

God's message of salvation was written down so that people who lived after the time of Christ could hear it and believe it. Each generation, culture, and language group needs to hear that message in a way that they can understand. Bible translators have worked hard to accomplish that goal.

---

*The grass withers, the flower fades,
but the word of our God stands forever.
Isaiah 40:8*

Assignments for Lesson 84

In Their Words — Read William Tyndale's translation of 1 Corinthians 13 (page 186).

Literature — Continue reading *Here I Stand*.

Student Review — Optional: Answer the questions for Lesson 84.

Himalaya Mountains

Lesson 85 - Bible Study

Grace

"What must I do to be saved?" was the desperate question of the jailer in Philippi to Paul and Silas (Acts 16:30). It is the question of all who realize their spiritual situation without Christ. Every religious group attempts to answer that question according to its understanding of the truth. The Gnostics said that one is saved by acquiring inside knowledge available to only a few. Some in the Roman Catholic Church said that one can be saved (or at least remain saved) by performing good works. Luther said that a person is justified on the basis of faith alone. To see how the Bible answers this question, we will study a passage that summarizes the grace of God and how a person is saved: Ephesians 2:1-10.

You Were Dead

In Ephesians, Paul is explaining to the Christians in Ephesus (1) how they came to be part of the glorious fellowship of Christ and members of one another and (2) how they need to live as a result of this astounding new identity. He prays that they will know the greatness of God's power and the riches of the glory that God has prepared for his people (Ephesians 1:15-23).

To appreciate this, they had to understand that they were once spiritually dead (Ephesians 2:1). They were dead, but they walked in their sins

"[T]here is not one in a thousand who does not set his confidence upon the works, expecting by them to win God's favor and anticipate His grace; and so they make a fair of them, a thing which God cannot endure, since He has promised His grace freely, and wills that we begin by trusting that grace, and in it perform all works, whatever they may be." —Martin Luther, Treatise on Good Works *(1520)*

Lesson 85 - Bible Study: Grace

"[Divine Grace] is a gratuitous affection by which God is kindly affected towards a miserable sinner, and according to which he, in the first place, gives his Son, 'that whosoever believes in him might have eternal life,' and, afterwards, he justifies him in Christ Jesus and for his sake, and adopts him into the right of sons, unto salvation." —Jacob Arminius, from a 1608 speech

(Ephesians 2:2). In other words, they were dead men walking. Life outside of Christ is no better than this, however it might be filled with pleasures. They lived according to the ways of the world, the ways of Satan. Christians are no better than anybody else on the basis of their track record (Ephesians 2:3). We are not better people because we believe, or because we come from a Christian family, or because we attend a particular kind of church. Because of our sins, we become by our very nature an object that deserves God's wrath.

God Made You Alive

God, however, did not exercise His wrath toward us while we were sinners. Instead, because of His great love, He mercifully made us alive in Christ even when we were dead in our sins. This is grace (Ephesians 2:4-5). When we didn't deserve it, God gave it to us. Even though we didn't earn it (and couldn't earn it--we were, after all, dead), we received it anyway because of God's loving and merciful nature.

The nature of this grace is that God seated us with Christ. As Christ is on His throne in heaven, we are seated with Him and participate in His reign. In that position God lavishes upon us the riches of His grace from now into eternity (Ephesians 2:6-7). God does not just barely tolerate us, allowing us to stand in the shadows of His kingdom when He would really rather not have us there at all. It is not as though we were wandering peasants whom God placed in a hut on His manor. Instead, He brought us into the castle and gave us a seat at the head table. Even the hut would be grace when we didn't deserve it, but God has an abundance prepared that He wants to give to those whom He makes alive in Christ.

Saved by Grace Through Faith

"For by grace you have been saved through faith," Paul summarizes in Ephesians 2:8. The Christian is saved; he is saved by God's grace—an act of love and mercy when he did not deserve it; and this comes about on the basis of faith. The apostle says that this does not come from ourselves but is instead the gift of God. Some people think that the word "that" in verse 8 refers to faith, that we are incapable of believing and that God gives faith to those whom He wills to save. However, if we are dead men capable of walking, the Bible teaches that we are also capable of choosing to believe. All of the many appeals in the Bible for people to come to faith support this.

Comparison of Bible Versions (Ephesians 2:8-9)

Wycliffe	For bi grace ye ben sauyd bi feith, and this not of you; for it is the yifte of God, not of werkis, that no man haue glorie.
Tyndale	For by grace are ye made safe thorowe fayth and that not of youre selves. For it is the gyfte of God and commeth not of workes lest eny man should bost him silfe.
Geneva	For by grace are ye saved through faith; and that not of yourselves, it is the gift of God; not of works, lest any man should boast himself.
KJV	For by grace are ye saved through faith; and that not of yourselves: it is the gift of God: not of works, lest any man should boast.
Amplified Bible	For it is by free grace (God's unmerited favor) that you are saved (delivered from judgment and made partakers of Christ's salvation) through [your] faith. And this [salvation] is not of yourselves [of your own doing, it came not through your own striving], but it is the gift of God; not because of works [not the fulfillment of the Law's demands], lest any man should boast. [It is not the result of what anyone can possibly do, so no one can pride himself in it or take glory to himself.]
NIV	For it is by grace you have been saved, through faith—and this is not from yourselves, it is the gift of God—not by works, so that no one can boast.
NLT	God saved you by his grace when you believed. And you can't take credit for this; it is a gift from God. Salvation is not a reward for the good things we have done, so none of us can boast about it.
The Message	Saving is all his idea, and all his work. All we do is trust him enough to let him do it. It's God's gift from start to finish! We don't play the major role. If we did, we'd probably go around bragging that we'd done the whole thing!
Hawai'i Pidgin	God like do plenny fo you guys, cuz dass how he stay. He like hemo you guys from da bad kine stuff you guys stay in, if you guys trus God strait out. No mo notting you guys can do by yoaself. God make lidis fo you guys. Dass jalike one spesho present God get fo you guys. Da tings you do by yoaself, eh, no talk big, cuz no worth notting.

In the Greek of verse 8, both grace and faith are feminine nouns, while the referent "that" is neuter. The word "that" is referring to the entire idea of salvation that is expressed in the previous phrase. The salvation we have by grace through faith is nothing we earn; it is God's gift. Paul rephrases his meaning in verse 9, where he says that salvation does not come as a result of works. We have no reason to boast pridefully about something that was given to us when we were dead.

As saved people, we have a new identity, a new nature. We were by nature objects of wrath (verse 3). Now we are God's workmanship, something that God has made anew. He took us when we were a lump of worthless clay that was His enemy and molded us into a beautiful vessel that He could use for His good purposes. Once we walked in our sins, but now we can walk in the good works that God planned for us to do (Ephesians 2:10).

What Grace Says

Grace says something profound about God. We have all messed up in our lives and are not able to go back and make things right on our own. Ephesians

Lesson 85 - Bible Study: Grace

says that the person in sin does not even want to go back and make things right. This is what we have done with our lives. Ephesians 2:1-10 tells us what God has done about our lives. He has provided a way of salvation that is available to us through faith. God acts on the basis of His nature, not on the basis of what we deserve--and that is grace! Someone has said that our salvation is the eighth day of God's Creation. God created the world in six days, rested on the seventh; and then from the time of the sin in the Garden forward, His creative powers have been devoted to recreating humanity in Christ.

Grace also says important things about man. It says we once were dead spiritually but God made us alive. It says that once we lived for the world but now we can live for God's purposes. Grace says that once we were fit only to receive the wrath of God, but now we are fit for serving Him. It says that we have blown it but that we are worth God's very best: the giving of His Son.

Grace reveals important truths about our lives. First, God says that we are to use our lives for Him. If this sounds unreasonable, remember that we have no room to negotiate with God on how we are to live. After all, we were once dead and He gave us a new life. Grace says that we can see every day as an opportunity to live in God's grace and be thankful for it. Grace teaches us to deny ungodliness and live righteously in the present age while we await the coming of Christ (Titus 2:11-15).

Cheap Grace, Costly Grace

The German theologian Dietrich Bonhoeffer, who died in a Nazi concentration camp during World War II, wrote in *The Cost of Discipleship* that some people have cheapened grace by how they respond to it. Cheap grace is the idea that since everything has been taken care of by Christ, we can live as we please. Cheap grace makes no demands on you. It is, as Bonhoeffer says, grace without discipleship, grace without the cross.

What the New Testament teaches is costly grace. Biblical grace was won at a tremendous price—the death of Christ—and thus it will cost us something also. For Christians to live with ingratitude and to live in the ways of the world, from which Christ died to redeem us, is the height of insult to God. Costly grace is beyond rule-keeping and minimum-essentials religion. When God's grace gets inside you, you will be different from the inside out.

The Proper Response to Grace

A gift so costly, amazing, and life-changing demands an appropriate response. If someone gave you a new car, it would be inappropriate to mutter "Thanks" and then go on as though it hadn't happened. The gift of God's grace deserves a response in keeping with the significance of the gift.

Yet, no response we can make earns us grace. Salvation is the gift of God so that no one can boast. Faith does not earn us salvation; faith is the proper response to grace. Repentance does not earn us salvation; repentance is the response of being convicted by grace. Baptism does not earn us salvation; baptism is done to us and puts us in touch with the source of grace (Romans 6:3). A life of good works does not earn us salvation; such a life is how those who have been saved should live.

Dietrich Bonhoeffer with a Group of Young Men, 1932

The Catholic system, the Protestant reaction, the doctrinal squabbles, and the religious wars all tend to cloud the basic truth: we were dead in sin, and God makes us alive in Christ by grace through faith. The way of Christ is not about ecclesiastical hierarchies or worldly power or political control. It is about people being made new and living for the One who saved them.

And He has said to me, "My grace is sufficient for you, for power is perfected in weakness." Most gladly, therefore, I will rather boast about my weaknesses, so that the power of Christ may dwell in me.
2 Corinthians 12:9

Assignments for Lesson 85

Bible — Recite or write Ephesians 4:4-6 from memory.

In Their Words — Read the excerpt from *Institutes of the Christian Religion* and "The Day of Grace" (pages 187-191).

Literature — Continue reading *Here I Stand*.

Project — Complete your project for the unit.

Student Review — Optional: Answer the questions for Lesson 85 and take the quiz for Unit 17.

18

The Age of Exploration

Summary Developing concurrently with the Reformation, the Age of Exploration affected culture, religion, science, and government. We will survey European exploration and focus especially on Christopher Columbus. England's defeat of the Spanish Armada in 1588 affected colonization in the Americas and the balance of power in Europe. We will also take a look at housing and home furnishings. The Bible study examines an exploration in the Bible: the twelve Israelite spies going into Canaan.

Lessons
86 - Discovering New Worlds
87 - Key Person: Christopher Columbus
88 - Key Event: The English Defeat of the Spanish Armada
89 - Everyday Life: Homes and Household Furnishings
90 - Bible Study: Exploring the Promised Land

Detail of 1570 Map by Abraham Ortelius Showing the Americas

493

Memory Work: Learn Luke 12:29-31 by the end of the unit.

Books Used:
The Bible
In Their Words
Here I Stand

Project (choose one):

1) Write 300 to 500 words on one of the following topics:

- Conduct research on one of the explorers mentioned in this unit, other than Christopher Columbus. Study his life as well as his explorations. If applicable, include any controversies regarding his exploration. See Lesson 86.

- Write a book review of *Here I Stand* by Roland Bainton. Summarize the book, tell what you liked, what you didn't like, what you learned, and what you would like to know more about.

2) Make a board game to play with your family about the Age of Exploration. The game should include facts about different explorers and their accomplishments.

3) Research foods that were introduced to Europe from the New World during the Age of Exploration. Prepare a meal that features several of these foods.

Lesson 86

Discovering New Worlds

Nations and individuals live within boundaries. People have to respect the boundaries of time, space, and their own physical strength. Nations must respect the political boundaries that define themselves and other countries. When people and nations do not respect boundaries, problems arise.

However, some boundaries are self-imposed. A person might convince himself that he is unable to accomplish a given task when in fact he could accomplish it if he had the will to do so. A people might have believed in its own limitations for so long that the limits might as well have been imposed upon them.

Expanding the Boundaries

For centuries, most people in Europe stayed within the boundaries of what they called the known world. Those boundaries consisted of the Sahara Desert, the borders of India, the wastelands of Central Asia, and, to the west, the vast Atlantic Ocean. Invaders had occasionally come to Europe from Asia, but not since Alexander the Great had a European force pushed as far beyond Europe as he had. What lay beyond the visible limits of the Atlantic was the subject of fearful and ignorant speculation.

Europeans had heard of mysterious and fabulous kingdoms to the east, but it was only when Marco Polo traveled beyond the accepted boundaries to China (Cathay as it was then known) and returned to tell his story that Europeans began to consider the possibility of new boundaries.

Some technological boundaries began to come down during the Renaissance. Better navigational tools became available. The Chinese had invented the magnetic compass, which was introduced to Europeans by Arab traders. Improved ships and sails brought closer the possibility of longer sea voyages. The rise of national monarchies enabled more funds to be devoted to explorations that smaller kingdoms could not afford. An increasing sense of possibilities for man encouraged people to think about going exploring to find adventure, to satisfy human curiosity, to amass wealth, and to spread the Christian faith to other people.

The Portuguese eventually reached Japan after going around Africa and crossing the Indian Ocean. The painting above, attributed to Japanese artist Kano Domi shows Portuguese traders passing a Japanese home (c. 1600).

The country of Portugal faced two significant boundaries in the 15th century. First, Italian merchants controlled Mediterranean trade as well as traffic in Oriental spices through Arab dealers. Second, Portugal faced the wrong way—on the western coast of Europe—to be able to make a dent in that trade; or so many people thought. With the advances in navigation mentioned above, some in Portugal began to think about stretching the boundaries. A few Portuguese royalty and businessmen wondered if a way might be found to delve into the lucrative spice trade by sailing to Asia themselves, without having to deal with either the Italians or the Arabs. One way was to find a route around Africa, while a handful of dreamers wondered if it might be possible to reach Asia by sailing west.

Prince Henry of Portugal (called the Navigator) encouraged exploration on behalf of his country. Portuguese explorers brought back wealth from the gold mines of West Africa, a region that became known as the Gold Coast. Later in the 15th century, Portuguese vessels pushed farther and farther down the western coast of Africa. In 1488 Bartholomew Dias reached the southern tip of Africa before returning home. He called the place the Cape of Storms because of the violent weather there. King John II of Portugal renamed it the Cape of Good Hope because he knew that Dias had given his people hope of finding a water route to Asia. In 1497 Vasco da Gama rounded the Cape, sailed up the eastern coast of Africa, then launched out across the Indian Ocean and arrived in India in 1498. Trade with India, China, and the Spice Islands (now known as the Moluccas) began to bring Portugal the wealth that people had dreamed about.

Response from Spain

As Portugal was expanding its boundaries—and its trade possibilities—its neighbor Spain became jealous. Ferdinand and Isabella had succeeded in expelling the Jews and Muslims in 1492 and in bringing peace to the country. Christopher Columbus gained the support of the royal couple for his famous voyage.

The Cantino Planisphere is a 1502 Portuguese map showing the results of Portuguese exploration in North and South America, Africa, and Asia.

Lesson 86 - Discovering New Worlds

The Nao Victoria was the first known ship to sail around the world. After Magellan's death, it returned to Spain under the command of Juan Sebastián Elcano. This replica of the ship is located at the Nao Victoria Museum in Punta Arenas, Chile, on the southern tip of South America.

Europeans began to send numerous expeditions to explore the new lands that had been unknown in Europe previously. Amerigo Vespucci was an Italian explorer who represented a Medici bank in Spain and who reported on what he found in the new world. In 1507 a German mapmaker named for him the lands Amerigo had found: America.

As competition heated up between Spain and Portugal, a treaty was signed with the approval of the pope in 1494 that divided the world between them. An imaginary north-south boundary line was drawn 1100 miles west of the Azores, islands off the western coast of Africa. Spain was permitted to explore and claim lands to the west of the line, while Portugal was given access to lands east of the line. Spain thus received the rights to most of the New World, but a few years later Portuguese explorers landed in and claimed Brazil, which protruded east across the treaty line. In Brazil the Portuguese used the work of African slaves to carve out sugar plantations and to mine for diamonds and emeralds.

Spain sent many expeditions west. In 1513 Ponce de Leon landed on the North American continent and explored what became Florida while he was looking for a fabled fountain of eternal youth (he didn't find it). That same year, Vasco de Balboa crossed a narrow strip of land in Central America and became the first European to view the Pacific Ocean from the New World.

The voyage led by Ferdinand Magellan that began in 1519 was intended to extend Spain's claims to western lands and to find a western passage to Asia. He found it around the tip of South America (Cape Horn) and eventually arrived in the Philippines. There Magellan got into a quarrel with the natives, and he and others in his party were killed. Of the five ships in Magellan's entourage that left Spain in 1519, one returned to Spain in 1520 having sailed around the world. With a continent theirs for the taking and western travel to Asia obviously difficult, Spain abandoned its quest to develop trade with Asia and instead concentrated on developing possibilities in America.

Other Countries

Other European nations did not recognize the treaty that divided the world between Portugal and Spain. These other countries wanted a share of the expanding global pie. One goal they shared was the hope of finding a passage through America to Asia to avoid having to go around Cape Horn.

John Cabot, an Italian, sailed in 1497 for England and explored a New Found Land (Newfoundland) in North America. In 1524 France sponsored another Italian, Giovanni de Verrazano, who explored the North American coast where English colonies would one day be founded. That same year, Jacques Cartier journeyed up the St. Lawrence River and explored the interior of the continent. In 1609 the Dutch hired the Englishman Henry Hudson, who sailed up the Hudson River before realizing that it was not the passage to India he hoped to find. Hudson later discovered the bay in Canada named for him.

As Portugal turned eastward and came to dominate the spice trade, other European countries besides Spain chased them also. The Netherlands and then England and France sent expeditions to islands off the coast of Southeast Asia, known in Europe as the East Indies. They did this to break the virtual trade monopoly that Portugal had developed there.

The Spanish Empire in America

Spain was able freely to develop and exploit vast sections of the New World with little interference from other European countries. Stories of wealthy kingdoms in the New World drew the Spanish on. Although those kingdoms did not exist, Spain did extract considerable wealth from its American empire.

The Spanish crown gave *conquistadors* (conquerors) the right to set up their own little kingdoms in the Americas as long as they gave a cut to the throne. In 1519 Hernando Cortes and his small army made alliances with tribes in Central America who disliked being subject to the Aztecs. The Aztecs themselves agreed to be allies with the Spanish but then revolted against them. The Spanish in 1521 easily defeated the Aztecs, destroyed their capital, and built a new settlement that became Mexico City. The Aztecs had not developed the wheel and did not have access to iron or to horses. They also were weakened by diseases such as smallpox which the Spanish brought to their land.

In South America, Francisco Pizarro fought the Incas between 1530 and 1535, conquering them and taking control of their empire. Once again, the Spaniards had horses and better weapons and the natives were weakened by disease. This pattern was repeated in many places in the Americas.

The conquistadors established their domains and required the natives to work as little better than slaves until Spanish law outlawed the practice in 1542. The Spanish shipped many products from the western hemisphere back to enrich Spain, including

This illustration from Universal History of the Things of New Spain *depicts the Spaniards disposing of the bodies of Montezuma and Itzquauhtzin, two local leaders. The work was created by Bernardino de Sahagún, who came to New Spain (Mexico) as a missionary a few years after the conquest of the Aztecs. He spent fifty years studying Aztec culture and created the twelve-volume set of books in cooperation with Aztec students and artists. Sahagún also translated the Psalms and Gospels into the Nahuatl language.*

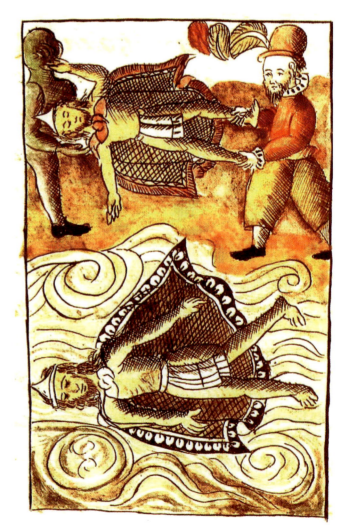

Toasted Cacao Beans Grown in Mexico

silver, gold, cacao (chocolate), coffee, lumber, tobacco, and sugar (for its own appeal and as the main ingredient in molasses and rum). Plantations were established to grow sugar cane, and the Spanish began to import thousands of slaves from Africa. Most of the slaves were captured and sold to the Spanish by their fellow Africans. Conditions on the slave ships were horrible. Many Africans died before reaching the New World.

Although the coming of other Europeans to settle in America limited the growth of Spanish territories, Spain retained control of its American colonies almost completely unchallenged until the 1800s. England managed to wrest control of Florida from Spain, but that was a notable exception. When the Spanish empire in America did begin to unravel, it was because of encroachments by the United States and by revolutions of subject peoples, not because of challenges from other nations in Europe.

Other European Settlements

By the late 1500s, the Netherlands had become a powerful international presence. Colonies of Netherlanders (also called Dutch) were created at New Amsterdam at the mouth of the Hudson River and along the river north to Albany. In 1655 the Dutch seized a Swedish colony near what became Wilmington, Delaware.

French explorers settled the St. Lawrence River valley and other parts of Canada. In 1673 Marquette and Joliet paddled their way down most of the length of the Mississippi River. Nine years later, LaSalle completed the journey and named the region at the mouth of the river Louisiana after the French king Louis XIV.

The English established colonies along the Atlantic coast from Massachusetts to Georgia and in the West Indies. The two predominant motivations for English colonial settlements were economic gain and religious freedom. In 1664 the English ousted the Dutch from New Amsterdam and renamed it New York. English forces and their Indian allies in 1763 defeated the French forces and their Indian allies in what is called the French and Indian War (part of the Seven Years' War that included conflict in Europe and India). The French gave up control of Canada, despite a large French-speaking population there. As a result, English control over most of North America was complete.

This painting, Robert Clive and Mir Jafar after the Battle of Plassey, 1757, *by Francis Hayman (British, c. 1760) depicts a scene from India. The British East India Company and the French East India Company vied for control of the region, working with various local allies. Mir Jafar, a general under the Nawab of Bengal, made a secret agreement with the British commander Robert Clive to lose the battle. This event paved the way for British control of India.*

Analysis of the Age of Exploration

Foreign trade was valuable to Europeans, but forming colonies in the New World and in Asia (called colonization) was even more attractive. This gave the colonizing nations direct access to raw materials, which could be returned to the home country and made into goods that could then be sold in international trade.

Trade and colonization, however, were expensive and risky propositions. Those involved always faced the initial costs, the dangers of bad weather and attack by natives, and the possibility that the ultimate selling price of the goods would not justify the endeavor. All of these factors came into play at various times and places, but the risks did not deter nations from seeking the profit to be gained. Exploration and colonization came to be major factors in world affairs.

To help with the costs, the practice of insuring a venture became commonplace. A relatively small premium protected investors if the effort did not work out. In addition, entrepreneurs spread the risk among several investors in the form of a partnership or joint stock company. Some companies and individuals received charters from their governments and acted as the government in those colonies. To finance some economic ventures as well as military actions, governments and individuals sometimes used loans from banks.

The prevailing economic philosophy in Europe in the 1600s was mercantilism. This approach held that (1) a nation was stronger economically by maintaining its gold supply and developing a positive balance of trade (more exports than imports); (2) a better return was possible through the selling of finished goods than through trade in raw materials, so companies began to build factories to manufacture goods; (3) colonies helped a nation's economy to grow by providing raw materials and by being a market for finished goods; and (4) the government should support and be intimately involved in the process by financing ventures, making rules and regulations favorable to such ventures, and supporting industries such as shipbuilding that made exploration, trade, and colonization possible.

Europe experienced an economic boom because of the increases in exploration, colonization, and trade. Italy lost its predominance in foreign trade, and the balance of economic power shifted to Spain, France, England, and the Netherlands. An increase in gold reserves was part of the greater wealth.

By the late 1700s Britain was the most powerful nation in the world, politically, economically, and militarily. The successful American independence movement slowed but did not stop this growth. Colonization by European countries continued into the 20th century.

Not everything about European world expansion was good. A focus on material wealth often led to ruthless exploitation of native populations and natural resources. African slaves were forcibly removed from their homes and used to enhance the wealth of a relatively few people. For many people, success came to be defined in economic terms.

Colombo, Sri Lanka, has been an important trading port for hundreds of years. Greeks, Persians, Romans, Arabs, and Chinese all traded there. During the Age of Exploration, Colombo was controlled successively by the Portuguese, the Dutch (as pictured here about 1670), and the English. Sri Lanka (also known as Ceylon) gained independence from Britain in 1948.

Lesson 86 - Discovering New Worlds

We must also remember that a genuine missionary impulse lay behind the efforts of some European explorers and colonizers. Most of the national rulers who supported or encouraged these ventures wanted to see the people of other lands become Christians. Priests and missionaries commonly accompanied the soldiers and colonizers to teach the gospel to the people they met. Not every motive and action of these evangelists was good, but certainly the Christian message was spread to new lands through their efforts.

We cannot completely separate the Christian motive from the economic and imperialist motives because, to the Europeans of the period, these motives were wrapped up together. Evangelism, rule by a Christian monarch, and economic gain were all part of the identity of European nations.

The boundaries within which Europe had lived for centuries were now forever changed. The issues that had concerned a continent now affected the entire world. As the European vision of the world expanded, the world in a sense became smaller.

Then He said to them, "Beware, and be on your guard against every form of greed; for not even when one has an abundance does his life consist of his possessions."
Luke 12:15

Assignments for Lesson 86

In Their Words — Read "Of the Isle of Cuba" by Bartolomé de las Casas (pages 192-194).

Literature — Continue reading *Here I Stand*. Plan to finish it by the end of this unit.

Student Review — Optional: Answer the questions for Lesson 86.

Detail from Inspiration of Cristobal Colon
Jose Maria Obregon (Mexican, 1856)

Lesson 87 - Key Person

Christopher Columbus

In 1451 Cristoforo Colombo was born in the Italian city-state of Genoa. His father, Domenico, was a wool weaver, and his mother, Suzanna, was the daughter of a wool weaver. He had four brothers and a sister. Colombus likely gained a basic education as he learned the wool craft, but his interest turned to the sea.

Columbus began working on ships at age fourteen. After years of sailing in the Mediterranean, he ended up in Portugal at age twenty-five. Tradition says that French privateers attacked and burned his ship on its way to England, and that he had to swim to shore.

His brother Bartholomew became a mapmaker in Lisbon, Portugal, which was a center for those interested in the sea. Christopher and Bartholomew worked together for a while before Christopher married Felipa Perestrello e Moniz. The young couple moved to the Madeira Islands off the coast of Africa, of which Felipa's father had been governor previously. Their son Diego was born there, and Felipa evidently died soon after.

The English translation of Colombo's name is Christopher Columbus. He used the Portuguese version Cristováo Colom when in Portugal and the Spanish version Cristóbal Colón when living in and sailing for Spain.

Preparation

The fall of the Byzantine Empire to Ottoman Turks in 1453 motivated European nations to seek a water route to Asia. They hoped to bypass the Muslim-controlled Middle East and deal directly with the Asians.

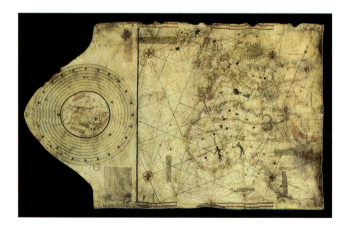

This map from about 1490 is thought to have come from the workshop of Bartholomew Columbus. On the right is a map of Europe and Africa. It includes a representation of Iceland, which Christopher visited in 1477, according to his son. On the left is a round map of the world showing Europe, Africa, and Asia.

Lesson 87 - Key Person: Christopher Columbus

Columbus began to develop his "Enterprise of the Indies," a plan to sail west to reach the lands of the east. He studied maps and charts and learned from sailors and scholars. However, since he overestimated the size of Asia and underestimated the size of the earth, Columbus was in for a surprise.

Columbus sought support from King John II of Portugal, but the king's Council of Geographical Affairs rejected the proposal. Columbus then moved to Spain. The kingdoms of Portugal and Spain at this time were competitors in acquiring new colonies. They were not on friendly terms, but they were not ready for all-out war.

Columbus spent time at a monastery in southern Spain. Some of the friars encouraged his plans. Friar Antonio Machena discussed geography with Columbus and introduced him to Friar Juan Pérez, who introduced him to the royal court of Ferdinand V and Isabella I.

Ferdinand and Isabella were cousins who joined two leading Spanish kingdoms through their marriage. Their five children included Catherine of Aragón, the first wife of England's Henry VIII, and Joanna the Mad, mother of Spanish King and Holy Roman Emperor Charles V. They were staunch

---

Paolo dal Pozzo Toscanelli (1397-1482) was an Italian scholar who corresponded with Columbus. Toscanelli's 1474 map depicted China, Japan, and other Asian islands with a navigable ocean between them and Europe and Africa. The 1884 illustration below shows Toscanelli's map superimposed over a map showing North and South America.

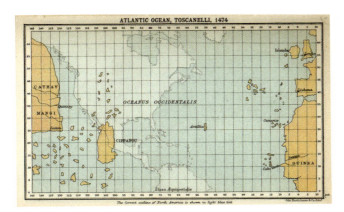

As seen above, Columbus made notes and drawings in his copy of The Travels of Marco Polo.

Catholics who initiated the Spanish Inquisition with the pope's authority.

Columbus went to Seville in 1485 and lived for a time at the queen's expense. Ferdinand and Isabella were not ready to back Columbus' ambitious plans, especially in the midst of their war against the Moors in Granada. A committee rejected Columbus' proposal in 1487.

During this time, Columbus developed a relationship with Beatriz Enríquez de Arana, a peasant woman. They never married, but Beatriz bore Columbus a son in 1488. This son, Ferdinand (also called Fernando), accompanied his father on his final voyage to the New World and wrote a biography of his father.

Columbus again sought royal favor in 1491. He asked for one-tenth of the riches gained in the journey and the titles of admiral, viceroy, and governor. These would give him royal authority to judge commercial disputes and to direct all civil and military affairs in lands he discovered. Ferdinand and Isabella rejected Columbus again.

Tradition says that as Columbus was riding away, Luis de Santángel asked the monarchs to reconsider. As Ferdinand's treasurer, he thought the possible rewards were worth the investment. However it happened, the king and queen changed their minds and prepared a contract with Columbus for the voyage.

A Reproduction of the Niña Built in 1991

The First Voyage

So in fourteen hundred and ninety-two, Columbus sailed the ocean blue. Three ships, each about 80 feet long, carried a total crew of about ninety sailors. No priests, soldiers, or settlers were on board the *Niña*, the *Pinta*, and the *Santa Maria*.

The trio of ships left Spain on August 3. They stopped in the Canary Islands, repaired the rudder of the *Pinta*, and continued into the unknown on September 6. Without reliable means of navigation in unfamiliar seas, Columbus relied on his highly trained nautical senses. In the early morning of October 12, just over one month after leaving the Canaries, Rodrigo de Triana, a lookout on the Pinta, cried "Tierra! Tierra! (Land!)" A reward had been promised to the man who first saw land. Columbus claimed the prize for himself, saying that he had seen lights earlier.

Columbus and a few crew members landed on the island, bearing banners and claiming it for Spain. They met and traded with the natives. Thinking that he had landed in the Indies of East Asia, Columbus called them *indios*, or Indians. He called the island San Salvador ("Holy Savior"). The precise location of Columbus' initial landing is uncertain, so the island called San Salvador today might not be the same one.

Native guides took Columbus to other islands. He thought that Cuba was a promontory of China, even though the natives told him it was an island. He also sailed along the island of Hispaniola.

One of Columbus' officers had sailed away with the *Pinta* for reasons unknown, and the *Santa Maria* had been damaged by a reef. The Spaniards built a fort from her lumber and left thirty-nine men in what they called Christmas Town. The *Pinta* came back on January 6, and with the *Niña* soon set sail for Europe. A storm separated the ships before they reached home.

Columbus and the *Niña* ended up in Lisbon, Portugal, where King John arrested him. Columbus got word to Spain that he had returned, and John released him in March. Columbus returned to the Spanish port he had left on March 15, 1493. The *Pinta* had arrived in northern Spain earlier, but it came to the southern port where Columbus landed.

Success and Failure

Ferdinand and Isabella welcomed Columbus back with great honor. Columbus displayed his exotic booty of parrots, gold, and human beings. Persuading the monarchs to equip a second voyage was less difficult than his previous attempts.

Columbus wrote to Pope Alexander VI to head off possible Portuguese interference with his claims. Alexander set a Line of Demarcation running north and south in the Atlantic Ocean. New discoveries east of the line would belong to Portugal. New discoveries west of the line would belong to Spain. The two countries agreed to move the line farther west the next year. This decision led to Brazil becoming a Portuguese territory while most of Central and South America came under Spanish control.

In September of 1493, Columbus set off on his second voyage with 17 ships and about 1,200 settlers. Columbus' brothers Bartholomew and Diego joined him. When they reached Hispaniola, they discovered that the Spanish settlement had been destroyed and the occupants killed. The village of friendly natives was also burned.

Lesson 87 - Key Person: Christopher Columbus

The Spaniards established another settlement called Isabela. Some of them became ill and others did not want to work. Columbus decided to force the natives to work for the new community. While he went off exploring, he made his brother Diego governor of Isabela.

The community did not get off to a good start. Some settlers returned to Spain and others sent letters home complaining about the situation. A Spanish official arrived in October of 1495 to investigate. Columbus put Bartholomew and Diego in charge and left for Spain in March of 1496. Ferdinand and Isabella received Columbus cordially, but they did not authorize a third voyage for over a year.

Columbus left Europe again on May 30, 1498. This time he sailed farther south, to the coast of South America. After seeing the large mouth of the Orinoco River in modern Venezuela, Columbus realized that he might have found a continent unknown in Europe.

A revolt against Columbus' authority on Hispaniola lasted two years. Columbus finally regained control, but conditions did not significantly improve. Columbus sought assistance from Ferdinand and Isabella, but they sent Franciso de Bobadilla to replace him. When Bobadilla arrived in 1500, he arrested Columbus and his brothers and sent them to Spain in chains. Ferdinand and Isabella ordered the restoration of Columbus' personal items, but they did not restore his titles.

In 1499 Vasco da Gama had opened a direct trade route between Portugal and India around the southern tip of Africa. Exploration was continuing along the coasts of North and South America. Columbus was 50 and in poor health, but he wanted to try his hand again. The Spanish sovereigns equipped him for a fourth and final voyage.

On May 9, 1502, Columbus left Spain with his fourteen-year-old son Ferdinand, his brother Bartholomew, and his crew. Trials beset this expedition, and Columbus and his men ended up stranded on Jamaica. Their ships became unseaworthy. When the natives on the island stopped providing food, Columbus used his astronomical tables against them. He threatened to take away the moon's light. When a lunar eclipse fulfilled his prediction, the islanders decided to renew trade.

Two of Columbus' sailors set out in canoes paddled by natives on a 450-mile journey by sea to get help from the governor on Hispaniola. Columbus

The Virgin of the Navigators by Alejo Fernández (Spanish, c. 1536) was painted as an altarpiece for a chapel in Seville, Spain. It features the earliest known surviving portrait of Columbus (far left). In the shadows beneath Mary's cloak are Native Americans who had been converted to the Catholic faith because of the explorers who had come to their land.

finally returned to Spain, arriving on November 7, 1504.

Queen Isabella died on November 26. Columbus was also quite ill, but he spent the next several months seeking the restoration of his titles of governor and viceroy and his share of the riches from the West Indies (now generally known as the Caribbean Islands). He never regained his titles or as much money as he believed he deserved.

Legacy

On May 20, 1506, Columbus prayed, "Into your hands, O Lord, I commit my spirit." His two sons, his brother Bartholomew, and his faithful sailor Diego Méndez were with him when he died. His body was buried in Spain but moved to Hispaniola later in the 1500s. His remains were moved again to Cuba in 1795. Uncertainty shrouds his exact final resting place.

Columbus did not discover the New World, since humans had been living there for hundreds of years. Columbus did, however, establish a connection between the Old World and the New that changed history.

Europeans brought the gospel to New World and introduced new ideas that many Indians embraced. However, the Europeans also implemented a colonial system that involved oppression, which was a tragic contrast to the gospel of peace. Those who claim to follow Christ should treat others with justice and kindness. Columbus and other Europeans who came after him often failed to do this in their dealings with native peoples and with Africans brought to the Americas as slaves.

We like our historical characters to wear either white hats or black hats, to be completely good or completely despicable. Like us, they are a mixture. Some did more good, while others caused more harm. Our job in studying history is to understand the truth as best we can, to learn from it, and to contribute good to the world in which we live now.

As far as the east is from the west,
so far has He removed our transgressions from us.
Psalm 103:12

Assignments for Lesson 87

In Their Words Read the excerpts from the Journal of Christopher Columbus (pages 195-199).

Literature Continue reading *Here I Stand*.

Student Review Optional: Answer the questions for Lesson 87.

Depiction of Sea Battle Between English and Spanish (English, 16th Century)

Lesson 88 - Key Event

The English Defeat of the Spanish Armada

In the last half of the 1500s, Spain was the most powerful nation in Europe. It had a rapidly expanding collection of colonies in the New World, its income from those colonies and other foreign trade had made her rich, and it wielded enormous power in Europe. By the end of the century, however, Spain was on its way to losing its position of power. Its military might had been weakened, its empire had peaked, and it would soon begin to lose some of its stature in Europe.

Changes such as these do not occur overnight, but in the case of Spain a single event was a dramatic turning point. That event was the defeat of the Spanish military fleet, called the Invincible Armada, at the hands of the upstart English navy in 1588. This English victory shifted the balance of power in Europe and initiated a series of events that influenced the makeup of the world today.

The Power of Spain

The ruling Hapsburg dynasty of Austria was a powerful Catholic family. Under Charles V, the Hapsburg Empire reached its greatest size. Charles inherited the throne of Spain from his grandparents, King Ferdinand and Queen Isabella, and the thrones of Austria and the Netherlands from his other grandparents. Charles became king of Spain in 1516. Three years later, the princes of Germany elected him Holy Roman Emperor.

During the Protestant Reformation, Charles tried to force the German princes to accept the authority of the pope. Many of them resisted, however; and Charles agreed to the Peace of Augsburg in 1555 that allowed each prince to determine the state religion in his own territory. The Spanish people generally accepted Charles' rule over them, even though he spent much of the nation's resources on wars elsewhere in Europe.

Charles abdicated his throne in 1556 and retired to a monastery. He gave the rule of Austria to his brother Ferdinand, who was elected Holy Roman Emperor. To his son Philip II he gave Spain, the Spanish colonies in the New World, the Netherlands, and the city-states of Naples and Milan in Italy.

During the reign of Philip II (1556-1598), Spain reached the height of its power. Philip ruled as absolute monarch with authority that he believed came from God. In addition to having significant political and financial power, Philip sent missionaries across Europe to convert Protestants to the Catholic faith.

Trouble in Northern Europe

One trouble spot for Philip was the Netherlands. This tiny northern European country had been a rising economic power since the Middle Ages. Its people, many of whom had become Calvinists, resented being ruled by a Spanish Catholic. In 1566 when Philip tried to enforce anti-Protestant laws, the Dutch rebelled. Protestants attacked Catholic churches, and many Catholics became Protestants. Spain sent 20,000 troops, who killed almost that many Dutchmen. Spanish authorities seized Dutch property and imposed heavy taxes.

The seven northern provinces (which had Protestant majorities) declared their independence in 1581 as the Dutch Netherlands. The ten southern provinces (predominantly Catholic) remained loyal to Spain as the Spanish Netherlands. They became Belgium in 1830. Fighting lasted for many more years, but Philip was not able to regain any of the seven provinces he had lost. The Dutch Netherlands became an international trading power over the coming decades.

Royal Intrigues in England

Henry VII came to the throne of England in 1485 and consolidated the power of the Tudor dynasty. During this period, Spain and England were allies because of their common Catholic faith, their common enmity with France, and their common interest in trade with the Netherlands. Henry's son, Henry VIII, was a strong ruler who broke with Rome and made a mess of things with his many marriages. The break with Rome cooled English relations with Spain. Henry's only son who survived infancy came to the throne as a child and reigned only six years. Henry's older daughter, Mary, claimed the throne in 1553. She was a Catholic who persecuted Protestants and tried to reinstitute the Catholic Church as the state religion of England.

Philip II of Spain was a fervent Catholic who wanted to increase the power of the Church. Mary felt the same way. It must have seemed most advantageous to their cause, and most worrisome to their opponents, when they were married in 1554. Philip ruled England jointly with Mary and ascended to the throne of Spain two years later. However, Mary died in 1558 and Philip's right to the throne of England expired according to their pre-nuptial agreement.

The younger daughter of Henry VIII, Elizabeth, became queen of England at her sister's death. Elizabeth I was a Protestant, so once again her fellow Protestants took over government positions. Catholics were on the outside, though they were not persecuted as much as Protestants had been under Mary. English Catholics hoped to regain the throne through Mary Queen of Scots, whose grandmother was a sister of Henry VIII. However, Mary fled Scotland because of Protestant opposition. When she came to England, Elizabeth put her under house arrest.

In 1570 the pope excommunicated Elizabeth, declared that she was no longer queen, and urged Catholics to remove her. The decree carried no authority in Elizabeth's mind, but it did provide justification for Catholic attempts to take the English throne. Elizabeth's support for the revolt against Spain in the Netherlands provided further fuel for her Catholic opponents.

Dutch and Spanish ships clashed at the Battle of Haarlemmermeer, 26 May 1573, *painting by Hendrick Cornelisz Vroom (Dutch, c. 1621).*

Lesson 88 - Key Event: The English Defeat of the Spanish Armada

This stone signal station was one of many built along the southern coast of England in 1588. If the Spanish fleet was observed, a fire could be put on a wooden pole protruding through the roof that would send word to other stations.

War with Spain

In England Catholic plots against Elizabeth continued. Upon the urging of her advisers, Elizabeth had Mary Queen of Scots executed in 1587 on the charge of treason, even though Mary was not a subject of Elizabeth. This prompted Philip II of Spain to prepare for an invasion of England.

Philip sent his impressive fleet of ships into the English Channel to ferry loyal troops from the Netherlands into England. He hoped that, once his forces were in the country, English Catholics would join the Spanish forces to oust Elizabeth. The key to England's hopes lay with the ability of its navy to stop the Armada.

Elizabeth sent out the English fleet. Though less numerous than the Armada, the smaller English ships were able to outmaneuver the Spanish fleet and utilize long-range guns to sink many Spanish vessels. The English also sent fire-ships among the Spanish, who feared that they were laden with bombs. A sudden change of wind (later called a Protestant wind) swept the remnants of the Spanish fleet into the North Sea. They were pursued by the English as far as Edinburgh, Scotland. Additional Spanish ships were destroyed by the weather, and the rest were helplessly scattered. The English victory could hardly have been more complete.

The Result of the Victory

The immediate result of England's success was that the Catholic threat to the English throne was ended. England was securely under Protestant control. The defeat weakened Spanish sea power, so Spain was not able to expand her overseas empire nor defend it as well as before, although she continued to rule her American colonies for more than two centuries. Spanish influence continued to be strong in Europe for another century or so, but the cost of Philip's continuous wars drained the Spanish treasury. The later persecution by the Spanish Inquisition of Moriscoes—Muslims who had converted to Christianity—drove hundreds of thousands of farmers and businessmen from the country. Imports of gold and silver from the New

Numerous commemorative medals were issued in England related to the defeat of the Spanish Armada. This one has the Latin-Hebrew phrase Flavit Jehovah et Dissipati Sunt *("God blew, and they were scattered").*

World, impressive through the 1500s, declined in the 17th century. Philip's successors were not strong leaders, and regional rivalries within Spain resurfaced.

Meanwhile, England was emboldened to stretch its colonizing muscles with the encouragement of Elizabeth and her successors. Several settlements were established in the West Indies, but the most successful colonies were planted along the Atlantic coast of North America. The Spanish presence in Florida and in what would become the southwestern United States posed little threat to the British. The colonizing power to the south of the British colonies was Catholic Spain and to the north was Catholic France, but the religion of the colonies that became the United States was overwhelmingly Protestant. In addition, the naval power that began to rule the waves was Protestant England, not Catholic Spain. A tide had turned in world history because of England's defeat of the Spanish Armada.

Elizabeth I of England, the Armada Portrait
George Gower (English, c. 1588)

---

*He has done mighty deeds with His arm; He has scattered those who were proud in the thoughts of their heart.
He has brought down rulers from their thrones,
And has exalted those who were humble.*
Luke 1:51-52

Assignments for Lesson 88

In Their Words — Read the excerpts from Captain Cuellar's Narrative (pages 200-204).

Literature — Continue reading *Here I Stand*.

Student Review — Optional: Answer the questions for Lesson 88.

Traditional Hearth, or Irori, in a Japanese Home

Lesson 89 - Everyday Life

Homes and Household Furnishings

Modern American homes are generally comfortable in all seasons and are filled with possessions. We even get rid of possessions through Goodwill stores and garage sales. Throughout most of world history, however, only rulers, nobility, and persons of great wealth had many possessions.

We marvel at American pioneers who could fit all their clothing and household goods into one covered wagon. Actually, most people in the history of the world could have done that easily. When explorers found new lands, people often wanted to settle there. They gathered a few possessions, traveled to the new area, and built homes there.

Bible Homes and Furnishings

People of the Bible lived in both portable tents and permanent houses. Abraham moved from place to place and lived in a tent (Genesis 13:18). Women, like Leah and her maids, sometimes had separate tents (Genesis 31:33). In the story of the tower of Babel in Genesis 11, the people spoke of building a city with baked bricks and tar for mortar. Leviticus 14:40-45 talks of houses of stone and plaster. In Deuteronomy, God commanded the Israelites to write commandments on the door frames and gates of houses (6:9). He also commanded that they build a parapet on the roof to protect people from falling off. The roofs of many houses were flat and were used for sleeping (Joshua 2:6-8), prayer (Acts 10:9) and work (Rahab laid stalks of flax in order on her roof). Deuteronomy 20:5 speaks of dedicating a house.

Rahab's house in Joshua 2:15 was on the city wall of Jericho. Deborah talked of a window and lattice (Judges 5:28). In 2 Kings 4:8-10, we read the story of a prominent woman of Shunem who often showed hospitality to Elisha. She asked her husband if they could make him a little walled upper room, supplied with a bed, a table, a chair, and a lampstand. Jeremiah speaks of a roomy house with spacious upper rooms, cut-out windows, paneling of cedar, and bright red paint (Jeremiah 22:14). The house where Jesus and the apostles had the Last Supper had a guest room (Mark 14:14).

Egyptian Houses and Furniture

Homes of the wealthy in Egypt were made of mud bricks, covered with plaster, and then whitewashed. Remember that making mud bricks was the task of Israelite slaves in Egypt. The burial chambers of Tutankhamen were filled with beds, bedding, chests containing clothing and jewelry, pottery vases, dishes, and various types of seating from stools to thrones. One chair, as seen at right, was carved of cedar. A scene decorates the back, and animal feet decorate the bases of the legs.

Wood was scarce in ancient Egypt, so furniture was made of several different kinds of wood, such as acacia or sycamore from Egypt and imported juniper or cedar from Syria. The Egyptians sometimes inlaid their furniture with ivory or ebony imported from other parts of Africa. Because Egyptians buried their dead in dry tombs, many examples of their furniture have survived.

Greek and Roman Houses

The houses of wealthy Greek families had a central courtyard. Often the men's rooms were on the street side of the house and the women's rooms were at the back. Though few examples of Greek furniture survive, we know about it through sculptures and paintings on vases. Wealthy Greek women sat on a comfortable chair called a *klismos*. Greek stools often had animal-shaped feet.

Roman houses were similar to those of the Greeks. Roman chairs were made from bronze, iron, or wood. Sometimes women had wicker chairs. Romans also enjoyed dining couches where they ate formal meals in a reclined position.

Homes in the Middle Ages

Poor peasants lived in tiny huts without windows. An etching by Adriaen van Ostade (1610-1685) revealed the interior of a Dutch peasant home of that time. The furniture consisted of a chair, a small table, and two stools. Baskets rested

The Pazyryk Carpet is the oldest known surviving knotted carpet. Found in a tomb in Siberia, it dates from about 400 BC. It features multiple colors and various patterns and designs.

Lesson 89 - Everyday Life: Homes and Household Furnishings

Homes Around the World

1. Ancient Puebloan people in North America constructed living complexes in cliff faces with access by rock stairs or ladders. An example from Chihuahua, Mexico, is shown at right.

2. Snowhouses, commonly called igloos, have been built by Inuit peoples for centuries in northern North America. At left is a view of the entrance from inside an igloo.

3. In Ghana, homes of the Ashanti had four rectangular rooms built around a central courtyard with elaborate wall decorations. An 1817 illustration is shown at right.

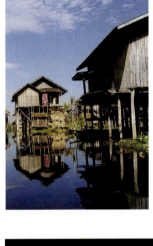

4. Stilt houses have been built for millennia in wet areas. The dwellings pictured at left are located in Nyaung Shwe, Myanmar.

5. Traditional homes of the Maori in New Zealand are called *wahne*. Built with a low, sloped roof, they were used primarily for sleeping. This photo is from the 1870s.

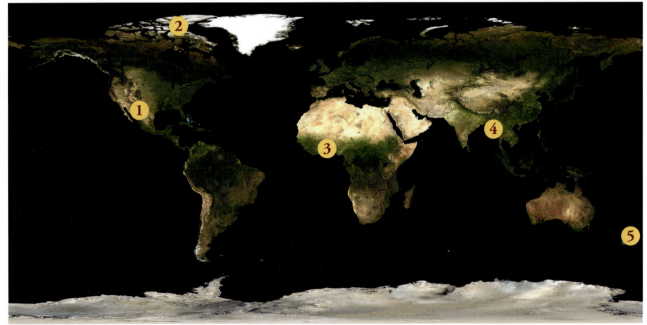

on shelves and the floor. The room had a large chimney with a place to cook. Meat hung from the ceiling. A basket cradle sat on the floor. In one corner were stairs and then a ladder to the loft above.

Merchants and craftsmen living in town had two-story homes with a workshop or store on ground level and one large room above. Here families cooked, ate, and slept, adults in beds built into the corners and children on pallets on the floor. Furniture included a few stools, chests for storage and seating, and a dining table. Chairs were so rare that they became symbols of wealth and power, reserved for the head of the family or a guest. From this practice, we get the word chairman.

Homes in the Renaissance and the Age of Exploration

During the Renaissance, the poor often lived in rented rooms. Many moved often, usually within the same neighborhood. As the economy grew, they were able to buy glass, earthenware, linens, painted chests, and printed images to decorate their walls.

Wealthy citizens built grand palaces, which housed parents, children, relatives, and servants. They filled them with fine furnishings and newly-available objects such as printed books and glass mirrors.

The lady of the house invited guests to tour the first floor of her home with its reception room, bedroom, study, and perhaps dining and music rooms. In the 1587 book *Institutione Della Sposa* by Italian Pietro Belmonte, new brides were instructed to:

Guide your guests around the house and in particular show them some of your possessions, either new or beautiful, but in such a way that it will be received as a sign of your politeness and domesticity, and not arrogance; something that you will do as if showing them your heart.

Therefore everyone who hears these words of Mine, and acts on them, may be compared to a wise man, who built his house on the rock.
Matthew 7:24

Assignments for Lesson 89

In Their Words — Read the excerpt from the Log of Jacob Roggeveen (pages 205-207).

Literature — Continue reading *Here I Stand*.

Student Review — Optional: Answer the questions for Lesson 89.

Sunset in the Negev Desert Near Yeruham, Israel

Lesson 90 - Bible Study

Exploring the Promised Land

When most Europeans in 1492 looked at the Atlantic Ocean, they saw a barrier. When Christopher Columbus looked at the Atlantic, he saw an opportunity. Columbus knew that sailing across it would be a challenge, but he envisioned sailing west as the answer that many Europeans were looking for to the problem of how to get to Asia more easily. Everybody saw the same ocean, but the difference was in how they saw it. Columbus' vision opened a new world for the Europeans and for world history, though the results were not what anyone expected.

When God was preparing to lead the Israelites into the land He had promised to give them, He had the people send twelve spies into Canaan to find out all they could about the land. Ten of the spies thought it was an insurmountable problem, while two believed that they could conquer the land with God's help. All of the spies saw the same land, but the difference was in how they saw it. The ten looked at Canaan through eyes of fear and doubt, while the two saw with eyes of faith. How these ancient explorers saw the land before them affected the history of their people from that time forward.

Let us consider this exploration that God initiated and see what lessons we can learn for our own lives. Read the account in Numbers 13 and 14 as you study this lesson.

God's Call to Send the Spies

Numbers 13:1-20. After God had brought the Israelites out of Egypt into the wilderness, He gave them His law at Mount Sinai. The people constructed the tabernacle according to the plan God had shown Moses. When Israel had been freed from bondage for about two years, the Lord prepared to lead them into the land He had promised to give them. God said that He was going to give Israel this land. In other words, there was no question in God's mind that He was going to do it.

God told Moses to select one man from each of the twelve tribes who was a leader in his tribe. These were men who were respected and whose word would be respected. Each tribe had a representative so that the whole nation would have ownership of the exploration and its results. The two whose names we remember were Joshua and Caleb. The spies were

This woodcut by Albrecht Altdorfer (German, c. 1515) shows the spies returning carrying the fruit of the Promised Land.

to go into the land and see: see what the land was like, see what the people living there were like, and see what the land produced.

Spying Out the Land

Numbers 13:21-33. The spies entered the land, made mental notes of what they saw, and collected evidence of what it was like. They cut down a single cluster of grapes that was so large two men had to carry it on a pole. The men spent forty days looking over the land and its people and then reported back to Moses and the Israelites on what they saw. They could see that it was a fertile land and quite desirable, but what loomed larger in their eyes were the people. It was their assessment that the Canaanites were strong and their cities well-fortified. The people living in the land appeared to be giants to the awe-struck spies. When the majority report of the spies was finished, the Israelites were dismayed and in turmoil.

Then Caleb spoke up. He had seen the same evidence, but he had seen it with an entirely different vision. Caleb was convinced that they should go up and take the land because he believed they could do it with God's help. The ten fearful spies began talking again, and the Israelites listened to them. The ten revealed the presence of the grasshopper syndrome in their hearts: in their eyes, they seemed like little grasshoppers before the huge Nephilim in Canaan.

Israel's Reaction, God's Reaction

Numbers 14:1-45. The congregation of Israel went into grief and mourning at what they believed to be their plight. They moaned that it would have been better to have died in Egypt than to be slaughtered in this ill-conceived plan into which Moses had led them. They planned to appoint a leader (probably meaning a real leader, not that knuckleheaded Moses) and go back to Egypt. Rather than argue with the people, Moses and Aaron went into grief and mourning themselves because of the Israelites' attitude. The two men fell on their faces before the people. Joshua and Caleb spoke up and said that the Lord would bring them into the land if He was pleased with them, but the two spies warned the people not to rebel against the Lord. The people responded by wanting to stone Joshua and Caleb.

God threatened to destroy the faithless people, but Moses told God that the Egyptians would think He was not powerful enough to bring the Israelites into Canaan. Moses then repeated God's own words to Him, reminding Him that He is slow to anger and abounding in mercy. Moses asked

Lesson 90 - Bible Study: Exploring the Promised Land

God to forgive the people who wanted to cast him off as their leader. God did forgive the people, but He determined that none of the armed men twenty years old and older (i.e., those who should have known better) would enter the Promised Land. Instead, they would spend forty years in the wilderness, one year for every day the spies had been in Canaan, and die in the wilderness without ever entering the Promised Land. This was true for all except Joshua and Caleb, who never doubted that God could accomplish what He had promised.

The next day, the Israelites admitted that they had sinned; but they also announced that they were now ready to take Canaan, in defiance of the word God had spoken the day before. Moses warned them not to try an assault on Canaan, but they did so anyway and were defeated. True to His word, God kept the Israelites in the wilderness for forty years until that generation of adults had died out.

Lessons from the Story of the Spies

The majority is not always right. Five-sixths of the spies and almost all of the Israelites were convinced that they could not conquer the Promised Land, but they were wrong. What is favored by the majority and what appears to be popular is no basis for living and making decisions. People (including you and I) can be easily influenced by an idea that appears to offer short-term reward or by a persuasive speaker who has a hidden agenda. We have to live by what is right in God's eyes, regardless of how popular that is at any given moment.

We become what we fear. The Israelites were afraid that they could not conquer Canaan and would die in the wilderness. Because of their faithlessness, that is exactly what happened to them. They did not conquer Canaan and they died in the wilderness. If we fear failure, we are more likely to fail by simply trying to avoid failure. If we fear what people think, we will become captive to the opinions of others. If we fear God, on the other hand, we will treat Him with respect and will become more like Him. Fear (except for the fear of God) is no motive to live by.

Look at your world through the eyes of faith. Anyone can make excuses and can see roadblocks and reasons why something cannot happen. The person who trusts God sees what is possible and looks beyond the problems to the solution. The eyes of doubt and fear focus on what is seen, which often includes difficulties. The eyes that see as God wants us to see focus on the unseen: the unseen and powerful God and the goal that God can help us accomplish.

The Israel Ministry of Tourism has used as a logo an image of two men carrying a large bunch of grapes on a pole. They have also shown two men carrying other objects on a pole to illustrate other attractions in Israel.

The explorers of the 15th and 16th centuries caught a vision for what was possible, despite the risks; and they changed the world. Joshua and Caleb caught the vision of what God promised, despite the difficulties, and entered the Promised Land. As you explore the life that God gives you, look beyond the difficulties and potential roadblocks and see what God can accomplish through you.

But My servant Caleb, because he has had a different spirit and has followed Me fully, I will bring into the land which he entered, and his descendants shall take possession of it.
Numbers 14:24

Assignments for Lesson 90

Bible — Recite or write Luke 12:29-31 from memory.

In Their Words — Read "Holy Sonnet 10" by John Donne and "On His Blindness" by John Milton (pages 208-209).

Literature — Finish reading *Here I Stand*. Literary analysis available in *Student Review*.

Project — Complete your project for the unit.

Student Review — Optional: Answer the questions for Lesson 90 and for *Here I Stand* and take the quiz for Unit 18.

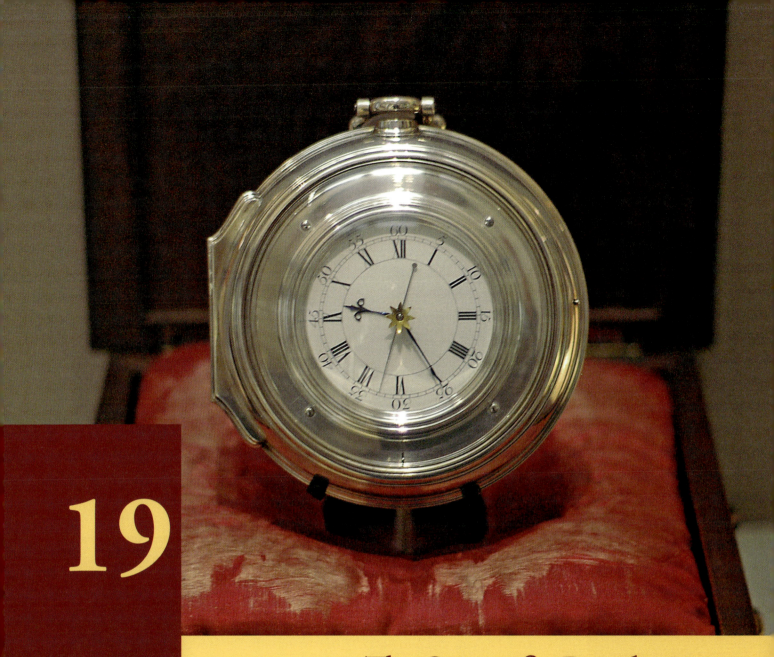

19

The Scientific Revolution

Summary As the world unfolded before Europe through exploration, a new way of looking at the world unfolded with the Scientific Revolution. We will look at some of the key persons and important developments of the period, especially Isaac Newton and Galileo's battle with the Catholic Church. The everyday life lesson looks at clothing through the centuries. The Bible study examines the value of life.

Lessons
91 - A New View
92 - Key Event: The Heresy Trial of Galileo Galilei
93 - Key Person: Isaac Newton
94 - Everyday Life: Clothing Through the Centuries
95 - Bible Study: The Value of Life

John Harrison (1693-1776) was an English carpenter and clockmaker who spent forty years developing a series of chronometers to help sailors measure longitude.

Memory Work — Learn John 8:31-32 by the end of the unit.

Books Used
The Bible
In Their Words
A Tale of Two Cities

Project (choose one)

1) Write 300 to 500 words on one of the following topics:
   - Write about recent developments in one field of science, such as astronomy, medicine, botany, genetics, or another field.
   - Write a response to this question: "Are natural laws and belief in a God who answers prayer mutually exclusive?" See Lesson 91.
2) Create for yourself one of the articles of clothing pictured in Lesson 94.
3) Interview a scientist (or university professor of science) who is a Christian about how faith influences his or her work. Compose at least 10 questions ahead of time. You can conduct your interview by phone or in person. Be respectful of your interviewee's time and keep the interview within an hour. If possible, make an audio recording of the interview.

Literature

For this and the next unit you will read *A Tale of Two Cities* by Charles Dickens. The story focuses on an Englishman and a Frenchman during the French Revolution and the great sacrifice that one of them makes for the other. Like any Dickens novel, however, the story is rich with colorful characters and fascinating plot twists. It is one of Dickens' best-known novels and certainly the most famous book on the French Revolution. The novel is probably his most serious work and does not have the humor and wit that are in works such as *The Pickwick Papers* and *David Copperfield*. The opening and closing paragraphs of *A Tale of Two Cities* have become some of the most famous lines in English literature.

Charles Dickens was born in 1812 in Portsmouth, England. He was a popular and successful writer by the time he was 25. When he wrote *A Tale of Two Cities* (1859), his career had been through significant turmoil, and he had left his wife to take up with a younger woman. The darkness of his personal life is reflected in the darkness of this novel. The French Revolution had begun some seventy years before the publication of this book, which means that the subject was as recent as World War II would be in a novel published today. Among Dickens' many other works are *Oliver Twist*, *A Christmas Carol*, and *Great Expectations*. He was the most popular writer of Victorian England. Dickens died in 1870.

Dickens gave public readings of his work in Great Britain and America. This image of Dickens reading appeared in Harper's Weekly *in 1867.*

Tycho Brahe in His Observatory (1598)

Lesson 91

A New View

Man's understanding of the world was changing rapidly. As we noted in an earlier lesson, change is unsettling and threatening for some while it is exciting and strengthening for others. Over a relatively short period of time, Europeans had begun to see that the Roman Catholic Church was not the only way to approach God and that the world was full of vast, unexplored territories. Building on work by Muslim and Asian scholars of previous centuries, European scientists in the 16th and 17th centuries challenged the way that mankind observed and understood the universe in which we live.

The Traditional Understanding

As the ancients, such as the Greeks Aristotle and Ptolemy, studied the world, they drew conclusions based on appearances and on what seemed to be common sense. It seemed, for example, that the earth was stationary and was orbited by the sun, the moon, the planets, and the stars in perfect circles (the only other known planets until 1781 were Mercury, Venus, Mars, Jupiter, and Saturn). All of the heavenly bodies, people believed, were encased in transparent spheres that were progressively further from the earth. Beyond everything visible was a final sphere that moved in the opposite direction, driving the heavenly bodies from east to west.

Whereas life on earth was subject to change, as was observed with the changing seasons and the realities of birth and death, the firmament seemed to be governed by a different set of laws where nothing changed. This understanding was accepted by Christians with one major addition. For believers, the most important fact was that God had created the universe, set it in motion, and guided its daily operation. He was the Prime Mover and constant Sustainer of everything that was. The answer that believers had for any question was that the universe was in the hands of God. He understood everything even if humans did not.

A Greek astronomer of the third century BC, Aristarchus, theorized that the earth moved around the sun; but Ptolemy rejected the idea for two reasons. First, it did not fit with Ptolemy's observations; and second, it did not fit with Aristotle's theory of motion. Aristotle believed that objects on earth tend to remain at rest unless a force is applied, and continued motion required continued force. With different rules in the heavenly realms, however, the movement of the objects in the sky did not require initial or continuous force.

521

New Observations, New Theories

However, the traditional theory did not adequately explain all of the observed phenomena of the heavens. Nicolaus Copernicus, a Polish priest and amateur astronomer, published a book in 1543 theorizing that the sun was at the center of the universe with Earth and the other planets rotating around it. Copernicus did not challenge Aristotle's beliefs about motion, nor did he question the theory of heavenly spheres. He simply exchanged the places of the earth and the sun.

As simple as that sounds, more than a century passed before his theory won general acceptance. First, it contradicted Aristotle and Ptolemy, who were assumed to be correct almost without question. Second, Catholic leaders condemned Copernicus' work because it differed with the official Church doctrine that the earth was the center of the universe. Third, Copernicus' ideas needed experimental confirmation, which he was not able to provide. Copernicus escaped official condemnation by the Catholic Church because he died soon after his work was published.

Later in the 16th century, Danish astronomer Tycho Brahe posited that the sun and moon revolved around the earth and the other planets revolved around the sun. He believed that the earth was too heavy to move and that the rest of the ideas of Copernicus contradicted the Bible.

Brahe gathered data which was analyzed by his co-worker, German mathematician Johannes Kepler. The data did not fit with circular orbits, so Kepler hypothesized elliptical orbits and found that the information fit together well. The planets moved on a regular basis, and Kepler discovered that the square of the time a planet takes to orbit the sun is proportional to the cube of its average distance from the sun. Thus Kepler showed that heavenly bodies were subject to exact, knowable laws. He could not explain how they moved, however, and theorized that the sun and planets were magnets, with the sun pulling the planets in their orbits as it rotated.

When the Italian astronomer Galileo Galilei turned his crude telescope (a three-foot lead tube with a two-inch lens) to the skies beginning in 1609, a vast treasure of new information opened before his eyes. He saw phases of Venus, which showed that the planets were not self-lighted; and he observed that Venus moved in relation to the sun. Galileo discovered moons orbiting around Jupiter, giving evidence that more than one center for orbits existed in space. He also saw more stars in a more distant firmament, which challenged the accepted belief of a fixed universe. Galileo determined that the sun was the center of the universe and that the earth and the other planets revolved around it.

Copernicus, Kepler, and Galileo were fervent believers. Their work was not intended to challenge faith in God or the Bible. Leaders in the Catholic Church felt challenged, however, and forced Galileo to recant his published findings. He spent the rest of his life in quiet study on the subject of motion.

Englishman Francis Bacon (1561-1626) addressed the process of learning. He encouraged experimentation and observation as the key to increasing reliable knowledge. He also favored inductive reasoning, in which data yields a general conclusion, as opposed to Aristotle's method of

Astronomer Copernicus, or Conversations with God
Jan Matejko (Polish, 1873)

Lesson 91 - A New View

Developments in Medicine

The Scientific Revolution brought changes in the medical field as well. The second century AD Greek physician Galen had been accepted for over a thousand years as the authority in medicine. However, he never dissected a human body; and he was simply wrong in several of his explanations for the functioning of many parts of the body.

Andreas Vesalius of Brussels was one of the first to challenge Galen's conclusions openly, primarily in his book On the Fabric of the Human Body, *published in 1543, the same year that Copernicus' work appeared. His book was filled with illustrations of different parts of the human body such as the circulation system, seen at right. Vesalius is credited with beginning the modern science of anatomy.*

About the same time, Paracelsus of Switzerland disproved Galen's belief that chemical changes were impossible. In the early 1600s, William Harvey of England showed how blood circulated through the body, disproving the traditional view that blood was stationary in the body.

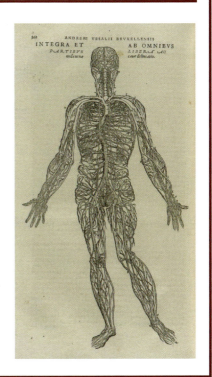

deductive reasoning, which starts with a premise and finds examples to support it.

Rene Descartes (1596-1650) of France showed the value of deductive reasoning, however, by starting with the simplest and least questioned truth and then reasoning out to a complete framework of understanding. To Descartes, the first step in understanding was expressed by the statement, "I think, therefore I am." He attempted to extrapolate his philosophy from that, including belief in God.

The main significance of both Bacon and Descartes was that they were not satisfied with relying on what had always been thought to be true or on what had appealed to common sense.

The Enlightenment and Deism

Philosophers of the day believed that mankind was living in an unprecedented age of knowledge and understanding. People were emerging from a period of intellectual darkness, they said, into the brightness of scientific light. Now that man had come to understand the operation of the universe and (it seemed) no longer needed superstitions and the prop of religious belief, the world had been enlightened by the truth. This period, from the publication of Newton's *Principia Mathematica* in 1687 to the start of the French Revolution in 1789, is called the Enlightenment. French writers were the most enthusiastic about promoting the dawning of this new age. Collectively they came to be known as the *philosophes* (the word comes from the Greek and means "lover of wisdom").

Newton and Descartes were, like Galileo and most other scientists of the day, believers in God. They did not work to undermine religious faith, but others used their accomplishments to do so. Science had shown that the earth was not the center of the universe and that the universe appeared to be much larger than previously thought. The previous structure of scientific knowledge had assumed that man was the center of Creation. Now he was seen as simply one tiny part of a vast cosmos that operated like a smooth-running machine.

Many scientists saw the findings of science as proof of God's wisdom and power. Some tried to separate their religious beliefs from their scientific work. Many writers and thinkers of the Enlightenment, however, began to see no need for God. Since the universe had been shown to operate by natural law, the guiding hand of an Almighty Deity did not appear to play a part. Religious activity such as prayer and worship seemed unnecessary if not illogical.

Still, the question of the origin of the universe demanded an answer. The answer proposed by some observers was that God had started the universe and instituted natural laws but then had backed away from its ongoing operation. This view came to be called Deism. In Deism, God was acknowledged; but pursuing a relationship with Him and especially submitting to Him were unnecessary. Deism became a popular position for many intellectuals in the 18th century, but it gradually lost its appeal as a religion that lacked emotion and offered no personal meaning. Some people, who did not want to believe in and submit to God, abandoned faith in God altogether.

Impact of the Scientific Revolution

The advances in knowledge that the Scientific Revolution made possible have given us a more accurate and complete understanding of the physical world than that which most people had prior to 1500. Science has made possible the amazing accomplishments in technology, transportation, communication, medicine, and other fields that we have seen in the last few centuries. The world is much better off in physical terms because of what has been done.

However, an even more fundamental change has taken place since the Scientific Revolution began: the way that most people in Western Civilization perceive the world. Before the Scientific Revolution, most people looked at the world primarily from a spiritual or religious point of view. They would ask

Edward Herbert (1583-1648) was a British soldier, diplomat, and philosopher. He argued that these five truths were the essence of true religion: the existence of a Supreme Being, the need for worship, a requirement of good behavior, the proper place of repentance, and the reality of divine reward and punishment. Herbert has been called the Father of English Deism, even though he believed that God heard and responded to prayer.

questions such as, "What is the will of God in this matter? What is the spiritual or eternal meaning of this event? How does this knowledge honor God?" Today, most people think about the world from a scientific perspective. It is much more common for people today to think in terms of, "How does this work? What natural phenomena caused this event? How will this knowledge help me or help mankind?"

One way to visualize this change is to think about today's "experts," the people that others look to for answers (the people whom reporters would call for a comment, for example). Before the Scientific Revolution, most people in Europe would have thought of the religious leader as the person with the most important insights. In medieval England, the local minister was called the parson. This term was a variation of person; in other words, the minister was the educated person in the community with whom others had to interact on just about any matter. The minister was the person who gave people hope.

Today, the scientist (whether in biology, history, psychology, economics, or another field) is most respected and is sought out for his viewpoint. The scientist is the person who has the most respected education. The scientist is the person who gives people hope—hope for a cure, hope for a solution to our problems. The spiritual perspective seems irrelevant to many. Not all truth is scientific truth that can be observed or proved in a laboratory, but today non-scientific truth has come to be treated as less important.

Even areas of study that are not related to the physical world have come to be called sciences. Thus, the study of politics has become political science. The study of society has become social science. Homemaking has become domestic science. Objective study in these areas is considered to be superior to subjective speculation, but not every aspect of these areas of human life is scientific.

Meanwhile, the study of religion has been relegated to the field of electives. Religion is held to be only a matter of opinion.

However, science is inexact because more can always be discovered. The currently accepted findings of science are not the last word, even though they might be portrayed as such. When Aristotle ruminated on the nature of the world, he believed that his findings were the last word. When the *philosophes* of the Enlightenment uttered their profound conclusions, they thought they had reached the pinnacle of understanding. When evolution first enjoyed its heyday, it was hailed as the explanation mankind was waiting for. In every case, what was announced was not the last word. In addition, scientists have their own prejudices that influence what they do. Just wait long enough, and you will see that the assured results of today will change. The wisest course is a healthy skepticism—not of God and the Bible, but of science and of what are considered today's assured results of scholarship.

Science, as important and worthy as it is, is not the savior of man, however much it is promoted as such. Some *philosophes* believed that knowledge

Immanuel Kant

Immanuel Kant (1724-1804) was a German philosopher who recognized the limits of reason. Kant believed that gaining scientific knowledge is only part of the mental process that humans follow to understand reality. Science cannot, he said, directly address questions that go beyond the material world, such as the existence of God, the immortality of the soul, and moral oughtness. In such matters as these, people must use conscience and intuition. Kant's best known work is Critique of Pure Reason *(1781). In it, Kant said, "Two things fill the mind with ever-increasing wonder and awe, the more often and the more intensely the mind of thought is drawn to them: the starry heavens above me and the moral law within me."*

Kant was correct in saying that science and reason are not the final word. The door he left open, however, led to the position that everyone is his own authority on such questions as the existence of God. The explanation for the two things that filled him with awe is, of course, God. However, if my conscience and intuition lead me to a conclusion different from yours, how can either of us say the other is wrong? We need God to do that.

was so powerful that, as knowledge of the world increased, mankind might prove to be perfectible; and thus all wars, poverty, crime, prejudice, injustice, and other scars on human life could be eliminated. It didn't happen. The Enlightenment period came to an end with the horrors of the French Revolution. The excesses and failings of the French Revolution were ended by the return of an absolute monarch in Napoleon. Napoleon was followed a few years later by another revolution in France and by revolutions in other European countries.

In the 20th and 21st centuries, we have seen much good accomplished and much progress made in human life. However, we have also witnessed Communism, Nazi Germany, two world wars, regional conflicts, and international terrorism. One cannot look at the last two hundred years of world history and say that this is the way of enlightenment and progress in the society of ever more perfect man. These tragedies have happened because man's central problem is not informational. It is spiritual, and this leads to moral failings. These moral failings are the heaviest problems for humans to bear. No telescope, calculator, computer, or laboratory will ever be able to resolve the sin that is in human hearts. That requires the application of the old-fashioned answer of faith in God.

The Scientific Revolution raised a question that humanists cannot adequately answer. If God does not exist or is irrelevant to human life, and if man is only one more element of a purely physical universe, what is the nature and purpose of human life? Secular humanists have no satisfying answer to this. The correct answer is that God does exist and does matter. His Creation—from the wonders of the atom to the wonders of the amazing but finite universe—gives Him glory and honor. Man is made in His image and is intended to serve Him and to worship Him. Only One is Lord; and science is a servant, not a master.

The heavens are telling of the glory of God;
And their expanse is declaring the work of His hands.
Psalm 19:1

Assignments for Lesson 91

In Their Words — Read "The Spacious Firmament on High" by Joseph Addison (page 210).

Literature — Begin reading *A Tale of Two Cities*. Plan to finish it by the end of Unit 20.

Student Review — Optional: Answer the questions for Lesson 91.

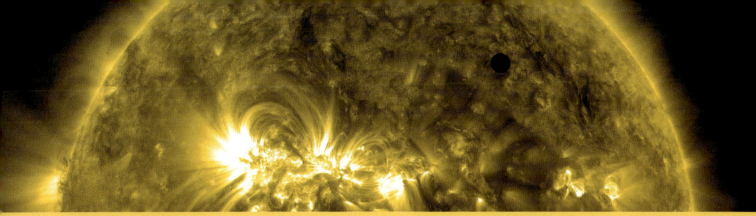

Venus Passing In Front of the Sun, 2012

Lesson 92 - Key Event

The Heresy Trial of Galileo Galilei

It was a showdown between scientific views and religious views—not science and the Bible. The conflict between astronomer Galileo Galilei and officials of the Roman Catholic Church teaches us about prejudice, fear, knowledge, and the interpretation of Scripture.

Galileo's Work and Faith

In the 1590s, Galileo came to accept the Copernican theory that the earth revolves around the sun. He discussed it with many people. His thinking was confirmed years later when he began using a telescope to study the heavens. He hoped that the telescope would lead others to accept the Copernican theory, but he was wrong. People strongly held the belief that the sun moved around the earth and that Scripture supported this belief.

Johannes Kepler (1571-1630) was a German astronomer who also studied planetary motion. In a 1610 letter to Kepler, Galileo wrote, "My dear Kepler, what would you say of the learned here, who, replete with the pertinacity of the asp, have steadfastly refused to cast a glance through the telescope? What shall we make of this? Shall we laugh, or shall we cry?"

All of the evidence indicates that Galileo was a humble believer who simply wanted to learn about the universe so he could share his understanding with others. After the firmament opened up to him through the telescope, Galileo expressed "infinite thanks to God for being so kind as to make me alone the first observer of marvels kept hidden in obscurity for all previous centuries."

Galileo Galilei Showing the Doge of Venice How to Use the Telescope, *Giuseppe Bertini (Italian, 1858)*

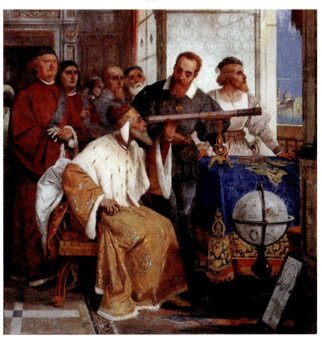

527

A Replica of One of Galileo's Telescopes

Objections to Galileo

Galileo was honored for his discoveries in 1611 at the Collegio Romano. Then in late 1613, Roman Catholic clergy began attacking the theories of Copernicus. Just over a year later, a Dominican friar lodged a complaint with the Inquisition in Rome against Galileo for his support of Copernicus. Galileo went to Rome to defend his views. In February 1616 the Church issued a statement that the theories of Copernicus were absurd and heretical.

Two days later, Cardinal Bellarmine warned Galileo not to "hold, teach, or discuss" the Copernican theory. A document that was later brought forward says that Galileo was forbidden from discussing the theory either orally or in writing. The next month, Copernicus' book was added to the Index of banned books.

Following years of continued writing and research, Galileo was told by the pope in 1624 that he could discuss the ideas of Copernicus as long as he treated them as an hypothesis. However, after the publication of Galileo's *Dialogue Concerning the Two Chief World Systems* in 1632 (previously approved by the Secretary of the Vatican), the pope stopped its distribution and Galileo was ordered to appear before the Inquisition.

In April 1633 the ill and aged Galileo was questioned for two weeks by the Court of Inquisition. Finally, on June 22, the judgment against Galileo was announced. It banned Galileo's book, imprisoned him indefinitely, and instructed him to perform penance. Seven of the Cardinals on the Court of Inquisition signed the sentence; three did not.

The verdict was relatively lenient because Galileo was not resistant to Church authority. Some historians believe that Galileo had done what he could to make his point and now he had to pay the ecclesiastical price and move on. The Cardinals offered to absolve Galileo of guilt if he made a formal recantation, which he did. According to legend, after he finished his statement, Galileo muttered under

Portrait of Galileo Galilei
Justus Sustermans (Dutch, 1636)

Lesson 92 - Key Event: The Heresy Trial of Galileo Galilei

his breath, "Nevertheless, it does move"; but this has little historical credibility.

Galileo lived out his days under house arrest. His 1638 petition to the Inquisition to be freed was denied. Galileo, by then totally blind, died in 1641.

Analysis of Galileo's Trial

Many questions in science and theology come down to a matter of perspective. Two different people can come to vastly different conclusions when they look at the same questions from different perspectives.

From the perspective of the earth, the sun clearly rises in the east and sets in the west. That is a natural and logical way to describe what we see. Galileo tried to look at the situation from a different perspective. He perceived from that different perspective that the earth actually orbits the sun in a large, complex solar system.

There is no conflict between science and the Bible. Conflicts arise when different people insist that their perspective is the only valid one and that anyone who believes differently is malicious. We should all be willing to admit that we have room to grow and change in our understanding of how the world works.

Modern Evaluation of Galileo

In 1992 the Vatican admitted its mistake in condemning Galileo 359 years earlier. After a thirteen year study, a commission appointed by the pope returned a verdict of not guilty for Galileo. They said that the Inquisition acted in good faith in 1633 but could not separate faith from the long-held belief that the earth was the center of the universe.

With the Catholic Church already under attack from Protestants, the Inquisition at the time feared that the new ideas would undermine Catholic tradition. Pope John Paul II (in office from 1978-2005) said that the trial had become "the symbol of the church's supposed rejection of scientific progress, or of 'dogmatic' obscurantism opposed to the free search for truth." In 2011 the Roman Catholic Church took part in a celebration in Rome of the 400th anniversary of Galileo's first public demonstration of the telescope.

In 1610 Galileo discovered the four largest moons of Jupiter. He named them the Medicean stars in honor of the Medici family. Later astronomers renamed them the Galilean satellites. NASA launched the Galileo *spacecraft to study Jupiter and its moons in 1989. After making 34 orbits around the planet, the spacecraft crashed into Jupiter in 2003. The image above is a composite of photographs taken by* Galileo *of (left to right) Io, Europa, Ganymede, and Callisto.*

*And you will know the truth,
and the truth will make you free.
John 8:32*

Assignments for Lesson 92

In Their Words Read the excerpts from *The Life of Galileo Galilei* (pages 211-216).

Literature Continue reading *A Tale of Two Cities*.

Student Review Optional: Answer the questions for Lesson 92.

Galileo's contributions to science have been honored by stamps in multiple countries, including Kazakhstan and Indonesia.

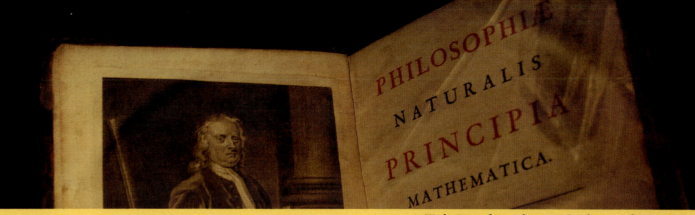

Title Page from the 1726 Edition of Principia

Lesson 93 - Key Person

Isaac Newton

*Nature and Nature's laws lay hid in night:
God said, Let Newton be! and all was light.*
— Alexander Pope (1688-1744)

Early Life

Isaac Newton was born in Woolsthorpe-by-Colsterworth, England, in 1642. His father died shortly before his birth, and his mother remarried when he was three. His grandmother played an important role in raising him. He attended local schools, but they did not hold his interest. Newton enjoyed learning on his own, tinkering with sundials, windmills, kites, and a mechanical carriage.

Newton's mother lost her second husband in 1656. She took her son out of school so that he could learn farming. One of Newton's former teachers recognized his intelligence, however, and encouraged his mother to let him attend Cambridge University. Newton was admitted in 1661 and received his bachelor's degree in 1665.

Pursuing Science

A plague shut down Cambridge for a time, and Newton returned to Woolsthorpe for almost two years. He developed his scientific theories through observation and experimentation. From the testimony of Newton and those who knew him, a falling apple did influence his thoughts about gravity; but the apple did not fall on his head.

Newton returned to Cambridge in 1667 and received a fellowship. He built a reflecting telescope the next year, which the Royal Society, an association of English scientists, inspected and publicized. Newton's experiments with prisms had shown him that lenses refract light, which limited the power of

Newton was born at Woolsthorpe Manor (pictured at right). He performed experiments there related to light and optics. The apple tree that influenced his theory of gravity might have been on the property.

Unit 19 - The Scientific Revolution

Newton deduced from his experiments with prisms that a white beam of light actually contains multiple colors of light that can be separated.

Newton's Laws of Motion

Newton studied planetary motion and discussed the subject with Edmond Halley (of comet fame). Halley took an interest in Newton's findings and encouraged him to publish them. Halley even paid for the cost of printing *Philosophiae Naturalis Principia Mathematica* (*Mathematical Principles of Natural Philosophy*), which appeared in 1687. Newton's main theme was gravitation, and he showed how that principle affects a variety of events in our universe. He also laid out three scientific laws about motion, summarized below:

1. If an object is at rest, it will remain at rest, or if an object is in motion, it will remain in motion in a straight line at a constant velocity, unless outside forces act upon it.

2. The acceleration of an object of constant mass is proportional to the force acting upon it (force = mass times acceleration).

a lens-based telescope. Mirrors, on the other hand, reflect the full spectrum equally.

In 1669 Newton gave his mathematics professor, Isaac Barrow, a manuscript about calculus. Newton called this branch of math the fluxional method. Gottfried Wilhelm Leibniz, a German, was developing a similar system independently of Newton; and the Leibniz notational method became the standard. Later in life, Newton and Leibniz disputed who invented calculus first. Newton evidently developed the ideas first, but Leibniz published them first.

Calculus combines algebra, arithmetic, and geometry for the study of concepts such as comparing a variable's rate of change in relation to another variable and calculating the area of space bounded by curves. Calculus is used today in physical and social sciences.

Barrow retired in 1669 and recommended Newton as his replacement, so Newton became a professor of mathematics. He became a fellow of the Royal Society in 1672, and the Society published his paper on the nature of white light. After this publication, some scientists began to criticize Newton's views. Though most of the criticisms were unfounded, Newton grew frustrated with the distractions and stopped publishing for a few years.

Newton's Discovery of the Refraction of Light
Pelagio Palagi (Italian, 1827)

Lesson 93 - Key Person: Isaac Newton

3. For every action, there is always an equal and opposite reaction. (Newton gave the example of a horse pulling a stone with a rope. He said that the stone would also pull back on the horse.)

Public Life

Also in 1687, Newton protested the order of King James II to allow a Catholic monk to become a Master of Arts at Cambridge without taking the oaths of allegiance to the Crown. James wanted to restore Catholic supremacy in England, and the University considered the request improper. The Glorious Revolution of 1688 deposed James II, and Newton became a member of the Convention Parliament from 1689 to 1690.

Newton became warden of the mint in 1696. He modified the production of coins to fight against counterfeiting. He moved up to the well-paid position of master of the mint in 1699 and held that post until his death. Queen Anne knighted Newton in 1705. Sir Isaac Newton had become a major figure in European science.

Newton resigned from his position at Cambridge in 1701. The Royal Society elected him president in 1703 and re-elected him every year. He published another major work in 1704 called *Opticks*. The *Principia* had been published in Latin, but *Opticks* was written in English. He released two more editions each of the *Principia* and of *Opticks*.

His Faith

Some historians and scientists have been reluctant to acknowledge the influence of Newton's faith upon his work. It was central to his character and his pursuit of knowledge. He began his study of the Bible as a boy. Teachers and fellow students recognized his knowledge of Scripture.

Newton believed that God created the universe and gave it order. With that premise, he considered it "unphilosophical" to pretend that the world came out of chaos or simply by natural laws. He saw that study of Scripture and study of the world complement each other because God gave us both of them.

Newton enjoyed exploring the numbers in the Bible. He wrote a *Chronology of Ancient Kingdoms* in which he sought to connect events from Egyptian, Greek, and Hebrew history. He used astronomical references in ancient works to calculate the dates of events. He also wrote *Observations upon the Prophecies of Daniel and the Apocalypse of St. John*.

His moral uprightness was evident. He never married and devoted himself to his work. He sought to be fair in his disputes with other scientists.

Portrait of Sir Isaac Newton
James Thornhill (English, c. 1712)

Unit 19 - The Scientific Revolution

He was also humble about his accomplishments, saying that if he had seen farther than other men, it was because he had stood on the shoulders of giants who had gone before him. He compared himself to a boy playing on the seashore, finding a smooth pebble or a pretty shell now and then, while the ocean of truth lay undiscovered before him.

Newton died on March 20, 1727, in a village outside London. He was the first scientist to be buried in Westminster Abbey. Newton's contributions to science were immense. His work laid a foundation for the investigations of scientists and philosophers in coming decades. Though some of Newton's ideas have been modified, scientists still accept and use many of his basic principles.

Newton's Tomb at Westminster Abbey

*For since the creation of the world His invisible attributes,
His eternal power and divine nature, have been clearly seen,
being understood through what has been made,
so that they are without excuse.
Romans 1:20*

Assignments for Lesson 93

In Their Words — Read the excerpt from *Opticks* by Isaac Newton and the hymns by Isaac Watts (pages 217-221).

Literature — Continue reading *A Tale of Two Cities*.

Student Review — Optional: Answer the questions for Lesson 93.

Clothing from the Pacific Islands

Lesson 94 - Everyday Life

Clothing Through the Centuries

Despite what many museums and books say to the contrary, the first humans wore clothing. At the very first they were naked and not ashamed; but after the first sin in the Garden of Eden, they sewed fig leaves together to make loin coverings for themselves. God then showed loving care by making garments of animal skin for Adam and Eve (Genesis 2:25, 3:21).

Since ancient times, people have grown plants and raised animals to supply raw materials for making cloth. They have spun fibers into threads, woven the threads into fabric, and cut and sewn the fabric into garments. Today some people in the world still work through that entire process, but most buy clothes ready-made. Most of the world's clothing is made by machines. Still, God provides the plants and animals. Farmers care for them. Factory workers spin the thread and produce the cloth. Other factory workers, often poorly paid, cut and sew the garments we wear today.

The images on this page and the next three pages are taken from *Costume History* by Auguste Racinet, a multi-volume encyclopedia filled with elaborate color illustrations that he published in the late 19th century.

Egypt

Clothing in ancient Egypt consisted largely of linen skirts and tunics for both men and women, garments suited for the hot desert. Dyes were known and used, but garments were often left white.

Greece and Rome

Greek and Roman clothing was similar. Men generally wore knee-length robes while women wore ankle-length robes.

> **Fancy Clothes in the Bible**
>
> *People from foreign lands brought garments as gifts to Solomon (1 Kings 10:25). Proud women denounced in Isaiah 3:16-26 wore headbands, various types of jewelry, veils, headdresses, sashes, amulets, robes, tunics, cloaks, undergarments, and turbans. Ezekiel mentions sandals of porpoise skin (16:10) and embroidered work, fine linen, and white wool (27:16-18).*

India

The Indian sari, a long piece of cotton or silk fabric wrapped around the body over a short, fitted bodice, has been worn since ancient times.

Sápmi/Sameland

Commonly known as the Laplanders, the Sami people live in far northern Scandinavia and Russia. Their traditional clothing is designed to withstand extreme cold.

Persia

Different ethnic groups wore a variety of clothing depending on their religious and cultural background.

Japan

The kimono (meaning literally "thing to wear") is a traditional garment for men and women that is wrapped around the body and tied with a sash. Notice the platform sandals on the right below.

France

In the late Middle Ages, hose for male nobles became popular. Sometimes each leg was made with a different color fabric.

Lesson 94 - Everyday Life: Clothing Through the Centuries

Chile

Traditional Chilean dress combines elements of native and European clothing. The chamanto, worn by men and women, is a colorful poncho; and the chupalla is a hat made out of straw.

The Netherlands

The ruff developed in Europe in the 1500s and remained popular longest in Holland. Originally a small collar designed to protect the shirt or jacket from getting dirty, the ruff, worn by men, women, and children, grew in height and circumference.

Turkey

The fez, a red felt hat with a black tassel, was popular during the Ottoman period in Turkey.

Scotland

The kilt developed in the 16th century. A traditional kilt is 60 inches wide and at least five feet long, up to seven yards. A tartan is a pattern of multi-colored horizontal and vertical bands.

Germany

The military became a major force in Prussia during the 18th century. Officers had previously supplied their own clothing, but uniforms and rank insignia became more common in the 1700s.

The Sewing Machine

Walter Hunt and Elias Howe were early inventors of sewing machines, but neither was successful at marketing them. Isaac Singer succeeded in the 1850s by hiring female salespeople and by selling sewing machines on an installment plan. In addition to its New York headquarters, Singer's company established operations in Scotland, France, and Brazil, becoming one of the first U.S.-based multinational companies.

Switzerland

Traditional Swiss clothing for women often featured elaborate embroidery.

West Africa

In the 19th century, a robe or tunic worn over baggy trousers was typical. A rectangular cloth was sometimes wrapped over one shoulder and under the opposite arm along with elaborate headdresses.

Russia

The Russian Empire and the more recent Soviet Union included many indigenous people groups. The three figures on the left below represent the Mordvin, Tatar, and Kalmyk people groups. The other three are wearing ethnic Russian clothing.

Balearic Islands

Majorca, Minorca, Eivissa, and Formentera are the four largest islands of the Balearic archipelago. They have been part of Spain for centuries, and the traditional clothing shows Hispanic influence.

A Short Timeline of the History of Making Cloth and Clothing

2000 BC	Peru	Cotton is cultivated and used to create cloth.
1500 BC	China	Weavers begin to make silk fabric.
600 AD	Egypt	Woodblock printing is used to print patterns on cloth.
c. 1000	India	Textile workers in India use a wheel to spin yarn.
1400s	Netherlands	The modern steel needle with an eye for thread is invented.
1589	England	Clergyman William Lee builds the first knitting machine.

Lesson 94 - Everyday Life: Clothing Through the Centuries

1700s	Hawaii	Hundreds of thousands of feathers are attached to a woven netting to create *'ahu 'ula,* cloaks worn by Hawaiian chiefs. An example is shown at right. 
1764	England	James Hargreaves, an illiterate weaver, invents an automatic spinning jenny that greatly increases yarn production.
1770s	England	Pins are painstakingly made by hand. Each of several workers specializes in one minute part of the process to create the final product.
1771	England	Richard Arkwright's water-powered spinning machines are installed in a mill along a Derbyshire river. Before, spinners had worked at home; now they began working in factories.
1785	England	Edmund Cartwright, a clergyman, designs a mechanically-powered loom. Two years later he builds a working model. Before that, looms had been powered by people and water and animals (such as donkeys, cows, and Newfoundland dogs).
1792	U.S.A.	Eli Whitney invents the cotton gin. By quickly removing seeds from the cotton fibers, it makes cotton a profitable crop, which encourages the use of slaves.
1829	France	Tailor Barthelemy Thimonnier patents a sewing machine.
1832	U.S.A.	John Howe develops a pin-making machine that can compete with hand manufacture. 
1856	England	Mauvine, the first synthetic fabric dye, is accidentally created by English chemist William Perkin. A letter from Perkin's son is shown at right with a sample of fabric dyed in mauvine.
1863	U.S.A.	Following a suggestion from his wife, Massachusetts tailor Ebenezer Butterick creates the first sewing pattern with sizes.
1873	U.S.A	Jacob Davis from Latvia and Levi Strauss obtain a patent for denim "waist overalls" with metal rivets in 1873. Today we call them jeans.
1914	U.S.A.	The first practical zipper, invented by Swedish immigrant Gideon Sundback, goes on sale, called a Separable Fastener.
1935	U.S.A.	Nylon, a highly elastic thread made from plastic, is invented at the DuPont company by scientists attempting to make artificial silk. The first commercial product made from it is a toothbrush. Nylon stockings come in 1940.
1950s	U.S.A.	Clothing made from polyester fibers, also developed by researchers at DuPont, becomes commercially available.
2013	China	Over half of all the clothing sold in the world is manufactured in China.

Of old You founded the earth,
and the heavens are the work of Your hands.
Even they will perish, but You endure;
and all of them will wear out like a garment;
like clothing You will change them
and they will be changed.
Psalm 102:25-26

Assignments for Lesson 94

In Their Words — Read "The Memorandum of Martha Moulsworth / Widdowe" (pages 222-225).

Literature — Continue reading *A Tale of Two Cities*.

Student Review — Optional: Answer the questions for Lesson 94.

Lesson 95 - Bible Study

The Value of Life

Life is full of amazing possibilities. Modern technology enables us to communicate almost instantaneously and relatively inexpensively with people around the globe. Fascinating work opportunities continually open up in fields that were unheard of twenty years ago. The average person can travel farther, learn more, and live longer than most of our ancestors could.

One of the most remarkable legacies of the Scientific Revolution has been the progress in medical technology. Researchers invest billions of dollars and countless hours in developing improved surgical procedures, prescription drugs, and other treatments and procedures to help people live longer and live better.

However, those who are the most vulnerable—the unborn, the chronically ill and handicapped, and the elderly—face real threats. Abortion gives women a choice but takes away the choice of living for millions of the unborn. Those who need continuing care face the possibility of that care being denied them when health care is rationed by government.

God, as the Giver of life, places great value on the gift of life. The Bible has much to say about how we should view the precious life that God gives to human beings.

Life Is From God

God created life (Genesis 1:11-12, 20-25). As a special act of Creation, He created man (Genesis 1:26-27, 2:7). David praised God for His wonderful work in forming him in his mother's womb:

For You formed my inward parts;
You wove me in my mother's womb.
I will give thanks to You,
  for I am fearfully and wonderfully made;
Wonderful are Your works,
And my soul knows it very well.
My frame was not hidden from You,
When I was made in secret,
And skillfully wrought in the depths of the earth;
Your eyes have seen my unformed substance;
And in Your book were all written
The days that were ordained for me,
When as yet there was not one of them.
                    Psalm 139:13-16

Medical technology has shown the amazing intricacy of an unborn baby's body from the early stages of pregnancy. We are also learning about an unborn child's reactions to external stimulations.

This is confirmed in the reaction of the unborn John the Baptist when Mary came into the house where Elizabeth was (Luke 1:41). The word for baby in this verse is the same word used elsewhere in Scripture for a child after he is born. What a pregnant woman carries within herself is a person, a human, a child.

Life Is in the Blood

God taught Israel to respect life. God made humans and animals such that blood is the river of life in the body. A study of biology shows how true this is. Blood carries nutrients to and removes waste from every cell in the body. White blood cells fight infection in the body.

When an Israelite made an animal sacrifice to the Lord, he was to bring the blood of the animal as well to have it poured onto the altar (Leviticus 17:1-9). The worshiper was to realize the seriousness and the sacredness of a blood sacrifice. He was not to take it lightly.

> *For the life of the flesh is in the blood, and I have given it to you on the altar to make atonement for your souls; for it is the blood by reason of the life that makes atonement. (Leviticus 17:11)*

This commandment was to instill in the Israelites an awareness that would help them to understand the atoning sacrifice that Christ made of His own blood, His life for ours.

The Israelites were not to eat blood (Leviticus 17:10-14; compare Genesis 9:4). A common pagan practice was to drink the blood of animals that they sacrificed in the belief that the worshipers would gain the life and strength of the slain animal. On some occasions pagan warriors were known to drink the blood of their enemies to try to obtain their qualities. God's people were to have no part of this.

Life is too precious and holy for men to drink the source of life as a pill or potion to work magic in them. If an Israelite even ate the meat of an animal that had not been properly slaughtered, he was considered unclean (Leviticus 17:15-16). The provisions against eating blood and eating improperly slaughtered animals were so important that the Holy Spirit made them essential for new Gentile Christians in the early church (Acts 15:28-29).

The Life of the Elderly

"You shall rise up before the grayheaded and honor the aged, and you shall revere your God; I am the Lord" (Leviticus 19:32). God gives life, and in His wisdom He gives length of life. God also defines quality of life, and we do not. We do not have the wisdom or perspective to decide when

Portrait of an Elderly Lady and a Girl
George Beare (British, 1747)

someone has lived long enough or that he has such a poor quality of life that he no longer deserves to live. This, however, is not the same as a situation in which family members decide about whether to continue medical treatment for a loved one near death. In such a situation, continuing what is called heroic treatment is often not prolonging life but is instead prolonging death.

It is a far different kind of decision to say that a person is too weak or too feeble-minded to continue living and so the best thing to do is to put that person to death. This practice is called euthanasia (from the Greek meaning good death). It might sometimes appear that the elderly or infirm person would be relieved of his burden of misery with such an action. However, that is not a decision we can make. It happens in the lives of some persons that their main purpose becomes letting others around them serve them and thus grow as servants. To watch a loved one suffer from illness or old age is difficult, but as humans we dare not take it upon ourselves to decide who is worthy of living.

The decision of who should live and who should not is far too serious to make a government policy. Hitler decided that Jews did not deserve to live. Stalin decided that his opponents did not deserve to live. What if a future leader decides, as some have in the past, that Christians do not deserve to live?

Taking Life is God's Decision

Cain's murder of Abel was a terrible stain on humanity because a human took it into his own hands to determine that another person should not live (Genesis 4:4-10). Life is too precious to be taken in anger or hatred. Jesus extended the application of this when He said that even hating another person will cause one to be guilty. Rather than hating others, God's people are to be about the business of reconciling with others (Matthew 5:21-26).

Algerian Woman with Child
Pierre-Auguste Renoir (French, 1882)

The Lord took life on occasion, but only in extreme circumstances. It was only when evil had increased tremendously on earth that God brought the flood (Genesis 6:5-7). As the ultimate plague on Egypt, after God had given Pharaoh many chances to obey Him, God caused the death of all the firstborn throughout the land of Egypt to convince Pharaoh to let His people go (Exodus 12:29-30).

The Law of Moses did not call for prison sentences for those who committed wrongs. Instead it called for beatings, and in extreme cases, the death penalty. Capital offenses in the law included:

- striking one's parents or kidnapping someone (Exodus 21:15-16);

- sacrificing a child to Molech; cursing one's father or mother; adultery,

homosexuality, and other sexual sins (Leviticus 20:2-16);
- being a medium or spiritist (Leviticus 20:27);
- blaspheming the name of the Lord (Leviticus 24:16);
- taking the life of another person (Leviticus 24:17);
- Sabbath-breaking (Numbers 15:32-36);
- being a rebellious son (Deuteronomy 21:18-21).

These sins were capital crimes because they showed disrespect for the Giver of life and for the lives of others. The person who committed one of these sins forfeited the right to continue his life because he had violated the lives of others. God also gives governments the right to "bear the sword" so that those who do evil will face the consequences of their actions (Romans 13:1-5).

Respect for Life

Science has revealed to us the intricacies and marvelous systems of life that God created. Medical science has enabled us to care for human life and health. This knowledge and ability, however, do not put us on a level equal with God. God gives life, and all we do and learn is done with the lives and talents He gives us, as persons made in His image.

Life is indeed a precious gift from God, one for which we should thank Him every day. We should use our lives wisely for His purposes. It is sad to watch someone throw his or her life away by giving in to drugs, alcohol, gambling, or some other self-destructive behavior. What a waste to use your one precious life for something degrading or harmful! This dishonors God just as taking another person's life does. As people who have been given life—and then given another chance at life in the new birth—Christians need to protect and cherish life and to help others see its value and sacredness.

The thief comes only to steal and kill and destroy;
I came that they may have life, and have it abundantly.
John 10:10

Assignments for Lesson 95

Bible Recite or write John 8:31-32 from memory.

In Their Words Read the excerpt from *Pensées* and "Awake, My Soul, and with the Sun" (pages 226-228).

Literature Continue reading *A Tale of Two Cities*.

Project Complete your project for this unit.

Student Review Optional: Answer questions for Lesson 95 and take the quiz for Unit 19.

20

The Age of Revolution

Summary Changes kept coming: changes in how people understood the size and breadth of the earth, changes in scientific understanding, and then changes in government and society. This unit examines three major political revolutions in Western culture, those that took place in England, the United States, and France. We also look at the life and influence of a key philosopher of the period, John Locke. The everyday life lesson looks at eating. The Bible study deals with real freedom, namely spiritual freedom in Christ.

Lessons
96 - Revolutions in England and America
97 - Key Event: The French Revolution
98 - Key Person: John Locke
99 - Everyday Life: Eating Through the Centuries
100 - Bible Study: Freedom and Responsibility

A huge mob confronted the French King in the 1789 Women's March on Versailles.

Memory Work

Learn Galatians 5:13-14 by the end of the unit.

Books Used

The Bible
In Their Words
A Tale of Two Cities

Project (choose one)

1) Write 300 to 500 words on one of the following topics:

- A broadside was a document that stated a case in the strongest terms possible. Write a broadside calling for revolution in one of the countries discussed in this unit. Make a big headline across the top, and make smaller subheadings throughout the document. Cover both sides of the page and end with a call to action.

- Write an essay on this topic: "The French Revolution was a highly imperfect attempt to solve a highly imperfect situation." See Lessons 96-97.

2) Create a video as if you were broadcasting a television newscast during the American or French Revolution. Choose an event to feature, and then research further details of the event to include in the newscast. You can be the anchor, or you can ask another person to be the anchor with a script written by you. You can also include an interview with an expert as part of your newscast, and/or interview two different experts with differing views. Your newscast should be at least four minutes long.

3) Write a song or poem of at least sixteen lines about freedom.

Statue of William III in Bristol, England

Lesson 96

Revolutions in England and America

The pattern of government in European countries at the start of the 1600s was absolutism: complete power in the hands of a monarch who could rule as he wished. However, cracks appeared in the foundation of absolutism over the next two centuries. By 1800 republican revolutions had taken place in England, France, and the United States; and the theoretical underpinnings of absolutism had been destroyed. Even where kings continued to rule, many of them gave broader rights and freedoms to the people, if for no other reason than to maintain their thrones.

Absolutism had developed as a means to control domestic strife and to allow countries to compete politically and economically on the world stage. However, as the middle (business) class grew in wealth and power, its members wanted a place at the political table. They demanded greater freedom and equality, but we must understand what they meant. Middle class merchants wanted freedom from the economic restraints of mercantilism and freedom for their own kind (certainly not the working class) to voice their opinions. Equality for the middle class meant being considered equal to the nobility. As a rule, they did not want the lower classes to be equal with them.

The philosophical drive behind these political changes came from the Enlightenment, with its faith in man's reason and its opposition to hereditary privilege and political absolutism as irrational traditions. In addition to this philosophical change, social, political, and religious factors were all at work in the movements of the times. In this unit we will trace developments leading to the republican revolutions of the 17th and 18th centuries. In the next unit, we will outline the development of modern Europe as a whole, which was greatly influenced by the revolutions to which we now turn.

Theory of the Divine Right of Kings

It was the age of the great dynasties in Europe: the Bourbon family in France (epitomized by the reign of Louis XIV, 1643-1715), the Hohenzollern dynasty in Prussia, the Hapsburgs in Austria, the Romanovs in Russia, and, beginning in 1603, the Stuart dynasty in England. The justification for their claim of absolute power was best expressed by James I of England, who held to the divine (God-given) right of kings to rule. The monarch, in James' view, was put in place by God and ruled on God's throne.

Since the mid-1500s, the British Parliament has been meeting at the Palace of Westminster. Most of the current structures, commonly known as the Houses of Parliament, were built after an 1834 fire. Big Ben is the name of the large bell in the Clock Tower. This 1904 painting, Houses of Parliament, London, Sun Breaking Through the Fog, *by French artist Claude Monet is one of a series he made in the early 1900s showing the building from the same point of view at different times of day and in different weather. (See also the photo on the cover of this book.)*

His absolute power could not be questioned. Neither Parliament nor any other institution could place any restraints on his power.

This was not what the English Parliament, trying to flex its own political muscle, wanted to hear. Parliament was dominated by Puritans, who wanted to purify the Anglican Church of its abuses and Catholic tendencies and lessen the powers of the king and the Church hierarchy. This put them at odds with the absolutist king who was head of the Church. James I, who persecuted Puritans at times, met the opposition in Parliament by simply going around them. When he needed more revenue and Parliament balked, James dismissed Parliament and then brought back feudal fines and increased customs duties on his own initiative. These were actions that he could take legally, but they cost him support in Parliament.

The English Civil War

The contest between the throne and Parliament continued when James' successor, his son Charles I, approached Parliament with a request for more revenue. Parliament replied by demanding that he sign the Petition of Right, which said that the king could not acquire new revenue without the approval of Parliament and that the king could not imprison someone without cause. Charles agreed, Parliament passed the revenue, and Charles promptly dissolved Parliament. He ignored the Petition of Right and ruled for eleven years without calling Parliament into session. Charles persecuted Puritans and other non-conformist (non-Anglican) Protestants and suppressed opposition to his rule.

In 1638 Charles I tried to impose the Anglican Church on Scotland. The Scots rebelled and began an invasion of England. Charles summoned Parliament in 1640 to ask for funds. This body came to be called the Long Parliament because it met off and on for twenty years. Instead of rubber-stamping Charles' request, Parliament tried and executed two of Charles' advisers for malfeasance in office. The king responded by sending an army

Cromwell at Dunbar *by Andrew Carrick Gow (British, 1886) depicts the Parliamentarian army at the site of a 1650 battle in Scotland.*

Lesson 96 - Revolutions in England and America

into Parliament and arresting five of its leaders. Parliament gathered its own troops, and civil war erupted in 1642.

Support for both sides crossed economic, social, and religious lines. Generally speaking, the King's Cavaliers (the word comes from cavalry or the French *chevalier* and means mounted troops) were supported by the nobles and the rural population. The Parliamentary forces (called the Roundheads for their simple haircuts that made a statement against the long hair of the royalty) were backed by the middle class, townspeople, and the Puritans.

Oliver Cromwell took over the Parliamentary army in 1645 and led them to victory over the Cavaliers. Charles I was captured, tried, and executed in 1649, an act for which many in England feel embarrassment and remorse even to this day. The House of Commons abolished the monarchy and declared England to be a republic (also called a commonwealth) with Cromwell as its leader. He was a man of high ideals who wanted to rule England by Puritan values. He offered toleration for all Protestants but not for Catholics.

Cromwell banned theaters, newspapers, and other forms of entertainment. He also crushed a Scottish uprising and oversaw the brutal suppression of a rebellion of Irish Catholics. Cromwell then encouraged Protestants to settle in Ireland, especially in the northern part of the island. Some in Parliament were not satisfied with Cromwell's leadership, so with Parliament divided Cromwell simply dismissed them in 1653. He ruled as Lord Protector until his death in 1658.

The Restoration and The Glorious Revolution

After Cromwell died, his son ruled for a short time; but Puritan government was wearing thin in merry old England. In 1660 Parliament asked Charles II, the son of the late Charles I, to return from exile in France to be made king. Given the events of the previous few years, both Charles and Parliament were cautious in their relations with each other. Charles was a worldly leader but proved to be popular.

Thomas Hobbes (1588-1679)

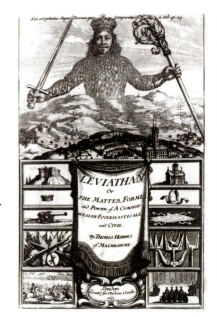

The writings of political philosophers during this time sometimes influenced and sometimes were influenced by the events taking place. In 1651, partly in response to the chaos of the English Civil War, philosopher Thomas Hobbes of England published the book Leviathan *(title page shown at right). He saw man as evil and given to selfishness. If left without government, human life would be "solitary, poor, nasty, brutish, and short." Man's one redeeming feature is his reason, Hobbes said, which leads him to sacrifice some of his freedom for the security of a strong government. Society and state result from this social contract.*

Hobbes' justification for an authoritarian government was that it avoided anarchy. However, his rationale was not based on any divine right but on human reason. Obedience was the best thing for people to do simply from the standpoint of self-interest. Law and order serves the individual better than rebellion and disorder. Hobbes' arguments did not convince the Puritan Roundheads. Cromwell ruled with a strong hand because he thought it was the will of God that he do so.

In 1673 Parliament passed the Test Act, which required all office holders and members of the army to be Anglican. However, matters were not settled yet. Charles was a closet Catholic who wanted to restore Catholic power and prominence in England. He made a secret treaty with France to obtain money that he needed, in return for which he promised to restore the Catholic Church in England as soon as possible. Charles also joined the French in a war against the Dutch Netherlands. During this war England seized New Amsterdam from the Dutch in America and renamed it New York.

Charles' brother James II inherited the throne in 1685. James was openly Catholic, and in 1688 his second wife gave birth to a son, a male heir to the throne, whom James had baptized in the Catholic Church. This was too much for the Protestant Parliament, which secretly invited into the country William of Orange of the Netherlands and his wife Mary, who was James' oldest child, the daughter of his first wife, and thus a defensible heir to the throne.

When James II fled from England, Parliament declared that he had abdicated and offered the throne to William and Mary. The next year, the new monarchs signed a Bill of Rights, guaranteeing certain protections to individuals and insuring that a Catholic could not assume the throne.

The long constitutional nightmare for England was finally over, and so was the theory that a monarch had absolute power (royal absolutism). The terrible civil war had been followed within a few years by a Glorious (also known as Bloodless) Revolution, which made the clear statement that Parliament no longer sat by the approval of the king, but the king sat by the approval of Parliament. England now had a limited monarchy, meaning that the king or queen did not have absolute power. The representative assembly, Parliament, increased its power significantly during the 17th century.

The British government of today began to take shape during this period. Political parties developed, with Tories generally supporting the crown and Whigs favoring limitations on the power of the king. The king appointed advisers who came to head departments of government. As a group, they were called the cabinet.

Cabinet members were also members of Parliament. There they could influence legislation that they wanted to see passed. Cabinet members usually were from the majority party in the House of Commons. A cabinet remained in power until they lost the confidence of Parliament, and then the king ordered new elections.

English vs. Irish

Later in 1689, James II attempted to foment a rebellion in Catholic Ireland. King William led a force against him and defeated the Irish army at the Battle of the Boyne. Parliament passed a series of harsh anti-Catholic laws for Ireland, including ones forbidding Catholics from serving in the Irish Parliament and from buying or inheriting land from Protestants. This legislation was part of a long series of actions by the English that contributed to the bitterness felt by many Irish toward England.

Battle of the Boyne Between James II and William III
Jan van Huchtenburg (Dutch, c. 1700)

Lesson 96 - Revolutions in England and America

After a miscarriage early in their marriage, William and Mary had no children. After Mary died in 1694 and William died in 1702, Mary's younger sister Anne became Queen. Queen Anne reigned until her death in 1714.

In 1701 Parliament had passed the Act of Settlement, which declared that only an Anglican could become monarch of England. It also stated that since Anne did not have any surviving children, the line of succession would go to Anne's cousin Sophia of Hanover in Germany. Sophia died before Anne, so Sophia's son George inherited the throne.

George I began the dynasty that is still on the throne of Great Britain today, although its name was changed to Windsor when Britain fought Germany in World War I. George I could not speak English and knew nothing about English politics. Sir Robert Walpole helped the king and took over running the government. He is considered to be the first prime minister.

George III came to power in 1760. He believed that the monarchy had given up too much power to Parliament and the cabinet, so he reasserted himself as the head of government. Some of his policies angered people in the British colonies in America and eventually led to the colonies declaring their independence.

Revolution in the American Colonies

British colonists in America had become increasingly concerned about their rights during the 1700s. The English government controlled trade to and from the colonies for the benefit of England, not the colonies. Parliament levied heavy taxes on the colonies to pay for debts incurred in the French and Indian War, taxation that was imposed without any American representation in Parliament. British troops were quartered in the private homes of Americans. The colonists had thought that winning the French and Indian War would help them be free, but the result was a heavier burden for them

Before becoming queen, Anne and her husband, Prince George of Denmark, suffered the loss of numerous children to miscarriage, stillbirth, and early infant death. This 1694 portrait by Sir Godfrey Kneller shows Anne with Prince William, her only child to survive infancy. William died in 1700 at age eleven. In response to this tragedy, Parliament passed the Act of Settlement in 1701.

to bear. The response by the British government to colonial complaints and requests was to impose more regulations and more taxes.

As British troops moved through the Massachusetts countryside in April of 1775 to seize a patriot arsenal and to arrest suspected patriot leaders, Americans fired on the troops. Thus began the war for independence. In July of 1776, the Continental Congress approved the Declaration of Independence, which declared the United States to be a free and sovereign country. The document, written largely by Thomas Jefferson, was filled with Enlightenment ideas about the natural rights of man and the correctness of removing an oppressive government from power.

The American army, although it was ill-fed and ill-equipped, defeated the strongest military force in the world. The Americans were highly motivated and fought on their home turf. The colonies received assistance from France, which was always eager to help England lose a war. The leadership of George Washington inspired the new nation to victory, and America upset the world superpower just as England had done to Spain in 1588.

After a period of weak national government under the Articles of Confederation, the United States implemented a Constitution which created three branches of government—legislative, executive, and judicial—and set up a system of checks and balances among them. A Bill of Rights was soon added to the Constitution to protect individual liberties.

The Enduring Legacy of the American Revolution

The English and American Revolutions successfully challenged absolutism and the divine right of kings in the name of the people. The new ideas of the Enlightenment were put into practice and appeared to be working. The American Revolution firmly established the principles of political freedom and individual rights that were later echoed in country after country around the world.

Still, the English and American Revolutions were not victories for pure democracy. The idea that "all men are created equal," for instance, was not applied to slaves. In addition, for most political leaders at the time, democracy was a dangerous concept, conjuring up images of mob rule by the ignorant masses. Relatively few people in England had the right to vote. In the United States, voting requirements were set by the states but generally included the requirement that the voter own property. Fairly early in the American republic, property requirements were dropped and all adult male citizens could vote. However, no women could vote and no slaves could vote. Even with these limitations, the American experiment was a model of freedom for other peoples in the world.

Every man's way is right in his own eyes,
but the Lord weighs the hearts.
Proverbs 21:2

Assignments for Lesson 96

Bible The readings for this week relate to Lesson 100. Read Galatians 1.

In Their Words Read the excerpts from the English Bill of Rights and from the letter by Edmund Burke (pages 229-231).

Literature Continue reading *A Tale of Two Cities*. Finish it by the end of this unit.

Student Review Optional: Answer the questions for Lesson 96.

The Execution of Robespierre and His Supporters (French, 1794)

Lesson 97 - Key Event

The French Revolution

The revolution in France was inspired in great measure by the American Revolution (and to a degree by the events in England of the 1600s), but it was by no means simply a duplication of the American experience. The American Revolution was primarily political, while the issues in France included economic and religious concerns as well as political ones. The American colonists wanted to be free from the king who had governed them from across an ocean, while the French Revolution took place in the country of France itself. The American conflict was clearly "us versus them," American patriots fighting English loyalists, but in France the political stances ranged across the spectrum from royalists to radical democrats.

The revolution in America followed a fairly straight line of events, from declaration to war to new nationhood, with a peaceful adjustment that followed from the Articles of Confederation to the Constitution. In France the revolution went through several phases, in which Frenchmen shed the blood of thousands of their fellow countrymen. The United States never wavered from the republican form of government it adopted, while the French revolutionary period was followed by the dictatorship of Napoleon and then a limited monarchy. Eventually the French people gained an outcome similar to that accomplished in America, but the route they took to that point was much more costly and tortured.

Cardinal Richelieu and the Power of the Monarchy

The 1500s were a period of instability in France, marked by considerable fighting between Catholics and Huguenots (HYOO-ga-nots). Named for Besançon Hughes, a Swiss reformer, the Huguenots were Calvinist Protestants. The Edict of Nantes, signed in 1598, gave Huguenots the freedom to worship as they pleased and the right to build church buildings in certain places.

King Henry IV worked to strengthen the French nation and his authority over it; but he was assassinated in 1610, and his ten-year-old son, Louis XIII, came to the throne. The French nobles forced a meeting of the Estates General (the advisory body to the king) to try to reassert their power, but they could not agree on issues among themselves. The king dismissed them in 1614, and the Estates General did not meet again for 175 years.

The prime mover in French politics during the reign of Louis XIII was his adviser, Roman Catholic Cardinal Richelieu. Richelieu's goal was to increase the power of the throne. He limited the political rights of Huguenots, destroyed castles that belonged to nobles in the provinces, encouraged overseas trade and investment in that trade by nobles, and allowed wealthy merchants to buy titles of nobility, which created nobles who were loyal to the throne. Over the course of Richelieu's tenure, power and prestige flowed to the French throne.

The Reign of the Sun King

Louis XIII died in 1643. His son was only four years old, so the boy's mother reigned in his place. She was assisted by Cardinal Mazarin, who followed the policies of Richelieu. Mazarin died in 1661; and Louis XIV, now twenty-three, declared that he was going to assume his full powers as king. For the next fifty-four years, Louis XIV dominated France and Europe. He was the epitome of the absolute monarch and the embodiment of the principle of divine right. Louis XIV was called the Sun King because his symbol was a sun and because, in his mind, he was as important to France as the sun is to the world. He once expressed his opinion of his significance to the state with the phrase, "*L'etat, c'est moi*" ("The state, it is I").

Louis XIV placed royal agents throughout the country to collect taxes and administer the king's policies. He increased the size of the army, both to fight more effectively abroad and to quell any disturbances at home. The finances of Louis' reign were overseen by Jean Baptiste Colbert, who increased taxes, enabled more efficient collection of taxes, and encouraged foreign trade. Although nobles did not pay taxes, Colbert hoped that increased trade activity would mean more income for the lower classes, who did pay taxes. New industry was encouraged (and taxed) and import tariffs were raised. Colbert also oversaw improvements in transportation and encouraged the growth of French overseas colonies.

A staunch Catholic, Louis canceled the Edict of Nantes. As a result, many Huguenots fled to England, the Dutch Netherlands, and America. The king also greatly expanded the Palace of Versailles, which stood twelve miles outside of Paris. This impressive structure took twenty-seven years to complete and sat on 20,000 acres of manicured grounds.

Philosophy in France

Two influential political philosophers of the mid-1700s contributed ideas that led to the revolutions in America and France.

Baron de Montesquieu (1689-1755, pictured at right) was a French aristocrat. He praised the separation of powers among the legislative, executive, and judicial branches of government that he saw in England. He also believed that a system of checks and balances among the branches would keep one branch from becoming too powerful.

Jean Jacques Rousseau (1712-1778, pictured at left) was born in Geneva but spent many years in France. He believed that all people were equal and were basically good. He believed in the theoretical noble savage and said that society corrupted people. As he put it, "Man is born free and is everywhere in chains." In Rousseau's ideal society, people would contract with each other, not with a ruler, to decide by majority vote what was best for all.

The move to Versailles placed the seat of government safely away from the sometimes turbulent setting of Paris. Louis' reign became the model for other European monarchs. French fashions became the rage across the continent, and French became the language of international diplomacy.

Louis' philosophy of government was best expressed by Jacques Bossuet, a bishop who wrote in 1670 that the authority of the king was given by God and thus was sacred and absolute. The king was like a father to his country, and the word of the king was not to be questioned. To resist the king was to resist God.

The sun rarely set on the Sun King's war-making efforts. Thirty of his fifty-four years on the throne were marked by foreign conflict. The most serious was the War of Spanish Succession, which began in 1701. Louis' grandson became king of Spain, and French forces occupied the Spanish Netherlands to support his rule. Many in Europe feared that the thrones of Spain and France would be united. Other European countries joined forces against France and struck at France at every opportunity. The war finally ended in 1713 with the Treaty of Utrecht, which said that the crowns of Spain and France could never be united. Louis XIV died in 1715.

Clouds Begin to Gather

The French economy was strong through most of the 1700s until the 1770s, when poor harvests cut food production. Regulations that gave the king strong powers hampered new trade and manufacturing. Rules imposed by local guilds put limitations on small businesses. Moreover, the French national debt was growing oppressive. The government owed the money to bankers because of loans the government had taken out to pay for its many wars, including the French and Indian War and French assistance to the United States during the American War for Independence.

Louis XVI, who came to the throne in 1774, was a careless and self-indulgent leader. His finance

Construction of the Château de Versailles
Adam Frans van der Meulen (Dutch, 1669)

minister, Robert Turgot, tried to improve economic conditions by cutting government expenses, lowering taxes on food, and limiting the power of guilds. He tried to impose a tax on the nobility, but the provincial parlements, especially the one in Paris, refused to approve the proposal. Since Turgot's effectiveness had reached its limit, the king dismissed him in 1776. France limped along until 1786, when the national debt crisis became so bad that bankers refused to loan the French government any more money. Poor harvests hurt the already staggering French economy even more. Desperate for a solution, Louis XVI summoned the Estates General to meet in 1789 to approve new taxes.

The Estates of France

French society was divided into three classes, or estates. The first estate was the clergy, from high-ranking Church officials (some of whom were also nobles) to parish priests. Local priests ran their parishes; kept birth, death, and marriage records; cared for the poor; and collected taxes or tithes from the lower classes. The Church owned vast amounts of land, but the First Estate paid no taxes.

The Second Estate was made up of the nobility and accounted for less than two percent of the population. This class included officers in the army. In general the Second Estate was also exempt from paying taxes.

The commoners made up the Third Estate. This included the bourgeoisie (merchants, manufacturers, lawyers, doctors, shopkeepers, and artisans) as well as city workers and rural peasants. This group paid the most taxes and resented the nobility and their privileges. The bourgeoisie was the wealthiest group in the Third Estate, and the peasants were the largest group. Peasants were not feudal serfs, but they paid feudal dues and were required to give unpaid service to the king and their lords (such as working on road construction for a certain number of days per year). Peasants also had to pay tithes to the Church and land rent to the nobles. The growing wealth and changing makeup of the Third Estate was an indication that society was changing, but the accepted structure of society did not reflect this change. The situation was ripe for trouble.

The Revolution Begins

The Estates General had not met since 1614. As the body convened in May of 1789, a dispute arose over how the body was to vote. Traditionally, the estates met separately and the entire delegation of each estate had a total of one vote. This meant that the first two estates could always defeat the Third Estate two to one. Members of the Third Estate, however, now called for all the estates to meet together and for each delegate to have a vote. They hoped that their numbers, augmented by sympathetic clergy and nobles, would constitute a majority.

Louis XVI ruled that the estates would meet separately as they had traditionally done. The representatives of the Third Estate then declared themselves to be the only true National Assembly and committed themselves to writing a constitution for the country. The king banished them from the Estates General, whereupon the delegates of the Third Estate, joined by some reform-minded nobles and clergy, met at a nearby indoor tennis court. They took an oath that they would not disband until they had written a constitution. After a tense interlude, the king ordered the first two estates to join the third. They met together in a national assembly, but deep divisions existed. Most of the reformers were not radicals. They sought a limited constitutional monarchy like the one in England. A few radicals urged equality of all people throughout the classes.

By July, little had been done. The peasantry and the people of Paris had gotten no relief, and the crisis of a lack of food was mounting. When it was learned that Louis XVI was gathering troops at Versailles, citizens of Paris began arming themselves. On July 14, 1789, crowds stormed the Bastille, an armory and prison which symbolized the old regime, to seize weapons. They believed that political prisoners were being held there, but they found only seven people

This 1789 French cartoon shows a peasant carrying a clergyman and a noble on his back. The caption reads, "You should hope that this game will end soon."

Lesson 97 - Key Event: The French Revolution

incarcerated. Disturbances spread to the countryside in what was called the Great Fear. Peasants heard rumors that the nobles were planning to attack them, so the peasants turned on the nobles first.

Amid these developments, the National Assembly began to act. They eliminated privileges that had been enjoyed by the clergy and nobility and declared that all men were now eligible for Church and government positions. In August the Assembly also published the Declaration of the Rights of Man and Citizen, which was written largely by the Marquis de Lafayette with help from Thomas Jefferson. This document stated the revolutionary principles which the leaders of the National Assembly hoped to include in the new system of government.

The Declaration passed the Assembly on August 26, 1789, but the king refused to sign it. In October, with the food shortage continuing, thousands of Parisian women marched in the rain to Versailles. They demanded that Louis XVI and his wife, Marie Antoinette, return to Paris with them so that they could be closely watched. The royal couple agreed to do so and wore the tricolors of the revolution as they did. The National Assembly also moved to Paris.

The Assembly soon declared freedom of religion in France and took away the privileges of the Roman Catholic Church. In 1790 legislation gave the government control of the clergy; and people were given the right to elect their bishops and priests. The government began selling land that the Church had owned in order to raise revenue. When this happened, Catholics began condemning the revolution in significant numbers.

A New Constitution and Assembly

A constitution was finally completed in 1791. It created a limited monarchy and called for separation of powers among the branches of government. The king was given a veto over laws passed by the Legislative Assembly, but he could only delay enactment and not prevent it altogether. The estates of society were removed. Only those who owned

The Storming of the Bastille
Jean-Pierre Houël (French, 1789)

considerable property could vote for members of the legislature. Some 50,000 people were able to vote under this constitution.

Few people were happy with the constitution. Radicals wanted to see the monarchy eliminated altogether, while the nobles thought the document went too far in limiting royal power. Some 100,000 nobles eventually left the country, including over half of the officers in the army. These nobles advised the kings of other European countries to take action against what was happening in France in order to reclaim France from the hands of the mob and to protect their own positions.

In June of 1791, Louis XVI and Marie Antoinette tried to escape the country, but they were recognized and arrested. In August the king accepted the terms of the new constitution and was restored to his position. Delegates to the Legislative Assembly were elected and convened in October. As they arranged themselves in the meeting hall, the moderate revolutionaries sat on the right side of the room while the radicals gathered on the left. This was the origin of designating conservatives as the right and liberals as the left. The radicals were even further divided. A group called the Jacobins (ZJOCK-o-bins) wanted to extend the right to vote to all adult males. Over the next few months the Jacobins and their leader, Maximilien Robespierre, gained the upper hand.

Tensions on the international scene increased also. Many European rulers, having seen revolutions in the United States and now France, were afraid that their country would be next. Meanwhile some of the revolutionary leaders in France wanted to export the revolution to other countries in order to make their position more secure and to help other people gain freedom from oppression.

The emperor of Austria, who was Marie Antoinette's brother, was especially wary. In the spring of 1792, war erupted between Austria and France. France would be involved in war for the next twenty-three years. The revolutionary army was poorly led and torn by internal strife. On one occasion, for instance, a French regiment insisted on voting to decide whether to move against the opposing army. By August Austrian and Prussian troops were closing in on Paris. In response, the French pulled together under the banner of "Liberty, Equality, Fraternity." Soldiers marched from the city of Marseille singing a patriotic song that came to be called the "Marseillaise" and was eventually made the national anthem. The revolutionary forces defeated the Prussian army, and the other invaders retreated.

As a counter-measure to the atheistic Cult of Reason promoted by the radicals, Robespierre created a Cult of the Supreme Being. Robespierre's "Supreme Being" was rather nondescript, and nothing was said about Jesus. This painting by Pierre-Antoine Demachy depicts the June 8, 1794, Festival of the Cult of the Supreme Being. Neither of these Cults lasted very long.

The Paris Commune

The turmoil led to uprisings in the provinces. On August 10, 1792, revolutionaries took over Paris and established a new government called the Commune. Commune forces captured the king and queen and demanded yet another national constitution. In this tense time, a constitutional convention was elected. When it assembled, the convention voted to abolish the monarchy and establish a republic. This raised the issue of what to do with the king: try him for treason or simply imprison him. A major division over the issue arose between the radicals and the moderates. Then evidence came to light which showed that Louis XVI was plotting with nobles who had left the country to crush the revolution. The Convention found the king guilty by an overwhelming vote, but the decision to execute him passed only narrowly. Louis XVI was put to death on January 21, 1793. The radicals marked those who opposed the execution as enemies of the revolution.

French revolutionary forces captured the part of the Netherlands then controlled by Austria. The National Convention promised to aid the citizens of other nations in their desire to gain freedom. In March of 1793, Great Britain, the Dutch Netherlands, and Spain joined Prussia and Austria in opposing the French. This appeared to be an imposing force arrayed against the unstable government. Within France few people could see much benefit from the ongoing war, and some feared that the revolution had gone too far. Counter-revolutionaries began springing up in outlying cities.

The Reign of Terror

Also in 1793, the National Convention established the Committee of Public Safety and gave it almost dictatorial powers. It initiated a campaign against all its enemies real or perceived in what came to be called the Reign of Terror, which lasted from July of 1793 to July of 1794. Radical leader Robespierre, who was honest but inflexible, led the

Committee. Secret police roamed the cities and countryside arresting anyone suspected of opposing the Committee or the revolution.

The Reign of Terror operated through intimidation and guilt by association. Trials for treason were held almost daily. An estimated 20,000 to 40,000 Frenchmen, mostly commoners, were condemned to the guillotine. Marie Antoinette was one victim. The Reign of Terror quelled revolts against the current authorities. As a result, the Committee put more military forces in the field to oppose invaders. In mid-1794 many began thinking that the Committee of Public Safety had gone too far. The National Convention ordered Robespierre arrested, and in July of 1794 Robespierre himself was executed. With that, the Reign of Terror ended.

The Directory

Popular reaction to the excesses of the revolution began growing with the execution of Robespierre. In 1795 another constitution was enacted. The new government was called the Directory, with a legislature and a five-man executive branch (the leaders of which were called directors). The country was divided into administrative departments about the size of American counties. Voting rights were extended to adult males who could read and who owned a certain amount of property. The middle and wealthy classes gained power under this government while the Roman Catholic Church essentially lost its political power.

The Directory lasted from 1795 to 1799. It was not an efficient government. Many good men had left the country or been executed. Several members of the legislature were corrupt and sold their votes to the highest bidder. When commodity prices rose, riots broke out again. The Directory built a large army to help it maintain power and to fight the forces of other countries. One man who rose to prominence and gained power as a military leader during this time was Napoleon Bonaparte.

Assessing the French Revolution

The French Revolution was an attempt to bring republican reforms supposedly on the basis of the philosophy of reason to the largest and most populous country in Europe. The revolution and the Napoleonic Era that followed it changed Europe, affected European relations with the United States, and had the greatest impact of any event in western Europe until 1917.

In this 18th-century caricature, Robespierre executes the executioner after killing everyone else in France. The guillotine, introduced in 1792, was named after a French physician involved in its design. The last execution by guillotine in France occurred in 1977. Capital punishment was abolished there in 1981.

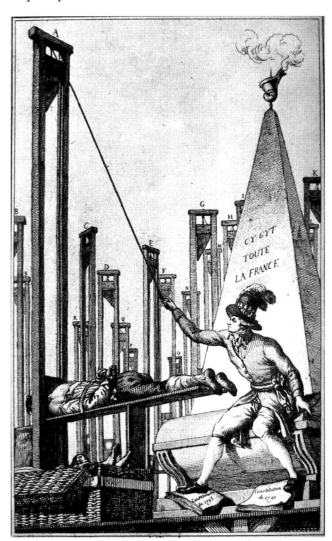

The abusive privileges of the French monarchy had been bad for the country, but a decade of revolution full of hatred and violence was a faulty solution. The period of instability only ended with a new emperor, Napoleon. The terror and chaos were a terrible price to pay for greater democracy and equality. The excesses of the period might have delayed the coming of democracy in other countries as kings and nobles feared mob rule and held power more tightly.

The new emperor brought stability to France, but he created turmoil in Europe. The Napoleonic Wars and their aftermath were important elements in the making of modern Europe. In addition, more domestic political revolutions in Europe were still to come. We will take up this story in the next unit.

Like a roaring lion and a rushing bear is a wicked ruler over a poor people.
Proverbs 28:15

Assignments for Lesson 97

Bible Read Galatians 2-3.

In Their Words Read the Declaration of the Rights of Man and of the Citizen (pages 232-233).

Literature Continue reading *A Tale of Two Cities*.

Student Review Optional: Answer the questions for Lesson 97.

Temple of British Worthies

Lesson 98 - Key Person

John Locke

John Locke's political ideas concerning the composition and role of government were known by American colonists in the mid-1700s. Locke's arguments influenced the development of the U.S. Constitution and thus indirectly the governing documents of many modern countries.

Locke was born in Wrington, England, near Bristol, in 1632. He studied at Westminster School and at Christ Church, Oxford, and became a tutor and lecturer at the latter. He studied both medicine and philosophy.

In 1667 Locke became friend, adviser, and physician to Lord Ashley, the first earl of Shaftesbury. Shaftesbury had a life-threatening liver infection; and Locke oversaw treatment, including a dangerous surgery, that proved successful.

Shaftesbury helped Locke obtain government employment. Locke served as secretary for the Royal Committee on Trade and Foreign Plantations and for the Lords Proprietor of Carolina, one of whom was Shaftesbury. Locke and Shaftesbury in 1669 wrote the Fundamental Constitutions of Carolina for the American colony. This document, which gave considerable power to the upper class, was unpopular with the colonial settlers. After several revisions, it was abandoned in 1693.

Shaftesbury opposed the rule of King Charles II. He ended up imprisoned in the Tower of London, charged with high treason. A jury acquitted Shaftesbury, but he fled to Holland, where he died in 1683.

During this turmoil, Locke spent several years in France and the Netherlands. He returned to England after the Glorious Revolution created a more welcoming environment for his views.

King William I appointed Locke to a post on the Board of Trade in 1696. Locke resigned in 1700 because of poor health and died in 1704.

Philosophy

Locke developed the philosophical idea of empiricism. He believed that the human mind is a blank slate at birth and that we acquire knowledge through experience. He did not think that people

---

The Temple of British Worthies, pictured above, is a private monument in the gardens of Stowe House in Buckinghamshire, England. Built in 1735, it features busts of historical figures considered important by the family who owned the property. The bust of John Locke is featured above at right.

What Else Was Happening? (1650-1800)

1. Hudson's Bay Company (HBC) was founded in 1670 after two French fur traders received backing from English businessmen. Now headquartered in Toronto, Canada, HBC has maintained a continuous existence in diverse industries (though no longer in fur). It is the official clothing supplier for the Canadian Olympic team.

2. The Fulani, or Fula, people are an ethnic group that live in West Africa (see photo at right). During the 18th century, Muslim Fulani established a federation known as Fouta Djallon. Fouta Djallon thrived economically, in part through the slave trade, until it was absorbed into the French colonial empire in 1896.

3. The Polish-Lithuanian Commonwealth prospered during the 16th and 17th centuries. After a period of decline, the national Sejm (parliament) adopted the Constitution of May 3, 1791, following the example of the United States. The new government was short-lived, as hostile neighbors completely took over the nation by 1795.

4. For centuries, the Banda Islands were the only known source of spices from the nutmeg tree. Arab traders had kept the location secret from Europeans; but the Portuguese came in the 1500s, followed by the Dutch. Dutch traders killed a large percentage of the native population and maintained control of the islands until the early 1800s.

5. Mount Fuji, a volcano long considered a holy site in Japan, is the country's highest mountain at 12,389 feet. It has often been the subject of poems and art. *Fine Wind, Clear Morning* (shown at left) by Japanese artist Katsushika Hokusai (1760-1849) is from *Thirty-six Views of Mount Fuji,* his series of woodblock prints. The last major eruption of Mount Fuji occurred in 1707-08.

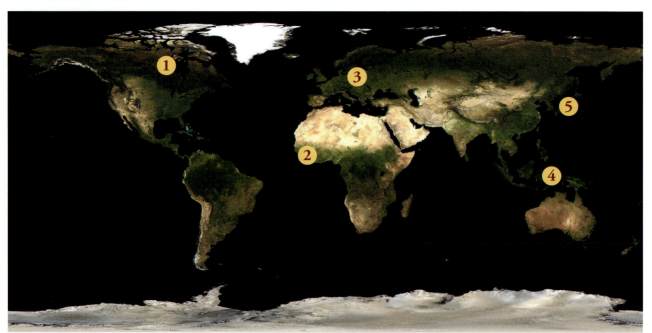

could have spontaneous ideas unrelated to what they already knew. Locke published his observations in the *Essay Concerning Human Understanding* (1690).

An alternative philosophical model is called rationalism. This approach emphasizes the role of reason in identifying and developing knowledge. Its advocates included René Descartes, Baruch Spinoza, and Gottfried Wilhelm Leibniz.

Politics

Locke also expressed his views on political matters in *Two Treatises of Government* (also published in 1690, see title page at right). He criticized the idea that a king has a divine right to rule without restraint from his subjects. He argued that the people, not the state, have ultimate sovereignty.

Locke believed that humans are inherently good. As a result, they can create governments that protect their rights to life, liberty, and property, and that resolve disagreements over those rights. He maintained that the people have the right, and even the obligation in certain cases, to change their government if it no longer serves its proper purpose.

Faith

Unlike many philosophers of his time and later, Locke maintained belief in God and appreciation for the Bible. In his essay *Some Thoughts Concerning Education* (1693), he stated that children should have a firm foundation in the Bible before they studied the physical sciences (or "natural philosophy" as the field was called then). If children studied the physical and visible world without recognizing spiritual and invisible forces, they might be prejudiced against recognizing God's direction of nature. (Locke did not have children of his own, but he tutored the children of others.)

Locke also wrote a book called *The Reasonableness of Christianity* (1695). In this work, he argued that, while nature testifies of God's

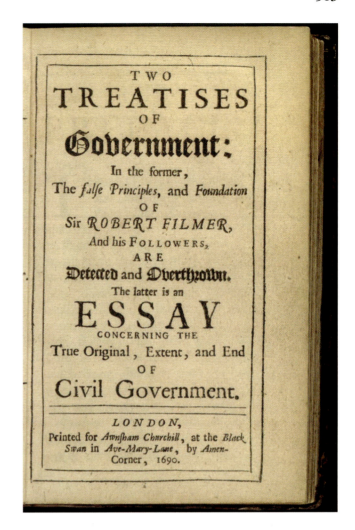

existence, man still needs divine revelation to understand and follow God; and this is the message that Jesus brought. People have developed moral principles throughout history, but they have been unable to develop a satisfactory moral code on their own. The New Testament, confirmed by the miracles of Christ and the authority of God in Christ's work, tells us what God requires of us to be saved. Locke also criticized those who make the plain principles of Scripture unnecessarily complex and attempt to impose their interpretations on everyone else.

Because he believed in God and the Bible, Locke advocated civil toleration for those of other religious faiths. The Fundamental Constitutions of Carolina included this interesting section:

> But since the natives of that place, who will be concerned in our plantation, are utterly strangers to Christianity, whose

idolatry, ignorance, or mistake gives us no right to expel or use them ill; and those who remove from other parts to plant there will unavoidably be of different opinions concerning matters of religion, the liberty whereof they will expect to have allowed them, and it will not be reasonable for us, on this account, to keep them out, that civil peace may be maintained amidst diversity of opinions, and our agreement and compact with all men may be duly and faithfully observed; the violation whereof, upon what presence soever, cannot be without great offence to Almighty God, and great scandal to the true religion which we profess; and also that Jews, heathens, and other dissenters from the purity of Christian religion may not be scared and kept at a distance from it, but, by having an opportunity of acquainting themselves with the truth and reasonableness of its doctrines, and the peaceableness and inoffensiveness of its professors, may, by good usage and persuasion, and all those convincing methods of gentleness and meekness, suitable to the rules and design of the gospel, be won ever to embrace and unfeignedly receive the truth . . . .

Memorial Stone at Christ Church, Oxford

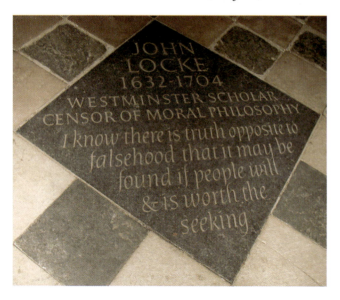

John Locke was born in his grandmother's cottage next to the cemetery of All Saints' Church in Wrington. The entrance has stone busts of John Locke and Hannah More (1745-1833), an author, educator, and philanthropist who spent half of her life in Wrington.

Locke composed more than one open letter regarding toleration, arguing that the civil magistrate did not have authority over men's souls. He said that believers should be more concerned about rooting out sin in their lives than about rooting out unorthodox members. He also wondered at the arrogance of those who thought they could explain, through mandatory creeds and confessions, the things necessary to salvation more clearly than the Holy Spirit did through Christ and the Apostles.

Conclusion

Thomas Jefferson, serving as U.S. minister to France in 1789, wrote a letter to American artist John Trumbull on the eve of the French Revolution. Jefferson described a painting he wanted to have made featuring Francis Bacon, John Locke, and Isaac Newton, because "as I consider them as the three greatest men that have ever lived, without any exception, and as having laid the foundation of those superstructures which have been raised in the Physical & Moral sciences, I would wish to form them into a knot on the same canvas, that they may not be confounded at all with the herd of other great men."

Lesson 98 - Key Person: John Locke

*For rulers are not a cause of fear for good behavior,
but for evil. Do you want to have no fear of authority?
Do what is good and you will have praise from the same;
for it is a minister of God to you for good.
But if you do what is evil, be afraid;
for it does not bear the sword for nothing;
for it is a minister of God, an avenger who brings wrath
on the one who practices evil.
Romans 13:3-4*

Assignments for Lesson 98

Bible Read Galatians 4-5.

In Their Words Read the excerpt from *Two Treatises of Government* (page 234).

Literature Continue reading *A Tale of Two Cities*.

Student Review Optional: Answer the questions for Lesson 98.

Tea Plantation in the Cameron Highlands of Malaysia

Lesson 99 - Everyday Life

Eating Through the Centuries

Since the French are known for their cuisine, this is a good time to explore some of the history of food. We begin with the most important meal ever eaten on earth.

The Lord's Supper

On the night before Jesus died, He shared a meal with His disciples. In a borrowed guest room, He washed their feet and told them to remember Him in the bread and the fruit of the vine. He had already told them that He is the bread of life. He had said that those who come to Him will not hunger or thirst (John 6:35). And He had taught them that He is the vine and we are the branches (John 15:5).

In this meal He said that the bread was His flesh and the fruit of the vine was His blood (Matthew 26:26-29). After Jesus died, rose again, and ascended into heaven, His disciples continued to remember Him in the Lord's Supper.

Food in the Beginning

The first time food is mentioned in the Bible is in the first chapter of Genesis. God told the first people that He had given them every plant yielding seed and every tree which has fruit yielding seed for food (1:29). He planted a garden and caused to grow every tree that was good for food. God put Adam in the garden to cultivate it. He told him to eat freely from any tree of the garden, except the tree of the knowledge of good and evil (2:8-17). Then God created Eve. The first sin on earth involved food (chapter 3). After the fall, the ground was cursed because of Adam. God told him that in toil he would eat of the ground all the days of his life and that he would eat the plants of the field. By the sweat of his face, he would eat bread (3:17-19). After the flood, God added meat to people's diet (9:1-4).

Bible Meals

Abraham served his visitors bread cakes, curds, milk, and calf meat. He stood by them as they ate under a tree (Genesis 18:6-8). The Passover meal included lamb roasted over a fire, unleavened bread, and bitter herbs (Exodus 12:8). After His resurrection Jesus prepared a meal for His disciples. He invited them to come and have breakfast. He gave them bread and fish (John 21:10-15).

Lesson 99 - Everyday Life: Eating Through the Centuries

Foods Mentioned in the Bible					
Nuts	**Fruits**	**Grains & Beans**	**Seasonings**	**Vegetables**	**Animal Products**
almonds pistachios	apples figs grapes mandrakes melons olives pomegranates	barley millet spelt wheat hyssop lentils beans	caperberries cassia cinnamon coriander cumin dill mint mustard rue saffron	bitter herbs cucumber garlic leeks onion	butter cattle cheese curds eggs fish game goat lamb milk quail

Reclining on Couches

In Exodus 32:6 the Israelites sat down to eat and drink, but in other passages diners reclined (see Amos 6:4-7). When Jesus ate with a Pharisee in Luke 7:36-39, he reclined. Jesus and His disciples reclined around the table at the Last Supper (John 13:12-20).

At formal dinners Romans lay on couches to eat. The Latin word for dining room was *triclinium*, which referred to three dining couches arranged in a U-shape. Each couch was large enough for two or more persons. Diners reclined on the couches, leaning on one elbow and reaching for food from a table in the center of the room. Many couches were made of bronze. Headboards and footboards were decorated with ivory and precious metals. They had thick mattresses covered with bright cloth and pillows. When a Roman family ate alone, they often enjoyed their meal in their enclosed courtyard. The father reclined on a couch, while the mother sat in a chair beside him. They ate from one table. The children sat on stools at their own table.

Eating on Benches

In the Middle Ages, monks sat on hard wooden benches while they ate. In the homes of the wealthy, benches were sometimes part of the wall paneling. At dinnertime, tables were put in front of the benches and people ate on only one side of the table.

Peasant Meals

A peasant would have eaten mainly bread. Drinks included goat's milk, ale, and light wine. What you ate depended on where you lived. If you lived in southern Europe, you might have had

This Roman triclinium dates from the first century. A modern wooden frame has been built into the original bronze fittings. Straps around the wood would have supported a mattress covered with textiles.

Unit 20 - The Age of Revolution

Steamed buns originated in China and spread to other countries in Southeast Asia. Sometimes filled with meat, the buns are known as salapao *in Thailand, where this street vendor has a variety for sale.*

olives, fruits, and berries. People in northern Europe ate more meat. Meat was pickled in salt to keep it from spoiling. It was served with cloves, cinnamon, nutmeg, allspice, ginger, and pepper. Fish was preserved by drying it and salting it. On Columbus' voyages he took dried beans, salt pork, sardines, raisins, olive oil, wheat flour, biscuits, cheeses, wine, vinegar, and garlic.

Bread

Bread is one of the most important foods in the world. It is highly nutritious when made from whole grains. Bread is so important that Jesus called Himself the bread of life.

The first flour was ground on grindstones. Greeks invented a water-powered mill for making flour around 85 BC. By 650 AD Persians were using windmills to grind grain. In the 1100s Europeans also began using windmills to grind grain.

Farming Improvements

Since ancient times farmers have used a yoke to make it easier for oxen to pull plows. By the 600s Germans were using the moldboard plow which could turn the heavy clay soil of northern Europe. With it a pair of oxen could plow a strip a "furlong" length after which they rested. The amount of land a pair of oxen could plow in a day using a moldboard plow was an "acre." Patrick Bell of Scotland invented the first successful mechanical reaper. The American Cyrus Hall McCormick patented his reaper in 1831.

A Short Timeline of Food-Related Inventions

1802	Austria	Zachaus Andreas Winzler made gas fuel in his home, piped it to his kitchen, and used it for cooking. He gave a series of dinner parties in 1802 in an unsuccessful attempt to make gas stoves popular. They were not common until the late 1800s.
1811	France	Nicolas Appert won a contest sponsored by the French government offering a cash prize for finding a way to supply high-quality food to the military. Appert heated food in glass jars and sealed the tops with cork (see example at right). Later he replaced the glass with tin cans. At first the cans had to be opened with a hammer and chisel.
1828	Netherlands	Casparus van Houten was a Dutch chocolate maker who patented a process for pressing fat from roasted cacao beans. This led to the creation of cocoa powder, which is used to make chocolate bars and candies.

Lesson 99 - Everyday Life: Eating Through the Centuries

1855	England	In the 1850s, many inventors made tools for opening cans, but Robert Yeates patented his claw-shaped opener with a bull's head in 1855.
1860	U.S.A.	L. O. Colvin, an American engineer, patented a milking machine using vacuum suction that became popular in England and in the United States. 
1862	France	Louis Pasteur invented a method for heating milk to kill bacteria. It kept milk from spoiling as rapidly and stopped it from carrying tuberculosis and brucellosis. The *Portrait of Louis Pasteur* at right is by Albert Edelfelt (Finnish, 1885).
1871	France	Chemist H. Mege-Mouries developed imitation butter, which is now called margarine. The first recipe was beef suet, milk, water, and chopped cow's udder. It tasted awful.
1872	U.S.A.	Native Americans chewed chicle, a natural gum. American Thomas Adams added licorice flavor to chicle and created the first commercial chewing gum. He named it Black Jack.
1879	U.S.A.	Inventor Margaret Knight pioneered machine manufacture of paper sacks with square bottoms like the ones used for groceries today.
1882	New Zealand	The first large-scale shipment of refrigerated meat was successfully transported to England on the ship *Dunedin*. The journey took three months, and the ship used three tons of coal a day to keep the hold of the ship cool.
1886	U.S.A.	John Pemberton, an American pharmacist, invented Coca-Cola. It was called "the esteemed brain tonic and intellectual beverage."
1891	U.S.A.	The first home electric stove was sold by the Carpenter Electric Company of St. Paul, Minnesota. The electric stove had been used in a few restaurant kitchens as early as 1889.
1930	U.S.A.	The McGraw Electric Company introduced the pop-up electric toaster.
1946	U.S.A.	Percy LeBaron Spencer, an American, discovered the cooking powers of microwaves when a chocolate bar melted in his pocket while he stood in front of a magnetron. A magnetron is the electronic tube at the heart of a radar transmitter. The first patents for microwave ovens were awarded in 1946. One early model (shown at right) was six feet tall and weighed 750 pounds. It was installed on the NS *Savannah*, one of only four nuclear-powered cargo-passenger ships built. 

Containers for Eating, Cooking, and Storing Food

When Elijah asked the woman of Zarephath for water and bread, she mentioned the flour in her bowl and the oil in her jar (1 Kings 17:8-15). Likely these were pottery vessels made of clay. At the wedding in Cana where Jesus and His mother were guests, there were six stone waterpots that held twenty or thirty gallons each. The servants filled them with water and Jesus miraculously turned the water into wine (John 2:1-10). After Jesus fed fish and barley loaves to the 5,000, the leftover fragments were gathered into baskets (John 6:12-13).

Glassworkers in Egypt, Greece, and Phoenicia began making glass containers around 1500 BC. They filled a bag with sand and then dipped the bag into molten glass.

Knives, Spoons, and Forks

Knives have had many utilitarian uses since ancient times. Ancient Greeks used spoons, but only for eating eggs. The first forks were used for carving meat. Arab nobility were using table forks by the seventh century AD. The wealthy of Byzantium used table forks by the tenth century. A Byzantine princess married an Italian nobleman and brought forks to Italy in the eleventh century. Gradually they spread to the upper classes of France and England. There was resistance to their use. Some even protested that since God gave people hands, why did they need forks? Forks are listed in a few wills and household inventories of the Middle Ages. They were made of precious metals and might have even been considered investments.

In 1743 Thomas Boulsover, a cutlery-maker in Sheffield, England, fused silver to ingots of copper and then rolled them into sheets, making silver plate. The silver plate was then used to make cutlery. This reduced the price of cutlery and made it available for more people. In 1913 Sheffield native Harry Brearly invented stainless steel, which further reduced the price of tableware.

For the Sweet Tooth

God promised the Israelites a land flowing with milk and honey (Exodus 3:8). Samson found honey in a lion's carcass; he ate some and shared it with his parents (Judges 14:8-9). Sweet cane is mentioned in Isaiah 43:24 and Jeremiah 6:20. There is evidence that sugar refining has been practiced in India since about 1000 BC. In 325 BC Alexander the Great invaded India. His men were impressed with the syrup Indians could make.

May I Get You Something to Drink?

Three common modern drinks are hot chocolate, coffee, and tea. The first to reach Europe was hot chocolate. In 1519 Cortez brought cacao beans from Mexico to Spain, where they were used to make a popular beverage.

Chopsticks have been in widespread use in Asia for hundreds of years. Chinese chopsticks are about 10 inches long. Japanese chopsticks (shown below) are shorter and have tapered ends. Chopsticks are also used in Korea and Vietnam. They are commonly made of bamboo, porcelain, metal, or plastic.

Lesson 99 - Everyday Life: Eating Through the Centuries

Fast Food Restaurants in the United Arab Emirates

People in Ethiopia and Yemen were drinking coffee during the Middle Ages. One story says that a sober goatherd named Kaldi had goats with the same mild disposition. One day his normally calm goats ate some red berries and started dancing. Kaldi ate some and started dancing, too. A passing monk saw them and spread the word about coffee. Coffee drinking spread in the Arabian world, perhaps first from monastery to monastery and then into the Muslim culture. Venetian merchants brought it to Europe in 1615, and coffeehouses quickly spread to many European cities.

The tea plant grows wild in China and India. Tea trees can grow to be 100 feet high. Monkeys have been trained to throw the leaves down. In cultivation, growers keep them trimmed to about three feet high. Tea is mainly associated with Asia and Great Britain. It has been known in China and Japan since ancient times, but it was unknown in England until the 1600s. The first tea was brought to England by sailors working for the East India Company. They brought tea packets home as gifts. The first recorded commercial sale was at a London coffeehouse in 1657. At first China controlled the growing tea market, but in 1822 a tea bush was found growing wild in northern India.

False Teeth

All this information about food is interesting, but what if you have no teeth? Around 700 BC people in Etruia, Italy, were using false teeth. They were animal teeth attached with straps of gold. Around 1770 French pharmacist Alexis Duchateau had problems with his teeth. He and his partner Nicholas Dubois de Chemant perfected false teeth. Springs held the porcelain teeth in place. Twelve thousand sets were made.

Coffee Farmer in Brazil

*But He answered and said, "It is written,
'Man shall not live on bread alone, but on every word
that proceeds out of the mouth of God.'"*
Matthew 4:4

Assignments for Lesson 99

Bible   Read Galatians 6.

Literature   Continue reading *A Tale of Two Cities*.

Student Review   Optional: Answer the questions for Lesson 99.

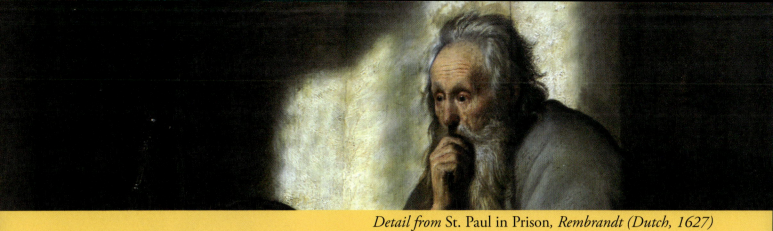

Detail from St. Paul in Prison, *Rembrandt (Dutch, 1627)*

Lesson 100 - Bible Study

Freedom and Responsibility

Freedom is a cherished gift in the hearts of men and women. We value our political and religious freedoms in America, and people around the world look to the United States as a beacon of hope when freedom is threatened or non-existent. However, the most important freedom a person can have is freedom from sin that is found in Christ. This freedom is one that someone can have even if he is not politically free. A Christian in jail in China is more free than a politically-free American who does not know Christ.

Freedom carries with it responsibility. A child sometimes wishes that he was an adult so that he could "do whatever he wants to." However, any responsible adult will tell you that the freedom that comes with adulthood carries many responsibilities, such as obeying the law and carrying out family duties. Also, political freedom must be respected and protected by responsible citizenship. The same is true with freedom in Christ. It carries responsibilities that the believer must take, or he will abuse and potentially lose his spiritual freedom.

The spiritual freedom enjoyed by Christians in Galatia was threatened by false teachers who wanted to return them to spiritual bondage. Paul wrote to the churches in Galatia to remind them of how they had gotten where they were spiritually and to encourage them (1) not to submit to a yoke of slavery again and (2) not to abuse their freedom in Christ by living by the flesh. Open your Bible to Galatians so you can refer to the book as you read the following discussion.

Who Discipled Paul?

Galatians 1:1-10—Paul was amazed that the Galatian Christians were so quickly deserting the gospel for another doctrine, a different gospel that was not true. They had answered to God with their lives on the basis of faith in Christ, but now they were answering to mere men and following men's rules.

1:11-2:10—The apostle then described his own walk with the Lord. The outstanding fact he wanted to emphasize was that he did not learn the gospel from men, nor did he answer to men about his ministry. He learned the message through a revelation of Jesus Christ (1:11-12). God revealed His Son to Paul, and then Paul went away for a time to Arabia. He did not go to Jerusalem until three years later, and those who heard about his conversion praised God for him (1:13-24). Then, fifteen years later, he went to Jerusalem again, not to seek approval from the apostles but "because of a revelation" (perhaps the prophecy of Agabus about a famine which led to Paul taking a contribution from Antioch to Jerusalem; see Acts 11:27-30). The leading figures in the church in Jerusalem welcomed Paul and gave him their approval (Galatians 2:1-10).

2:11-21—Paul was so unconcerned about what other people thought of him that he even opposed Peter to his face when Peter did not act right regarding Gentile believers in Antioch. He reminded Peter that a man is justified by faith in Christ, not by any works that one might perform. Paul died to the law-keeping approach to religion so that he might live according to God (2:11-19).

Paul was co-crucified with Christ, which meant that he (as an independent, self-willed person) no longer lived. Instead, Christ lived in him; and Paul lived for the One who gave Himself for Paul. Paul did not want to return to living by rules because if he did, Christ would have died needlessly (2:20-21). Thus Paul did not answer to any other human about his spiritual life. He was free from having to do that because he knew that he answered to God for his salvation and his life in Christ.

The Way Is By Faith

3:1-25—The apostle was concerned that the Galatians were returning to the way of fleshly accomplishment after beginning their walk with Christ by the Spirit. The way to God was by faith, which had been clear from the time of Abraham. The Law, which was an important part of God's working with mankind, was not able to impart righteousness. The Law was a child-conductor to lead us to Christ, where salvation is available by faith. Now that we have arrived at justification by faith in Christ, we no longer need a child-conductor to get us there.

3:26-4:31—Paul knew that his readers were children of God on the basis of their faith because

In The Pilgrim's Progress *by John Bunyan, the main character is described as having a burden of sin on his back. The burden only falls away when he reaches the cross. This illustration is by William Blake (c. 1824).*

they had been baptized into Christ and thus had put on their Jesus-clothes. In Christ, they were now Abraham's seed and heirs of God's promise of justification (3:26-29). As sons of God, born again in the fullness of Christ, they no longer had to live like slaves. Why would they want to submit to slavery again by following rules taught by men? False teachers were trying to manipulate them and make them feel spiritually dependent on man-made rules to be right with God (4:1-20), but even the Law says that Abraham's child of promise and his descendants are free (4:21-31).

Christ Set Us Free

5:1-26—Christ set us free spiritually to enjoy the freedom we have in Him. Christians do not have to answer to others. However, we must not use that freedom irresponsibly. We must not serve the flesh, but instead we must love one another (5:1-15). The way to do this is through walking by the Spirit, not the flesh. The deeds of the flesh are a distinctive kind of behavior. The deeds of the flesh that Paul describes are selfish, self-indulgent, and divisive. They do not belong in the kingdom of God (5:16-21). The evidence or fruit of the Spirit's presence in a person's life is an entirely different kind of behavior. It is loving, self-denying, and respectful of others. Those who belong to Christ have crucified the flesh and seek to live by the Spirit (5:22-26).

This is what freedom in Christ means. It means we are free from bondage to sin. We are free from the penalty of sin. We are free from being driven by the lusts of the flesh to chase after whatever we think will give us immediate pleasure. We are free from hurting people in the name of self-interest. We are free from worrying about what other people think of us and from answering to the most persuasive voices we hear. We are free from living by the flesh, which is what got us into spiritual trouble in the first place.

6:1-18—Freedom in Christ means that we can gently help a brother entangled in sin. We can bear each other's burdens, share with others, and devote ourselves to doing good (6:1-10). The false teachers who were trying to rob the Galatians of their freedom merely wanted to look impressive by having a large following. By contrast, all that Christians should boast about is the cross of Christ that sets us free and makes us a new creation (6:11-18). "The world has been crucified to me," Paul says, "and I to the world." In other words, a Christian has been freed by the cross from the world being his master; but now free of the world's demands, he is bound by the cross to lay himself down in service to the world (6:14).

A Christian's Rights

Do Christians have rights? Absolutely! We have the right to approach the throne of grace with confidence (Hebrews 4:16). We have the right to consider ourselves sons of God and to call God Abba (the Aramaic word for Daddy, suggesting an intimate relationship; Galatians 4:6-7). God gives us rights as His children that we need to use.

Paul talked about rights that he had as an apostle in 1 Corinthians 9:1-14. The important thing about those rights, however, was that he gave them up for the good of others (1 Corinthians 9:15-23). A Christian must not insist on his rights because that causes division and pride. Paul sometimes used his rights as a Roman citizen to avoid a beating and to have his case heard by Caesar; but he used those rights to further the gospel.

A Christian answers to God and not to men, but we must respect and obey those with earthly authority over us unless doing so causes us to disobey God. Ignoring rules and civic laws because we answer to Christ makes us appear to be a nuisance and makes the way of Christ unattractive. Christian slaves were free in Christ, but they needed to obey their earthly masters to make the gospel attractive to their masters and to others (Titus 2:9-10). Christianity needs to be seen as making people better, not making them troublemakers.

Opening of Paul's Epistle to the Galatians from an Illuminated Manuscript

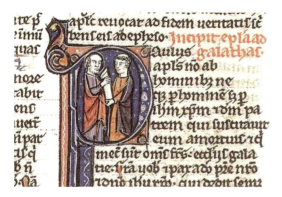

Christians are free in Christ. This is a freedom that no king, no Congress, no judge, no jailer, and no executioner can take away from us. We need to glory in that and live as people free from the bondage of sin and the bondage that people impose on each other. As servants of Christ, we get to give up our rights to bless others. We can be peacemakers rather than dividers.

For you were called to freedom, brethren;
only do not turn your freedom into an opportunity for the flesh,
but through love serve one another.
Galatians 5:13

Assignments for Lesson 100

Bible — Recite or write Galatians 5:13-14 from memory.

In Their Words — Read the excerpt from "Serbia for Cross and Freedom" and "God Moves in a Mysterious Way" (pages 235-237).

Literature — Finish reading *A Tale of Two Cities*. Literary analysis available in *Student Review*.

Project — Complete your project for this unit.

Student Review — Optional: Answer the questions for Lesson 100 and for *A Tale of Two Cities*; take the quiz for Unit 20; and take the fourth history, English, and Bible exams.

21

The Making of Modern Europe

Summary The nineteenth century in Europe began in upheaval as the French Revolution gave way to the Napoleonic Era. The century ended with a new superpower in Europe—Germany—and with a mad scramble among European nations for overseas colonies and political alliances. During the 1800s, Europe witnessed continuing political turmoil and the process of unification in Italy and Germany. This unit also provides a brief history of art, and the Bible study deals with honesty.

Lessons
101 - Key Person: Napoleon
102 - Revolution, Reaction, and Reorganization
103 - Key Event: Unification in Italy and Germany
104 - Everyday Life: A Short History of Western Art
105 - Bible Study: Honesty

Cavalry Skirmish in the Village
Alexander Bogdanovich Villevalde (Russian, 1881)

Memory Work

Learn Matthew 16:24-27 by the end of the unit.

Books Used

The Bible
In Their Words
North and South

Project (choose one)

1) Write 300 to 500 words on one of the following topics:
   - Write a speech in which you try to persuade your listeners either to participate in an 1848 revolution or to oppose a revolution that took place in that year. See Lesson 102.
   - What are the best ways to enact reform in government?
2) Copy a painting by an artist mentioned in Lesson 104 in the medium of your choice (paint, colored pencil, pencil, ink, pastels, etc.).
3) Make a poster showing at least eight flags of modern European nations. Next to each flag, give information about when it was adopted and the meaning of the colors and/or symbols.

Literature

North and South is a novel set against the backdrop of the Industrial Revolution in England in the mid-1800s. Richard Hale, an Anglican clergyman in the quiet village of Helstone in southern England, develops doubts about Anglican doctrines and resigns his position. He becomes a tutor in the industrial city of Milton in the north of England. The main characters are Margaret Hale, who is Richard's daughter, and John Thornton, a factory owner. Members of the Hale and Thornton families as well as other people connected to them are also important characters.

The main theme of the novel is prejudice. People of the rural south of England are prejudiced against the people of the industrial north, and vice versa. Margaret is prejudiced against Mr. Thornton, and Thornton's mother is prejudiced against everyone who does not admire her son. Factory owners and factory workers are prejudiced against each other. Through the events of the story, these prejudices are broken down; and people learn to accept and respect each other.

The book does an excellent job of describing the social and economic issues of industrialization. With the material progress and employment opportunities that industry offered, the trade-offs included exploitation (or perceived exploitation) of workers, environmental problems, and a dependence on other nations for supplies and markets. These are not just theoretical economic concepts; the issues affect real human beings, sometimes at the level of life or death.

Elizabeth Gaskell (1810-1865) was a popular and highly praised author in her day. This work is her fourth novel, which was serialized in 1854-1855 in *Household Words*, edited by Charles Dickens. Two other works by Gaskell are *Cranford* and *Wives and Daughters*, which was unfinished at the time of her death. Gaskell was the daughter of a minister in London. She married a minister, and they settled in the industrial city of Manchester in northern England.

Battle of the Pyramids, *Louis-François Lejeune (French, 1808)*

Lesson 101 - Key Person

Napoleon

On August 15, 1769, Napoleone Buonaparte (his name became Napoleon Bonaparte in French) was born in Ajaccio on the island of Corsica. His parents Carlo and Letizia had eight children, of whom Napoleon was the second.

Corsica had been under the control of Genoa in Italy for most of the time since 1312. The Corsicans established a republican government in the mid-1700s, and Genoa sold the island to France in 1768. The Corsicans fought for independence, but the French defeated them. Napoleon's father Carlo had sided with the Corsicans, but when the French took control, he became a prosecutor, a judge, and a count in the French aristocracy. Thus Napoleon was born a French citizen.

Carlo used his influence to secure training for Napoleon in France. He studied at the École Militaire in Paris. When he graduated at age sixteen he became a second lieutenant in the artillery. Napoleon was about 5' 6" tall and was later called The Little Corporal, but his ability to make quick decisions as a leader of men allowed him to rise in the ranks.

The French Revolution began in 1789 as citizens protested the power of the king and abuses of the existing government. In 1791 Napoleon became a lieutenant colonel in the Corsican National Guard. The people of Corsica proclaimed independence from France in 1793. Because of his ties to France, Napoleon left the island and returned to France.

Rising Prestige

The city of Toulon in southern France had revolted against the new French government. British ships assisted the revolt. Napoleon joined the French army besieging the city. When an artillery general was wounded, Napoleon took command and led his guns into position to fire on the British fleet. By driving away the British, he contributed to the fall of the city to French troops. In 1795 he broke up a royalist mob in Paris by firing over the crowd and giving them, as he put it, a "whiff of grapeshot." Napoleon received a promotion to brigadier general when he was twenty-four.

Napoleon became commander of the French army in Italy in 1796. He enhanced his reputation as an astute leader by defeating the Austrians in several battles. He created the Cisalpine Republic in northern Italy and was able to supply France with large amounts of treasure from the region.

In 1798 he led a force against Egypt, which the Ottoman Empire ruled at the time, and proceeded to conquer the country. However, the British navy

579

under Horatio Nelson destroyed the French ships; so Napoleon and his soldiers were stranded in Egypt. Napoleon changed the Egyptian government according to principles of the French Revolution. He ended serfdom and feudalism and promoted civil rights for the citizens. In 1799 he won another battle against the Ottomans, but he did not capture his goal of Syria.

The Emperor

Napoleon left his army in the Middle East and returned to France as a hero. He became part of a *coup d'etat* against the revolutionary government. He and his companions took control in November 1799. Napoleon became first consul of the Consulate and received immense authority. He claimed to be acting only to maintain order and to defeat the enemies of France.

Napoleon had a desire to rule effectively and powerfully. In a sense, he wanted to recreate the glory days of the Roman Empire, ruling France and as much of the rest of Europe as he could. In 1802 Napoleon was declared First Consul for life, a move overwhelmingly endorsed by a popular vote. Two years later, the pope traveled from Rome to crown Napoleon Emperor of the French in the Cathedral of Notre Dame. As the pope approached Napoleon with the crown, Napoleon took the crown and placed it on his own head. Napoleon did not want to answer to anyone.

As emperor Napoleon kept in place many of the republican reforms of the previous years, but he maintained firm control of the government. New reforms instituted by Napoleon created a more efficient government and equalized the tax burden on all Frenchmen. The Cult of Reason, which the radical revolutionaries had put in place instead

Coronation of Emperor Napoleon I and Coronation of the Empress Josephine in the Notre-Dame de Paris
Jacques-Louis David and Georges Rouget (French, 1807)

Lesson 101 - Key Person: Napoleon

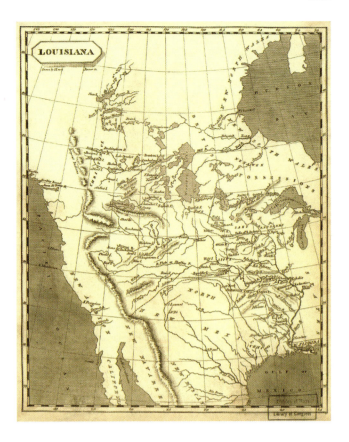

Napoleon agreed to cede the Louisiana Territory in North America to the United States of America in 1803. The United States doubled its territory for $15 million. This 1804 map shows the Gulf of Mexico in the lower right, the Pacific Ocean on the left, and the Rocky Mountains snaking from north to south.

of the Catholic Church, was itself replaced; but the Church was clearly subservient to Napoleon's rule. Under the Concordat of 1801, the French government appointed Catholic bishops but the pope had authority over them. Napoleon was an unbeliever, but he knew the value of having the Catholic Church on his side. The Church agreed not to demand back property that had been seized during the revolutionary period.

All adult males could vote, but they only elected candidates. Napoleon chose those who actually served. The day of the bureaucrat had arrived, which ushered in the model of modern administrative government. Public offices went not to those who were well-connected but to those who were well-qualified. Napoleon created the Bank of France (in a move influenced by the new Bank of the United States) to issue money and stabilize the French economy. A system of *lycees* (similar to a modern high school plus community college) offered public education. Napoleon was supported by members of all social classes but received the strongest backing from the bourgeoisie.

During this period of reorganization, Napoleon continued his military exploits. He defeated the Austrians again and moved the eastern border of France to the Rhine River. Napoleon's government also streamlined the judicial system and reworked French laws into a new code that was named the Code Napoléon in 1807. This system spread to the regions that Napoleon conquered. Except in Spain, freedom of religion was allowed. Constitutions were drawn up in each country that included universal male suffrage, parliamentary systems, and bills of rights.

Britain, Russia, and Austria joined forces to prevent Napoleon from expanding his empire. Napoleon considered an invasion of England, but he chose to focus his efforts on the continent. For several years, he led his forces to victory, capturing kingdoms and setting up his brothers and brother-in-law as their rulers.

Spain joined France in a war against Portugal in 1807, and Napoleon put his brother Joseph on the throne of Spain in 1808. This marked the beginning of a long war on the Iberian Peninsula. Great Britain and Portugal supported Spanish insurgents against the French. Napoleon spent some time in Spain and obtained victories leading troops himself; but after paying a great cost in lives and treasure, the French withdrew from Spain in 1813.

Fall From Power

Napoleon married Joséphine de Beauharnais, a widow with two children, in 1796. Her husband had been guillotined by the revolutionaries. Both Napoleon and Joséphine were unfaithful to each

Portrait of Joséphine de Beauharnais
Andrea Appiani (Italian, c. 1808)

other, and they did not have a happy marriage. When it became clear that Joséphine could not bear Napoleon an heir, she agreed in 1809 to a public divorce ceremony in which they declared their affection for each other.

Napoleon married Marie Louise in 1810. She was the daughter of the Austrian emperor, a member of the Hapsburg dynasty. She bore him a son the next year, and Napoleon hoped this child would one day be able to take his place among the kings of Europe.

Napoleon began an invasion of Russia in 1812 after cordial relations with Alexander I of Russia had broken down. He marched his army of some 400,000 soldiers plus support personnel to Moscow, but he was unable to secure a decisive victory against the determined Russians. The Russian winter aided Russian arms as Napoleon began a long retreat. By the end, the French army was reduced to a small fraction of its original strength.

In 1814 Europe was arrayed against Napoleon, and his commanders refused to continue the struggle. Napoleon abdicated his throne and went into exile on the island of Elba. The next year, unwilling to resign himself to inactivity, he escaped and returned to France. He created a new constitution and rebuilt his army.

Opposing nations were unwilling to make peace with him, however; and he marched into Belgium to face combined British, Dutch, and Prussian forces. Napoleon was defeated in the Battle of Waterloo by the allied army under Arthur Wellesley, Duke of Wellington. It was a bloody battle with some 60,000 total casualties.

Though some in France still supported him after that battle, he lost the support of the government. He surrendered to the British, and they exiled him to the island of St. Helena, far off the coast of Africa in the southern Atlantic. He lived there nearly six years before his death on May 5, 1821.

This daguerreotype of Maria Louise was taken in 1847, the year she died.

Lesson 101 - Key Person: Napoleon

His Legacy

King Louis-Philippe of France requested the return of Napoleon's remains in 1840. They were buried in Paris and a great tomb was constructed. Napoleon's son, recognized as Napoleon II by his followers, died at age twenty-one in Austria.

Napoleon Bonaparte claimed high ideals in his pursuit of honor and glory. He said that the happiness of France was his aim, and he looked beyond France to the establishment of a federation of free people in Europe. His efforts helped to spark other national revolutions in the 1800s, and his governmental reforms have had a lasting effect on European politics. However, Napoleon's thirst for power led to much suffering on the continent and ultimately led to his own downfall.

Napoleon commissioned the Arc de Triomphe in 1806 to commemorate his military victories. It was completed in 1835 after his death. This photo was taken just before French World War I pilot Charles Godefroy flew a plane through the arch in 1919.

For what will it profit a man if he gains the whole world and forfeits his soul? Or what will a man give in exchange for his soul?
Matthew 16:26

Assignments for Lesson 101

In Their Words — Read the excerpt from *Talks of Napoleon at St. Helena* (pages 238-239).

Literature — Begin reading *North and South*. Plan to finish it by the end of Unit 22.

Student Review — Optional: Answer the questions for Lesson 101.

Detail from The Black Stain, *Albert Bettannier (French, 1887)*

Lesson 102

Revolution, Reaction, and Reorganization

For twenty-five years, Europe watched in wonder and fear as France was shaken by revolution and then was ruled by the autocratic hand of Napoleon. The kings of other countries worried that revolution would come to their lands. Then when Napoleon led his armies across the continent, those kings mobilized their forces to confront him.

The Congress of Vienna

After Napoleon abdicated in 1814, the chief minister of Austria, Clemens von Metternich, called a meeting of the leaders of Europe in Vienna to rebuild the continent according to their royalist vision. In this Congress of Vienna, nine kings, dozens of princes, and hundreds of diplomats converged on the Austrian capital and spent ten months deliberating, bargaining, and deciding. They were interrupted for a time when Napoleon made his comeback attempt in 1815, but his defeat at Waterloo enabled the leaders to return to their discussions with that threat removed.

Along with Metternich, the key players at Vienna were the Russian czar, the king of Prussia, and the prime minister of Great Britain—in other words, the leaders of the countries that had most to do with defeating Napoleon. Also present and playing an important role was Maurice de Tallyrand, the representative of France. Tallyrand had been Napoleon's foreign minister; but as Napoleon's end neared, Tallyrand secretly gave assistance to foreign enemies of the emperor in the hope of receiving a place in the post-Napoleon government. The cunning Tallyrand promoted restoration of the Bourbon monarchy; this won favor in Vienna and enabled France to keep its overseas territories. The workings of Metternich and Tallyrand meant that (1) even though Napoleon had defeated Austria several times, Austria played a prominent role in post-Napoleonic Europe and (2) France was spared harsh treatment in the decisions reached in Vienna.

Two influential principles that guided the deliberations at Vienna were legitimacy (meaning the right of kings to rule their lands) and balance of power (the desire to keep one country in Europe from being able to dominate others). The Congress, and thus the participating nations, recognized the oldest surviving brother of the slain Louis XVI as the legitimate king of France. He assumed the title of Louis XVIII (the son of Louis XVI had died in 1795 and was considered by royalists to be Louis XVII). The royal families of Spain, Portugal, and Sardinia

Lesson 102 - Revolution, Reaction, and Reorganization

(an island nation off of Italy) were restored to their thrones after periods of unrest in those nations. The Dutch and Austrian Netherlands were united under the Dutch king. Thirty-nine German states were joined together as the German Confederation, which was led by Austria. Switzerland was recognized as an independent country. Great Britain was given the right to control several overseas colonies, which helped to build the growing British Empire. Many deals that were made involved assigning disputed territories in Europe to the control of various countries.

Another result of the Congress of Vienna was the formation of alliances among powerful nations that were designed to stop problems before they escalated into full-fledged war. The leaders of these nations agreed to hold meetings when conflicts arose instead of resorting immediately to arms. These alliances led to a period known as the Concert of Europe.

The delegates to the Congress of Vienna were strong monarchists and defenders of the status quo. They largely ignored other philosophies that were gaining ground in Europe, most notably the desire for republican reforms and the increasing interest in nationalism, which was the desire of national ethnic groups to rule themselves. As a result, the Vienna meeting put the lid back on the cauldron of Europe, but the mixture of ingredients inside the cauldron continued to heat up.

Riots in Brussels in 1830 led to the formation of the new country of Belgium out of the Netherlands. The majority of those who lived in this area spoke French and were Roman Catholic, which made them different from the Dutch Protestants who ruled them. This change was successful in large measure because it was supported by the middle class of Belgium. The Triumphal Arch in Cinquantenaire Park in Brussels was intended to be part of the fiftieth anniversary celebration of Belgium's independence in 1880. It was finally completed in time for the 75th anniversary in 1905.

Revolutions Erupt Again

The seeds planted by the French Revolution and the ideals of reform and republican government that it represented bore fruit in other parts of Europe. In the German Confederation, students at several universities called for the unification of the German states. Metternich reacted in 1819 by announcing the Carlsbad Decrees, which limited free speech and freedom of the press. Attempts at revolutions in Spain and Naples in the 1820s led to an Austrian army being dispatched to Naples and a French force to Spain to quell the disturbances and strengthen the rule of the monarchs in those countries. However, Spain's empire in the New World was severely weakened in the 1820s when several South and Latin American countries followed the lead of the United States and declared their independence from Spain. Greece successfully gained its independence from the Ottoman Empire in 1829.

In France the new government under Louis XVIII displeased monarchists, who wanted the king to have more power, as well as republicans, who were unhappy that only a relatively small number of wealthy individuals could vote. Louis' successor, his brother Charles X, wanted to compensate French nobles for lands they lost during the French Revolution. When the National Assembly refused to go along, Charles dismissed the body and called for new elections. Surprisingly, the reformers (also called the liberals) won a majority of seats in the Assembly. Charles responded with the July Ordinances of 1830, which dissolved the National

The Ottoman dynasty had existed since 1453 and reached the height of its power in the mid-1500s. In the 19th century, the Ottomans still oversaw a large area from the Middle East to the Balkans, but their control was weakening. This illustration of Istanbul is from about 1900.

Unit 21 - The Making of Modern Europe

The Revolutions of 1848

The year 1848 saw unrest in a number of European countries. The results were mixed, but they demonstrated that the spirit of reform and popular rule was very much alive throughout the continent.

In February of 1848, the French prime minister canceled a large public banquet because he feared an outbreak of violence. What happened as a result of the cancellation was an outbreak of violence. Continued unrest caused Louis Philippe to abdicate and flee to England. Socialist reformers proclaimed the Second Republic, which was led by outspoken reformer Louis Blanc. Blanc created national workshops to give jobs to poor workers. However, those needing work outnumbered the jobs available, so some people simply received relief payments. Blanc financed this program through a property tax. This angered the urban middle class as well as peasants in the countryside who owned land. In the election to form the National Assembly, middle class moderates (not socialists) won a majority of seats.

The Assembly abolished the workshops, which prompted the workers to revolt. In the conflicts between workers and soldiers, some 10,000 persons were killed or wounded. The Assembly then issued a new constitution, which called for an elected legislature and president and gave all adult men the right to vote. However, the chain of events had left bitterness between the French middle class and French workers because neither group felt that it could trust the other.

In December of 1848, Louis Napoleon, a nephew of Napoleon Bonaparte, was elected president of France. Louis was a symbol of the order and glory of bygone days. He tried to please just about everyone, promising more jobs, encouraging trade, defending property rights, and supporting the Catholic Church. He developed a virtual dictatorship by 1851. The next year he assumed the title of Napoleon III, Emperor of the French. This change was endorsed by a popular vote (just as his

Assembly, ended freedom of the press, and restricted the right to vote even further. Demonstrations erupted in Paris, led by middle class reformers. When soldiers refused to break up the crowds and instead joined the demonstrators, Charles abdicated the throne and fled to England. The middle class leaders of this July Revolution were afraid that a full republic would trigger an attack on France by other European countries, so they instituted a constitutional monarchy and invited Louis Philippe, a cousin of Charles X, to be king.

Louis Philippe was considered to be the king from the middle class. He dressed in bourgeois fashions and often walked the streets of Paris to give the appearance of being an average person. However, Louis Philippe still favored the interests of the wealthy and a restricted electorate. The growing number of factory workers began to listen to the appeals of reformers, especially those who promoted the new idea of socialism, under which all business would be owned and operated by the government in the name of the people. This sounded good to the overworked and underpaid workers, but what they did not see was that socialism simply meant that a new, small band of elites would be telling them what to do as opposed to the old, small band of elites.

Lesson 102 - Revolution, Reaction, and Reorganization

uncle's assumption of the emperorship had been). Just as the first republic had ended with an empire, the second republic ended with the second empire.

The Austrian Empire was also shaken by revolts in 1848. Word of the overthrow of Louis Philippe caused students, workers, and middle class liberals to stage an uprising in Vienna and demand an end to feudalism and the ouster of Metternich. The frightened emperor dismissed Metternich in an attempt to mollify the crowds. Meanwhile, in Hungary, the Magyar people, led by the fiery Lajos Kossuth, demanded that their country be given a separate government. Czechs in Bohemia issued similar demands. Nationalists in Lombardy and Venetia in northern Italy revolted against their Austrian overlords.

Austrian forces eventually overcame all of these outbreaks. The Austrians, assisted by Germans living in Bohemia, occupied Prague and stopped the Czech revolt. Kossuth proclaimed a republic in Hungary in 1849, but Russia came to Austria's aid and overthrew the republic later that year. Louis Napoleon sent French troops to help Austria regain control over its Italian provinces.

Further Developments in France

Though Napoleon III maintained tight control over France, he did bring about some economic and social reforms and encouraged the growth of industry. His foreign policy saw many setbacks. The attempt to ally with and take over Mexico ended in embarrassing disaster. In 1870 war broke out between France and Prussia over who would become the next king of Spain (each side had an interest in seeing who became king there). The Prussian army defeated the French and captured Napoleon III.

Reformers in France organized a new government and declared the third republic. France was forced to sign a humiliating treaty of defeat with Prussia in which France gave the coal-rich provinces of Alsace and Lorraine to Prussia. This led to a deeply-held resentment of the German nation by many French. The painting on page 584 illustrates this. Alsace-Lorraine was colored black on French maps, and children were taught that it still belonged to France.

Radicals in Paris were furious over the treaty and fearful that the monarchist majority in the National Assembly would make further reforms impossible. In 1871 these radicals set up a government they called the Paris Commune. The National Assembly sent in the armed forces and crushed the uprising. Some 20,000 people died in the conflict.

Lajos Kossuth (1802-1894) was a leader in the failed Hungarian Revolution of 1848. Having learned English by studying Shakespeare and the Bible, he toured Great Britain and the United States in 1851-1852 to raise support for freedom fighters in Hungary. Kossuth spoke to crowds of thousands and met with influential people such as President Millard Fillmore, Daniel Webster, and Abraham Lincoln. Lincoln called him "the most worthy and distinguished representative of the cause of civil and religious liberty on the continent of Europe." However, Kossuth's efforts to gain financial and military backing were largely ineffective.

France was a splintered nation politically for the rest of the 19th century. Monarchists controlled the National Assembly, but even they were divided between supporters of the Bourbon dynasty (the line of Louises) and supporters of the house of Orleans (the line of Louis Philippe). As many as twelve political parties had representatives in the Assembly, which meant that governments were often formed by shaky coalitions of two or more parties. When an issue arose that divided the coalition, the government descended into turmoil once again. The government was also weakened by recurring scandals and corruption.

One particular scandal left many Frenchmen embarrassed and angry. In 1894 Captain Alfred Dreyfuss was accused of passing secrets to the Germans. Dreyfuss was the first Jewish officer in the general staff of the French army. Although he claimed to be innocent, Dreyfuss was found guilty and sent to prison. The verdict set off a wave of anti-Semitic feeling in France. Later revelations showed that another officer, a Catholic monarchist, was the true traitor; but the government refused to reopen the case. The controversy deeply divided the French people, with Catholics, monarchists, and the military on one side and republicans, leftists, and socialists on the other. In 1899 the French president issued a pardon to Dreyfuss.

Encouraged by what they saw as vindication of their position, republicans in the National Assembly were able to enact reforms for the workplace, including a maximum twelve-hour workday and the outlawing of hiring children under thirteen. The Assembly also cut the ties between the government and the Catholic Church, effectively ending the Church's position as the official state religion of France.

Developments in Russia

The Romanov dynasty had begun in Russia in 1613, when Russian nobles elected seventeen-year-old Michael as the czar. Michael ended the process of electing the czar and made the monarchy hereditary. He also gave the nobles complete control over the peasants on their land. The Russian system of serfdom was much like slavery. Russia also took Siberia to benefit from its natural resources, such as iron, timber, and fur. This move extended Russian control to the Pacific. The Romanovs ruled Russia until 1917.

Peter I (or Peter the Great) reigned in the late 1600s and early 1700s. He was determined to make Russia a more modern nation. Peter visited cities in Europe and brought back new industrial and agricultural methods. He also tried to impose changes on Russian society, including ordering the nobles to shave their long beards and requiring the

The Dreyfuss Affair received extensive newspaper coverage, such as in the issue of Le Petit Journal. *It also inspired posters, cartoons, postcards, music, and board games.*

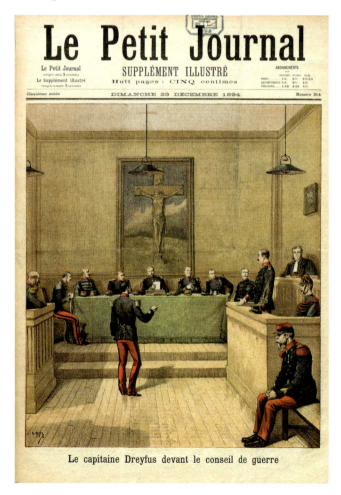

The Russian-American Company was chartered in 1799 to oversee economic activity in the Aleutian Islands, Alaska, and the Pacific Coast of North America. In addition to several outposts in Alaska and a few in Hawaii, the Russian-American Company established Fort Ross in California in 1812. Russian scientist I. G. Voznesenskii painted this watercolor of Fort Ross in 1841. That year the Russians sold the area to John Sutter (of California Gold Rush fame).

wives of nobility to wear French fashions. Peter established a more efficient government bureaucracy and defeated Sweden in 1709 to gain a seaport on the Baltic. He built a new capital, St. Petersburg, on the Baltic Sea, largely by the brutal use of peasant labor. His palace was a monument to his greatness as Versailles was to the French monarchy.

A series of weak czars ended in 1762 when Catherine II assumed the position from her late husband and became czarina. Catherine was a German princess, but she learned Russian and became a member of the Eastern Orthodox Church.

Catherine granted a charter of rights to the nobles but refused to give equivalent rights to the peasants. An estimated 34 million of the 36 million people in Russia were serfs during her tenure. Catherine (often called the Great) won a seaport on the Black Sea to the south. This warm water port was vital to Russian expansion, since its northern ports were blocked with ice during the winter.

Russia remained largely unchanged until the mid-19th century. The czars had absolute control, and both the serfs and the nobles were unmotivated to change and make progress in their lifestyles. In 1861 Czar Alexander II abolished serfdom. He gave the former serfs their freedom but no land. They had to buy the land they wanted to own, while the nobles were compensated handsomely by the government for land they gave up. As a result, many serfs were heavily in debt. These modest efforts at change in Russia suffered a setback when Alexander II was assassinated in 1881.

Alexander III did not want to continue the reforms begun by his father. Alexander III wanted all Russians to become members of the Orthodox Church. Jews living in Russia were a special target for persecution. They could not own land, they had to live only in certain areas, and their communities were the targets of merciless attacks called pogroms. Many Jews were driven out of Russia and moved to other countries in Europe and to the United States. A smaller number relocated to Palestine.

Nicholas II became czar in 1894 and encouraged rapid industrialization. This benefited the small number of Russian capitalists but brought severe hardship on the abused Russian labor force. The rule of the Romanovs came to be opposed by peasants, ethnic minorities, urban workers, and middle class liberals. Assassinations of government figures became commonplace.

In 1904 Russia lost a war to Japan over issues involving Pacific territories. This was an embarrassment to many Russians and led to further dissatisfaction with the existing regime. In 1905 a peaceful march in St. Petersburg to petition the czar for reforms ended in tragedy as troops opened fire, killing about one thousand marchers. After this event, discontent exploded in Russia. Nicholas promised to bring about reforms, but they did not happen.

The New Century

By the end of a century of turmoil, Europe had witnessed many economic changes and several political reforms including broader voting rights and, in some cases, entirely new forms of government. The ideologies of liberalism and socialism remained strong as did nationalist movements, as we will see in the next lesson. The political landscape was complicated in many countries as moderate and radical reformers were divided in their goals and conservative monarchists remained strong.

Europe itself became largely stabilized after 1870, but then conflicts developed overseas with increased competition for foreign colonies. This competition came about as a result of the desire for economic power combined with nationalistic pride. This colonialism was a factor in the outbreak of the Great War, also known as World War I.

A leader who is a great oppressor lacks understanding, but he who hates unjust gain will prolong his days.
Proverbs 28:16

Assignments for Lesson 102

In Their Words   Read "Anti-Semitic Riots" and "Where Love Is, God Is" (pages 240-250).

Literature   Continue reading *North and South*.

Student Review   Optional: Answer the questions for Lesson 102.

Celebration in Florence of the 150th Anniversary of Italian Unification (2011)

Lesson 103 - Key Event

Unification in Italy and Germany

The drives for unification in Italy and Germany in the last half of the 1800s ended for all practical purposes the remaining relics of small medieval kingdoms in Europe (with the exception of such tiny states as Luxembourg and Monaco). These unifications were the high point of the move toward nationalism during the 19th century. In addition, German unification set the stage for dramatic events in the 20th century.

The results were similar in each case, but the processes were quite different. Italy was unified from the bottom up, with popular movements leading to the end of small kingdoms. In Germany, unification occurred from the top down, as the Prussian leader Otto von Bismarck shrewdly engineered a Prussian-dominated takeover of the smaller German states.

Forces at Work in Italy

The peninsula of Italy had been covered with small kingdoms and city-states for centuries. The rulers of these kingdoms, which included Sardinia, Lombardy, Tuscany, and Sicily, wanted to maintain their power, which they knew they would lose if the peninsula united into one nation. These rulers generally opposed republican reforms. Since they saw such ideas as a threat to all of them, they wanted to stand together against such changes.

In addition, foreign countries controlled many parts of Italy; and those countries were reluctant to give up the territories that had been awarded or confirmed by the Congress of Vienna. Also, the papacy opposed unification because it would mean giving up control of the Papal States and because it would risk offending Austria, the strongest Catholic country in Europe.

However, reformers saw the possibility of better days with unification. The glimpse of freedom provided by the French Revolution encouraged liberals in Italy to think about what might happen in their land. They were tired of the fate of Italians resting in the hands of foreign kings.

Advocates of change promoted the idea of a representative government that would provide greater political freedom for all Italians. Pooling the resources of Italy could bring economic progress through modern industry and improved agricultural techniques. The idea of a unified Italy also had an emotional appeal to those who thought about the glory days of the Roman Empire and the international role that Italian city-states played in the Renaissance.

The Movement Takes Shape

Giuseppe Mazzini, an impassioned orator, formed a secret society called Young Italy in 1831 to hold meetings, publish materials, and pressure governments to consider unification. During the revolutions of 1848, Austria's two provinces in northern Italy attempted to win their independence but failed. The people of Sicily did succeed in ousting their king, and other kingdoms produced more liberal constitutions. Nationalists under Mazzini took over Rome and declared the Roman Republic in early 1849. The pope fled into exile. However, French troops (sent by Louis Napoleon to try to win the pope's favor) entered the city and restored the pope.

King Victor Emmanuel II, who came to the throne of Sardinia in 1849, strongly supported unification. A proposal by Count Camillo Cavour of Piedmont (part of the Kingdom of Sardinia) called for Italian unification under the Sardinian king. Victor Emmanuel named Cavour to be prime minister in 1852. Cavour initiated a program of public improvements and encouraged economic growth to show the rest of Italy what could be done.

Cavour was also a shrewd diplomat. When France and England went to war against Russia to limit Russia's power in the Ottoman Empire, Cavour influenced Sardinia to enter the war on the side of France and England. Sardinia had little interest in protecting the Ottomans, but when Russia was defeated in the Crimean War in 1856, Sardinia participated in the peace conference. There Cavour publicized the idea of Italian unification.

Unification Is Accomplished

Cavour gained support from Napoleon III of France for his goal of ending Austria's influence in Italy. The Sardinian prime minister made a secret agreement with France to draw Austria into war. France would help Sardinia against Austria, and in return the French would receive the provinces of

Giuseppe Barboglio (1838-1919), a Red Shirt in 1865

Nice and Savoy that were situated next to France but ruled by Sardinia.

Sardinia supported nationalist movements in the Austrian-held provinces of Lombardy and Venetia. Sure enough, Austria declared war on Sardinia, France sent their troops, and the Austrians were driven from Lombardy. Then France changed its tune and made a separate peace with Austria. Sardinia was given Lombardy, but no other provinces in northern Italy changed hands. The idea had been planted, however; and four provinces held elections in which the people voted for unification with Sardinia.

In southern Italy, the dashing military leader Giuseppe Garibaldi organized a volunteer army called the Red Shirts with Cavour's approval. Garibaldi planned to take over the kingdom of Sicily.

The Red Shirts took control of the Kingdom of the Two Sicilies in 1860, which Sardinia annexed later that year. Garibaldi began to move on Rome, which was still defended by French troops; but Cavour dissuaded the action because he feared a negative reaction to what would appear to be an attack on the pope.

In 1861 a parliament with representatives from all of Italy except Venetia and the area around Rome met and declared the kingdom of Italy with Victor Emmanuel as its monarch. A few months after this initial declaration, Cavour died. Five years later, Italy acquired Venetia from Austria. Then in 1870, French troops withdrew from Rome because of the Franco-Prussian War. Italian forces moved into Rome, and the people there voted to become part of the Italian kingdom. Italian unity was complete.

The move was not without its problems. The pope opposed unification and urged Catholics in Italy not to go along with the new government. In addition, southern Italians resented the dominance of Sardinians in the national government. Moreover, southern Italy was mostly rural while northern Italy began a program of rapid industrialization.

Background of the German States

The German people had long been divided into several small kingdoms. After the Protestant Reformation some leaders became Lutheran, which led to conflict with Catholic states. The strongest German Catholic kingdom was Austria, which was led by the Hapsburg dynasty. Austria also ruled Bohemia and Hungary.

In 1618 the Hapsburg emperor tried to restore the Roman Catholic Church to its former position of dominance in Bohemia, where many nobles had become Lutheran. War broke out among the German princes, and other nations in Europe became involved as well. Cardinal Richelieu of France, for instance, supported the Protestants to keep Austria from becoming more powerful. The Thirty Years' War devastated the German provinces. Because of the war, as well as famines and plagues, the population of the German provinces decreased by about one-third. The Treaty of Westphalia, which ended the war in 1648, forbade the Hapsburgs from imposing their rule on other German states.

The big political winner in Westphalia was Friedrich Wilhelm, the elector of Brandenburg and a Lutheran of the Hohenzollern dynasty. The Hohenzollerns had inherited the kingdom of Prussia. After the Thirty Years' War, Friedrich Wilhelm was determined to build a strong army to defend Prussia and the other lands that he held. This was the start of the military tradition of Prussia.

In later years, the Austrian emperor asked for Prussia's help against France. The elector at the time,

This gate leads into Vatican City from Rome. When Italy unified in 1870, King Victor Emmanuel annexed the papal states. The Catholic Church protested this infringement of its jurisdiction. The "Roman Question" lingered unsettled until 1929 when Italy and the Holy See signed the Lateran Treaty. The treaty established the Vatican City as a separate, sovereign state. Prime Minister Benito Mussolini signed on behalf of the king.

In October of 1817, three hundred years after Martin Luther's posting of his Ninety-Five Theses, German students gathered at Wartburg Castle to demonstrate their support for unification of the German states (illustration at right). Some of the students had fought against Napoleon's army wearing black, red, and gold uniforms. These became the colors of their movement, and eventually the colors of the German national flag.

Friedrich Wilhelm's son, agreed on the condition that the Holy Roman Empire recognize him as king of Prussia. Friedrich Wilhelm's grandson, who ruled from 1713 to 1740, strengthened the Prussian military and encouraged disciplined living by all Prussians. By the mid-1700s, the two strongest powers among the German states were Austria and Prussia.

The tumultuous year of 1848 brought another attempt at German unity. A riot in Berlin led the Prussian king, Friedrich Wilhelm IV, to promise reform. However, when he saw how other countries had squashed republican uprisings, the king dismissed a newly-elected assembly and issued his own constitution. In May of 1848, a parliament of nationalists from the various German states met in Frankfurt to work for peaceful reform and for German unity. The next year, the parliament offered the throne of a united Germany to Friedrich Wilhelm IV, but he refused because it was offered in the name of the people and not by the princes of Germany. He then ordered the parliament to disband.

The Road to German Unity

Several roadblocks stood in the way of a unified Germany. Austria, as a member of the German Confederation created in Vienna in 1815, feared that it would lose its influence among the German states. Austria was also afraid of the competition that a larger, Prussian-led state might pose. Many smaller German states wanted to maintain their

The Battle of the Nations took place in 1813 in Leipzig (in modern Germany). A coalition army of Russian, Prussian, Austrian, and Swedish troops defeated Napoleon's army and his allies. The Völkerschlachtdenkmal (Monument to the Battle of the Nations) was completed in 1913 to commemorate the 100th anniversary of the battle. It became a symbol of German nationalism. Adolph Hitler used it as a backdrop for public meetings. After the bitter conflict between Soviet Russia and Germany during World War II, the Communist government of East Germany decided to keep the monument as a memorial to German-Russian cooperation.

independence, and they believed that a unified Germany would be dominated by Prussia. Catholic German kingdoms feared a loss of power to Protestant Prussia. France and Russia opposed German unification because they thought that a larger German state led by the Prussians would threaten European stability.

All of these roadblocks the Prussians decided to overcome. In the 1850s, Prussia became the leading proponent of a unified Germany. Prussia had a strong government, a powerful army, and a growing industrialized economy. The Prussian leadership decided that a unified Germany would increase their power in Europe and the world. In 1861 King Wilhelm I of Prussia appointed Otto von Bismarck as both prime minister and foreign minister.

Bismarck was from a wealthy family and had served in the military. He believed in the power of the king, the military, and Prussia. He had no use for representative government, liberals, or the will of the people. Bismarck's goal was for a unified Germany to be the strongest nation in Europe. This would happen, he said, not with speeches and political majorities "but with blood and iron," that is, with military strength.

The Prussian prime minister pursued his plan with little regard for the law, honesty, or parliamentary approval. This approach was called *Realpolitik*, which meant that might made right and the end justified the means. When the parliament did not approve his plan to strengthen the military, Bismarck ignored the body and collected the taxes anyway.

In 1864 Prussia allied with Austria to seize two provinces from Denmark. Then, after obtaining agreements from France, Russia, and Italy to stay out of the way, Bismarck fomented a conflict with Austria over the province that Austria had gained. The Prussian army easily rolled over the Austrians in the Seven Weeks' War. Bismarck made peace relatively easy for Austria, but the Austrians lost some of their foreign territories and were forced out of the German Confederation. This Confederation was disbanded; and Prussia formed the North German Confederation of twenty-one states led, of course, by Prussia.

The last step to unity involved small German Catholic kingdoms near Austria. Bismarck persuaded them to form a military alliance with Prussia against France. France and Prussia came to be at odds over the successor to the throne of Spain. The Spanish government had offered its kingship to a Hohenzollern cousin of Wilhelm I. France strongly opposed this and wanted a promise from Wilhelm that he would not agree to this. Wilhelm refused to agree.

The Prussian king, who was at his vacation retreat at the time, sent a telegram to Bismarck describing his meeting with the French ambassador. Bismarck edited the telegram to make it appear that Wilhelm and the French ambassador had insulted each other. Bismarck then released the telegram to the public. People in both France and Prussia were outraged; France declared war on July 15, 1870; and the Franco-Prussian War was the result.

This 1867 political cartoon by Wilhelm Scholtz portrays Bismarck as a paper doll with multiple uniforms representing the multiple roles he filled in the Prussian government. It appeared in Kladderadatsch, *a German satirical magazine published from 1848 to 1944.*

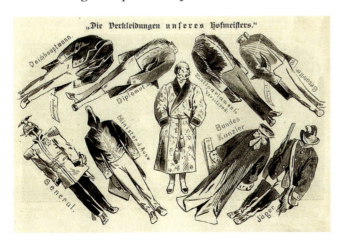

The Prussian military machine again was victorious. By the following January, all French resistance was gone. The French had to give up Alsace-Lorraine, and on January 18, 1871, at Versailles, Wilhelm I was proclaimed *kaiser*, or emperor, of all Germany. The German state included the North German Confederation, the southern German Catholic states, and Alsace-Lorraine. Germany was unified, and France had become a bitter enemy.

Consolidating German Unity

Not everyone in Germany was pleased with the outcome. Those who had exercised influence in Prussia feared that they would be swallowed up by an all-German government. German Catholics distrusted the Prussian Protestants. Liberals and reformers disliked Bismarck's conservative views. Once again, however, Bismarck outmaneuvered all opposition.

The Second Reich was a confederation of twenty-five states (Germans called the Holy Roman Empire the First Reich). Each state had its own king, duke, or prince. State leaders appointed representatives to an upper house of Parliament, while all males over twenty-five elected representatives for the lower house. The upper house could veto any measure, and the emperor

The Proclamation of the German Empire
Anton von Werner (German, 1885)

This 1878 illustration by Wilhelm Camphausen shows the Prussian Otto von Bismarck (right) with the captured French Emperor Napoleon III.

and (now Chancellor) Bismarck controlled the votes in the upper house.

Prussians dominated the new government. Compulsory military service, a Prussian tradition, was imposed throughout the empire. Army officers were Prussians. Legal and monetary systems were unified, and communication and transportation systems tied the huge empire together. Bismarck was suspicious of Catholic opposition to the unified government, so he began an attack on the Catholic Church. The Jesuit order was expelled from Germany, Church-run schools were closed, and Catholic clergy were forbidden from criticizing the government. However, these measures served to strengthen Catholic resolve. Bismarck later repealed the laws in order to gain Catholic support against a threat from the socialists.

Bismarck feared and hated the socialists. He had the parliament pass laws forbidding socialist printed materials and allowing police to break up socialist meetings. As with the Catholics, however, these repressive measures spurred the socialists to greater resolve. Bismarck then instituted some of the reforms advocated by the socialists, such as government sponsored insurance programs for workers, to weaken the socialists' cause; but socialists continued to win election to the parliament.

The Reichstag building opened in 1894 as a home for the German parliament. A fire in 1933 severely damaged the building, and it fell into disrepair. After German re-unification, it was rebuilt and put to its original use in 1999.

A Change of Leadership

Wilhelm II, the twenty-nine-year-old grandson of Wilhelm I, came to the throne in 1888. He shared Bismarck's desire for a strong Germany, but he was jealous of Bismarck's power. Wilhelm II believed in the divine right of his kingship, but he was impulsive and self-centered. In 1890 Wilhelm II forced the resignation of Bismarck after twenty-eight years in power.

In an attempt to win the support of German workers, Wilhelm II allowed the anti-socialist laws to lapse and continued the social insurance programs. The socialist Social Democratic Party continued to grow and became the largest party in the lower house of parliament. Wilhelm expanded Germany's colonial activities overseas to compete with Britain, France, and Russia. In the twenty years before World War I, Wilhelm doubled the size of the German army and built an impressive naval force. Germany eventually was second only to the United States in the manufacture of steel and became the leading industrial nation of Europe.

German national pride grew along with its economic and military growth. They took pride in their cultural heritage, their educational system, their world-renowned universities, and their military strength. Germany had become the nation to reckon with as the 20th century dawned.

Then he said to me, "This is the word of the Lord to Zerubbabel saying, 'Not by might nor by power, but by My Spirit,' says the Lord of hosts."
Zechariah 4:6

Assignments for Lesson 103

In Their Words — Read the Rallying Speech by Garibaldi and "The Wolf and the Seven Little Kids" (pages 251-254).

Literature — Continue reading *North and South*.

Student Review — Optional: Answer the questions for Lesson 103.

Detail from The Boating Party, *Mary Cassatt (American, 1894)*

Lesson 104 - Everyday Life

A Short History of Western Art

God is the original artist. In the Garden of Eden He caused to grow every tree that is pleasing to the sight (Genesis 2:9). People made in His image create things of beauty.

Artists for the Tabernacle

When the time came to build the Tabernacle, all the skilled women spun blue, purple, scarlet, and fine linen. All the women whose "heart stirred with a skill" spun the goats' hair used in its construction (Exodus 35:26).

Then Moses said that the Lord had called by name Bezalel and filled him with the Spirit of God, in wisdom, understanding, knowledge, and all craftsmanship to perform every inventive work. His skills included: (1) making designs in gold, silver, and bronze; (2) cutting stones for settings; and (3) carving wood. God also put teaching in Bezalel's heart and also in Oholiab. God filled them with skill so they could engrave, design, embroider, and weave. They could perform the work and make designs.

Other Israelites helped Bezalel and Oholiab. The Lord put skill and understanding in them also. Moses called each person "whose heart stirred him" to come to do the work (Exodus 35:25-36:2).

They made the Tabernacle and the priestly garments, decorating with cherubim, almond branches and blossoms, and pomegranates. They hammered and cast metal, embroidered, overlaid with gold, engraved, constructed with wood, and set precious stones (Exodus 36-39).

Mosaics and Glass

The Sumerians created mosaics of painted baked clay cones, as shown below. Pebble mosaics from the centuries before Christ have been discovered in Greece and Turkey. Romans excelled in the mosaic art form, placing them on ceilings, walls, and floors. Early Christian mosaics have survived on the walls of churches.

Ancient Egyptians made glass beads and were able to color glass. Syrians developed a method for blowing glass around 100 BC. Romans made mosaics from glass tubes in the first centuries after Jesus' birth. Europeans were making stained glass pictures as early as the 800s.

Among the earliest surviving windows are five larger-than-life figures in the clerestory of Augsburg (Germany) Cathedral, made in the early the 1100s. The portrayal of Jonah is shown below.

Painting

Egyptians painted scenes of mythology and everyday life. Human figures showed both the front and the profile at the same time on the same figure. Important people were portrayed as larger than other people.

The Minoans created beautiful paintings. Marine life, such as dolphins and octopi, were popular subjects. Few ancient Greek paintings have survived except on vases. One Greek mural that has survived from a tomb in Paestum, Italy, is a scene of a young man diving. It was painted around 480 BC.

Early Christian fresco paintings have survived in Roman catacombs. They date from the third and fourth centuries. Wide-eyed figures that seem to float became characteristic of early Christian art, especially in Byzantium. The style was used on icons, which were painted on wood and depicted Christ, Mary, or people referred to as saints.

During the Middle Ages, artists were generally anonymous. In Ireland and England, the most beautiful preserved paintings are manuscript illuminations with intricate calligraphy designs. Most European painting of the Middle Ages was created in monasteries, both in the British Isles and on the continent of Europe. During the early Gothic period lay people (non-clergy) began to set up workshops outside of monasteries. They created beautiful manuscripts for patrons.

Beginning in the Renaissance, European artists were known and praised by name. They worked for patrons, who paid them to decorate their homes and to record their accomplishments. Many surviving Renaissance paintings are portraits.

The subjects in European paintings of the Middle Ages appeared two-dimensional. Around 1290 Italian painter Giotto di Bondone learned to use light, shade, and color to make more realistic scenes. Cennino Cennini wrote a treatise on oil paints around 1390. Afterwards their use became popular. Oil on canvas began to replace the medieval use of frescos and of tempera on wood. Jan van Eyck of Bruges, Belgium, mastered the use of oil paints around 1400, using them to create rich detail. He also used oil glazes to reflect light.

Masters of the Italian Renaissance included Leonardo da Vinci (1452-1519), Michelangelo (1475-1564), and Raphael (1483-1520). One style of Renaissance painting emphasizing complexity and distortion was called Mannerism. One Mannerist painter was El Greco (1541-1614), who was born on Crete and worked in Spain. Among the master painters in northern Europe during the Renaissance were the German Albrecht Dürer (1471-1528), who excelled at painting the human figure, and Netherlander Pieter Bruegel the Elder (c. 1525-1569), who painted peasant life.

Baroque art of the 1600s was characterized by realism, the portrayal of movement, and contrasts between light and shadow. The Flemish Peter Paul Reubens (1577-1640) was a master of the Baroque period, but the most famous and beloved of Baroque painters was Netherlander Rembrandt van Rijn (1606-1669).

The Rococo style was popular in France and Germany in the early 1700s. It was light and

Portrait of Young Woman with Unicorn
Raphael (Italian, c. 1505)

delicate with elaborate ornamentation. The French Jean Baptiste Siméon Chardin (1699-1779) painted during this period, often choosing simple scenes of domestic life. A revival of interest in ancient Greek art followed in the Neoclassical period. One artist who painted in this style was American Benjamin West (1738-1820). Romanticism followed with picturesque paintings of nature and paintings that conveyed mood and emotion.

In the mid-1800s, many artists turned to realism. Some were innovators like Édouard Manet (1832-1883), who painted common people such as old beggars and people in cafés. Manet befriended well-known French painters Paul Cézanne (1839-1906), Edgar Degas (1834-1917), Claude Monet (1840-1926), Camille Pissarro (1830-1903), and Pierre-Auguste Renoir (1841-1919).

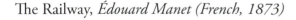

The Railway, *Édouard Manet (French, 1873)*

The Seine at the Grand Jatte, Spring
Georges Seurat (French, 1888)

The Impressionist style of painting, which emphasized light and used lighter colors than the old masters, became popular in the late 1800s. Mary Cassatt (1844-1926) was an American Impressionist who featured women and children.

An outgrowth of Impressionism was Pointillism, perfected by Georges Seurat (French, 1859-1891). Paintings in the Pointillism style are made up of thousands of dots of color that give the impression of a scene. Other post-impressionists were Paul Gauguin (French, 1848-1903), Henri de Toulouse-Lautrec (French, 1864-1901), and Vincent van Gogh (Dutch, 1853-1890).

Art critics have categorized modern art into several different styles. Some of these styles and representative artists include:

- Fauvism - Henri Matisse (French, 1869-1954)
- Expressionism - Paul Klee (Swiss, 1879-1940)
- Cubism - Pablo Picasso (Spanish, 1881-1973)
- Abstract - Kasimir Malevich (Russian, 1878-1935)

Unit 21 - The Making of Modern Europe

- Dadaism - Max Ernst (German, 1891-1976)
- Surrealism - Salvador Dalí (Spanish, 1904-1989)
- Synchronism - Georgia O'Keefe (American, 1887-1986)
- Realism - Andrew Wyeth (American, 1917-2009)
- Abstract Expressionism - Jackson Pollack (American, 1912-1956)
- Pop Art - Andy Warhol (American, 1928-1987)

Some artists use their work to advocate for or against issues that are important to them. The use of children as soldiers is a common tragedy in Africa. This work is Child Soldier in the Ivory Coast, Africa *by Gilbert G. Groud (Ivorian, 2007).*

Sculpture

Sculpture is three-dimensional art, either free-standing or relief. Throughout the centuries, sculptures have been made from various materials using one of three methods: carving, modeling, or casting. Carving is taking away from the original material. Modeling is adding material until the desired shape is achieved. Casting involves making a mold and then pouring molten material inside it. In the 20th century, a fourth technique called construction and assemblage was developed, in which various materials were put together to make a sculpture.

Most Egyptians never saw the magnificent sculptures of ancient Egypt because the sculptures were placed in temples, tombs, and palaces. Egyptian figures were more geometric and symbolic than realistic.

Mesopotamian sculptors during the Assyrian period were masters at portraying animals. Etruscans, inhabitants of the Tuscany region of Italy in the first millennium BC, carved elaborate tomb covers with life-sized human figures of terra-cotta.

The main subjects in classical Greek sculpture were idols, legendary heroes, athletes, young men and women, historical portraits, animals, and imaginary monsters. Classical Greek sculpture was based on imitation of the real world. This concept helped produce some of the most beautifully realistic sculpture in world history. The Greeks did not intend to glorify God with their art, but its beauty lies in the fact that it used materials that God made (stone, bronze, wood, clay, gold, ivory, and silver) and mimicked the beauty of His Creation.

Throughout the Roman Empire, sculptors decorated public and private buildings. They created triumphal arches which honored their heroes and depicted historical events. They also created honorific columns and altars. Private individuals even had their own histories preserved in funerary reliefs on tombs. The Romans often reused statuary to honor a new emperor, sometimes changing the head to a new person to be honored. Most Roman sculptures were fashioned from white marble, but some were created from bronze, gold, or silver. Few of these survive because they were melted down in the Middle Ages or later.

During the early Middle Ages, stone sculpture was not as common as during the Greek and Roman period, but examples of bronze statues and wood carvings have survived. Stone sculptures like those from ancient times were created again during the Romanesque period of the 11th and 12th centuries. They were sometimes placed on the outside of churches and were intended to attract and to instruct. A common theme was the Last Judgment. French, German, and Italian sculptors created remarkable sculptures during the Gothic period.

The marble sarcophagus of Junius Bassus, created in 359 AD, is an early Christian sculpture. It depicts several Biblical scenes, including Abraham and Isaac. A cast of the original is pictured below.

Unit 21 - The Making of Modern Europe

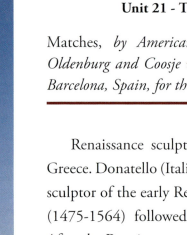

Matches, by American husband-wife team Claes Oldenburg and Coosje van Bruggen, was installed in Barcelona, Spain, for the 1992 Olympic Games.

Renaissance sculptors looked back to classical Greece. Donatello (Italian, c. 1386-1466) was a great sculptor of the early Renaissance, and Michelangelo (1475-1564) followed him as a master sculptor. After the Renaissance, styles of sculpture were often similar to styles of painting. In fact, many artists created both paintings and sculptures. Sculpture periods since the Renaissance have included Mannerism, Baroque, Rococo, Neoclassical, Romantic, Cubism, Futurism, Constructivism, Dadaism, and Surrealism. European sculptors of the 20th century were also influenced by the art of Africa and Oceania. Sculptors of the 20th century introduced abstract sculpture, assemblage and junk sculpture (using found objects), and earthworks which encompass large outdoor areas.

*Splendor and majesty are before Him,
strength and beauty are in His sanctuary.
Psalm 96:6*

Assignments for Lesson 104

In Their Words — Read "The Necklace" (pages 255-261).

Literature — Continue reading *North and South*.

Student Review — Optional: Answer the questions for Lesson 104.

Prussian Bombardment of Paris, 1870

Lesson 105 - Bible Study

Honesty

Count Cavour manipulated matters behind the scenes to draw Austria into a war that would prove costly.

Otto von Bismarck led other European nations to believe that certain things would happen if they stayed out of a Prussian war with Austria.

On another occasion, Bismarck edited a telegram by striking out certain words to make it appear that the Prussian king had insulted the French ambassador, hoping to incite the French to declare war.

The Bible is clear that lying is wrong. The deceptiveness of sin, however, leads us to want to shade the truth sometimes. We think that we are not lying but we know that we are not telling the whole truth. Telling the truth is an important element in building and maintaining trust in any situation.

God Tells and Expects the Truth

God cannot lie (Titus 1:2). In Him is no darkness at all (1 John 1:5). No deceptiveness is in His character (James 1:17). Satan, on the other hand, is a deceiver (Revelation 12:9). He is the father of lies. It is his nature to lie and deceive (John 8:44). He will even disguise himself as an angel of light (2 Corinthians 11:14), which sometimes makes it difficult to determine the truth. The contrast between the way of God and the way of Satan could not be more distinct.

God has always expected truthfulness from people. He did not accept the prevarications of Adam, Eve, and Cain (Genesis 3:10-13, 4:9). The Ten Commandments included a prohibition against bearing false witness (Exodus 20:16). For the Christian, telling the truth is part of putting off the old way of sin and putting on the new man of righteousness (Ephesians 4:25, Colossians 3:9-10). Revelation is clear that those who practice lying will have no part in heaven (Revelation 21:27, 22:15).

Saying something is true when it is not, denying something when you should admit it, and giving a false impression to another person are wrong. In the pursuit of truth, however, we need to be aware of other ways in which we can fail to be honest.

"I Was Only Joking"

A common deception is the mixed message, trying to say something without really saying it. "You did a good job cleaning your room. It's about time!" This is a mixed message. It is unclear whether the speaker is praising or criticizing.

"Like a madman who throws firebrands, arrows, and death, so is the man who deceives his neighbor and says, 'Was I not joking?'" (Proverbs 26:18-19). Mixed messages are a form of deception. When you use a mixed message, you leave the hearer guessing as to your true intention. When you have more than one message to send, make both of them clear. "You did a good job cleaning your room, but I am disappointed that it took you so long." Don't hide behind "I was only joking." Proverbs is right that this is as harmful to other people as throwing firebrands and shooting arrows.

"White Lies"

Society has accepted the use of white lies, which is telling a lie when you think the other person does not need to know the truth. You convince yourself that you are doing it not to deceive but to help or protect the other person. Many sitcoms have been produced with a premise such as one character telling an untruth to protect himself from embarrassment or to shield another person from some unpleasant reality.

Harm is done when a lie is told. It harms the relationship because trust is destroyed. It harms the person telling it because it hardens that person's conscience, and next time the lie might be a little bigger to cover more serious consequences. Lying does not protect; lying hurts. Truth honors the other person and protects the relationship.

"The End Justifies the Means"

In the incidents described at the first of this lesson, public officials used deception to get what they wanted. They believed in the goodness of their goals, but they thought that deception was the best means to achieve their goals. It reflects a low view of other people to think that they have to be manipulated in this way. It is not treating the other person the way you want to be treated (Matthew 7:12).

If the end is just, the means to obtain it can and should be just as well. To think otherwise is to rewrite the rules to suit yourself. We should be able to trust God to provide the ends that we need to reach if we follow proper means.

Governments are sometimes guilty of putting a spin on information to make its officials look good. Communist governments became adept at giving out false information to protect themselves. We have to be able to trust the information that our government and its officials give out. We have a right to expect this, even if it is information that we do not want to hear.

Truthfulness in "The Necklace"

The short story "The Necklace" is a good illustration of the pain that can be caused when people do not tell the truth. Madame Forestier should have been honest about the value of her necklace when she let Mathilde borrow it. All Mathilde wanted was to make a good impression, which she was able to do with cheap costume jewelry. At the same time, Mathilde should have told Madame Forestier the truth when she lost the necklace. If she had, she could have avoided years of misery.

Lesson 105 - Bible Study: Honesty

What Else Was Happening? (1800-1900)

1. The huge eruption of Mount Tambora (at right) in Indonesia in 1815 likely contributed to the Year Without a Summer in 1816 (also called Eighteen Hundred and Froze to Death). Summer cold, frost, and snow devastated crops in Asia, America, and Europe.

2. Since ancient times, people had theorized that a large landmass existed in the far south. In 1820 three separate ships (Russian, British, and American) sighted Antarctica. A Norwegian crew made the first confirmed landing in 1895 at Cape Adare.

3. Ivan Evseyevich Popov (1797-1879) was a Russian Orthodox missionary to Alaska (see 1818 painting by Mikhail T. Tikhanov of Aleuts at right). Popov arrived in 1824 with his family, learned local languages, and translated Bible portions. After his wife's death, he became a monk named Innocent, continuing his interest in the area as a Church leader.

4. As British settlers arrived in Tasmania, the native Palawa people were nearly wiped out by disease and violence. Fanny Cochrane Smith (1834-1905, pictured at right) was a Palawa woman. Wax cylinder recordings were made of her singing songs in her native language.

5. José Rizal (1861-1896) was a Filipino nationalist with Chinese, Japanese, and Spanish ancestry. He had wide interests as a doctor, author, artist, and scientist. Though Rizal did not push for revolution against Spanish authorities, he was convicted and executed for sedition. He was later hailed as a national hero of the Philippines.

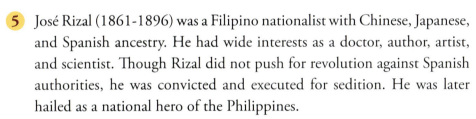

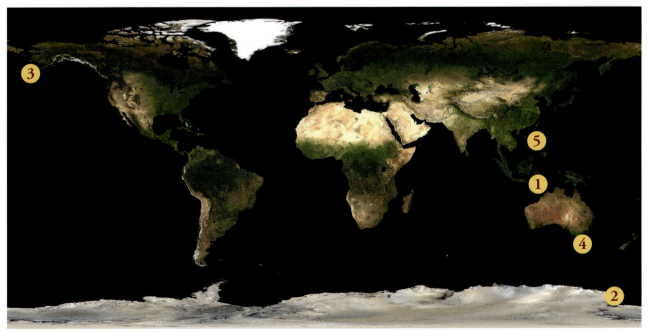

Both women in the story let their pridefulness get in the way of honesty and good judgment. Madame Forestier wanted to give the impression that she owned expensive jewelry, and Mathilde wanted to give the same impression to the other people at the party. Wanting to give a certain appearance and acting out of fear lead us into deceptiveness, and the cost of this deception is tremendous.

The Lie

Truthfulness and deceit involve more than individual statements. We can live in an atmosphere of deceit and mistrust. In Romans 1:25, Paul says that pagans "exchanged the truth of God for [literally] the lie." Worship of what is created instead of the Creator is part of the big lie that Satan wants us to believe. All of Satan's lies are part of the lie, such as: we find our worth in what we own; what people think of us is crucial to our well-being; pleasing self is what life is all about; and so forth.

The lie can be so pervasive that it is the atmosphere to which we become accustomed. To question the lie appears to risk getting along in life itself. The media help spread lies that deceive many people, such as: "Glamour is all that matters," "The issues discussed in the media are the most important ones," and "The Bible and godliness are old-fashioned and not worth mentioning."

Homeschoolers are trying to fight against the lies that dominate the way children are reared, such as: "Children have to go to school to be socialized properly," "The way of the public school system is the way education should be done," and "Children do not need to be sheltered."

Whenever we accept untruthfulness in ourselves or in others, we turn to that extent toward Satan and away from God. Christians must not blend in with common expectations and practices. Instead, we must be true to God, who is truth.

Two things I asked of You, do not refuse me before I die:
Keep deception and lies far from me, give me neither poverty nor riches . . . .
Proverbs 30:7-8

Assignments for Lesson 105

Bible   Recite or write Matthew 16:24-27 from memory.

In Their Words   Read "Day by Day" (page 262).

Literature   Continue reading *North and South*.

Project   Complete your project for the week.

Student Review   Optional: Answer the questions for Lesson 105 and take the quiz for Unit 21.

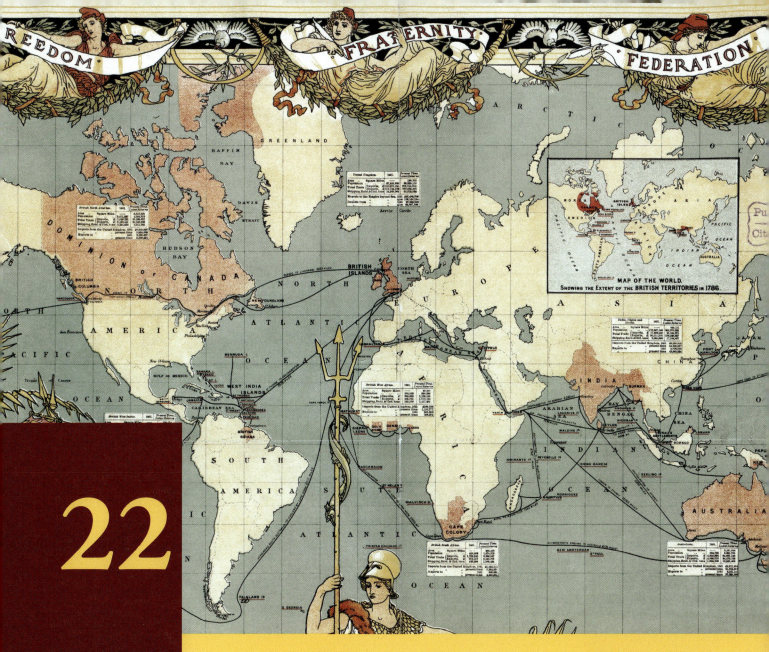

22

Britain: Industry and Empire

Summary With the biggest empire, the mightiest army and navy, and the greatest industrial output, most Britons believed that the 19th century belonged to Britain. As we look at Britain's industry and empire, we look at the failure of British policy in Ireland and the amazing life of George Müller, who cared for orphaned children in Bristol, England. We also have an overview of transportation in world history and a Bible study on kindness.

Lessons
106 - Britain in the 19th Century
107 - Key Issue: The Irish Question
108 - Key Person: George Müller
109 - Everyday Life: A History of Transportation
110 - Bible Study: Kindness

Detail from 1886 Map of the British Empire

Memory Work
Learn James 1:26-27 by the end of the unit.

Books Used
The Bible
In Their Words
North and South

Project (choose one)

1) Write 300 to 500 words on one of the following topics:

- Discuss successes and failures of British imperial policies. See Lessons 106-107.

- Describe an effort to serve others motivated by faith that you know about personally or have heard about. See Lesson 108. Tell who was involved, how it started, how it progressed, and the outcome.

2) Create a model of an historic means of transportation as shown or discussed in Lesson 109.

3) Put Christian kindness into action by taking over for a week a significant chore normally performed by another member of your family. See Lesson 110.

Clifton Suspension Bridge, Bristol

Lesson 106

Britain in the 19th Century

"The sun never sets on the British Empire."

The United Kingdom of Great Britain and Northern Ireland is slightly smaller than the state of Michigan. At the height of its power in the late 19th century, Britain controlled an empire that covered forty times the size of its homeland, or one-fifth of the world's land area. Some 400 million people lived within the British Empire. The Empire included Gibraltar in Europe; Egypt, Sudan, British East Africa, Rhodesia, and South Africa on the African continent; India, Singapore, Hong Kong, Burma, Borneo, and New Guinea in Asia; Canada in North America; British Guiana in South America; islands in the Caribbean; and Australia and New Zealand.

In addition, Britain was one of the world's leading economic and military powers. Its culture, including its language, literature, and technological advances, influenced and have continued to influence the world. The cultural heritage of the United States is primarily British. Despite the division caused by the American Revolution, the United States and Great Britain have been allies for most of the last two hundred years; and their continued cultural, political, and economic ties are strong. The story of Britain in the 19th century is an important part of world history.

A Revolution in Agriculture

The Industrial Revolution, which caused significant growth in Britain's economic power and led to the development of its world-wide empire, was preceded by a revolution in agriculture that contributed to its industrial transformation.

Isambard Kingdom Brunel (1806-1859) was an outstanding civil engineer in Britain who designed several landmark projects during his career. He oversaw construction projects for every aspect of railway travel, including over 1,000 miles of track and a two-mile long tunnel. Brunel helped connect London and Bristol (on the western coast of England) by rail in 1841. He also designed some of the first ocean-going steam vessels and worked on the project to lay the first transatlantic telegraph cable. The Clifton Suspension Bridge in Bristol, completed a few years after his death, is still in use and is a beautiful monument to his talent.

England is a country on the island of Great Britain, along with Scotland and Wales. Since medieval times, England has tended to dominate politics and government on the island. Wales was confirmed as an official part of the Kingdom of England in 1542, and Scotland was joined to England through the 1707 Treaty of Union (a copy of which is shown above.) In recent years, Scotland and Wales have regained limited home rule. Britain used to control the whole island of Ireland also, but now it governs only the northern part. The rest of Ireland is an independent country. The official name of the country we are studying in this unit is the United Kingdom of Great Britain and Northern Ireland. It is shortened in common usage either to the United Kingdom or to Britain.

Medieval crop rotation systems let one-third of the land lie unused each year. In the 1730s, Charles Townsend found that planting a different crop on the fallow land, such as clover or turnips, restored nutrients to the soil and provided feed for livestock. About the same time, the inventor Jethro Tull devised a seed drill that enabled farmers to plant seeds in straight rows instead of sowing them broadcast by hand. This meant that less seed was needed, and the fields were easier to maintain and keep weeded.

Also during this period, iron plows replaced wooden ones, which made breaking up the soil easier. Somewhat later, mechanical reapers and threshers replaced hand methods and greatly increased farm output. These advances led to higher food production, which in turn contributed to healthier lives and significant population growth. Increased population caused a greater demand for manufactured goods.

The Industrial Revolution

Industrial progress was a practical outgrowth of the Enlightenment, as inventors made use of scientific knowledge to help everyday life. The growth of world industry took place in two main stages. In the first, from 1750 to about 1850, Great Britain far outdistanced industrial activity in other countries. Political disruptions in France and the lack of unity in Germany held back development in those places. During the second period, between 1850 and 1914, the United States and Western Europe more aggressively developed their industrial capacities and surpassed Britain's level of production.

Until the mid-1700s, textile production had been centered in the home. Merchants hired individuals (usually women) and brought raw materials to their homes for the workers to make thread and cloth on individual spindles and looms. New inventions in the 1700s changed the textile industry. In 1733 John Kay developed the flying shuttle that replaced the hand shuttle and made the weaving process much faster. This caused a demand for more thread.

In 1764 James Hargreaves attached multiple thread spindles to one wheel. This spinning jenny enabled a worker to spin several threads at the same time. Five years later, Richard Arkwright invented a water-powered frame that held one hundred spindles. Edward Cartwright devised a water-powered loom that enabled one person to make 200 times more cloth than could be produced by hand.

Another major advance came in 1793, when Eli Whitney of the United States invented the cotton gin (short for engine) to separate cotton seeds from the boll more quickly. This led to a huge growth in cotton farming, especially in the United States where the increased demand for cotton led to greater dependence on slavery in the South. Great Britain was the main buyer of American cotton, and by 1830 Britain was the world's leading producer of cotton thread and cloth.

Factories, Iron, and Steel

The development of large, expensive machinery led to the creation of factories, where the machines could be brought together in one place. Rather than supplies being taken to the workers in their homes, workers came together and labored in factories for a set number of hours per day and for a set wage. The first textile mills were located by streams that ran the water-powered machines. In the 1760s, James Watt perfected a steam engine powered by burning coal. This enabled factories to be located in cities. It led to an increase in production as well as a greater demand for coal to produce the steam.

Coal was also needed for the production of iron. With improvements in iron processing, Great Britain quadrupled its output of iron between 1788 and 1806. Then in the 1850s, Henry Bessemer developed a way to produce high quality steel from iron. Steel is stronger than iron, and its production led to even greater economic growth.

Why Britain Led

Great Britain led the industrial revolution during the period before 1850 for several reasons. We have already mentioned advances in agriculture and a larger and healthier population. Labor-saving devices for farms meant that fewer workers were needed in agriculture, which freed laborers for industry. The island of Great Britain was blessed with considerable resources of coal and iron. Progress in transportation (outlined in Lesson 109) helped the production and distribution of finished goods.

Britain's involvement in overseas trade since the 1500s had opened markets for goods and had brought wealth into the country that could be invested in manufacturing enterprises. Government policies encouraged businesses to make profits. Britain's colonial empire provided raw materials and markets for British-made goods, and the country's large navy protected merchant ships.

During the second phase of the Industrial Revolution, other countries became rivals to Great Britain. Belgium utilized its deposits of coal and iron, its skilled labor force, and its available investment capital. The invention of the punch card loom in France helped that country's textile industry.

For many years, small farmers let their livestock graze in what were considered public lands. However, in the late 1600s large landowners began closing off their lands to control their animals and to define property boundaries. These enclosures were often marked by hedgerows in England and Wales and by stone fences in northern England and Scotland. This enclosure movement meant that many small farmers could no longer support their families with the land they had available to them. Many moved to the cities and became industrial laborers while others emigrated to the colonies to start anew. Hedgerows (such as those in Wales shown below) and stone fences are beautiful features of the British countryside today.

German unification led to industrial growth there. Finally, the United States utilized its vast natural resources and began developing its industrial capacity. During the 1880s, the United States passed Britain as the leading industrial nation in the world. Japan started later but quickly became an important participant in the world's industrial activity. Still, in 1892, three out of every four ships built in the world were built in Britain.

By the late 1800s, a complex international economy had developed, encouraged by ever-increasing production levels, an eagerness on the part of many countries to engage in international trade, and the availability of reliable transportation. Many nations followed Britain's lead in developing overseas colonies.

Effects of the Industrial Revolution

The Industrial Revolution changed the face of English commerce and society. More people lived in cities and relatively fewer lived in rural areas. In 1801 one-third of the British population lived in cities and towns. By 1851 the urban population had increased to one-half of the total. Most of those who lived in the cities were wage earners and their families. This was a change from the time when many men owned their own business or worked their own land.

As cities grew rapidly, the quality of city life declined. Factories, unregulated by environmental laws, belched thick smoke and other waste into the countryside. A certain part of the famous London fog was factory smog which blackened buildings and land. Factory workers received low pay for their six-day weeks and twelve- to fifteen-hour days, with no vacations, sick leave, health insurance, coverage for accidents, or other benefits. Many women and children worked in factories to help with the family income. Other women worked as domestic servants for the wealthy. A family might live in a single room, usually with inadequate water and no sanitation facilities.

The growing class of unskilled laborers felt powerless. They were dependent on the hard work they performed for what little income they received; they could not protest their conditions; and, not being landowners, they could not vote for candidates who might work to alleviate their plight. Middle and upper class members of Parliament had little sympathy for the workers. It was simply the workers' lot in life to work hard and yet be poor, many politicians believed. Between 1811 and 1816, bands of men called Luddites took to smashing the new machinery, blaming it for the hardships they faced. A demonstration at Manchester, England, in 1819 to press for reforms ended in tragedy when soldiers fired on the crowd, killing several.

Industrial Reforms

Reforms came slowly, with much difficulty and opposition. Workers formed associations, later called unions, to press for higher wages and better conditions. However, the middle and upper classes strongly opposed such organizations as dangerous bands of rabble. Higher wages and better conditions,

The Great Exhibition of the Works of Industry of All Nations took place in 1851 in London's Hyde Park. The Crystal Palace, pictured at left, was a huge display hall built of a framework of iron covered with glass windows. On view inside the Crystal Palace were the latest technological marvels of the day from many countries. The event attracted six million visitors in 140 days and is considered to be the first world's fair.

Sunday Schools began as a way for churches to teach academic subjects to children on their only day off during the week. Hannah Ball (1734-1792), an acquaintance of John Wesley, started a Sunday School in 1769 that continued long after her death, well into the 19th century. Robert Raikes (1736-1811) established a similar program in 1780, which spread to other cities in Britain. Within fifty years, about 25% of the children in the country were enrolled in Sunday schools. The statue of Raikes shown at left is located in Toronto, Canada. It was unveiled there because of an International Council of Religious Education convention that occurred on the 150th anniversary of Raikes' Sunday School.

factory owners complained, would drive up prices. When memories of the French Revolution were still fresh, laws banning unions were passed in England and elsewhere in Europe. The ban was repealed in Britain in the 1820s, but unions still could not picket or strike.

Lord Ashley, the 7th Earl of Shaftesbury, and a member of Parliament, came to believe that it was God's will for him to do what he could to improve conditions for factory workers. A Parliamentary commission in the 1830s heard testimony that confirmed the worst about the lives of workers and miners. The reform cause was helped by journalists and writers such as Charles Dickens, who publicized the miserable conditions in which workers labored and lived.

In 1833 Parliament passed the Factory Act, which limited the work day for nine- through thirteen-year-olds to eight hours and for fourteen- to eighteen-year-olds to twelve hours. The 1842 Mines Act forbade the hiring of any females and any boys under thirteen to work in mines. In later years, the Ten Hours Act limited the workday for women and children under eighteen to ten hours per day. This ten-hour limit was eventually applied to all workers.

Trade unions of skilled workers were able to negotiate with factory owners for their services, which opened the door for other laborers. In the 1870s, unions gained the right to picket and strike. Unskilled workers began to use their organizations to pressure for better wages. The 1889 London dock strike paralyzed the busiest port in the world, and its settlement brought significant improvements for dock workers and others.

In the last years of the 19th century, wages for British workers rose appreciably. Improvements in manufacturing methods allowed goods to be made more cheaply, and owners realized that higher wages enabled workers to buy more products. Employers also saw the benefits of safer working conditions and worker benefits. Factory codes, national insurance for accidents, and an old age pension were enacted. In the early 1900s, Parliament passed a minimum wage law and a workers' compensation program for those injured on the job.

Reforms came in other areas also. In 1829 Sir Robert Peel promoted the organization of a police force for London. The officers were called Bobbies in his honor, as they still are today. Other major cities soon followed this example. Later in the 1800s, London was cleaned up and renewed. Gas and later electric lights made streets safer. Streetcars enabled workers to live outside of the city center and commute to their jobs. Around the end of the 1800s, London and other major world cities built subway systems.

For most of history, formal schooling was available only to the children of families who could pay tuition or hire a tutor. In Britain small schools operated by churches, charities, and individuals made learning available to some degree; but the quality of education in them varied greatly. Many British children had to work to help support their families. Lord Ashley, who started soup kitchens for poor people, also created what were called ragged schools for poor children. In 1880 school attendance became compulsory for British children five to ten years old. Eleven years later, elementary education became free to all.

Political Developments in Britain

George III became king of Britain in 1760. He reigned for sixty years, though he was mentally ill for the last part of his reign. His son, George IV, served as regent for the last years of his father's tenure and occupied the throne himself from 1820 until 1830. His brother, William IV, ruled from 1830 to 1837. Victoria, granddaughter of George III, came to the throne as an eighteen-year-old in 1837. She reigned for almost sixty-four years, until her death in early 1901. The British monarch had little real power by the time Victoria became queen, but she was a much-loved ruler who became a symbol for Britain's strength and world-wide influence. The last two-thirds of the 1800s are known as the Victorian Era.

At the beginning of the 1800s, British government was dominated by the House of Lords. Only six percent of men were able to vote because of property requirements. The districts or boroughs represented in the House of Commons had not been redrawn for some time. This meant that rural areas where few people lived had more representation than larger cities. These rural districts were called rotten boroughs. The Reform Bill of 1832 redrew Parliamentary boroughs and lowered property requirements so that now twenty percent of adult males could vote. A reform movement in the 1830s called the Chartists proposed the secret ballot, universal male suffrage, and salaries for members of Parliament so people who were not independently wealthy could serve. Their proposals were rejected at the time, but eventually just about all of their ideas became law.

Significant economic legislation passed in the early part of the century. The slave trade was outlawed in 1807, and slavery was abolished throughout the empire in 1833. William Wilberforce, a devout Christian and member of Parliament, played a major role in the movement to abolish slavery. The Corn Laws of 1815 put high tariffs on imported grain (corn is the general British term for grain). This kept prices for grain and grain products high within Britain. After crop failures caused widespread hunger and led to the need for more imports, the Corn Laws were repealed in 1846.

The Liberal and Conservative Parties jockeyed for power throughout the 19th century. Each Party

This is the earliest known photograph of Queen Victoria, shown with her eldest daughter, who was also named Victoria (c. 1845).

Lesson 106 - Britain in the 19th Century

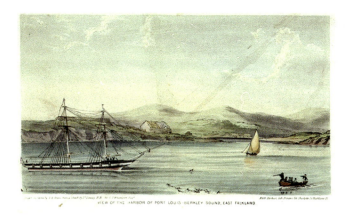

The Falkland Islands are an archipelago made up of two large islands and hundreds of smaller ones. They were uninhabited when Europeans began to explore the South Atlantic. Britain asserted its authority in 1833 against the claims of the United Provinces of the River Plate, a forerunner of modern Argentina. Lt. Robert Lowcay, a British Naval Officer stationed at the Islands, painted the watercolor at left around 1839. A long-running dispute between Argentina and the UK finally erupted in a brief war in 1982 that ended with the British retaining control.

gained and lost favor with the people from time to time. The two best known leaders in the latter half of the century were William Gladstone for the Liberals and Benjamin Disraeli of the Conservatives. Both men were prime minister more than once.

By 1885 almost all adult men had the right to vote. The two main parties competed for the new electorate of urban workers. However, many workers did not believe that either party truly represented their interests. In 1900 the Labor Party was formed with a special interest in promoting the rights of the working population. Today, the Labor and Conservative Parties are the two strongest political parties, while the Liberals hold a much smaller number of seats in the House of Commons. Another move toward popular government came in 1911 when the House of Lords lost the right to veto legislation. The House of Lords can only delay implementation of a law for a time, but they cannot kill it.

The British Empire

We noted in an earlier lesson how the English defeat of the Spanish Armada in 1588 opened the door for British exploration and colonization. The settlement of colonies became a major part of British foreign policy during the 1600s and 1700s. The first part of this lesson outlined the vast reach of British power around the world. Britain found the colonies to be lucrative enterprises. The loss of the American colonies that came about with American independence was a rare setback.

The British approach in the colonies was one of domination and an assumption of British superiority. British officials and businessmen did bring Western culture to far-off places, but they also tended to exploit the natives and give them few rights. On the other hand, British missionaries spread the gospel to many lands. The 1800s were the high point of British missionary outreach.

As the 1800s progressed, the movements for liberty and nationalism had an impact as some colonists began agitating for independence and some local natives tried to break free of British rule. Canada was given home rule in 1849. This meant that Canadians could elect their own Parliament to handle domestic affairs, but Great Britain oversaw Canada's foreign relations as part of the empire. Most of the first British settlers in Australia were convicts being resettled from Britain; but as the regular British colonial population there grew and was uncomfortable with the practice, convict-placement ended in 1840. Australia received the right of self-government in 1850, and New Zealand received it two years later. Australia instituted the secret ballot and granted women the right to vote in the late 1800s, several years before these reforms took place in Britain itself.

Empire-building involved more than simply taking over territory. In 1854 Great Britain became involved in a war to stop Russian aggression against Turkey (the Ottoman Empire) in the region of Crimea on the Black Sea. Russia eventually capitulated in 1856; but fighting, bad weather, and disease took a terrible toll. The British nurse Florence Nightingale led a group of almost forty nurses to the Crimea to care for the sick and wounded.

The British presence in India was threatened in 1857 by an uprising of Indian soldiers at Delhi. Hundreds of Europeans were killed. However, the rebellion languished because of poor leadership; and British forces regained control in 1858, killing thousands of Indians in revenge.

Completion of the Suez Canal in 1869 eliminated the need to sail around Africa to get to Asia from Europe. This strengthened British trade and Britain's control of its colonies to the east. The canal was built by a French company but was controlled by Egypt. In 1875 Prime Minister Disraeli bought enough shares of the canal company on behalf of Great Britain to give Britain control of the canal. The canal was important for continued British growth in Africa and Asia as other European countries joined the rush for colonies.

Over time, British colonies gained or demanded more autonomy. The British Commonwealth was formed in 1931. The Commonwealth is mostly a friendly association of nations. Each member country is considered to be of equal status with Great Britain.

Britain's dominant position in the world went unchallenged for most of the 19th century. However, the costs and responsibilities of maintaining its empire proved difficult, as it has for every empire in history. The events of the 20th century seriously affected Great Britain's position.

For the kingdom is the Lord's
and He rules over the nations.
Psalm 22:28

Assignments for Lesson 106

In Their Words   Read the selected British Poetry (pages 263-268).

Literature   Continue reading *North and South*. Plan to finish it by the end of this unit.

Student Review   Optional: Answer the questions for Lesson 106.

Gallarus Oratory, a Medieval Chapel in County Kerry, Ireland

Lesson 107 - Key Issue

The Irish Question

The English people have made notable contributions to the culture of the world throughout their history. However, English leaders made many grave mistakes in their relations with the Irish. This lesson focuses on "the Irish question" for several reasons. First, it is an example of how colonialism can be harmful to the people living in the colony. Second, the British policy had a direct impact on the United States, as we will see. Third, the conflict between the British and the Irish has continued into our own day; and much blood has been shed because of this on-going disagreement, based largely on ethnic and religious prejudice.

A Long-Standing Conflict

In 1171 King Henry II responded to a letter from the pope asking for help in bringing the Irish Catholic Church more in line with standards that Rome had set. Henry went to Ireland and declared himself ruler of the land. Some Anglo-Norman lords had already taken large areas of the island, and they along with Irish kings who ruled small kingdoms gave their allegiance to the English throne. However, England did not make it a priority to seek strict control over the entire island. The English had greatest control over Dublin and the area around it, which was called the Pale. This led to a phrase that describes something outside the bounds of propriety: "beyond the pale."

Henry VIII and succeeding monarchs made a more concerted effort to exercise tighter control over Ireland. The monarchy used military expeditions as well as the strategy of encouraging English settlement in Ireland. It was still the English trying to dominate the Irish; but the added insult now (except during Mary's brief reign) was that English Anglicans were seeking control over Irish Catholics, and the Irish were none too happy about it.

The official Church of Ireland, supported by taxes that Irish Catholics had to pay, was Anglican. In the early 1600s, some Irish nobles left to live in Europe. The English kings confiscated their lands and promoted additional settlement by Protestants, especially in northern Ireland. This led to further migration from Scotland into the region, which is why Northern Ireland is predominantly Protestant. This was also the source of the Scots-Irish settlers who migrated to the American colonies in the 1700s.

After the Glorious Revolution of 1688, Irish Catholics supported the Catholic James II in his attempt to gain the throne. William of Orange defeated James and his Irish Catholic supporters in the Battle of the Boyne. The Act of Union in 1800 joined Ireland to Great Britain. Ireland was represented in Parliament, but only by Anglicans at first. Irish Catholics could not be elected to Parliament until 1829.

Political and economic power in Ireland belonged to the Protestants, who had strong ties to Great Britain. Most Irish Catholics were poor and politically powerless. They had to pay rent to (usually absentee) landlords. Large estates had been so divided and sub-divided that many Irish had to support their families just by what they could grow on their tiny plots. During the early 1800s, a small movement arose among Irish Catholics to urge separation from Britain. The movement gained almost no support from Protestants, who preferred being part of the group in power as opposed to being Irish nationalists.

Then came the potato famine.

Devastation and Death

The mainstay of Irish farming and food was the potato. A blight on potato plants ruined the crop in 1845 and again the next year. The people of Ireland experienced a terrible famine, even though Irish farms continued to produce other crops, and the English in Ireland exported food from the country. At the beginning of the decade, the population of Ireland was just over eight million. As a result of the famine, about one million people died.

During the 1840s and 1850s, about two million Irish emigrated to the United States. A total of 3.8 million people, including some from Northern Ireland, came to America between 1820 and 1900. This migration is the reason for the huge Irish influence in America, especially in large cities such as New York and Boston. Most Irish immigrants stayed in the cities to look for work. They wanted nothing more to do with farming.

The British government did almost nothing to help the suffering Irish. The British had been willing to benefit from rent payments from Irish tenants and wanted control over the land, but they turned a cold shoulder when the Irish were in need. No protection was offered when tenants could not pay their rent and were evicted.

The Push for Home Rule

Many Catholics in Ireland believed that they had suffered enough at the hands of the British. The movement for home rule, if not complete independence, grew slowly but steadily. An Irish Home Rule Party was formed in 1870. It quickly gained fifty seats in the House of Commons and won even more after that. Some Irish turned to terrorism, which included bombings and occasional

Aid came to Ireland during the Great Famine from a variety of sources, including the pope, the Society of Friends, Irish soldiers stationed in British India, Ottoman Sultan Abdülmecid I, and the Choctaw, who had experienced famine on the Trail of Tears just a few years earlier. Reminders of the famine are located across Ireland and in Irish communities around the world. These statues in Dublin were created by Irish artist Rowan Gillespie (b. 1953).

Lesson 107 - Key Issue: The Irish Question

assassinations of British officials. The violence, however, hurt their cause.

Parliament enacted some reforms. An 1869 law exempted Irish Catholics from paying taxes to support the Anglican Church. Laws passed about a decade later protected Irish tenants from sudden eviction, provided for equalized rents, and enabled the Irish to buy land.

Both the Conservative and Liberal Parties opposed home rule for Ireland. They feared that the Protestants in Northern Ireland would lose political power if Ireland had its own Parliament. It was one issue on which the vast majority of British politicians were united. However, in 1885 Liberal leader William Gladstone had a change of heart and decided to support home rule. He faced an uphill battle in getting a bill through Parliament since he had to convince his own party first. Gladstone tried more than once to get a home rule law passed, but he was never successful during his career.

Home Rule and Irish Independence

Parliament finally passed a home rule law in 1914, but the northern Protestant-dominated counties vowed to resist. The British government promised to give Ulster (another name for Northern Ireland) separate treatment. Enactment of the law was suspended because of the outbreak of World War I. Guerrilla warfare between the Irish Republican Army (IRA) and British defense soldiers led to several years of uncertainty.

A treaty signed in 1921 between the British government and a group of Irish leaders called for an Irish Free State as a separate dominion within the British Empire, with the six northern counties exempted from the dominion. More extreme Irish Catholics refused to accept the treaty because (1) they wanted all of Ireland to be together and (2) they wanted less of a connection to Great Britain.

The Irish Free State began in 1922. A new constitution was written in 1937 and the country's

This 1893 map describing and illustrating a proposal for Irish home rule was published in Massachusetts, home to a large number of Irish immigrants.

name was changed to Eire (the Gaelic name of the island). In 1948 the Republic of Ireland was formed as an independent nation outside of the British Commonwealth. After that point, the focus of continued conflict became Northern Ireland.

Northern Ireland

Extreme partisans on both sides hurt the cause of peace in Northern Ireland. Catholic groups such as a new IRA wanted a united Ireland and claimed to defend the rights of the minority Catholics in the North. Protestant extremists continued to see Catholics as the enemy. The Protestant government in the North found it difficult to maintain order. In 1972 Parliament dissolved the Northern Ireland government and imposed direct rule on the region. This only intensified Catholic resistance.

After almost thirty years of sectarian violence, an agreement was reached in 1998 to form a new Northern Ireland Assembly and a North-South Ministerial Council to discuss matters of concern for all of Ireland. The Republic of Ireland agreed to give up all territorial claims on Northern Ireland. Paramilitary groups were slow to disarm, but finally in December 1999 Britain ended direct rule. The United Kingdom oversees certain aspects of government in Northern Ireland, but most matters are left in the hands of the Northern Ireland Assembly and Executive.

The Irish Question, as many Britons called it in the 19th century, has defied an easy answer. The British desire to control other lands and their prejudice against the people of those lands certainly contributed to the problem, but both Protestants and Catholics in Ireland have been guilty of hate and violence. Satisfying everyone's complete list of demands might not be possible; but with all groups working together, a better solution can be reached than what any one group might propose.

Wash yourselves, make yourselves clean; remove the evil of your deeds from My sight. Cease to do evil, learn to do good; seek justice, reprove the ruthless, defend the orphan, plead for the widow.
Isaiah 1:16-17

Assignments for Lesson 107

In Their Words — Read the selection from *Fairy and Folk Tales of the Irish Peasantry* (pages 269-270).

Literature — Continue reading *North and South*.

Student Review — Optional: Answer the questions for Lesson 107.

One of the Former Orphan Houses at Ashley Down, Bristol, England

Lesson 108 - Key Person

George Müller

George Müller was a man of faith and prayer who made a remarkable impact on children in Bristol, England, and people around the world.

Müller was born on September 27, 1805, in Kroppenstaedt, Prussia. His father, a tax collector, was not a spiritually minded man. Left without proper training, young George wasted the first twenty years of his life in selfish pursuits. Before he was ten, George frequently stole money that his father had collected, forcing his father to juggle the books. This was only one of his admitted sins.

His father wanted George to become a minister so that he would have a comfortable livelihood. He sent George to school in Halberstadt. George's mother died when he was fourteen, but even this did not affect his wicked lifestyle.

George received confirmation in the Lutheran Church, but his heart was not committed to the Lord. He attempted on his own strength to turn away from his evil habits; he failed, and the bad habits got worse.

In 1821 when his father received a position in another city, George asked his father to have him transferred to a different school. He thought that getting away from his bad companions would help him change. Müller was still not relying on God, however; and his efforts at self-reform failed again.

At age sixteen he ended up in jail for failure to pay a hotel bill. He made the acquaintance of a thief, and they swapped stories about their exploits. George not only told his actual vices but made up additional stories to prove his wickedness.

George's father arranged for his release and beat him when they met again. George went to another school and even tutored pupils himself. His external behavior seemed better, but he knew his heart was still wicked.

By the time he was twenty, he had some three hundred books in his personal library, but no Bible. He participated in the Lord's Supper twice a year, reforming his habits for a few days each time; but he continued his life of hypocrisy.

He entered divinity school and knew that he would have to change his lifestyle in order to obtain a parish. His careless living was injurious to his health. He sought relief through travel, but even the beautiful scenes of Switzerland became tiresome.

One of Müller's friends had been convicted of his sins and started meeting with a group of believers. He told George about it, and George wanted to attend with him. The simple fellowship made a strong impression on Müller, and his attitude and

623

actions began to change. He started to read the Bible and pray and attend church for the right reasons.

Müller considered becoming a missionary. He told his father about his new perspective, but his father was angry and disappointed with his plans. Müller began to minister to people in Prussia, though his understanding was still immature.

For his first preaching opportunity, he memorized a sermon by another man. He recited that sermon in the morning, but for the afternoon service he decided to read Matthew chapter 5 and comment upon it. He realized that his memorized sermon had been too complex for his country audience. He later determined that simple exposition of God's word is suitable for any audience, learned or illiterate.

To England

George Müller went to England in 1829 to meet with the London Missionary Society. The group was looking for someone to work among Jews. Müller began to preach in London and to read Scripture with Jewish boys. He decided that he did not need to work under the direction of a missionary society, and he and the society kindly broke off their plans together. He gained experience preaching to groups and ministering to individuals in several places, trusting the Lord to help him choose suitable messages from Scripture.

George Müller and Mary Groves were married on October 7th, 1830. Together they decided to trust the Lord for their daily provision as they went about their service for him. Often when their means were low, the Lord sent them unexpected and unsought gifts.

George and Mary had a stillborn child in 1831. In 1832 the Müllers moved to Bristol, England; and there Mary gave birth to a girl. They had a son in 1834, but he died fifteen months later, a few days after Mary's father died.

Scriptural Knowledge Institution

George Müller and his fellow-worker Henry Craik formed the Scriptural Knowledge Institution in 1834. They were disappointed that many contemporary religious societies allowed wealthy unbelievers to direct their operations and contracted debts for their work. Müller and Craik wanted their institution to establish and support schools for children and adults that promoted Biblical teaching; to distribute Bibles; and to assist missionaries whose work adhered to principles of Scripture.

An orphan boy who enjoyed attending one of their schools was forced to move to a poorhouse outside Bristol. This prompted Müller's thoughts on how to help poor children in the city.

Making a Home for Orphans

In 1835 Müller became convinced of the need to establish a home for orphans. He wanted to give the children a basic education, train the girls for household work and the boys for trade, and with God's blessing, lead them to a knowledge of Jesus Christ. By trusting God to provide the means for the creation and continuance of the home, Müller also wanted to give believers and unbelievers a testimony to God's faithfulness, showing that God was able and willing to answer the prayers of his people.

Bethesda Chapel in Bristol, Where Müller and Craik Ministered

Lesson 108 - Key Person: George Müller

People began to offer money and furnishings and to volunteer to help run the home. The initial home opened in April 1836 intended for girls ages seven to twelve. In November of that year another home opened for boys and girls under seven. In October of 1837 a home for boys seven and up was prepared.

Müller avoided asking individuals to contribute to his efforts and avoided purchasing anything that he could not pay for at once. He made public his intentions and trusted God to provide what was needed. God showed his faithfulness on numerous occasions when supplies ran low. A cart of wood arrived when the coal had run out. Once after feeding the orphans their evening meal, nothing was left for breakfast the next day. When Müller was out walking the next morning, a friend met him and gave him five pounds.

By 1845 Müller saw the need to move the Orphan Houses. Nearby residents had raised complaints about the noise of the orphans during play time, and the size and situation of the homes was not suitable for the number of orphans living there. He also wanted ground to grow food and space to provide outdoor work for the boys.

A London architect volunteered to design the new buildings and oversee construction. A land owner offered his property at a discount, and people donated over 10,000 pounds to build and furnish the new homes. Eventually five homes for the care of 2,000 children were constructed on seven acres at Ashley Down, just outside Bristol.

The Initial, Rented Orphan Homes in Bristol

The children had a regular schedule of work, play, and study. They were well-dressed and well-educated (too well-educated, according to some critics). They enjoyed special celebrations such as an annual field day and a Christmas party. Eventually boys were kept until age fourteen and girls until age seventeen, but the children did not leave unless they had an employment opportunity. Upon leaving, each child received clothing and a sum of money, along with a Bible and a special blessing from George Müller. During his life, some 10,000 children received care in the homes.

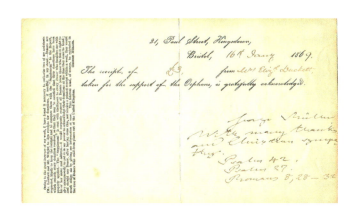

George Müller signed this receipt "with many thanks and Christian sympathy" acknowledging a gift of three pounds from a Mrs. Elizabeth Duckett in 1869. He listed Psalm 42, Psalm 27, and Romans 8:28-32. Müller's goal was for every donor to receive a written receipt within a week (unless they lived outside the United Kingdom, when the mail would take longer).

Author Charles Dickens heard rumors that the children in the homes were not getting enough food. After he visited the orphanage, he was convinced that the rumors were false. These photographs show various aspects of life for the children. Clockwise from right are a dining room, boys playing tug of war, girls at the swings on the annual outing to Purdown, the five New Orphan Homes at Ashley Down, girls in a schoolroom, and the Babies Dormitory.

Lesson 108 - Key Person: George Müller

A New Phase

George Müller's wife Mary died in 1870. Their daughter Lydia and her husband James Wright took a leading role in managing the homes about this time. George married Susannah Sanger in November 1871, and together they began a new phase in Müller's ministry.

From 1875 to 1892, George and Susannah made numerous missionary tours around the world. George preached in forty-two countries in Europe, Africa, Asia, Oceania, and North America. Since he knew English, French, and German, he could speak directly to a variety of audiences. Translators helped him in other places.

Müller's seven goals for his travels were to preach the simple gospel message, to help believers rejoice in their salvation, to encourage serious Bible study, to promote unity among believers, to strengthen their faith, to encourage separation from the world, and to help disciples fix their hope on the coming of Christ.

His Legacy

George Müller did not consider the orphans' homes to be his. He did not want his name attached to them. He saw them as God's homes. During his life, he was able to see the effect that his example had on believers who benefited from his example and on the children who lived in the homes.

In 1880 Müller received a letter from a man and wife, both former orphans in the homes. This couple had three orphan boys working for them as apprentices. With their letter, they included a donation for the continuing work:

Dear and honoured Sir, I desire to acknowledge with thanks the receipt of the second half of premium on account of C. B. You will be pleased to hear he is getting on very nicely with his trade, and his behaviour is all we could desire. The same can be said of J. D. He confesses his faith in the Lord Jesus Christ, in whom also J. D. is rejoicing. As regards ourselves, we daily continue to pray, as we have done for many years, for blessing on the dear Orphan Work, and those engaged in it. We greatly rejoice in its continued prosperity, as well becomes us, who have received such inestimable spiritual and temporal blessings through its instrumentality. Will you please use £3. 10s. of the enclosed for the support of one Orphan for three months, and the remaining 10s. for Foreign Missions? and accept with it the grateful love of two former Orphans.

George Müller, About Age Ninety

George Müller's tombstone was "erected by the spontaneous and loving gifts" of orphans who had received care in the homes he founded.

George Müller died in Bristol on March 10, 1898, at age ninety-two. His second wife Susannah had died in 1894. Concerning how the work he began might continue after his death, George had said, "My business is, with all my might, to serve my own generation by the will of God: in so doing I shall best serve the next generation, should the Lord Jesus tarry." His work did continue. His son-in-law James Wright helped to oversee the work after Müller's death, though Müller's daughter Lydia had died in 1890. Today, the George Müller Foundation carries on a ministry of care, faith, and evangelism in Bristol and around the world through the Scriptural Knowledge Institution.

George Müller spent his life in the confident belief that the God he served in the 19th century was the same God of past centuries who listens to the prayers of His children and gives them the help they need.

*Pure and undefiled religion in the sight of our God and Father is this:
to visit orphans and widows in their distress,
and to keep oneself unstained by the world.
James 1:27*

Assignments for Lesson 108

In Their Words Read "Real Faith" (pages 271-273).

Literature Continue reading *North and South*.

Student Review Optional: Answer the questions for Lesson 108.

The Karakoram Highway, opened to the public in 1986, connects China and Pakistan.

Lesson 109 - Everyday Life

A History of Transportation

Improved transportation in Britain helped industry grow as products could be shipped to more markets faster. Canal building began in Britain in the mid-1700s. The first practical railroad engine was unveiled in England in 1829. It could move at an amazing 36 miles per hour. Between 1850 and 1860, some 5,000 miles of railroad track were laid in Britain. With the advent of steel rails, trains could speed along at 60 miles per hour. Railroads helped business in many ways. Besides carrying goods faster and making more markets available, railroads increased the demand for coal and steel. At first, however, railroads frightened many people. Coach and canal owners feared the competition that rail lines presented. Property owners near the tracks as well as potential passengers disliked the fire hazard that engines presented. Some people wondered if humans could survive the outrageous speeds that trains traveled.

People have always found it necessary—or entertaining—to travel from place to place. From ships to bridges to trains to subways to the Channel Tunnel, the people of Britain have needed ways to get around the island and to get from there to the rest of the world. This is a good time to look back on the history of transportation.

Travel in the Bible

People in the Bible were often going from place to place. Noah and his family traveled on the ark. People spread out over the world from the tower of Babel. Abram moved from Ur to Haran and then to Canaan. Jacob and his family, seventy persons, moved to Egypt during a famine. Centuries later, the Israelites—hundreds of thousands of them—traveled across the Sinai Desert from Egypt to the Promised Land.

The most common means of transportation in Bible times was walking. Some people were able to afford camels (Genesis 24:10), donkeys (Numbers 22:21), or horses (2 Kings 18:23). Animals pulled wagons (Genesis 45:19), carts (Numbers 7:3-9), and chariots (Acts 8:25-40).

Long roads connected distant cities. Moses told the king of Edom they would go along the king's highway (Numbers 20:17). Moses told the Israelites to prepare roads (Deuteronomy 19:3). A highway went from Bethel to Shechem (Judges 21:19). Philip met the Ethiopian eunuch on the road that ran from Jerusalem to Gaza (Acts 8:26).

People traveled across water by boat, sometimes with human rowers (Jonah 1:13) and other times with wind power (James 3:4).

629

Roads, Tunnels, and Bridges

Roads made of brick or stone were built in ancient Persia, India, China, and Rome. Darius I built the 1,500-mile Persian Royal Road from Susa to the Aegean Sea. The Romans built the 350-mile Appian Way to connect Italy and Greece. Parts of it are still used today. A series of land routes connecting Rome and China was established over time. This network was called the Silk Road.

Spanish conquistadors built the first major American roads during the 1500s and 1600s. One stretched from Vera Cruz, Mexico, to San Francisco. Another went from Santa Fe, New Mexico, to St. Augustine, Florida. In the mid-1600s in England and in the late 1700s in the U.S., privately-operated turnpikes were popular. Turnpike owners charged tolls for the privilege of traveling on their roads.

Between 1816 and 1820 John McAdam of Scotland invented a way to improve the surface of roads. His roads were raised and drained well and made of crushed stone and gravel. Tar, a waste product of the gas industry, was added in the 1830s. The roads were called "Macadamized" roads. In 1921 the world's first highway opened in Berlin, Germany. It was called the Avus Autobahn and was also used as a racetrack.

The oldest remaining tunnel is on the Greek island of Samos in the Aegean Sea. Built in 687 BC, it is about 3,300 feet long. The first railroad tunnel in the world was the Mont Cenis, built in 1871 through the Alps between France and Italy. It is 8.5 miles long. The largest-diameter single-bore tunnel in the world contains two levels of traffic. It was built in 1936 through Yerba Buena Island in the San Francisco Bay in California. The

Percy Shaw, a British inventor, patented cat's-eye road studs in 1934. They were inspired by the eyes of a real cat that had helped him avoid driving off a cliff. In Ireland, as seen in this photo, yellow cat's eyes are used to mark the outside edges of roads.

longest highway tunnel in the world, completed in 2000, goes fifteen miles through a mountainous area in Norway. The Japanese islands of Honshû and Hokkaidô are connected by the world's longest undersea railway tunnel, opened in 1988. The Channel Tunnel connects the island of Great Britain with the mainland of Europe. The "Chunnel" has both a highway and a rail track. It was opened to the public in 1994.

The ancient Romans perfected the stone arch. They used it to build the first large-scale bridges. Some are still standing today. The largest remaining Roman bridge is in southern France and is 886 feet long. The Anji (or Zhaocheng) bridge in China was built in the seventh century AD. It is an arch of limestone wedges reinforced with iron.

Some bridges of the Middle Ages included a chapel. During the Renaissance, some bridges had shops on them. Rent from these shops was used to finance other public works. The first major bridge made completely of iron was the Ironbridge at Coalbrookdale, England, completed in 1779. Thomas Telford was a Scottish engineer who designed the Menai Suspension Bridge. Completed in Wales in 1826, it was the world's first major suspension bridge. The Forth Bridge over the Firth of Forth in Scotland was the first major structure built entirely of steel. This cantilevered bridge was completed in 1890.

Lesson 109 - Everyday Life: A History of Transportation

Norwegian Thor Heyerdahl (1914-2002) believed that ancient people had the knowledge and ability to make long sea voyages, such as from Africa to Central America. Many other scholars disagree with his theories about ancient travel, but he demonstrated the possibility by constructing boats using traditional methods. At right is Heyerdahl's ship called Kon-Tiki, *in which he and his team sailed from Peru to the Tuamotu Islands in Polynesia. The ship is now housed at the Kon-Tiki Museum in Norway.*

Reinforced concrete was invented in 1867 by a French gardener, Joseph Monier. He made flowerpots from concrete and wire netting. One of the first engineers to use reinforced concrete in bridges was the Frenchman Francois Hennebique. He designed bridges built at Viggen, Switzerland, in 1894, and Chaterallerault, France, in 1898.

Transportation on Seas and Oceans

Thousands of years ago ships in the Middle East had sails. An early clay model of a ship dug up at Eridu in Mesopotamia had a place to hold a mast and holes for ropes. Ancient Egyptians built boats from papyrus reeds and from timber.

The best shipbuilders of the ancient world were the Phoenicians. Other nations hired Phoenician sailors for their own navies. Most of Ancient Phoenicia is now part of Lebanon. Tyre was a coastal city. Ezekiel 27:1-9 gives a description of a Phoenician ship. The ship had a cedar mast and oak oars. The boxwood deck was inlaid with ivory. The sail was fine embroidered linen from Egypt and the awning was blue and purple.

The Phoenicians developed galley ships with many oarsmen. The galley was a better warship. Greeks also used galley ships. Some had two or even three levels of oarsmen. Romans developed galley ships that could carry as many as one hundred men.

When Arabs attacked Byzantine ports in the seventh and eighth centuries AD, their ships had lateen sails as had been used on Roman ships. The Chinese used a sailing ship called a junk. It had four or more masts. The sails were stiffened with bamboo battens to make them more efficient. By the 800s they regularly traveled in the waters of China, Japan, and Southeast Asia. Between 1405 and 1433, Chinese explorer Zheng He commanded a fleet of about 200 ships and voyaged across the Indian Ocean, the Arabian Sea, and the Red Sea.

This is a reproduction of one of the treasure ships used by Chinese Admiral Zheng He (1371-1433). It is located in Nanjing, China, a leading city of the Ming Dynasty during his life.

An 18th-Century Persian Astrolabe

Around 1090 Chinese and Arab sailors began using the magnetic compass. This made it possible to travel long distances on the ocean. Before that time the Chinese had used a lodestone spoon spinning on a brass plate to determine direction. The astrolabe had been used by astronomers for centuries. Between 1470 and 1480 European seafarers adapted it for use as a navigation instrument. These inventions paved the way for the great explorers of the 15th and 16th centuries.

Caravel ships used by European explorers in the 1400s had lateen sails on three masts: the foremast, the mainmast, and the rear mizzenmast. A larger version of the caravel, called a galleon, was used to haul cargo from newly-discovered lands. One famous galleon was the *Mayflower*. Frigates, sloops, brigs, and clippers were the sailing ships of the 1600s and 1700s. Today sailing ships are used for sport.

In 1731 the octant was invented by John Hadley of England and—independently—by Thomas Godfrey of Philadelphia. It used twin mirrors aligned with the reflection of the sun or a star to determine latitude. The marine clock (or chronometer) was invented in 1759 by Englishman John Harrison. It was accurate to 30 seconds a year. The sextant was an adaptation of the octant. John Campbell completed it in 1757. When they used it with a chronometer, sailors could measure their exact position on the sea.

The *Savannah*, the first steamship to cross the Atlantic Ocean, used steam for ninety hours and used sails for the rest of its month-long journey in 1819. As steamships developed, they included the following features: paddle wheels, screw propellers, iron and steel hulls, double- and triple-expansion steam engines, steam turbines, and diesel-powered steam engines. Today's cargo, passenger, and military ships are powered by petroleum or by nuclear energy.

Underwater Transportation

Aristotle wrote about diving bells used by soldiers of Alexander the Great to clear the Tyre harbor. They were bell-shaped wooden barrels worn over the head. By 1538 divers in Spain were using diving bells. Edmund Halley (of Halley's Comet fame) in 1716 invented a wooden diving bell with windows and leather tubes for air. Divers could stay underwater at a depth of about 60 feet for ninety minutes. Copper helmets came in the 1800s.

A Dutchman, Cornelius Drebbel, built for King James of England in 1620 the first submarine that could be controlled underwater. The submarine had a wooden frame covered with greased leather. It leaked badly, but oarsmen could row it down the Thames River thirteen feet below the surface. King James even took a ride himself.

This reproduction of Drebbel's submarine was successfully tested underwater.

Lesson 109 - Everyday Life: A History of Transportation

Venice, Italy, is built on 120 small islands separated by canals. Gondolas were the traditional means of transportation, though motorized craft are now widely used. This painting of The Grand Canal *is by Canaletto (Italian, c. 1738).*

Canals and Locks

At 1200 miles long, the Grand Canal in China is the world's oldest canal system. The concept is attributed to Yang Guang, second monarch of the Sui dynasty. It connected and expanded existing canals, the oldest of which dated from the fifth century BC. The system was dredged and modernized between 1958 and 1964. In 1817 work began on the Erie Canal, which linked New York City to the Great Lakes. It was completed in 1825. The Suez Canal in Egypt was completed in 1869. It allowed ships to sail from the Red Sea to the Mediterranean and cut the distance from Europe to India by about forty percent. In 1904 work began on the Panama Canal. When it opened in 1914 it linked the Pacific Ocean and the Caribbean Sea.

The invention of locks greatly improved inland water transportation. The Chinese used a simple lock as early as 984. Holland has had a usable lock system since 1373. In the late 1400s, Italians invented the pound lock, which is the forerunner of modern locks.

Trains

In 1803 Richard Trevithick, an English engineer, invented a railroad locomotive. In 1808 he was commissioned to build a locomotive demonstrating the power of steam. The locomotive was called Catch-Me-Who-Can. He exhibited it on a circular track in London.

The first practical demonstration of an electric train was at an exhibition in Berlin in 1879. In 1880 a French laundry began to use electric trains. After workers spread linen sheets in meadows to bleach them, they used electric trains to collect the sheets. The electric trains were cleaner than steam trains.

Bicycles

In 1839 Scotsman Kirkpatrick Macmillan invented the first bicycle. It was called a velocipede. In 1845 R.W. Thomason patented the pneumatic tire. In 1888 an Irish veterinarian, John Boyd Dunlop, adapted the velocipede to make a more comfortable bicycle for his son.

The Southern Fuegian Railway, designed as a freight railway for a prison colony at the tip of South America, was used during the first half of the 20th century. Service was restarted in 1994 for tourist trips, making it the southernmost operational railway in the world.

An 1887 German encyclopedia featured these illustrations of various models of the velocipede.

Internal Combustion Engines

In 1859 Etienne Lenoir, a Frenchman, built the first practical internal combustion engine. It did not compete with steam until German Nikolaus August Otto built a better one in 1878. Gottlieb Daimler, a German, made the first high-speed lightweight gasoline engines in 1884. In 1885 he invented the motorcycle. He used it to test the practicality of gas-powered road vehicles. The first motorcycle was made of wood.

Karl Benz of Germany made a tricycle with a single-cylinder gas engine in 1885. It went about eight miles per hour. Benz built a four-wheel vehicle by 1893. German engineer Rudolph Diesel built the first diesel engine in 1892.

Henry Ford worked as an engineer for the Edison Illuminating Company and experimented with engines in his spare time. He built his first car in 1896. He and eleven investors started the Ford Motor Company in 1903. After experimenting with Models A through S, they found that their financial future lay in an inexpensive car for the masses. By 1927 they had made 15 million Model Ts.

Air Transportation

Balloons. In 1783 paper-makers Joseph and Etienne Montgolfier launched the first passenger-carrying hot-air balloon in Paris. It flew for 5.5 miles.

Parachutes. In 1783 another Frenchman, Louis Lenormand, jumped from a tree and later a tower in the French town of Montpellier wearing a parachute. Leonardo da Vinci had suggested the device in one of his manuscripts, and the ancient Chinese might have understood the principle of the parachute.

Airships. In 1852 Henri Giffard, a French inventor, built the first airship that worked. It had a steam engine that drove it at 6 mph. An airship is different from a balloon in that it has a source of power.

This photo of a reproduction of the 1885 Benz Patent Motorwagen was taken in 2007 in Frankfurt, Germany.

Lesson 109 - Everyday Life: A History of Transportation

Alberto Santos-Dumont (1873-1932), son of a wealthy Brazilian coffee farmer, enjoyed reading the books of Jules Verne as a boy. After his family moved to France in 1891, he studied science and mechanics. He began experimenting with dirigibles (steerable balloons), winning a prize in 1901 that required flying around the Eiffel Tower. He also used an airship for personal transportation in Paris, often landing in front of a cafe.

In 1906 Santos-Dumont demonstrated his new heavier-than-air plane, the 14-bis (depicted in the French magazine shown above). This was after the Wright brothers' flights of 1903-1905, but since Santos-Dumont's flight was public and his plane took off on its own power, he is hailed in Brazil as the father of aviation. The first Brazilian astronaut, Marcos Cesar Pontes, flew on a mission to the International Space Station in 2006, honoring the 100th anniversary of Santos-Dumont's flight.

Glider. Englishman George Cayley built a glider big enough to carry a pilot. His reluctant coachman was the first to fly it. Afterwards, the coachman promptly quit his job. The German Otto Lilienthal made a hang glider around 1891. He made hundreds of flights in it.

Airplane. In 1903 Orville and Wilbur Wright flew their Flyer aircraft at Kitty Hawk, North Carolina. They had solved the problems of lift, control, and power.

Helicopter. Heinrich Focke introduced the first practical helicopter in 1936. It had two rotors turning in opposite directions. Near that time, Igor Sikorsky developed one in America that used a single rotor.

Jet. The first jet aircraft flew in 1939. It was built by German inventor Ernst Heinkel, who used information developed by Englishman Frank Whittle. Whittle had the idea for a jet engine in 1928, got a patent in 1930, and built a prototype in 1937.

Supersonic. A Soviet supersonic plane, the Tupolev Tu-144 was first tested in 1968, but production delays allowed the Concorde to become the world's first supersonic passenger aircraft. It was built jointly by British and French companies. The final Concorde flight was in 2003.

Cockpit of the Aérospatiale-BAC Concorde

London's Metropolitan Railway, the world's first underground line, opened in 1863. Steam locomotives pulled wooden carriages between two stations on a four-mile track. The next subways opened in Budapest, Hungary, and Glasgow, Scotland, in 1896; followed by Boston (1897), Paris (1900), Berlin (1902), and New York (1904). Today the London Undergound system (known as the Tube) has 270 stations along 250 miles of track. It carries over one billion passengers per year.

The chariots race madly in the streets,
They rush wildly in the squares,
Their appearance is like torches,
They dash to and fro like lightning flashes.
Nahum 2:4

Assignments for Lesson 109

Literature   Continue reading *North and South*.

Student Review   Optional: Answer the questions for Lesson 109.

Many poor Irish were evicted from their homes in the 1800s.

Lesson 110 - Bible Study

Kindness

The British government failed to show kindness to the Irish throughout their governing of Ireland, but especially during the potato famine of the 1840s. Much interpersonal and international conflict could be avoided if people practiced more kindness toward others.

God Is Kind

We should be kind to others first of all because our Father in heaven is kind. In his prayer, Nehemiah proclaimed, "You are a God of forgiveness, gracious and compassionate, slow to anger and abounding in lovingkindness" (Nehemiah 9:17). "His lovingkindness is great toward us," rejoiced the psalmist (Psalm 117:2). God has shown kindness to His people over and over.

Jesus told His followers, "Love your enemies, and do good, and lend, expecting nothing in return; and your reward will be great, and you will be sons of the Most High; for He Himself is kind to ungrateful and evil men" (Luke 6:35). We are not called to be kind just when others are kind to us. Instead, we are to be kind even when people are ungrateful and evil. Others deserve our kindness not on the basis of their actions but simply on the basis of what we are to do as God's people. Our kindness, like the kindness of God, is to be based not on the character of others but on our renewed character and on the character of our Father.

Our walk with God is to be influenced by God's kindness. Peter told his readers to long for the milk of the word in order to grow with respect to salvation "if you have tasted the kindness of the Lord" (1 Peter 2:2-3). Peter is not saying "if" you have tasted the Lord's kindness as much as he is saying "since" you have tasted the Lord kindness. He knows that all Christians, indeed all people, have been blessed by the kindness of God. Therefore we should long for the milk of God's word. One way that we demonstrate a renewed character is the way we respond to God's kindness.

The Lord's Commandment

Second, we are to be kind because God instructs us to be kind:

He has told you, O man, what is good;
And what does the Lord require of you
But to do justice, to love kindness,
And to walk humbly with your God?
  (Micah 6:8)

Compassion International is a global ministry that works through local churches to meet the spiritual, economic, social, and physical needs of children such as these in Uganda.

"Be kind to one another, tender-hearted, forgiving each other, just as God in Christ also has forgiven you" (Ephesians 4:32). We are to apply to "godliness, brotherly kindness" (2 Peter 1:7). "Love is patient, love is kind" (1 Corinthians 13:4). Kindness is part of the fruit of the Spirit that Christians are to bear, showing that the Spirit is working within us (Galatians 5:22).

The Lord's commands are not burdensome. We make them a burden if we try to rationalize our disobedience or if we split theological hairs about the meaning of this or that word, as the lawyer did when he wanted to justify himself by asking Jesus, "Who is my neighbor?" (Luke 10:29). The Lord's commandments will challenge us in areas in which we need to grow. This need to grow is what can be difficult. Kindness, like love, is not an emotion. It is a characteristic we are to demonstrate. Feelings of kindness will likely follow our actions of kindness, but we need to be kind even when we don't feel like it.

The Value of Others

Third, kindness demonstrates the value that we place on other people. It shows that we believe them to be worthy of our kindness. The lawyer who came to Jesus with questions wanted to draw a line on his kindness. He thought that some people did not deserve his kindness. In the story of the good Samaritan that Jesus told in response to the lawyer's question, the priest and the Levite who did not help the hurt man showed that they did not think he was worthy of their help (Luke 10:30-37).

Lesson 110 - Bible Study: Kindness

In the great judgment scene that Jesus described in which the sheep are separated from the goats, the goats would have gladly been kind to Jesus if they had realized His need because they believed He was worthy of it. The sheep, on the other hand, pleased God by their actions. They understood that all people deserve our kindness because of their intrinsic worth as human beings created in God's image (Matthew 25:31-46).

Examples of Kindness

In the description of the worthy woman in Proverbs 31, the writer says, "She opens her mouth in wisdom, and the teaching of kindness is on her tongue" (Proverbs 31:26). One important way that we can show kindness to others is by our words. Even things that need to be said and correction that needs to be given can be said with kindness. In fact, they will be more effective if they are spoken in this way.

The passages we have cited in this lesson provide illustrations of what it means to be kind. Treating others with justice; showing love, patience, and forgiveness; doing good without expecting payback; helping others who are in need; and speaking kindly to others are all ways that we can show kindness.

When the people of Israel asked Rehoboam, the son of Solomon, to lighten the heavy yoke of service that Solomon had placed on them, the elders of Israel advised Rehoboam, "If you will be kind to this people and please them and speak good words to them, then they will be your servants forever" (2 Chronicles 10:7). Rehoboam did not heed this advice, and as a result he sowed seeds of division among his people that caused problems for hundreds of years. If the British government had considered the advice of the elders of Israel with regard to their relations with the Irish, they could have spared both sides much heartache.

We are in this world to be a blessing to others, not to see what we can acquire for ourselves.

Giovanni de Fiesole (c. 1395-1455) was an Italian friar and painter. He was known as Fra Angelico ("Angelic Friar") for his modest and generous lifestyle. This is his depiction of The Last Judgment *(c. 1431).*

The way of Jesus is one of kindness toward others because of the way God is and because of the value of other people. If we are unkind, not only do we devalue others but we also devalue ourselves because all people share the same value in God's eyes.

One reason people are unkind to others is because they have a mistaken view of their own worth. Either they think too highly of themselves in comparison to others and feel no need to be kind, or they think of themselves as worthless and wind up doing worthless deeds. In either case, they are wrong. We are sinners loved by God and saved by His kindness, and as followers of the God of kindness we are to be kind.

He who oppresses the poor taunts his Maker, but he who is gracious to the needy honors Him.
Proverbs 14:31

Assignments for Lesson 110

Bible — Recite or write James 1:26-27 from memory.

In Their Words — Read the letter by Florence Nightingale (pages 274-275).

Literature — Finish reading *North and South*. Literary analysis available in *Student Review*.

Project — Complete your project for the unit.

Student Review — Optional: Answer the questions for Lesson 110 and for *North and South*, and take the quiz for Unit 22.

This is the April 1931 cover of the Soviet magazine Bezbozhnik ("The Atheist"). It depicts on the left men representing Capitalism, Religion, and Fascism preventing the workers of the world from following the example of the Soviets on the right.

23

A Revolution in Thought

Summary

The late 19th and early 20th centuries brought a series of new ideas that challenged existing beliefs. Karl Marx shook common notions about society and work. Charles Darwin challenged the traditional understanding of where we came from. Sigmund Freud published unsettling theories about who we are within. John Dewey proposed radical ideas about teaching children. Most threatening of all, higher critics took aim at the reliability of the Bible. We are still coping with the revolution in thought that these men encouraged.

Lessons

111 - Karl Marx
112 - Charles Darwin
113 - Sigmund Freud
114 - Everyday Life: Education and the Work of John Dewey
115 - Bible Study: Higher Criticism

Memory Work — Learn Colossians 3:12-15 by the end of the unit.

Books Used
The Bible
In Their Words
The Hiding Place

Project (choose one)

1) Write 300 to 500 words on one of the following topics:

- What is the best way to educate children? See Lesson 114.

- If you were asked to describe your views on the origin of the world, what would you say? See Lesson 112.

2) Create a collection of photos showing examples of God's handiwork in Creation. See Lesson 112. Compose your photos intentionally and artistically. Your finished project should be in the form of a slideshow on an electronic device, prints of the photographs displayed on a poster, or photos in book form. Include a minimum of twenty photos.

3) Write and illustrate a children's book on the history of education. See Lesson 114. Include several key groups and individuals who influenced education.

Literature

The horrors of Nazi oppression and concentration camps are vividly portrayed in Corrie ten Boom's classic book, *The Hiding Place*. Corrie (1892-1983) was the daughter of a watchmaker in the Netherlands. Her family were devout Christians. Nazi occupation of their country was bad enough, but the systematic persecution of Jews by the Nazis was even worse. The ten Boom family decided to do something to help, so they arranged a hiding place in their home for Jews.

The Nazis eventually found out about what they were doing and shipped the entire family off to concentration camps. There, Corrie's faith continued to shine; and she survived the horrible experience, though other family members did not. Corrie dedicated her life to telling others about her experiences and about how Jesus was real even in a concentration camp. It is a testimony to the power of God that people of faith were able to bear such a strong witness for Him during that awful time. This is a story that needs to be told.

Corrie ten Boom in later life.

Mysore, India (2004)

Lesson 111

Karl Marx

The Communists disdain to conceal their views and aims. They openly declare that their ends can be attained only by the forcible overthrow of all existing social conditions. Let the ruling classes tremble at a Communistic revolution. The proletarians have nothing to lose but their chains. They have a world to win. Working men of all countries, unite!

These chilling words come at the end of the Communist Manifesto, written in 1848 by Karl Marx and Friedrich Engels. Marx is one of the most influential thinkers and writers of the last two hundred years. His ideas gave justification to socialist theories and to the Communist revolutions of the 20th century. His concepts about economics have influenced many economists, philosophers, and politicians since his day.

Karl Marx was born in Germany in 1818. His father was a lawyer who held a position in the Prussian government. The Marx family was Jewish, but Karl's father had become a member of the Lutheran Church. Some historians believe that he did this to keep his job.

The younger Marx attended the University of Berlin to study law but became interested in history and philosophy. He earned a doctorate in philosophy in 1841. While in school, Marx became enamored with the views of history expressed by G. W. F. Hegel, which we will discuss below. As a young man, Marx developed a friendship and writing partnership with Friedrich Engels, the son of a wealthy textile manufacturer. Marx became increasingly radical in his opposition to capitalism. After receiving his doctorate, he became the editor of a newspaper and wrote such scathing editorials that the government shut the paper down in 1843.

Karl Marx, 1875

Marx moved to Paris and eventually to London. He returned to Germany during the 1848 revolution, but when it failed he returned to England and lived there the rest of his life. Marx and his family lived in near poverty conditions for many years while he wrote and researched. His later years were marked by illness and depression. His wife and oldest daughter died shortly before his own death in 1883.

Hegel and Feuerbach

G. W. F. Hegel (1771-1830) was a German historian and philosopher whose ideas have influenced many other philosophers. Instead of seeing history as a straight line of events or as a chain of events guided by God, Hegel saw the course of history as a swirl of often conflicting ideas that he called the historical dialectic. The dominant idea at any one time in history he called the thesis. However, some people always opposed the dominant idea and believed in the opposite idea; this he called the antithesis. As these ideas opposed each other and often influenced each other, the result was what Hegel called the synthesis. This synthesis became the new thesis, and the process began again. Hegel understood that this development was not always clear and neat, but he believed that this is how mankind progressed.

For instance, at one point the dominant idea or thesis of Western thought was the absolutism of kings. The antithesis was the desire by nobles for more political power. The synthesis was the practice of limited monarchy with power shared by a representative assembly whose members consisted of and were chosen by landowning men. This new thesis was then opposed by a new antithesis, namely those who wanted all males to be able to vote. The synthesis was a move toward broader voting rights.

Marx was also influenced by the writing of another German philosopher, Ludwig Feuerbach (1804-1872). Feuerbach believed that religion was an invention of man, a mere projection of

Feuerbach (pictured above) published Das Wesen des Christentums *in 1841. The 1854 English translation by Marian Evans (the novelist whose pen name was George Eliot) was called* The Essence of Christianity.

man's ideals into a system of beliefs about the supernatural which, in his thinking, did not exist. In creating this spiritual realm above himself, man alienated himself from himself. Man cast himself as a lowly creature who needed the church and the government to help him become better. Feuerbach believed in the ability of man to improve himself without what Feuerbach considered a fabricated belief system.

The Writings of Marx and Engels

An organization of working men in London asked Marx and Engels to write a statement of purpose for them. The result was the 1848 Communist Manifesto. Marx and Engels wrote many other books and articles, but their best known other work is *Das Kapital (Capital)*, a detailed study of economics. The first volume appeared in 1867;

Lesson 111 - Karl Marx

two later volumes were published by Engels after Marx's death.

Marx totally rejected belief in God and any spiritual reality. "Man is the world of man," he wrote; and he wanted "man to be the supreme being for man." The spiritual weapon to reach the hearts of men, he believed, was philosophy, a man-based belief system. "Religion is the sigh of the oppressed creature, the heart of a heartless world, and the soul of soulless conditions. It is the opium of the people." As a thorough-going materialist who completely rejected moral and spiritual absolutes, Marx believed that he could define his own values, identifying what was good, noble, and worthwhile from his own viewpoint.

Second, Marx did not see his perspective as merely his viewpoint. To him his conclusions were undeniable fact. Marx believed that, just as nature had laws that it obeyed, history had laws that mankind obeyed. A scientific study of history, he believed, led to inescapable conclusions—his.

Marx believed that the key to history was economics. Economic forces determine events, he said. The primary factor at any given place and time in history was what he called the mode of production, how goods in society were produced. In his day, the mode of production was controlled by the bourgeoisie or wealthy middle class. The proletariat (workers) were used by the bourgeoisie to produce the goods that fed the economy. The profit or excess value of the goods produced should go to the workers, Marx said; but instead it was taken by the capitalists while the workers suffered in misery. Picking up on an idea from Feuerbach, Marx said that man had become alienated from his true and better self by accepting the idea that he was working only for himself instead of for the good of all mankind. Thus the workers were chained to a system that victimized them but that they had accepted.

All of history, Marx claimed, was the story of class struggle. Capitalism had been the dominant thesis of history, but he believed capitalism was collapsing. Now it was time for the antithesis to emerge. He believed that the workers of the world would rise up, unite as one body, and overthrow the bourgeois capitalists. Since Marx believed that this was a good end, he justified the use of violence to achieve it. This overthrow would be followed by a temporary dictatorship of the proletariat, in which the workers (and the intellectuals like Marx, of course) would be in charge. Enemies of the system would have to be done away with, including Christians. Members of the Communist Party, i.e., those who could be trusted, would fulfill positions of responsibility in the government.

This statue by Ludwig Engelhardt is located in the Marx-Engels Forum in Berlin, Germany. Dedicated in 1986 under the Communist government of the German Democratic Republic (East Germany), it honors Marx (seated) and Engels (standing). After East and West Germany reunited in 1990, some Germans argued that the park should be removed. It was retained for historical and artistic reasons.

This period would transition into socialism, in which all modes of production would belong to the state. Then would come the phase of communism, in which each person would work according to his ability and receive according to his need. At this point, the state would simply wither away as unnecessary since the proletariat would be in charge and would not need to be controlled by a government. This would be the final dialectic that would end the Hegelian model.

Failings of Marxism

By rejecting any idea of the supernatural, Marx rejected as mere illusions the working of God and all spiritual motives that people have for what they do. He claimed to be scientific and objective in his analysis, but in fact he interpreted history to support the ideas he wanted to promote. Marx claimed that all of history was the history of class struggle; however, as important as economics and class struggle have been in history, these have not been the only issues.

Marx and Engels were disgusted by the working conditions they saw in mines and factories, and their condemnation of these exploitative practices was just. The owners and capitalist backers of these ventures should have cared more about the working conditions that their employees endured. However, most workers were not interested in overthrowing the government and the entire economic and political system. They simply wanted to be treated fairly and to be able to support their families. Marx also did not consider the patriotic feelings that workers had. This was much more powerful than any desire to unite with workers around the world.

The Influence of Marxism

Marxist thought has had an impact on others besides Communists. It has influenced the development of what is called democratic socialism, especially in Europe, as governments there have taken over more and more aspects of what was the private economy. Government-controlled health care is one example.

Two spinoffs of Marxism have been anarchism and liberation theology. Anarchism was the desire for a complete and immediate overthrow of government, although what was to happen after that took place was never clear. Anarchists assassinated several European heads of state in the late 19th and early 20th centuries. Max Stirner (1806-1856) was a German philosopher whose ideas contributed to modern anarchism. The sketch of Stirner at right was drawn by Friedrich Engels.

Liberation theology arose in the 20th century in South and Central America. Gustavo Gutiérrez (b. 1928, pictured below), a Peruvian Catholic priest, published A Theology of Liberation *in 1971. He argued that Christians should identify with the plight of the poor and work toward more just social systems. Combining these arguments with Marxist ideas, some proponents of liberation theology redefined the mission of Christ to say that He was an economic liberator. Sin to them was the ownership of wealth by a few and righteousness was the redistribution of wealth to the people. The overthrow of an oppressive government (to "liberate" the people, by violence if necessary) was seen as a positive step to bring this about. Liberation theology has been used as a religious justification for political radicalism.*

Lesson 111 - Karl Marx

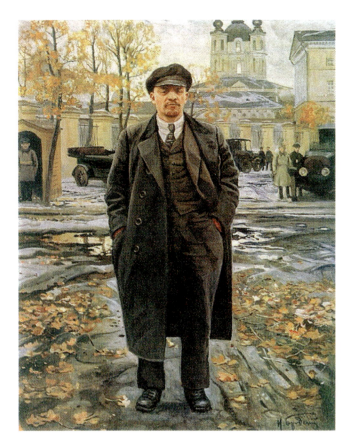

Lenin in Front of Smolny
Isaak Brodskiy (Russian, c. 1925)

The division of the world into the haves and have-nots is too simplistic. It does not take into account the middle class, those who have some. It also does not consider that some people choose to have relatively less because they are not motivated to work. The freedom to have more (whether for personal gain, to support one's family, or to give to others) is one of the attractions of capitalism and free enterprise. The absence of it under Communist rule is not appealing to many people. The so-called bourgeois capitalists create jobs and thus give people the opportunity to work. Capitalist success stories inspire others to better themselves economically.

In practical terms, the Marxist revolutions that took place never progressed to the withering away of the state. The Communist Party always stayed in control. Communist economies never were guided by the workers. Instead, they were controlled from the top down by bureaucrats loyal to the party who told the workers what they were supposed to do. Any failures of the system were blamed on capitalist interference or on the incomplete application of Marxist theories.

Marxism was the justification later used by Vladimir Lenin in Russia, Mao Zedong in China, and other Communist revolutionaries to seize power in the name of the people. However, after the revolutions, the people went from being (supposedly) oppressed by the capitalists to being oppressed by the terror tactics of the Communist Party. The predicted workers' paradise never materialized. Capitalism, meanwhile, saw its own revolution with the formation of unions and the institution of workplace reforms by government, although these changes did not come without unsettling periods, even some sporadic violence.

Thus while the capitalist West prospered and the rising tide of a free economy lifted the boats of even the working class, Communist countries were mired in continuing economic hardship that kept the ruling party in power. If the party ruled in the name of the people, the people sure had it rough. The elite leaders of Communist governments developed a luxurious lifestyle that did not differ greatly from that of the capitalist bourgeoisie they claimed to hate.

The Bolshevik, *Boris Kustodiev (Russian, 1920)*

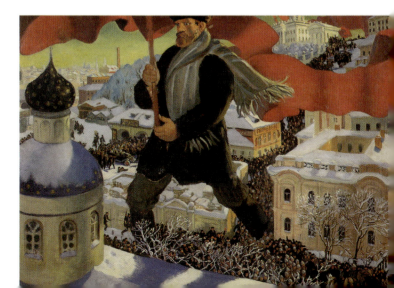

The Communist governments in the Soviet Union and Eastern Europe fell in the late 20th century in large measure because of these inner weaknesses of the Marxist system. Perhaps more than any other weakness, Communism leaves people impoverished spiritually and without hope. People cannot long endure under such a system. Communism still controls China, but the government there has adapted its practices to encourage closer ties with Western capitalists. The growth of Christianity in China shows the hunger for God in the human heart. Pure Marxism has not worked and will not work because it is based on false theories.

---

*For they exchanged the truth of God for the lie,
and worshiped and served the creature rather than the Creator,
who is blessed forever. Amen.*
Romans 1:25

Assignments for Lesson 111

In Their Words Read the excerpts from the Manifesto of the Communist Party and "The Man and His Newspaper" (pages 276-281).

Literature Begin reading *The Hiding Place*. Plan to finish it by the end of Unit 24.

Student Review Optional: Answer the questions for Lesson 111.

Finches in the Galápagos Islands

Lesson 112

Charles Darwin

Charles Darwin was born February 12, 1809, in Shrewsbury, England. He was the fifth child of a prominent family. Josiah Wedgwood, of china and pottery fame, was his mother's father. Erasmus Darwin, his father's father, was a physician and author. Charles' mother died when he was eight.

Darwin studied medicine at the University of Edinburgh but left for Cambridge to become an Anglican minister. According to his memoirs, he had questions about aspects of Church of England teachings, but he "did not then in the least doubt the strict and literal truth of every word in the Bible." He added, "Considering how fiercely I have been attacked by the orthodox, it seems ludicrous that I once intended to be a clergyman."

Darwin thought the lectures at Edinburgh dull and his academic studies at Cambridge a waste. However, he met Adam Sedgwick, a geologist who studied rock layers, and John Stevens Henslow, a distinguished botany professor and a generally well-studied scientist. Both of these men influenced Darwin's pursuits.

Henslow helped to arrange Darwin's famous voyage around the world. Darwin graduated from Cambridge in 1831. That year, at age twenty-two, he joined the survey ship HMS *Beagle* as a naturalist. The ship spent nearly five years at sea, skirting the coast of South America, sailing across the Pacific, touching New Zealand and Australia, crossing the Indian Ocean to Africa, and returning to England.

Darwin studied geological formations, observed animals and plants, and collected specimens. The six-week visit to the Galápagos Islands was one of the most famous stops. Darwin made numerous notes about the voyage but admitted that his lack of drawing skill and his limited knowledge of anatomy hindered his work.

Darwin married his cousin Emma Wedgwood in 1839. They had ten children. Darwin's family wealth allowed him to devote himself to study and writing.

HMS *Beagle* at Tierra del Fuego
Conrad Martens (English, c. 1833)

This 1837 diagram from one of Darwin's notebooks illustrates his idea of evolution as a branching tree of life. "I think case must be that one generation should have as many living as now. To do this and to have as many species in same genus (as is) requires extinction. Thus between A + B the immense gap of relation. C + B the finest gradation. B+D rather greater distinction. Thus genera would be formed. Bearing relation [next page] to ancient types with several extinct forms"

Developing His Theory

Darwin had formulated the basic theory of natural selection by 1839, but he spent twenty years continuing his research. By 1858 he had prepared a rough paper outlining his conclusions.

Alfred Russel Wallace, who left school at age fourteen, was a Welshman who had independently developed a theory of natural selection based on his scientific observations. Wallace sent Darwin a copy of his theory in 1858. Darwin arranged to have Wallace's paper and a working draft of his theory read before a meeting of the Linnaean Society. Darwin remembered little public notice of this presentation of his and Wallace's theories except for an Irish professor who said that "all that was new in them was false, and what was true was old."

For thirteen months, with several interruptions, Darwin collected his thoughts into book form. November 1859 saw the first edition of *On the*

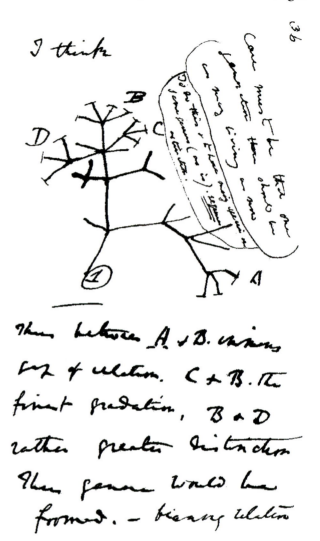

Darwin's "Thinking Path" at His Home, Down House

Origin of Species By Means of Natural Selection, or, The Preservation of Favoured Races in the Struggle for Life. Darwin considered it his most important work, and it was immediately successful. The initial printing of 1,250 copies was sold to subscribers on the first day, and 3,000 more copies followed. By 1876 the book had sold 16,000 copies in England and was translated into multiple languages, including Spanish, Bohemian, Polish, and Russian. It generated dozens of reviews and responses both praising and attacking it.

Darwin soon began work on the second edition as he dealt with a large amount of correspondence. He eventually published six editions of *The Origin of Species,* along with several other works. *The Descent of Man* was published in 1871. In this book Darwin wrote about his belief that humans had evolved.

Lesson 112 - Charles Darwin

Variation and Natural Selection

Darwin's theory of natural selection proposed that since animals are born with slightly different features, those with features best adapted to their environment will be most likely to survive and produce more offspring. He compared this with artificial selection (selective breeding) as practiced by humans, where the best animals for a given purpose (strongest, fastest, etc.) were favored for future breeding. Note, however, that this breeding is guided by human intelligence, while "natural selection" is supposed to be unguided.

Darwin suggested that all members of the horse-genus descended from a common equine ancestor. Whether or not that is true, it is a reasonable theory based on what we see in the selective breeding of animals and plants. However, evolutionists make a much more convoluted leap of logic when they suggest that humans and all other living creatures are descended from one-celled bacteria.

Some people in Darwin's day believed that God had created each individual species in each geographical location and that these species were immutable, or unable to change. Darwin made valid arguments against this idea, but the main problem is the vocabulary used.

Plants, animals, and humans do show variety. To say that modern "species" have natural variations within them does no violence to Scripture, and believers should not deny that such variations exist. The Bible uses the Hebrew term *meen*, translated "kind" in our English Bibles. It is used in Genesis 1 to describe the "kinds" of plants (v. 11), the "kinds" of sea creatures and birds (v. 21), and the "kinds" of land creatures (v. 24). The term is also used for the different animals on the ark (Genesis 6:20 and 7:14), clean and unclean animals (Leviticus 11 and Deuteronomy 14), and various types of fish (Ezekiel 47:10). This word is broader than the modern term "species."

Dogs and wolves, despite their wide variation in size and coloring, are grouped together into one species, Canis lupus. *However, the so-called "Darwin's finches" on the Galápagos Islands are now divided into fifteen different species in five different genera based primarily on their beaks. The illustration below is by John Gould, an ornithologist who examined Darwin's specimens from the Galápagos.*

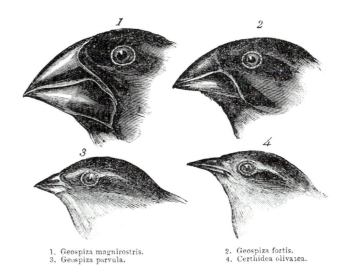

1. Geospiza magnirostris.
2. Geospiza fortis.
3. Geospiza parvula.
4. Certhidea olivasea.

The tradition of giving living creatures Latin names and trying to group them in broad categories (species, genus, family, order, class, phylum, kingdom) is an arbitrary one. The labels are used for the convenience of scientists, and scientists disagree about how to classify certain organisms.

Consider humans. According to the Bible, every human being is a descendant of Adam and Eve (and also Noah and his wife). Think of the amazing variety that has come from two individuals. The world has short people and tall people, people of various shades of skin from pale white to brown to dark black, and people with black hair and yellow hair and red hair and brown hair. The contrasts go on and on. And yet these are all human beings, made in the image of God.

We see similar variety among dogs, birds, fish, trees, and a host of other living things. The fact that different creatures of the same kind exhibit different features does not necessarily mean that they are "inventing" new genetic material through mutations. God evidently built in the potential for much variety when he created the first plants and animals and people.

Comparative Anatomy

Another purported line of evidence for evolution is the similarities we see among living creatures in the way they develop and the features they have. People share numerous features with animals such as eyes, arms, brains, and stomachs. Among different animals we see similarities. Does this mean that people and animals have descended from a common ancestor? Or does this mean that an Intelligent Designer knew that the same basic body structure was suitable for many living creatures?

Consider that automobiles from different manufacturers share the same basic features: engine, wheels, seats, trunk, and so forth. Does this mean that all automobiles are copied from one original car? Or does it mean that car makers have intelligently decided over the years that one basic car design is suitable for most transportation applications?

Comparative anatomy, like scientific classification, is not a reliable support because of its arbitrary nature. When evolutionary scientists find similar features in two creatures, they might classify them as either homologous structures or analogous structures. They describe homologous structures as those which were inherited from a common ancestor. They describe analogous structures as those which appear similar but arose separately in different evolutionary branches. This arbitrary distinction makes it easy to emphasize or de-emphasize evidence as it suits the situation.

Fossils

Darwin admitted that a lack of fossil evidence was among the most obvious arguments against his theory. If modern organisms have evolved from primitive forms through innumerable generations of variation, then the fossils should show those

Ernest Heckel (1834-1919), a German biologist and artist, strongly promoted Darwinian evolution. This illustration from his 1874 book Anthropogenie *purports to show similarities between the embryonic development of a human baby (far right) and various animals. Heckel argued that the growth of embryos demonstrates ("recapitulates") evolutionary history. Heckel's drawings were grossly inaccurate (he improved them in later editions); but copies of his earlier work were used for over a century as evidence for evolution.*

 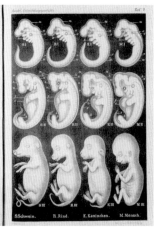

intermediate forms. His only answer was that the fossil record was not complete.

After a century and a half of effort to prove Darwin's theory with fossils, the results are still unsatisfactory. Some fossils are held up as examples of transitional forms, showing features of two widely different creatures. One of the best known is *Archaeopteryx*. The first largely-complete specimen was discovered in 1861, and a few other examples have been found. *Archaeopteryx* has wings and feathers like a modern bird, but it also has teeth, clawed fingers, and a bony tail unlike a modern bird. The consensus opinion at the 1984 International Archaeopteryx Conference was that *Archaeopteryx* was a bird, though paleontologists continue to debate its scientific classification.

Fossils provide a snapshot of a particular individual at a particular time and place. They cannot tell us who their parents were or who their descendants are. *Archaeopteryx* does not prove that dinosaurs evolved into birds. It is an unusual animal, but so is the platypus.

Instead of showing a gradual progression from simple organisms to modern creatures, the fossil record shows much continuity—dragonfly fossils look like modern dragonflies, jellyfish fossils look like modern jellyfish, ape fossils look like modern apes, and human fossils look like modern humans.

The Theory Today

Charles Darwin was not the first to propose evolutionary ideas, but his theories and writings gave them popular expression. Darwin's name is thus inextricably linked with the theory of evolution. Supporters of evolution today debate aspects of Darwin's ideas, such as the importance of natural selection, and whether evolution is the result of slow changes over time in a basically uniform environment or periods of rapid change in a world of catastrophes and mass extinctions. One thing we can say with confidence about the theory of evolution is that it is still evolving.

Berlin Specimen of Archaeopteryx lithographica

The word evolution is used in two different ways, and this causes some confusion. Can fish produce other fish with variations in size and markings? Yes, this is reasonable and possible. This is microevolution, small changes in fish offspring that are still fish. But can fish produce an amphibian that walks out on land, even after many generations of variations? No, this is a theoretical example of macroevolution, large changes from one type of creature to a radically different one.

When scientists and the media use the term evolution, they are generally referring to macroevolution, a belief that human beings and all living beings on earth are descended from a one-celled organism that came to life spontaneously millions of years ago. Many modern scientists have accepted this theory of evolution as true by faith, and they look for evidence to support their assumption. For those who want to ignore God, evolution is an attractive theory because it does not require a Creator God who has authority over His Creation.

Many scientists choose only to examine the evidence presented in the physical world. They do not admit the possibility of divine involvement. The physical world provides much evidence that points to God. It shows His power and creativity. However, simply looking at the world today cannot prove everything that happened in the distant past.

The best way to know what happened is to listen to Someone who was there. The Lord God Almighty was there, and He has informed us in the Scriptures about what happened. Ultimately, we must choose to accept the Bible's account of Creation by faith. "By faith we understand that the worlds were prepared by the word of God, so that what is seen was not made out of things which are visible" (Hebrews 11:3).

Since we accept by faith that the Biblical account is true, we can joyfully explore the evidence presented in the world around us and make educated guesses about how the evidence fits in with the Creation, with the sin of Adam and Eve, and with the flood. We should not feel compelled to modify the clear message of Scripture so that it fits with the latest scientific theories. If we doubt the truthfulness of the beginning portion of Scripture, then we will have reason to doubt the rest of Scripture. As Jesus said, "For if you believed Moses, you would believe Me, for he wrote about Me. But if you do not believe his writings, how will you believe My words?" (John 5:46-47).

Conclusion

A dubious story says that Darwin had a change of heart about evolution before his death on April 19, 1882. Since the account of one witness (a Lady Hope) is unsubstantiated by other contemporary accounts and denied by Darwin's children, we should ignore it. This excerpt from an 1879 letter gives some insight into Darwin's attitude (punctuation as in *The Life and Letters of Charles Darwin*):

> What my own views may be is a question of no consequence to any one but myself. But, as you ask, I may state that my judgment often fluctuates. . . . In my most extreme fluctuations I have never been an Atheist in the sense of denying the existence of a God. I think that generally (and more and more as I grow older), but not always, that an Agnostic would be the more correct description of my state of mind.

We must regret that someone with such promising capabilities and such opportunities for study failed to recognize God's goodness and power. We must regret, too, the effect that his theory has had on the moral and social fabric of our world. Darwin offered this summary of his life work:

Charles Darwin (Photo by His Son Leonard, c. 1874)

Therefore my success as a man of science, whatever this may have amounted to, has been determined, as far as I can judge, by complex and diversified mental qualities and conditions. Of these, the most important have been—the love of science—unbounded patience in long reflecting over any subject—industry in observing and collecting facts—and a fair share of invention as well as of common sense. With such moderate abilities as I possess, it is truly surprising that I should have influenced to a considerable extent the belief of scientific men on some important points.

However great the skill and influence of Charles Darwin, we cannot depend on him for an adequate description of the origin of life. We can learn to prepare ourselves for the time when "we shall all be changed," not by a random process of evolution, but by the mighty power of God (1 Corinthians 15:50-58).

In the beginning was the Word, and the Word was with God, and the Word was God. He was in the beginning with God. All things came into being through Him, and apart from Him nothing came into being that has come into being.
John 1:1-3

Assignments for Lesson 112

In Their Words — Read the excerpt from *On the Origin of Species* (pages 282-285).

Literature — Continue reading *The Hiding Place*.

Student Review — Optional: Answer the questions for Lesson 112.

Berggasse 19, Vienna, Austria

Lesson 113

Sigmund Freud

Sigmund Freud offered surprising new theories of human behavior based on his practice of psychiatry. His ideas have undergone intense critical examination. Although few psychiatrists and counselors are pure Freudians today, his work opened the door to a new way of looking at the inner person.

Freud's Life

Sigmund Freud was born in 1856 in a small town in Moravia (now in the Czech Republic). When he was a child, his family moved to Vienna, Austria, where Freud spent almost all of the rest of his life. Freud's family was complicated. Sigmund's father was forty and his mother was twenty when Sigmund was born, and they had seven more children together. The elder Freud also had children from his first marriage who were about the same age as Sigmund's mother.

The Freuds were Jewish, but they did not practice the faith except for observing Passover and Purim as a family. Sigmund was in the care of a Roman Catholic nanny when he was a small child. She took him to Catholic services with her. When Sigmund was two years old, his younger brother died.

Freud studied medicine and established his psychiatric practice in Vienna. He married in 1886. He and his wife had six children in eight years.

Sigmund Freud (pictured below, c. 1900) lived and worked at Berggasse 19 in Vienna for forty-seven years. The building now houses The Sigmund Freud Museum and a psychoanalytic library with 35,000 volumes.

Lesson 113 - Sigmund Freud

The pioneer in psychoanalysis wrote widely about his theories and developed an international reputation from about 1900 on. Many considered him to be self-centered and stubborn about the correctness of his views. Freud suffered from depression at times and occasionally took cocaine.

For about the last twenty years of his life, Freud suffered from cancer of the jaw and palate. He endured considerable pain and went through numerous operations. Freud was able to leave Nazi-occupied Austria in 1938 and move to England. The next year, by an agreement that they had made, Freud's physician administered heavy doses of morphine to him; and Freud died by this physician-assisted euthanasia.

Freud's Theories

When Sigmund Freud began his practice of psychiatry, the field was a fairly new discipline. Two techniques he used to treat patients were hypnosis and free association. In free association, he said words to patients and let them discuss whatever came to their minds.

Freud did not believe in God. He found support for his atheism in the ideas of Ludwig Feuerbach, who also influenced Karl Marx. In fact, Freud once wrote that religion was the "universal obsessional neurosis," that is, an indication of mental illness. The chief purpose of life to Freud was happiness, and the chief motivation in a person's life was his desire for pleasure.

In his view, the desire for pleasure starts in early childhood and continues throughout life. Freud traced most of the neuroses and psychiatric problems with which people struggle to abnormalities in their subconscious desires.

Freud divided the personality into three parts: the id (physical desires), the ego (sense of self), and the superego (similar to the conscience). The ego supposedly mediates between the want-to of the id and the ought-to of the superego, but all these parts

Freud studied in Paris with Jean-Martin Charcot, a neurologist who studied hysteria and hypnosis, often demonstrating his techniques with patients in front of audiences. This 1887 painting by French artist André Brouillet depicts one of Charcot's presentations. Freud hung a lithograph of this painting over the patient couch in his consulting room.

are influenced by desires for pleasure. Philosophers had held for some time that humans were basically rational; but Freud believed that man was basically irrational, driven by his desire for pleasure and by subconscious drives of which he was often not aware but which could be identified by psychoanalysis. Identifying these desires could help a person live within the demands of his superego, bring inner peace, and help him live a stable and productive life. Religion, rather than being part of the solution, was to Freud part of the problem.

Analyzing Freud

Freud's ideas have largely carried the day in the analysis of our inner selves. Such terms as the subconscious and the ego and such ideas as the impact of early childhood experiences have entered into common usage because of Freud's writings. The Bible, of course, talks about the conscience and the importance of training children in the way they should go; but Freud's ideas were attractive because he seemed to be a "modern" and "scientific" authority.

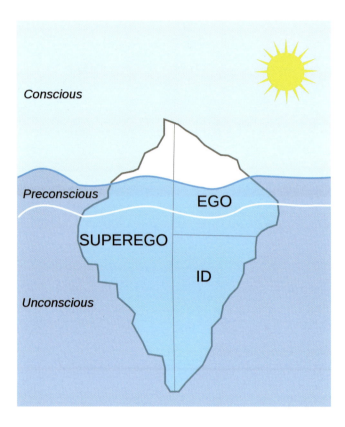

Freud's model for understanding the way we think has been compared to an iceberg. In this model, all of the id is "under water," or subconscious, as is most of the superego. A smaller portion of the ego is subconscious. His earlier model had identified thoughts and memories as conscious, preconscious, or unconscious.

Changed attitudes about right and wrong have come about because of the way Freud's opinions have been interpreted by the general public and by those who have tried to capitalize on or market Freud's ideas. All of these changes, however, are built upon a faulty foundation.

The scientist is supposed to be an objective observer of the phenomena he is considering. However, if a person's early childhood has a profound formative effect on his outlook, we can only assume that Freud's childhood had such an effect on him. In addition, it appears that Freud developed his ideas first and then analyzed his patients in that light.

Perhaps Freud analyzed other people on the basis of what was going on inside of him as much as what was going on inside of them. Freud considered himself an objective scientist, but in reality he was a subjective observer. Perhaps he even suffered from some of the psychiatric troubles he diagnosed in others.

Freud's theories can be challenged in a number of ways. First, Freud denied the spiritual realm. The Bible, however, teaches that the spiritual impulse

Albert Einstein

Another German who had a profound influence on the world was the physicist Albert Einstein (1879-1955). In articles published in 1905, Einstein presented his special theory of relativity which showed the relationship between matter and energy. Most of the rest of his life was devoted to working out the consequences of this theory. Einstein's work influenced the development of atomic energy and our understanding of space and time. Einstein grew up in a non-observant Jewish family. Unlike Marx and Freud, Einstein believed that the universe provided evidence for the existence of a divine source, but he did not believe in the personal God of the Bible.

Einstein Lecturing in Vienna, Austria, 1921

Lesson 113 - Sigmund Freud

and the guidance of God are real and are good. To deny the spiritual is to dismiss the very nature of a human being as God made us. Any analysis that does not recognize the spiritual nature of man is flawed from the start.

Second, the drive for pleasure does not fully explain all human actions. A farmer working to repair fences to keep control of his livestock, a mother staying up all night with a sick child, and a man risking his life for his family or his country have motivations that go beyond pleasure.

Third, our desire for pleasure is not always good. We often desire things that are harmful for us or for other people. When we give in to these harmful desires, we commit sin. According to Freud, no God told us "Thou shalt" or "Thou shalt not." Any standards that humans believe in and follow are, by this theory, mere human constructs with no eternal value. Since Freud saw desires for pleasure behind every action, he would be hard-pressed to declare which expressions of those desires were right and which were wrong.

Effects of Freud's Theories

Freud did not advocate completely irresponsible behavior. However, his theory that all desires for pleasure were normal gave the green light for others to promote immoral behavior, especially in the area of sexuality.

God made us male and female. He gave us sexual desires, and He gave us instructions on how to control those desires and how to enjoy them within marriage. Promiscuity, pornography, immodesty, and other forms of sexual sin distort the goodness of God's design. We must keep all of our desires for pleasure, including sexual pleasure, under the Lordship of Christ.

With Freud we have another example of where human life winds up if we leave God out of the picture. If we fail to understand our nature as revealed in the Creation story, and if we fail to recognize our spiritual need as revealed in the gospel story, we wind up where any analysis winds up that is built on inaccurate presumptions and incorrect data: lost.

This statue of Sigmund Freud in London is located near where he lived for the last few months of his life. Behind the statue is one building of the Tavistock Clinic. This mental health facility was founded in 1920 by Dr. Hugh Crichton-Miller, a specialist in treating World War I veterans suffering from shell-shock.

*Therefore consider the members of your earthly body
as dead to immorality, impurity, passion, evil desire,
and greed, which amounts to idolatry.
[A]s those who have been chosen of God,
holy and beloved, put on a heart of compassion,
kindness, humility, gentleness, and patience . . . .
Colossians 3:5, 12*

Assignments for Lesson 113

In Their Words — Read the excerpt from "Science Gives Us a New Explanation of Dreams" (page 286).

Literature — Continue reading *The Hiding Place*.

Student Review — Optional: Answer the questions for Lesson 113.

Schoolteacher and Children in Pokhara, Nepal

Lesson 114 - Everyday Life

Education and the Work of John Dewey

The place to look for the best method of education is in the Bible. From the beginning God has been our teacher. He taught Adam in the Garden of Eden. God gave the Israelites the Law of Moses to teach them how to live. He sent prophet after prophet to teach His erring people. After speaking to the Israelites in the prophets, in the last days He spoke to us in His Son (Hebrews 1:1-2).

Jesus, the Master Teacher

Everything we need for life and godliness comes to us through the true knowledge of Jesus (2 Peter 1:3). Jesus taught important truth with His words, but He also taught important truth by the way He lived among us as a man. Jesus is the Word that God wants us to learn. God sent Jesus to earth to explain Himself to us (John 1:1, 18).

Unlike the scribes and Pharisees, Jesus taught as one with authority (Matthew 7:29). Jesus said that His teaching was not His own, but was from the One who sent Him. He said that anyone who is willing to do God's will will know whether His teaching is of God (John 7:16-17).

Using objects in the world that people already knew about, Jesus imparted spiritual lessons. He taught, for example, about seed falling on different types of soil, tares growing among the good grain, leaven, and good and bad fish in a net (Matthew 13). He also taught parables that used as illustrations the way people act. Some of these stories include a servant who did not show mercy (Matthew 18:23-35), a king who hosted a wedding feast for his son (Matthew 22:1-14), and a rich fool who built big barns but then died (Luke 12:16-21).

Jesus took advantage of teaching opportunities in a variety of locations. He taught by the sea (Mark 4:1), in synagogues (Matthew 4:23), in a boat (Luke 5:3), on a mountain (Matthew 5-7), and in the temple (Matthew 26:55). One crucial aspect of Jesus' teaching is that He felt compassion for people and told them what they really needed to hear for their own good (Mark 6:34).

Parents and Grandparents Teaching

God knows the importance of teaching in families. He chose Abraham so that he might command his children and his household after him to keep the way of the Lord (Genesis 18:19). During the Feast of Unleavened Bread, each father was to talk to his son about what the Lord did for him when he came out of Egypt (Exodus 13:1-8).

The Israelites were not to forget what their eyes had seen but were supposed to make it known to their sons and grandsons (Deuteronomy 4:9). They were to have God's words on their hearts and teach them diligently to their sons, when they sat in their houses, walked by the way, lay down, and rose up (Deuteronomy 6:6-9; 11:19-20).

Psalm 78:1-8 is a reminder to teach the next generations the praises of the Lord. Proverbs tells children of the blessings of listening to the teaching of their fathers and mothers. A father's instruction and a mother's teaching are a graceful wreath for the head and ornaments about the neck (Proverbs 1:8-9). Proverbs instructs parents to train up a child in the way he should go (Proverbs 22:6). In the first verses of Joel, the Lord through Joel instructed the elders and all the inhabitants of the land to tell their sons what had happened. These sons were to tell their sons, and those sons were to tell the next generation (Joel 1:1-3).

Educational Philosophers Through the Centuries	
The Sophists Greek 400s BC	A group of wandering teachers called Sophists claimed they could teach any skill or subject to anyone willing to learn. Their specialties were grammar, logic, and rhetoric.
Socrates Greek c. 469-399 BC	Socrates sought to discover and teach universal principles of truth, beauty, and goodness. He believed true knowledge existed within all. Socrates asked questions that forced students to think deeply about the meaning of life, truth, and justice.
Plato Greek c. 427-347 BC	In *The Republic*, Plato described a society ruled by intelligent philosopher-kings with a second class of warriors and a lower class of workers. The education system in this imaginary republic prepared each class for its role.
Aristotle Greek c. 384-322 BC	Aristotle founded his school, the Lyceum, in Athens. He believed man was basically rational and could discover and follow the natural laws governing the universe. Aristotle believed reason would cause educated people to live in moderation.
Cicero Roman 106-43 BC	In his book *De Oratore*, Cicero recommended that orators study grammar, rhetoric, logic, mathematics, astronomy, ethics, military science, natural science, geography, history, and law.
Quintilian Roman c. 35-100 AD	Quintilian wrote that education should be based on developmental stages from childhood to adulthood, with lessons adapted to the student's readiness and ability. The statue of Quintilian at right is in his birthplace of Calahorra, Spain.
Thomas Aquinas Italian 1225-1274	Thomas developed the practice of Scholasticism, an attempt to use revelations from the Bible alongside human reason. He combined the philosophies of Aristotle and Augustine.

Lesson 114 - Everyday Life: Education and the Work of John Dewey

Desiderius Erasmus Dutch 1466?-1536	Erasmus encouraged the study of Scripture and also archaeology, astronomy, history, and mythology. He produced a Greek New Testament and a Latin translation more accurate than the Vulgate.
Philipp Melanchthon German 1497-1560	Melanchthon, a student of Martin Luther, wrote a school code for one area of Germany which influenced all of Europe. The code called for government supervision of schools and government licensing of teachers. His portrait, by Lucas Cranach the Elder, is shown at right. 
John Amos Comenius Czech 1592-1670	A bishop of the Moravian Church, Comenius encouraged teachers to use children's senses. He wrote one of the first illustrated children's books which taught Latin using pictures as well as the student's own language.
J. H. Pestalozzi Swiss 1746-1827	 Pestalozzi believed children were naturally good, that education should nurture and preserve innocence, and that teaching should use the senses. He said that schools should resemble secure, loving homes; and he established schools for poor and orphaned children. The 1879 painting at left by Konrad Grob shows Pestalozzi with orphans in Stans, Switzerland.
Friedrich Froebel German 1782-1852	Froebel was largely self-taught. He established the first kindergartens (literally "child's garden") in Prussia. The curriculum included games, songs, stories, folk heroes, cultural values, building activities, and group participation.
Herbert Spencer English 1820-1903	An advocate of Social Darwinism, Spencer coined the phrase "survival of the fittest." He opposed public schools, saying they would create a monopoly for mediocrity by catering to students with low ability. Spencer himself was mainly self-educated.
Horace Mann American 1796-1859	Horace Mann helped create the first state board of education in the U.S. (in Massachusetts). He advocated non-religious public schools and a uniform curriculum for all students. 
Ellen Key Swede 1849-1926	Key, pictured at right about 1915, inspired the progressive education movement. She emphasized the needs and potentials of the child rather than religion or the needs of society. Key herself was educated at home by tutors.
Jean Piaget Swiss 1896-1980	Piaget described four stages of intellectual growth: birth to age two—gaining motor control and learning about physical objects; ages two to seven—naming objects and reasoning intuitively; ages seven to twelve—beginning to deal with abstract concepts like numbers and relationships; and ages twelve to fifteen—beginning to reason logically and systematically.

A Short History of Formal Education

People around the world recognize that the major goal of education is to prepare children for life. For most of history, parents have taught their own children. In keeping with the teachings of the Bible, many families have passed on faith in God through many generations. In non-Christian cultures as well, parents have taught their cultural values to their children. Girls have learned from their mothers how to care for families and homes. Boys have learned to do the work their fathers did.

Some children, especially those from wealthy families, have been taught at home by paid tutors or went away from home to study in formal schools. Long before the birth of Christ, schools were often connected with temples. Egyptian priests taught writing, the sciences, mathematics, and architecture. Also in ancient Egypt, children of royal or wealthy parents learned at the palace.

Boys preparing to be scribes learned to write. Writing practice exercises with teacher corrections still survive from antiquity. A library-type storage place for manuscripts was called a "house of life." Indian priests taught Hinduism, grammar, and philosophy. Formal education in China emphasized philosophy, poetry, and the religious teachings of philosophers like Confucius and Lao-tzu.

Formal schooling practices varied from one Greek city-state to another. In Athens only the sons of citizens went to formal school. Tutors educated some girls at home. In Sparta boys were educated for military service and girls received athletic training so they could be healthy mothers to produce future soldiers.

Wealthy Roman boys were sent to a primary school called an *aludus*. In secondary school they were taught by Greek slaves called pedagogues, learning Latin and Greek. Some then went on to study oration. Since ancient times, Jewish rabbis have encouraged parents to teach their children religion, law, ethics, and vocational skills. In addition to learning from their parents, many Jewish children have also attended synagogue schools to study the Torah (the Old Testament Law) and the Talmud (teachings of Jewish rabbis) and to learn the Hebrew language.

During the Middle Ages, the Roman Catholic Church operated parish, chapel, and monastery schools for elementary students. One of the main

Sergey Rachinsky (1833-1902) taught botany at Moscow University and was acquainted with author Leo Tolstoy and composer Peter Illyich Tchiakovsky. He published the first Russian translation of Darwin's On the Origin of Species *in 1864. Rachinsky spent the latter decades of his life organizing and teaching in rural schools for peasant children. He emphasized the need for religious education. This painting, titled* Mental Calculation. In Public School of S. A. Rachinsky *is by Nikolay Bogdanov-Belsky (Russian, 1895).*

purposes of these schools was to teach Latin. Some women learned in religious communities or convents, which had libraries and schools to teach nuns how to abide by the rules of their particular order. Some schools operated by merchants and craftsmen taught basic education and trained young men for specific occupations. Knights were trained in military tactics and chivalry. The famous European universities of Bologna, Padua, and Salerno in Italy; Paris in France; and Cambridge and Oxford in England began when Thomas Aquinas and others encouraged a combination of the faith of the Bible and the philosophy of Aristotle.

During the Renaissance, the wealthy continued to send their children to schools. Some middle class families began to do so as well. Private tutoring continued also. Young men followed a humanist course of studies at the high school level. Women studied art, dancing, music, needlework, and poetry. During the Reformation, reformers established primary schools that taught in the children's own languages. Curriculum included religion, reading, writing, and arithmetic. Reform educators wrote catechisms, which were primary books that taught religious doctrine using questions and answers. High school students continued to study Greek and Latin. A German high school was a gymnasium; an English one was a grammar school; and a French one was a lycee.

In the 1800s, France, Germany, Italy, the United Kingdom, and other European countries organized national public school systems. Some New World countries organized similar systems. In the 1700s almost all schools in the U.S. were voluntary, privately-funded institutions. By 1918 all states in the U.S. had government-run schools and compulsory attendance laws.

The Influence of John Dewey

John Dewey was born in 1859 in Burlington, Vermont. He was educated at the University of Vermont and received a doctorate from Johns Hopkins University. He taught at the Universities of Michigan, Minnesota, and Chicago and at Columbia University in New York. At the University of Chicago he and his wife Alice experimented with his Laboratory School, the so-called Dewey School.

As a philosopher, Dewey was a pragmatist. A pragmatist believes that there is no absolute truth. Pragmatists assert that all truth, knowledge, morality, and politics must be tested in practice to see if they produce desirable results. They believe that values such as goodness, justice, and truth are changeable and depend on context. Pragmatists maintain that humans are progressing in a Darwinian fashion and therefore knowledge, truth, and values are progressing also. They see all ideas and institutions as tentative hypotheses and as tentative solutions to the world's problems. Pragmatism was popular for a while in England, France, and Italy; but it was most widely-accepted in the United States. Critics of Dewey believed that adherence to pragmatism would cause morals to degenerate.

John Dewey at the University of Chicago, 1902

The particular branch of pragmatism to which Dewey ascribed was developed at the University of Chicago by Dewey and his associates. It is called instrumentalism. In instrumentalism, all that matters is a particular situation and what a person thinks he should do in that situation.

The idea of situation ethics was a natural result of instrumentalism, which rejects outside authority and standards. This form of ethics is concerned only with what will accomplish a desired goal in a given situation. A person who adheres to situation ethics will lie or steal or do anything he deems is appropriate in a particular circumstance.

John Dewey focused on the education of children because that was an effective way to engage in social engineering. By training children to think the way he and his fellow philosophers thought, they could orchestrate changes in the general populace.

Allowing pragmatist philosophy into the realm of public education was a dangerous step. Forcing children to go to school through compulsory education laws makes it easier to practice social engineering to make students into the kind of adults desired by those in authority.

Government-run education continues to get more complicated and more expensive. Politicians and educators are constantly calling for new programs and for more money to fix perceived problems. In response, many parents have chosen to put their children in private schools, and increasing numbers have turned to homeschooling.

The idea that absolute truth does not exist has led to problems in schools and in society. How will a society ever create a perfect school environment for teaching children if there is no absolute truth? If truth is ever-changing, then education will be ever-changing. Christians believe that there is absolute truth and that it will set us free. This belief should be the foundation of education.

The fear of the Lord is the beginning of knowledge;
Fools despise wisdom and instruction.
Proverbs 1:7

Assignments for Lesson 114

In Their Words   Read the excerpt from *Moral Principles in Education* (pages 287-288).

Literature   Continue reading *The Hiding Place*.

Student Review   Optional: Answer the questions for Lesson 114.

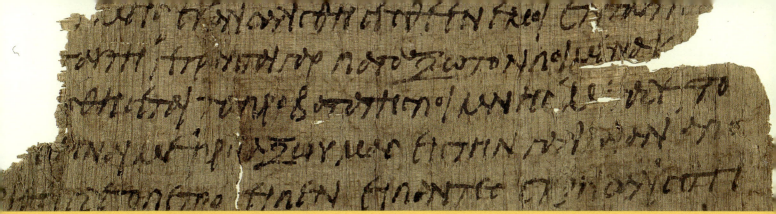

Manuscript Portion of Matthew (Third Century)

Lesson 115 - Bible Study

Higher Criticism

During this period when new ideas came to be promoted about the origin of the Earth, the nature of history, the inner person, and the purpose of education, some Biblical scholars, influenced by the same type of worldly thinking, began to question the nature of the Bible and how we should understand God's Word.

The Meaning of Higher Criticism

In Biblical studies, textual criticism (sometimes called lower criticism) seeks to determine the exact wording of the original Biblical books based on analysis of the thousands of handwritten copies (called manuscripts) that are available to us. No original autograph of a Biblical book is known to exist; that is, we do not have the very ink and papyrus of Isaiah, Matthew, Paul, or any other Biblical writer. We do have ancient copies of their books. In addition to manuscripts of the books of the Bible, portions of the Biblical text have been preserved in letters, commentaries, and religious documents in many languages.

God inspired the writing of the original books, and we believe that He guided the copying process; but the copies we have do contain some variations. For example, if two lines in the work being copied end with the same word, a copyist might have accidentally skipped the second line and thus left out a portion of text. A copyist working on Matthew might have added words to make the account of an incident there the same as the account in Mark, even though other manuscripts of Matthew do not include those words.

No points of truth or doctrine are involved in these minor variations. These textual variances are amazingly few considering the large number of hand-copied manuscripts that are known. Scholars involved in textual criticism do not challenge the truthfulness or inspiration of the Biblical text; their faith in the Word is often strengthened as they see the evidence of its preservation over the centuries.

However, another discipline of Biblical study, variously called higher criticism, literary criticism, or form criticism, does challenge the traditional understanding of the inspiration and authority of God's Word. Higher criticism became widespread during the last half of the 19th century. It seriously undermined the respect that many people had for the Bible, and it shook the faith and practice of many churches.

667

The Claims of Higher Criticism

The traditional understanding was that the books of the Bible were written by those who claimed authorship or those who were attributed as the authors: Moses wrote the Pentateuch (as supported by references to it in the rest of Scripture as the work of Moses), David wrote the Psalms attributed to him, Matthew wrote Matthew, Paul wrote the letters that have his name, and so forth. Higher critics began to make the claim that the Biblical books were not always what they seemed. Jean Astruc (1753) and J. G. Eichhorn (1787) raised questions about sources that Moses might have used in writing the Pentateuch. These scholars believed that passages which used YHWH as the name for God and passages that used Elohim as the name for God were from two different documents that Moses combined in writing the Pentateuch. These earlier documents were abbreviated J (for the German rendering of YHWH as JHWH) and E.

In the mid-1800s, scholars continued to look into the Pentateuch and claimed to find two more documents that were sources for the Pentateuch. They said that Leviticus came from a priestly source (abbreviated P) and that Deuteronomy (abbreviated D) was written by someone other than Moses. Thus was developed the documentary hypothesis that the Pentateuch was compiled from four sources, J, E, P, and D, with the final version coming much later than the time of Moses. A humorous observer joked that, according to this theory, the Pentateuch was was not "Mosaic" (written by Moses) but was simply a mosaic.

Julius Wellhausen added another dimension to higher criticism in the 1870s. He published his theory that monotheism in Israel evolved through various stages from an early practice of polytheism to the worship of God described in the Old Testament. Wellhausen dated the Old Testament books at various points during this supposed evolution.

F. C. Baur, 1830s

Wellhausen said that Moses was a shadowy figure who almost certainly could not have written the Pentateuch. His theory was an attempt to go behind the Biblical text to determine how the religion of Israel developed. Undoubtedly Wellhausen was influenced by the ideas of Hegel and Charles Darwin concerning social change and evolution.

F. C. Baur (mid-1800s) developed a theory about the growth of ideas in the church which purported to show that Paul could not have written several of the letters which bear his name. Baur was influenced by the dialectical ideas of Hegel and wanted to show that the teachings of the New Testament evolved over time, with some letters dating from the second century AD. Another avenue of New Testament scholarship examined the four gospel accounts to look for sources that might lie behind them and to determine whether the ideas in them might have come from later than the time when Matthew, Mark, Luke, and John could have written them.

Lesson 115 - Bible Study: Higher Criticism

Assumptions of Higher Criticism

Higher critics assume first that the Bible is not the inspired, authoritative Word of God. Instead, they believe it to be a collection of documents that shed more light on the writers, the process of editing and compiling the books, and the development of religion in Israel and the church than they do on God.

Second, the process of higher criticism accepts Hegel's dialectic and Darwin's theory of evolution as established facts. The worship of God and the life of the church, they say, could not have begun as the Bible presents them. Instead, they must have been the ideas of man that developed through social evolution and the process of thesis-antithesis-synthesis.

A third assumption of higher critics is the denial of miracles and predictive prophecy. To these critics, miracle stories are myths that were intended to impress the original audience and to teach some lesson about God or morality. Since the critics did not believe that inspiration is possible, they said that prophets could not know the future. Therefore, the critics claimed that passages which predicted future events were actually written sometime after those events.

Fourth, higher critics assume that their reasoning process is more reliable and accurate than what is written in the Bible. Their exaltation of reason followed the trend of the times and said that 19th century Biblical scholars with their own presuppositions knew the truth better than the primitive peoples of ancient times who simply copied various sources almost willy-nilly and who were so gullible as to believe phony letters to have been written by the apostle Paul. In other words, the scholars trusted their reason and the theory of evolution more than they did the Word of God.

Failings of Higher Criticism

Ever-Changing Theories. Higher critics have sometimes presented their theories as the "assured results" of their study. However, those results are often amended by later scholars who have differing opinions. New theories are even more imaginative than the ones they replace. For instance, scholars were not satisfied with the theory of four documents behind the Pentateuch, so they claimed to find more sources. At times it seems as though the only limit to what might be proposed is the imagination of the one proposing it. This makes it difficult to know exactly what is being put forth as the final answer.

Truth of the Bible Questioned. One thread that weaves through all of the higher criticism is the belief that the Bible cannot be trusted to be factually true. The chronology of the Bible, the higher critics say, was just a fabrication by later writers. Many letters claiming to have been written by Paul are, according to these theories, pious forgeries. In fact, all parts of the Bible have been subjected to the

The University of Tübingen in Baden-Württemberg, Germany, was the center of higher criticism in the 19th-century. The University had been founded in 1477. The Alte Aula (Old Hall), pictured below, was the main assembly building of the University from about 1547 to 1845.

scrutiny of the critics. This assault on the Bible has made it increasingly difficult to present the Bible as God's authoritative word to a skeptical public.

Basis for Living and Worshiping Removed. The attack by scholars on the authenticity and accuracy of the Bible has led many people to question its authority over their lives. When people think of the Bible as a collection of truisms and not as a life-changing source of spiritual truth, they do not have the same motivation to follow its teaching in their daily lives. Perhaps this explains why attendance has generally declined in recent decades in churches where the authority of the Bible is minimized.

Liberal critics ignore or downplay the evidence that supports the authority and truthfulness of the Bible. It takes more credulity to believe the complex and ever-changing ideas of the critics than it does to believe in the simple message of Scripture. The traditional view of Scripture has been ably defended. The different names used for God, for instance, are stylistic variation and not evidence of multiple sources.

One response to higher criticism was a series of pamphlets published in the United States in the early 20th century called *The Fundamentals*, which restated traditional Christian doctrines. This is why those who believe in these Biblical teachings came to be called fundamentalists.

Nothing that has emanated from scholars, linguists, textual critics, or archaeologists has threatened the rock of certainty which is the Bible. The Bible stands as true as ever.

For the word of God is living and active and sharper than any two-edged sword, and piercing as far as the division of soul and spirit, of both joints and marrow, and able to judge the thoughts and intentions of the heart.
Hebrews 4:12

Assignments for Lesson 115

Bible — Recite or write Colossians 3:12-15 from memory.

In Their Words — Read "Pied Beauty" and "That Holy Thing" (page 289).

Literature — Continue reading *The Hiding Place*.

Project — Complete your project for the unit.

Student Review — Optional: Answer the questions for Lesson 115 and take the quiz for Unit 23.

24

The World at War

Summary The first half of the 20th century saw two world wars that took millions of lives and brought to an end the idea that man had progressed beyond the desire for armed conflict. In this unit we examine the causes of the Great War, the unsatisfactory conclusion of it, the events leading up to the Second World War, and the shape of international relations after that conflict. We focus on the inspiring leadership of Britain's Winston Churchill and look at the cultural history of Japan to understand a country that once was an enemy and is now an ally. The Bible study is on peace.

Lessons
116 - The Great War
117 - World War II
118 - Key Person: Winston Churchill
119 - Everyday Life: The Cultural History of Japan
120 - Bible Study: Peace

Abandoned Boy in London, 1945

Memory Work Learn Psalm 46:1-3 by the end of the unit.

Books Used The Bible
In Their Words
The Hiding Place

Project (choose one)

1) Write 300 to 500 words on one of the following topics:

- Write about life on the home front during World War II. See Lesson 117. Life in the United States will be the easiest to research, but try to find out what it was like to live in Britain or France or another country during the war.

- Looking at wars through the scope of history, why do you think nations go to war?

2) Interview a person who remembers World War II about their experiences during the war. Compose at least ten questions ahead of time. You can conduct your interview by phone or in person. Be respectful of your interviewee's time and keep the interview within an hour. If possible, make an audio recording of the interview.

3) Memorize Psalm 46.

Europe at the Beginning of the Great War

German Infantry, 1914

Lesson 116

The Great War

A new century was dawning that held new possibilities for mankind. Technology and inventions were developing at an astounding rate. The world economy was changing from an agricultural base to an industrial base. People across the globe were connected through communication as never before. The possibilities for future progress seemed limitless. Surely, many thought, mankind was entering an era when old ways and old prejudices would disappear.

Then reality hit with two world wars, new weapons of death, the rise of terrible totalitarian regimes that took the lives of millions of people, and years of economic uncertainty that affected the entire globe. All this brought cynicism and despair to the hearts of many. The political, military, and social conditions in which people lived changed drastically from 1914 to 1945.

Prelude to War

The first two-thirds of the 19th century in Europe saw a growing industrial revolution and continuing political revolutions. Then from 1870 forward came a period of rapid overseas expansion with European colonization of Asia and Africa. Several motives drove this expansion: a desire for wealth and economic growth, a mission to "civilize" those who had a different cultural background, and a belief that national power and prestige were enhanced by building a colonial empire.

The partitioning of Asia and Africa by European nations was largely completed by 1914. The lands that were colonized were indeed modernized by the Europeans (and after 1898, by the United States), but those changes came at a price paid by the native people who were often manipulated and oppressed.

Europe appeared to be at peace. No major war had taken place since the end of the Napoleonic Wars in 1815. The nations of Europe were witnessing reforms in their government, and European economies were booming. However, dangerous storm clouds were gathering.

International Competition

Colony-grabbing created a sense of competition among the larger nations of Europe. Each wanted to have more, and all were looking at each other suspiciously. This fed a growing spirit of nationalism that went beyond the earlier desires for a unified country. Now nationalism meant a belief that your country was better than others and deserved to expand its power and reach as fully as possible.

One symbol of national pride was a strong army that could defend national interests when necessary. Germany had already developed a powerful military force by 1900, and other European nations tried to catch up with it. In this mindset, nations were quick to consider military action when a potentially troubling situation arose. The goal was to maintain peace through a position of strength so that other nations would not threaten, but every nation wanted to be the strongest. This resulted in a huge arms race. In addition, several nations wanted to add to their strength by forming alliances with other countries to be partners if any one nation in the alliance was threatened.

Bismarck of Germany feared that France might try to attack Germany in revenge for its loss in the Franco-Prussian War. As a result, Germany created a military alliance with Austria-Hungary in 1879. This Dual Alliance was later expanded to the Triple Alliance when Italy joined. France, meanwhile formed an alliance with Russia in 1894 to protect against any expansionist moves of Germany. This meant that Germany faced the possibility of a two-front war, against France to the west and Russia to the east, should conflict erupt. Britain, which still ruled the seas, became threatened by the German naval build-up. As a result, Britain made an informal mutual defense agreement with France. This group of three was called the Allies or the Triple Entente (French for "understanding," or "intent").

Moreover, no international law existed to govern such competition and potential conflict. Conferences at The Hague in the Netherlands around the turn of the century attempted to formulate such law, including a ban on the use of poison gas (a new weapon of mass destruction) and the creation of an international court of arbitration where countries could take their complaints before turning to military action.

The Powder Keg

Many observers saw the Balkan peninsula, which lies between Austria and Turkey, as a powder keg that combined all of the factors which threatened the uneasy peace of Europe. The dying Ottoman Empire clung to some areas of the Balkans where Islam was strongest. Austria, which had formed

Exploring the Poles

The early 1900s saw the exploration of the North and South Polar regions. Exploration in the North had historically been motivated by the desire to find a northwest passage from the Atlantic to the Pacific Ocean. On a journey from 1903 to 1905, Norwegian explorer Roald Amundsen (1872-1928) managed to get through the  *icy waters north of Canada. The difficulty of the trip showed that development of the passage for regular use was not practical. Claims regarding who got to the North Pole first have been disputed. Robert Peary (1856-1920), an American, is generally recognized as the leader of a team that reached the North Pole in 1909. Amundsen flew with a team over the North Pole in 1926 in the* Norge *airship (shown at left).*

The Antarctic region was the scene of seal hunting beginning in 1790, when Americans first ventured into the area to pursue this trade. Amundsen led a team that arrived at the geographic South Pole in 1911. British explorer Ernest Shackleton led an expedition in 1914 that attempted to cross the continent of Antarctica, but his ship Endurance *(pictured at right) became trapped in the ice. Though his crew was stranded through the winter of 1914-1915, all 28 members were eventually rescued.*

Lesson 116 - The Great War

Archduke Franz Ferdinand and His Wife, Sophia

a dual monarchy with Hungary in 1867, annexed Bosnia and Herzegovina in the Balkans in 1908. However, the peninsula was home to a mixture of ethnic groups that resented both Ottoman and Austrian control. These groups wanted the opportunity to live in a free country of their own, but they were victims of the nationalistic expansion of others.

The strongest nationalist feelings were held by the Slavs, who lived in several of the small countries in the Balkans. Serbia, a predominantly Slavic nation, gained its independence from the Ottoman Empire in 1878. Many Serbians, including its government, wanted to see a Pan-Slavic state that would include all Slavs in a single political unit. The Slavs were encouraged in their desires by Russia, which shared their Slavic ethnic background, and by France and Great Britain, which opposed Austria-Hungary. Russia, France, and Great Britain all hoped for a slice of the Balkans to feed their hunger for empire.

However, matters in the region were even more complicated. Russia and Great Britain had historic conflicts in the Black Sea area, dating from the Crimean War in the mid-1800s. In addition, Germany was building a Berlin-to-Baghdad railroad to expand its eastern trade routes. The rail line passed through the Balkans and the Ottoman Empire, and governments in those regions did not want to stand in Germany's way.

Austria-Hungary feared that if Slavic nationalism pulled any of its territory in the Balkans out of its grasp, the tide of nationalism would ripple throughout the region and damage the Austrian Empire. If Austria were weakened in this way, the Triple Alliance would also be weakened.

The Spark in the Powder Keg

Serbian nationalists, unable to oppose Austrian rule in Bosnia and Herzegovina directly, resorted to terrorism. One Serbian terrorist group was the Black Hand. Its goal was to unite Bosnia and Herzegovina with Serbia as a Slavic state. On June 28, 1914, the heir to the Austrian throne, Archduke Franz Ferdinand, and his wife, were in Sarajevo in Bosnia on a visit that was intended to remind the Bosnians who was in charge. As the royal couple rode through the streets of Sarajevo, Gavrilo Princip assassinated the archduke and his wife. Princip was a member of the Black Hand and a Slavic Serb.

After receiving assurances from Germany that it would support any action against the perpetrators, Austria-Hungary used the killings to put pressure on Serbia and the Pan-Slavic movement. About one month after the assassinations, the Austrian government issued an ultimatum to the government of Serbia. Austria demanded that Serbia suppress all anti-Austrian activities and dismiss all officials who harbored resentment toward Austria-Hungary. Austria also demanded that Serbia allow Austrian investigators to come into Serbia to investigate the assassination. Austria wanted an answer to all of this within 48 hours.

Trial in Sarajevo of Conspirators in the Assassination

The Black Hand group was not directly sponsored by the government of Serbia, but some Serbian officials were sympathetic to the group's agenda and apparently even knew of the assassination plot. Refusing the Austrian demands would almost surely lead to war, but agreeing to the last demand would sacrifice Serbian sovereignty. Therefore, Serbia agreed to all of the demands except the last one.

Germany advised caution, but Austria-Hungary ignored this advice and ordered a mobilization of its troops to prepare for war. Then the dominoes began to fall. Russia began a partial mobilization of its forces to be ready to help Serbia. Five days after issuing the ultimatum, on July 28, 1914, Austria-Hungary declared war on Serbia. The Russian czar then ordered a full mobilization. Germany requested that Russia cancel its mobilization; when it did not do so, Germany declared war against Russia on August 1 and (attempting to pre-empt the inevitable) declared war against France on August 3.

These wounded soldiers from British India are at a hospital in England. They are being entertained by a gramophone and a bagpiper. The photographer was H.D. Girdwood, a Canadian who was in India at the outbreak of the war. He went to England with Indian troops and took propaganda photos for the British government.

Russian Troops in a Trench at the Battle of Sarikamish, Turkey, c. 1915

When German forces moved across neutral Belgium to invade France, Britain, in keeping with its commitment to defend Belgium, declared war against Germany on August 4. Japan entered the war on the side of the Allies, while the Ottoman Empire declared its support for Austria-Hungary. Italy was neutral at first, but it came into the war for the Allies in 1915.

The Course of the War

Germany, hoping to avoid a two-front war, planned to strike France quickly and defeat it, and then move against Russia. Germany plowed through Belgium and into northern France, but the advance was stalled by British and French resistance. From this point until the end of the war, the western front was largely a stalemate involving fixed positions, fighting from long trenches facing across "no man's land," and occasional attempts in various places by both sides to break through the enemy's lines. Neither side gained much ground on the eastern front either.

The war saw the introduction of new weapons, such as tanks, airplanes, and poison gas. Casualties were enormous. The four years of conflict affected

No Man's Land, Flanders Field, France, 1919

more people, saw more armed forces engaged, and spread over more land area than any war in history. More than twenty nations were directly involved, and it became known as the Great War.

The upheaval of the war added to domestic unrest in Russia. A Communist revolution took place there in October of 1917. The new government sued for peace with Germany the next month. Under the treaty, Russia gave up about one-fourth of its land and population in order to end the slaughter and begin to rebuild. The Communists saw the conflict as the war of the deposed czar, not a war that they chose.

French Photos from The Great War

Russia's departure was offset by the entrance of the United States into the war. President Woodrow Wilson had declared America's neutrality when the war began, and most Americans were satisfied with this stance. The United States was much less connected to affairs in Europe and Asia than it is now, and neutrality seemed to be a viable option. The country's historic ties with England were offset by pro-German sentiment among many German immigrants in the U.S.

In 1915 a German submarine sank the RMS *Lusitania,* a British ship carrying military supplies and passengers, including some Americans. This incident caused public outcry, but it did not lead to immediate U.S. entry into the war. German aggression against Atlantic shipping increased, and evidence surfaced of an attempt by Germany to recruit Mexico into an alliance against the United States. On April 2, 1917, Wilson asked Congress for a declaration of war against Germany, which came a few days later. When large numbers of American troops began arriving in Europe in late 1917 and early 1918, they added pressure on the armies of the Central Powers that were beginning to crumble. Germany accepted Wilson's call for "peace without victory" and began negotiating for an armistice (a truce to halt the fighting). A revolt against the German government broke out within Germany. A republic was declared on November 9, and Kaiser Wilhelm II fled to the Netherlands the next day. On November 11, 1918, at 11:00 a.m., Germany signed the armistice that ended the fighting.

The Versailles Peace Conference

The leaders of the Allied powers met in Versailles, France, to hammer out the terms of a peace treaty. The goal of the European allies, who had borne the brunt of the war, was to make Germany pay. President Wilson brought high ideals about creating an international arrangement to prevent future wars.

Separate treaties were drawn up with each of the Central Powers. When Germany and its allies complained about the proposed terms, the Allies threatened to renew their war effort. To humiliate the Germans, France had the German representatives sign the treaty in the Hall of Mirrors in Versailles, where Bismarck had declared the German Empire several years before.

Germany was forced to give Alsace-Lorraine back to France and to give up its overseas empire and the lands it had captured from Russia. The German government had to dismantle its armies and much of its merchant marine. New political arrangements were made on the global map. Poland was reconstituted as a sovereign nation. Austria and Hungary were separated, the country of Turkey was all that was left of the Ottoman Empire, and the pan-Slavic nation of Yugoslavia, the issue that had started it all, was created in the Balkans. The principle of self-determination for ethnic groups was generally followed, though not in every case.

The hardest terms for Germany to swallow were the admission of guilt for causing the war and the demand to pay heavy reparations to the Allies. Only part of the reparations were ever paid because of the struggling German economy. The guilt clause created bitterness in Germany that helped lead to the next war.

The Effects of the War

Of the sixty million soldiers mobilized into active duty around the world, about nine million died. The total of all deaths, civilian and military, from fighting and from other war-related causes such as disease was thirty million.

Fall of the Ottoman Empire

The Great War delivered a death blow to the Ottoman Empire. Because it was on the losing side, the Ottoman government lost almost all of its territories. The picture at left shows Ottoman officials attempting to surrender Jerusalem to two British sergeants in 1917.

In 1919 Greece seized land in Asia Minor that was still ruled by the Ottoman Turks. A group of Turkish nationalists led by Mustafa Kemal ousted the Greeks. The Ottoman Empire was abolished in 1922, and a republic under Kemal was instituted in 1923. Kemal was called Ataturk ("Father of the Turks"). He led sweeping changes to modernize Turkey.

During and immediately after the Great War, the Muslim Ottoman government approved persecution against the Armenians, who were Orthodox Christians. The Armenian population of Asia Minor dropped by an estimated 1.5 million from 1914 to 1922. Hundreds of thousands were killed or died because of disease and starvation during removal from their homes. Survivors resettled in other areas, particularly Syria. The modern government of Turkey denies that this was genocide, a deliberate and organized attempt to exterminate the Armenians.

The Battle of Verdun (France) between French and German troops lasted for ten months in 1916 and involved over two million soldiers. Around 300,000 men were killed or went missing and were presumed dead. Hundreds of thousands more were wounded. The Douamont Ossuary, shown in the background above, contains the remains of over 100,000 unidentified French and German soldiers. In the foreground is the largest French military cemetery of the Great War with 16,000 graves.

More broadly, the war changed the outlook of many in the world. Liberalism, reason, and progress did not seem to be workable answers any longer. In many countries the aristocracy lost power, and the younger generation was disillusioned. Many grasped for something to believe in. Past abuses by people claiming to follow Christ and the views of higher criticism had turned many people, especially in Europe, against Christianity. Philosophies that became popular were socialism, skepticism, and nihilism (nothingness). Another force arose in Italy and Germany which promised a new day: the extreme nationalism of Mussolini and Hitler.

The costs of the war and its devastation made recovery difficult. The United States responded by turning inward. Wilson was the moralist at the peace conference, but his proposal for a League of Nations as a way to prevent future wars received only lukewarm acceptance both abroad and at home. The U.S. Senate voted to reject the Versailles peace accords with its provision for a League of Nations, and the U.S. made separate treaties with the Central Powers.

Between the Wars

In the United States, economic recovery from the war started slowly. This was complicated by a Red Scare, a fear that the Communist Revolution in Russia might be duplicated in the United States. Economic recovery did come during the 1920s. The U.S. even started to become the economic center of the world. However, the economic downturn of the Great Depression affected the U.S. and the world economies.

In Europe, the road to recovery was especially difficult. Britain moved not toward more capitalism (since its resources were limited) nor toward revolution (since the British disliked both extremes of Communism and Fascism), but instead toward what was called the welfare state, with private enterprise continuing but with the government taking a much larger role in managing the economy. The British government even assumed control of some vital parts of the economy when leaders felt it necessary. France struggled back and built a line

Much of the Middle East was put under British control after the Great War. Iraq became an independent country in 1932 under the leadership of King Faisal I. Iraq became a member of the League of Nations that year. This photo shows the king giving a speech in Baghdad celebrating that event.

of fortifications along its border with Germany, known as the Maginot Line.

The League of Nations came into existence, but the United States was never a member. Germany and the Soviet Union were not allowed to be members. The League was never a force to be reckoned with in handling international conflict. Nations generally took matters into their own hands when they saw fit, without consulting the League.

The two world wars of the first half of the 20th century were connected. They were the result of (1) the competitive international colonial system, (2) intense nationalistic feelings that erupted into conflict, and (3) the attempt to create a balance of power among European nations. The Great War occurred as a direct result of these factors. The incomplete settlement of these and other issues set the stage for World War II only twenty years later.

He makes wars to cease to the end of the earth;
He breaks the bow and cuts the spear in two;
He burns the chariots with fire.
Psalm 46:9

Assignments for Lesson 116

In Their Words Read the excerpt from *Three Times and Out* (pages 290-293).

Literature Continue reading *The Hiding Place*. Plan to finish it by the end of this unit.

Student Review Optional: Answer the questions for Lesson 116.

U.S. Troops Preparing to Land in France on D-Day

Lesson 117

World War II

Fascism and Nazism

Several factors contributed to the rise of authoritarian leaders in Italy and Germany: reaction to the settlement of the Great War, failure of the democratic governments in those countries, the rise of a militant nationalism, and the appeal of these leaders to the interests of both the upper class and the working class.

Italy did not have a long tradition of democracy. Its post-war government was weak, the country suffered severe economic problems, and its gains from being on the winning side of the war were minimal. The Communist and Catholic political parties were strong; but the Communists split, leaving the door open for Benito Mussolini to step forward as a national savior.

Mussolini was the son of a laborer. He began getting an education to become a teacher, but he turned to political agitation and became the editor of a socialist newspaper. Mussolini opposed Italy's involvement in the Great War at first and fled to Switzerland to avoid serving. Later, however, he encouraged participation. The Socialist Party expelled him, and Mussolini served in the war until he was injured in 1917.

Following the war, Mussolini spoke out harshly against Soviet Communists and the Italian government. He organized the Fascist Party, named for the fasces, a bundle of rods that was a symbol of strength during the Roman Empire. The group wore black shirts and became known for bullying other political parties. Mussolini effectively played on people's fears and came across as a strong leader, which won him wide support. He was backed by the army and by Italian industrialists, who feared socialists and who were frustrated by the failures of the existing government.

When in 1922 Mussolini and his followers marched on Rome to defend the capital from the Communists (though no Communist threat was known to exist), the constitutional monarch, Victor

Benito Mussolini and Adolf Hitler, 1940

Emmanuel III, asked Mussolini to form a new government. Mussolini then changed the election laws in his favor and took control of Parliament. Soon the Fascists were the only legal political party.

In Germany, Adolf Hitler, a German veteran of the Great War, joined and soon became leader of the National Socialist (Nazi) German Workers Party in the German state of Bavaria. Like Mussolini, Hitler appealed to the fears of the people: fears related to the struggling economy and to what he saw as the dangers of ethnic impurity. For Hitler, the fault for Germany's problems lay with those who had humbled Germany and especially with the Jews, who in his mind wielded too much power and were a blight in society.

In 1923 Hitler failed in an attempt to seize the state government of Bavaria. He was imprisoned for more than a year. During this time he wrote *Mein Kampf (My Struggle)*, in which he outlined his goals for conquest. Hitler, like Mussolini, was supported by the middle class, who feared both chaos and Communism.

After his jail term, Hitler and his Nazi party continued to grow in power. In 1933 the aging German president asked Hitler to form a government as chancellor. The Nazis did not have a majority in the legislature, so Hitler called for new elections in the hope of gaining a majority. A week before the election, a fire destroyed the legislative building. It was probably set by the Nazis, but Hitler blamed the Communists and declared martial law. The Nazis pushed through legislation that gave Hitler dictatorial powers for four years. By the end of the year, Hitler's opponents were in exile or in jail; and the Nazis had gained total control. The army and the industrialists supported Hitler as their best hope.

Hitler implemented policies based on his belief in the superiority of the Germanic people and his hatred of the Jews. The Nazis instituted discriminatory laws against the Jews. Hitler forced them to wear identifying badges, their synagogues were burned, and the "final solution" of destroying them in concentration camps was begun.

The Star of David

In the early 1940s, Jews in Nazi-occupied territories had to wear badges with the Star of David and the word Jude, *German for Jew. The origin of the Star of David as a symbol of Judaism is unclear.*

According to tradition, David's armies displayed it on their shields or had shields in that shape (the Hebrew word translated star actually means shield); but evidence of its use in ancient times is limited. The symbol of intertwined triangles was used by other people groups in the Middle East and North Africa, and it might have had a connection to magic at one time. As shown at left, the hexagram appears as part of a design in the Leningrad Codex, the earliest surviving complete copy of the Hebrew Bible (c. 1000 AD).

The Zionist Movement, led by Theodor Herzl, chose an official flag design that included the Star of David between two horizontal blue bars. This became the model for the modern flag of Israel. The Magen David Adom ("red star of David") is the national emergency organization of Israel, associated with the International Federation of Red Cross and Red Crescent Societies.

Lesson 117 - World War II

International Aggression

Internationally, Germany, Italy, and Japan supported each other in seizing land. Japan invaded Manchuria in China in 1931. The League of Nations recommended sanctions against Japan, but the British were reluctant to support the move and the United States was on the sidelines. Japan's defiance of the League encouraged other aggressors.

Italy annexed Ethiopia in 1936 and resigned from the League of Nations. Later that year, Italy and Germany announced a mutual defense pact. Mussolini declared that the axis of the world now ran between Rome and Berlin. Thus the two countries became known as the Axis. Japan joined them the next year. The premise of the agreement was to defend against Communist aggression, but actually they were planning to be as aggressive as they accused the Communists of being.

Meanwhile, in 1935 Hitler had announced that he was going to rearm Germany in defiance of the Treaty of Versailles. Hitler said that Germany needed more *lebensraum* (living space), which meant that he planned to invade other countries. In 1938 Hitler took over Austria. Hitler also gave aid to Francisco Franco, the leader of a fascist rebellion in Spain. Franco won, but Spain was never a major factor in World War II. Many in Britain and France were alarmed at the actions of Italy and Germany; but most British and French were opposed to becoming involved in another war, and their governments were ineffective in dealing with the aggressors.

In 1938 France and Germany agreed for Hitler to take over a German-speaking part of Czechoslovakia without complaint (he took the rest of Czechoslovakia six months later). Hitler then turned his attention to Poland, and as a result, the Soviet Union began looking for security of its own. The Soviets, while supposedly considering a defense pact with Britain and France, on August 23, 1939, shocked the world by announcing a non-aggression treaty with Germany. Secret provisions called for the two countries to divide up Poland and the rest of Eastern Europe.

On September 1, 1939, German forces invaded Poland. This is usually seen as the start of World War II. France and Britain declared war on Germany two days later, but they provided minimal practical support to the Poles at first. The Soviets moved into eastern Poland on September 17, and most Polish resistance was crushed by October. The government of Poland never formally surrendered to the invaders, and Polish troops served with Allied forces throughout the war.

Emperor Hirohito ruled Japan from 1926 until his death in 1989, the longest reign in Japanese history. The photo above shows him at his enthronement. Though the Emperor officially had supreme authority over the country, the day-to-day affairs of government were largely in the hands of others. Military leaders had a great influence on government policy, and historians still debate the role that Hirohito played in Japan's military expansion of the 1930s.

War in Europe and the Pacific

In 1940 Germany took over Denmark and Norway. Hitler then moved against France by avoiding its defensive Maginot Line and going through the Netherlands and Belgium. The German attack isolated about 300,000 British troops against the English Channel near the town of Dunkirk in northern France. To help evacuate its soldiers, Britain summoned every available vessel, large or small, in a stunning mobilization of citizens. As the Germans moved on Paris, Italy came into the war on the side of Germany. France fell to the Germans in June of 1940. To humiliate the French, Hitler had French officials sign the document of surrender in the same rail car in which German officials had signed the armistice in 1918 to end the Great War.

This left Britain as the only declared enemy of Germany that could offer any meaningful military resistance. Hitler planned an invasion of England, and in mid-1940 he began sending German aircraft to bomb Britain in order to soften their resistance. The Germans were able to cause significant damage on the ground; however, the British Royal Air Force thwarted the German air attack, and the invasion never happened. Prime Minister Winston Churchill called this Battle of Britain "their finest hour."

Pilots from other countries joined British airmen in fighting the German Luftwaffe, including Australians, Canadians, New Zealanders, South Africans, Belgians, Czechs, and Poles. The pilots pictured below are from the No. 303 ("Kościuszko") Polish Fighter Squadron

The next year, German forces invaded the Soviet Union. Russian resistance and the Russian weather caused the assault to stagnate, and the Germans eventually had to retreat. Meanwhile, on December 7, 1941, Japan launched an air assault on the United States' military installation at Pearl Harbor in Hawaii (which was a U.S. territory, not a state, at the time). Japan had been moving aggressively throughout the Pacific and decided to make a pre-emptive strike against the U.S. in the hope of eliminating any opposition to their moves.

Before the attack on Pearl Harbor, the United States had begun supplying military equipment to the Allies through a program called Lend-Lease. The bulk of this aid went to Britain and the Soviet Union, with smaller amounts going to Free France, China, and other Allies. After the Japanese attack, the U.S. entered the war against Japan, Germany, and Italy. The U.S. government oversaw the transformation of the domestic economy to focus heavily on wartime production. Located far from the main scenes of conflict, and with access to extensive natural resources, the United States was able to generate huge quantities of military supplies for the Allied war effort.

In 1942 reinforcements of fresh American troops began to help turn the tide against the Axis in the Pacific, in North Africa, and in Europe. American forces cleared the Japanese from the island of Guadalcanal northeast of Australia and began the slow task of island-hopping toward Japan. The Allies defeated German forces in northern Africa and then moved into Italy. Mussolini was imprisoned by other Fascists, and Axis fighting in Italy was taken over by the Germans. The new Italian government that was formed after Mussolini's overthrow joined the Allies. After many difficult battles, the Allies entered Rome on June 4, 1944.

Meanwhile, a giant Allied assault was planned for the northern coast of France to push the Germans out of France and then move east to invade Germany and end the war. The code name for the landing

Lesson 117 - World War II

was Operation Overlord, and the day of invasion, June 6, 1944, was called D-Day. Fighting was fierce, but the Allies secured the beaches and began moving inland. Paris was liberated on August 25, 1944. The push toward Germany was interrupted only in December of 1944, when the German forces broke through the Allied line and made a bulge back toward the west. This Battle of the Bulge was only a temporary setback, and the advance toward Germany continued.

Allied forces entered Germany on March 7, 1945. In Italy, Mussolini had been released by the Germans, but he was captured again by Italians and executed on April 28. Hitler committed suicide two days later. The German high command surrendered on May 7, and V-E (Victory in Europe) Day was celebrated the next day.

In the Pacific, the Allied advance toward Japan continued into the summer of 1945. Then in August, the United States dropped atomic bombs on the cities of Hiroshima and Nagasaki. Japan surrendered a few days later, on August 14 (V-J Day, Victory over Japan), and signed the surrender documents September 2, 1945. At last, the war was over.

Nazi Concentration Camps

Besides Jews and those who helped them, the Nazis imprisoned many others in concentration camps, including Gypsies, the handicapped, and political dissidents. The horrors of the concentration camps showed the depths of man's inhumanity to man; but even there, the best in mankind found ways to emerge.

Maximilian Kolbe was a Catholic priest from Poland who was a prisoner at Auschwitz. In August of 1941, after a prisoner escaped, the prison warden chose ten men at random to die of starvation as revenge. One of the condemned, Franciszek Gajowniczek, cried out in anguish for his wife and children. Kolbe stepped forward to take Gajowniczek's place, and he was allowed to do so. Ten days later, after leading the other nine in prayers and hymns, Kolbe was put to death by lethal injection. Gajowniczek lived to return to his family. He dedicated his life to telling others about the man who died in his place. Gajowniczek died in 1995, having lived long enough to see Poland freed from Communism.

Dietrich Bonhoeffer was a German Lutheran minister when Hitler seized power. Bonhoeffer left Germany for a time, but he decided to return to minister to suffering believers. He opposed the Nazi regime and became involved with a group of Germans who attempted to kill Hitler. Bonhoeffer was arrested and placed in a concentration camp. He was executed by the Nazis in April of 1945, just a few days before the camp was liberated by the Allies. Bonhoeffer is known for his insightful writings that reflect his deep commitment to following Jesus. Among his books are The Cost of Discipleship, Letters and Papers from Prison, *and* Life Together.

Viktor Frankl was a Jewish psychiatrist who spent several years in a prison camp and survived. He observed that prisoners who had a purpose for their lives had a better chance of making it than those who gave up hope. In his book that recounts his experiences and tells what he learned, Man's Search for Meaning, *Frankl wrote that we can survive almost any how if we have a why.*

These survivors of a concentration camp in Austria were liberated by Allied troops in May 1945.

Effects of the War

The toll of the Second World War was even greater than that of the first. Some seventy million people were mobilized, with seventeen million casualties. Including the six million Jews murdered by the Nazis, the total loss of life, military and civilian, caused by the war is estimated at fifty million. The conflict was total war as never before, with civilian populations heavily involved in the war effort and often the target of military attack.

After the Great War, the defeated nations were harshly punished. The Allies implemented a different policy toward the defeated nations after the Second World War. Rather than punishing Germany, Italy, and Japan, the United States sought to help and rebuild them. The Marshall Plan, named for U.S. Secretary of State George Marshall, provided loans and other economic aid to war-torn Europe.

Japan was occupied by American troops and forced to eliminate its military. The country underwent a transition to a democratic government imposed by the American occupation forces. Americans helped to rebuild the Japanese economy. Japanese businesses borrowed American techniques and in some cases, became more proficient at using them than the Americans had been.

The decades after the war also saw a significant increase in missionary activity. Christians who had served in the military had seen a diverse world that needed Christ. Some of these Christians came home,

Women in Berlin Doing Their Washing, July 1945

went to Bible college, and then went back overseas as missionaries. The 1950s saw a revival of spiritual activity around the world.

The war brought major changes to the British Empire, which lost its prominent position in world affairs. After supporting a fight against the oppressive Axis governments, people living in British colonies argued that they had a right to self-determination of their governments. Most of the British colonies achieved independence in the 1940s, 50s, and 60s.

One issue that America had to face was treatment of African Americans. Thousands had served capably during the war, though in segregated units. When these soldiers returned home, many blacks recognized that they had been fighting for freedom for others when they did not have complete freedom and equality in America themselves. The

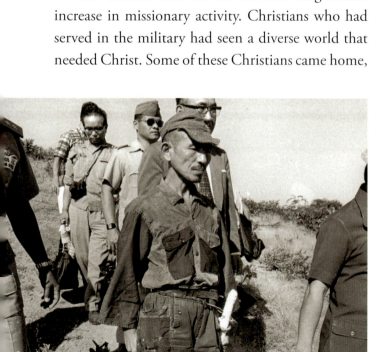

For years after the end of the war, isolated Japanese soldiers on Pacific islands refused to give up the fight. One of the last confirmed holdouts was Lt. Hiroo Onoda on Lubang Island in the Philippines. Along with three other Japanese, he eluded capture and refused to believe printed messages and radio reports that the war was over. Onoda was the only survivor when he was discovered in 1974. His former commanding officer was located in Japan and came to order him to give up. Onoda died in 2014 at age 91.

Lesson 117 - World War II

World War II Veterans Cemetery, Hausjärvi, Finland

Great Patriotic War (WWII) Memorial, Buryatia, Russia

The Kranji War Memorial in Singapore honors men and women from Australia, Canada, India, Malaya, the Netherlands, New Zealand, Sri Lanka, and the United Kingdom who died defending Singapore and Malaya during World War II.

Memorial for South African Soldiers, El Alamein, Egypt

*Memorial from the People of Cuba
Nagasaki Peace Park, Japan*

Unit 24 - The World at War

World War II influenced the development of such products as computers, electronics, radar, plastics, synthetics, jet engines, rockets, and atomic energy. ENIAC, the first general-purpose electronic computer (shown above), was developed for the U.S. Army.

civil rights movement in the United States became more active after the war. The United States became an international power with troops stationed around the world and a keen interest in international affairs.

The world was no longer dominated by European nations. In addition to the United States, the Soviet Union had gained a prominent role. Germany was divided between Allied-controlled (West) and Soviet-controlled (East) zones. The capital city of Berlin, which was entirely within East Germany, was also divided into Allied-controlled West Berlin and Communist-controlled East Berlin. Bonn became the capital of West Germany.

Communists made no secret of their desire to take over the world. In addition to Soviet control of East Germany and several countries in Eastern Europe, Chinese Communists ousted the Nationalist government and set up their own totalitarian regime. Communists gained control of North Korea and tried to invade the South. Communist guerrillas fought for control of Southeast Asia. The United States was the key adversary that fought against the expansion of Communism around the world.

The United Nations was created in 1945 to promote world peace, but a major purpose behind it was to balance the interests of the U.S. and its allies against the Soviet Union and its satellite nations. The uneasy relationship between the U.S. and the U.S.S.R. formed the basis of the Cold War, which dominated the last half of the 20th century.

If one can overpower him who is alone, two can resist him.
A cord of three strands is not quickly torn apart.
Ecclesiastes 4:12

Assignments for Lesson 117

Literature — Continue reading *The Hiding Place*.

Student Review — Optional: Answer the questions for Lesson 117.

Stalin, Roosevelt, and Churchill at Tehran, Iran, 1943

Lesson 118 - Key Person

Winston Churchill

Sir Winston Leonard Spencer Churchill epitomized the forces of freedom during the time when the world was at war. An eloquent speaker, a prodigious writer, a brilliant politician, and a world statesman, Churchill served some fifty years in Parliament, held many cabinet positions, and was twice British prime minister.

His Early Life and Career

Lord Randolph Churchill was a younger son in a prominent British family. He married Jeanette Jerome, an American from Brooklyn, in Paris after a whirlwind romance. They did not have a close or happy marriage. Their eldest son Winston was born into wealth and privilege at Blenheim Palace in England in 1874.

Winston attended the Royal Military College and entered upon a career in the British army. Churchill saw action in Cuba, India, and the Sudan. He was sent by a newspaper to cover the Boer War in South Africa. The Boers captured him, but he made a daring escape and became a national hero.

Churchill was elected to Parliament in 1900 as a Conservative, but four years later he switched to the Liberals. When the Liberal Party gained a majority in 1905, Churchill filled a succession of cabinet positions, including First Lord of the Admiralty (similar to the Secretary of the Navy in the American government) during World War I. Although the British navy was strong, it suffered an embarrassing defeat in the Gallipoli campaign to control the Dardanelles in Turkey, a defeat for which Churchill had to take the blame. He went on active duty in France for a time but then returned to government.

Losing his seat in the House of Commons in 1922, Churchill rejoined the Conservative Party and won back his seat in 1924. He served as Chancellor of the Exchequer (similar to the Secretary of the Treasury) until 1929. During the 1930s, he warned Britain about the increasing threat that Adolph Hitler posed; but few people in the war-weary country listened to him.

Blenheim Palace, Birthplace and Ancestral Home of Winston Churchill

His Finest Hour

When Prime Minister Neville Chamberlain's policy of appeasement toward Hitler proved to be a failure, Churchill became prime minister in May of 1940. The next month, British troops had to be rescued from Dunkirk, France. The Battle of Britain between the Royal Air Force and the German Luftwaffe commenced later that summer. Churchill used his powers of eloquence to rally his beleaguered nation during their darkest period.

Churchill was intimately involved in planning British war strategy. He developed a close relationship with U.S. President Franklin Roosevelt that helped bring aid from the United States before the Japanese attack on Pearl Harbor led to America's official entrance into the war. Churchill also supported giving aid to the Soviet Union when it was attacked by Germany, even though he had deep suspicions of Stalin and the Soviet agenda in the war.

Winston Churchill is probably best remembered for his stirring speeches, many given over the radio, when Britain was feeling the onslaught of the German offensive.

Mr. and Mrs. Churchill (Far Right) Visited Jerusalem in 1921

Churchill Visits the Ruins of Coventry Cathedral, 1941

Family Man

Winston Churchill first met his future wife Clementine Hozier in 1904. They met again in 1908 and were married later that year. The couple had five children—Diana, Randolph, Sarah, Marigold, and Mary. Marigold died when still a little girl in 1921. In 1922 the family settled in Chartwell House in southeastern England.

Clementine Churchill had come from a dysfunctional home also, but she and Winston were able to build a close and happy marriage. Soon after he became prime minister, she wrote him this note:

> I hope you will forgive me if I tell you something that I feel you ought to know.
>
> One of the men in your entourage (a devoted friend) has been to me & told me that there is a danger of your being generally disliked by your colleagues and subordinates because of your rough sarcastic & overbearing manner . . . I was astonished & upset because in all these years I have been accustomed to all those who have worked with & under you,

loving you — I said this & I was told 'No doubt it's the strain' —

My Darling Winston — I must confess that I have noticed a deterioration in your manner; & you are not so kind as you used to be.

It is for you to give the Orders & if they are bungled — except for the King the Archbishop of Canterbury & the Speaker you can sack anyone & everyone — Therefore with this terrific power you must combine urbanity, kindness and if possible Olympic calm. . . .

Besides you won't get the best results by irascibility & rudeness. They will breed either dislike or a slave mentality — (Rebellion in War time being out of the question!)

This letter is included in *Winston and Clementine: The Personal Letters of the Churchills*, a collection published in 2001 by their last surviving child, Mary Soames. During World War II, Mary served as an anti-aircraft gunner with the Auxiliary Territorial Service and traveled with her father as an aide on some trips overseas. The Churchills' daughter Diana had married before the war, but she still served in the Women's Royal Navy Service. Their son Randolph was a Member of Parliament during the war. Daughter Sarah worked in the Women's Auxiliary Air Force studying aerial reconnaissance photos.

Clementine made supporting her husband a priority, but she largely left the care of their children in the hands of others. Winston was a devoted father when he made time in his busy schedule. The three older Churchill children led very sad and troubled lives. The Churchill family did not attend church regularly, and Mary credits her childhood nurse "Nana," a cousin of her mother, with instilling in her a vibrant religious faith that guided her life.

Churchill With His Daughter Mary at the Potsdam Conference, 1945

Legacy

After the United States and the Soviet Union became fully involved in the war, Churchill had less of an influence in overall war strategy. He was, however, able to convince the Allies to attack Northern Africa and southern Europe (the "soft underbelly of the Axis" in Churchill's words) before commencing the D-Day invasion in northern France. In July of 1945, with Germany defeated and Japan on the run, the British electorate voted out the Conservative government and returned a Labor majority to Parliament. At the last meeting of the Allied leaders, new British Prime Minister Clement Atlee and new U.S. President Harry Truman (Roosevelt had died in April of 1945) were overshadowed by the stature of Soviet leader Josef Stalin.

Besides his public career, Churchill's writing of history was voluminous. He wrote a biography of his father; a four-volume biography of his ancestor, the first duke of Marlborough; a four-volume *History of the English-Speaking Peoples*; and a six-volume history of *The Second World War*. He also took up painting during the first World War and produced some 500 works of art during his life.

Churchill remained leader of the Conservatives after World War II. His party returned to power in 1951, and Churchill began his second term as prime minister. He was knighted by Queen Elizabeth II in 1953 but suffered a stroke shortly thereafter. Churchill stepped down as prime minister in 1955, but he continued to serve in the House of Commons until 1964, though his health continued to deteriorate.

Winston Churchill died in 1965. Queen Elizabeth II ordered and attended a major state funeral at St. Paul's Cathedral in London, which drew representatives from 112 other countries. The service was broadcast live on television stations across Europe. Thousands of mourners paid their respects along the route as his funeral train traveled from London to the Spencer-Churchill family cemetery at St. Martin's Church near Blenheim Palace.

Sir Winston Churchill continues to be honored as one of the most influential and popular prime ministers in British history.

*Like apples of gold in settings of silver
Is a word spoken in right circumstances.
Proverbs 25:11*

Assignments for Lesson 118

In Their Words — Read the excerpts from Winston Churchill's speeches (pages 294-297).

Literature — Continue reading *The Hiding Place*.

Student Review — Optional: Answer the questions for Lesson 118.

Ninna-ji North Garden, Kyoto

Lesson 119 - Everyday Life

The Cultural History of Japan

Japan is called Nihon or Nippon in Japanese. It means Origin of the Sun. In English it is sometimes called the Land of the Rising Sun. The islands that make up Japan are the peaks of a huge underwater mountain chain. As part of the ring of fire around the coast of the Pacific Ocean, it has forty active volcanoes (10% of the world's total) and as many as 1,500 earthquakes each year.

Japan is made up of over 3,000 islands. The largest island is Honshû, which includes Japan's capital city of Tokyo. The next three largest islands are Hokkaidô, Kyûshû, and Shikoku. The main four islands extend 1,200 miles from northeast to southwest and 900 miles from east to west. They are separated from each other only by narrow straits. Distant island groups include the Ryukyu (Nansei Shotô), Izu, Bonin (Ogasawara), and Volcano Islands (Kazan Rettô). Japan claims several more islands north of Hokkaidô. They have been in dispute since the end of World War II. Russia administers the islands now.

Mountains cover three-fourths of Japan's land area, though most people live in the lowlands and plains. The population per square mile is among the densest in the world. Because of the construction of tunnels and bridges and the availability of air transportation, the mountain and water barriers no longer isolate the Japanese from one another.

The Japanese have a great respect and love for nature, and it is often a subject of their art. Japan is home to over 17,000 plants and celebrates many flower festivals. Two-thirds of Japan is forested. Wood from Japanese cedar and cypress trees is highly prized. The Japanese harvest and cultivate seaweed for food. They enjoy the hobby of growing miniature bonsai trees in pots. Japan is home to a red-faced monkey called the Japanese macaque. Beautiful cranes, herons, storks, and swans are common.

The Japanese People

Japan is the ninth most populated country in the world. Around the time of Christ, the ancestors of the Japanese probably migrated onto the islands from the mainland of Asia and from the islands of the South Pacific. The only major language in Japan is Japanese, which is of unknown origin. Several dialects are spoken. Most of the people now use standard Japanese. It is spoken by the educated people of Tokyo and is the dialect most often used on national television and radio. Japanese was only an oral language until Chinese writing was introduced in the 400s.

Japan is a homogenous society with few minorities. The ethnic Japanese make up 98% of the total population. The Korean, Burakumin, and Ainu minorities have suffered discrimination. The Burakumin were "hamlet people" during Japan's feudal era. Though like other Japanese racially and culturally, they have been kept separate because historically they did jobs considered to be unclean such as slaughtering animals and disposing of the dead. Discrimination is illegal but still occurs.

Ainu—Indigenous People of Japan

The Ainu are an indigenous people of Japan and far eastern Russia. According to tradition, they lived in Japan long before the ancestors of the Japanese arrived there. Oral history suggests that the Ainu might be related to the Tlinglet people of the Alaskan coast. One research theory is that they are related to Siberia's Tungusic, Altaic, and Uralic peoples. The Ainu lived on the islands of Hokkaidô and Honshû. About 25,000 Ainu still live on Hokkaidô, with smaller groups living on other islands.

Traditional foods of the Ainu were deer, bear, salmon, herring, and other fish; wild plants; and crops of beans, millet, and wheat. They lived in grass huts with open fires. Cloth was woven from the inner bark fiber of the elm tree and was called attush.

Male and female Ainu wear earrings and have thick wavy hair, like Europeans and Semites. The men have heavy beards and muscular bodies. Traditionally Ainu girls were tattooed on their hands, lips, and arms during childhood. When the tattooing was completed by age fifteen or sixteen, she was eligible to be married. Males were also eligible for marriage at that age. When a person died, the Ainu burned his or her family's house and moved elsewhere.

As Japanese power grew, the Ainu fought unsuccessfully to maintain their territory and culture. In the mid-1800s, Japan prohibited several Ainu customs, including the wearing of earrings by men, tattooing women, and the burning of houses. In the late 1800s, Japanese took the best Ainu land and made it illegal for them to fish. A law was passed in 1899 to assimilate the Ainu into Japanese

Ainu Bear Sacrifice (Japanese, c. 1870)

Lesson 119 - Everyday Life: The Cultural History of Japan

life. One method it employed was the creation of separate elementary schools for Ainu children. They were not allowed to speak their native language in these schools. The Ainu language is spoken by very few people today, but some Ainu are attempting to revive it.

The discriminatory law was not repealed until 1997, when it was replaced with the Ainu Shinpo, a governmental policy seeking to protect and promote Ainu culture. The Ainu have been supported by Native Americans in the U.S. and the First Nations of Canada.

Japanese Religion

Most Japanese practice Buddhism, Shinto, or both. Shinto was mentioned in the first history of Japan written in 720. From 1868 to 1945, it was the state religion. Many Japanese combine Buddhism and Shinto, and both are integral parts of Japanese culture. Many visit Shinto shrines for weddings, New Year's Day, and the onset of adulthood at age twenty, but participate in Buddhist ceremonies for funerals and for Obon, the midsummer celebration that honors ancestors. A variety of newer religious groups, known as *shinkô shûkyô*, have attracted followers. Perhaps 2% of Japan's population are members of Catholic or Protestant churches.

Traditional Japanese Music

Kagura, a Shinto music performed on drums, rattles, and flutes, is played at Shinto shrines and at Shinto folk festivals. When music is performed at a Buddhist temple in Japan, it is chanted in Japanese, Sanskrit, or Chinese. It is accompanied by bells and chimes. At the Buddhist *bon-odori* festival, singers

Haiku

The haiku poem, a small observation about everyday life, grew out of longer Japanese poetic forms. Matsuo Bashō was a 17th-century Japanese poet who is recognized as a pioneer of the form. One of his poems, "The Rough Sea," is shown at right painted on a wall in the Netherlands.

Traditional haiku, formalized in the late 1800s, consisted of seventeen sounds ("on") in three lines with a 5-7-5 structure. English syllables do not exactly correspond to Japanese on, *but many haiku in English have seventeen syllables. Traditional haiku mentions a season of the year and has a break in thought, often indicated by a dash in English.*

> *Blossoms budding white,*
> *Blue sky days getting longer—*
> *Spring is all around.*

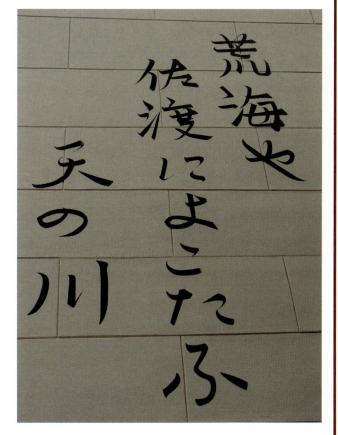

Thousands of people make submissions each year to publications devoted to haiku. Try writing your own!

A Shamisen Crafter with a Customer, c. 1909

and sometimes a flute, drum, and a three-stringed lute (*shamisen*) accompany the dancers.

Traditional woodwind instruments of the Japanese imperial court were a *ryûteki* (a flute), a *hichiriki* (a short double-reed pipe), and a *shô* (a mouth organ with seventeen bamboo pipes). Percussion instruments included a small gong called a *shokô* and two drums, a small two-headed one called a *kakko* and a large one called a *taiko*. Stringed instruments were the four-stringed lute called a *biwa* and the thirteen-stringed zither called a *koto*.

Traditional Theater and Dance

Japanese paintings and architecture show great respect for the natural world, but much of their traditional theater and dance has been rigid and unrealistic. The earliest known theater style was *gigaku*, performed by actors wearing masks. A formal, solemn style called *bugaku* followed. It is still performed at certain public ceremonies. *Sangaku* was popular in the 700s. It included juggling, tightrope walking, and sword swallowing. A ritual dance and play still performed today, the *Okina*, might date from the 11th century.

Japanese *nô* theater has been performed since the 1300s. These plays, inspired by Zen Buddhism, combine dance, drama, mime, music, and poetry. Costumes are rich and elaborate. It is performed by males only. When actors portray women or men of different ages than their own, they wear masks. *Nô* theater is serious, but the acts are interspersed with humorous *kyogen* farces.

A puppet theater style that developed in the 1500s and 1600s is called *jôruri* or *bunraku*. It combined puppets, chanters, and shamisen players. Kabuki theater also dates from that time. It is the most popular of all Japanese theater forms. It is a spectacle with great acting, music, and dance performed in brightly colored settings.

Japan has rich folk dance traditions. Many are religious. One form of Japanese dance is the rice-planting dance. It involves rhythmic movements that made planting rice more enjoyable. When Japanese women perform traditional dances, their movements are restricted by the tightness of the kimono. Leg and foot movements are quite small and controlled.

Geishas are a group of professional female singers and dancers in Japan. Traditionally they began their training at age seven and were bound to their employers by contracts arranged by their parents. They were basically slaves until and unless they married. Selling daughters was outlawed after World War II, but professional geishas still work in Japan. Today many are members of unions.

Maiko, such as those pictured below, are apprentices who learn the music, singing, and dancing of the geisha.

Japanese Martial Arts

Most of the two hundred varieties of martial arts originated in East Asia. Martial arts generally involve both physical and mental training. Eastern religions, especially Buddhism and Taoism, influenced the development of many martial arts.

Karate ("empty hand" in Japanese) became highly developed in the 1600s on Okinawa, which is now part of Japan. The origin of jujutsu ("art of gentleness") is unknown, but experts believe that elements of it were used by samurai warriors. Judo was developed in 1882 by a Japanese educator. It is based on jujutsu.

Ueshiba Morihei began teaching aikido ("way of harmony") after claiming to have had a vision about it in 1925. He integrated elements of the Zen religion (a fusion of Buddhism and Taoism) into aikido. Aikido is also derived from jujutsu. Kendo ("way of the sword") is a Japanese form of fencing. It is a twentieth century adaptation of kenjutsu ("art of the sword"), which was a form of mortal combat practiced by the samurai.

Sumo wrestling is a competitive martial arts sport that involves two heavy competitors. Each uses his weight either to push the other wrestler out of the ring or to make him touch the floor. It is based on the ancient sumai ("struggle") wrestling which began in 23 BC. It has many ritual elements. The *dohyo* (ring) is covered with a Shinto-style roof.

Art, Crafts, and Architecture

Traditional Japanese art and crafts include wood block printing, painting (on scrolls and screens), ceramics, calligraphy, lacquerwork, woven textiles, fans, dolls, and wooden cabinets. One traditional Japanese craft is silk thread embroidery on bright silk fabric. Stitches are long and soft. Preferred motifs are birds, flowers, bold lines, and abstract designs.

Most Japanese sculpture is directly related to Buddhism. Traditional Japanese architecture has excelled in building Buddhist temples and Shinto shrines; castles; and the *shoin*, a place to study and to receive guests. Many fine examples of modern architecture have been built since World War II.

Because Japan experiences as many as 1,500 earthquakes per year, the traditional Japanese house was lightweight, one-story, and easy to rebuild.

Kokeshi are wooden dolls made by hand in Japan. The traditional design is a cylindrical body without arms or legs, a rounded head, and painted clothing and facial features.

Inside walls made of paper on wooden frames were moved to make rooms larger or smaller. Traditional furniture includes chests and low tables. Floors covered with *tatami* (rice-straw mats) provided a place for kneeling or squatting at mealtime and for sleeping at night. Today many Japanese live in apartments in crowded urban centers.

The Tea Ceremony

Drinking tea has been part of Japanese culture for hundreds of years. The modern ritual tea ceremony has been traced back to the 1500s. It was originally held in a specially-built tea house made of bark-covered logs, woven straw, and other natural materials in the style of a rustic cottage. In the tea ceremony, the host leads guests in sharing a bowl of green tea as a celebration of harmony, respect, purity, and tranquility. In more elaborate ceremonies, the guests also eat sweets or even a full meal.

Beautiful ceramic vessels for use in the tea ceremony have been created. In the Momoyama period (1573-1603) each elegant vessel had a specific function and name. One famous type of tea vessel is Raku ware, which is asymmetrically-shaped and has a crackle glaze. Fine ceramic tea vessels are coated with green, brown, or purplish-brown glaze. Tea vessels, including cups, teapots, and water containers, are also made of lacquerwork.

Japanese Tea Ceremony

From the rising of the sun to its setting, the name of the Lord is to be praised.
Psalm 113:3

Assignments for Lesson 119

In Their Words Read "A Soldier's Regrets on Leaving Home" (page 298).

Literature Continue reading *The Hiding Place*.

Student Review Optional: Answer the questions for Lesson 119.

Hiroshima Peace Memorial

Lesson 120 - Bible Study

Peace

In our lives of turmoil, lived in busy families, in a nation on the run, in a world constantly at war, the great gift of God is the offer of peace. The twentieth century was marked by world wars as well as smaller wars in which the peace of the world hung in the balance. The twenty-first century has already seen more fighting taking place in various parts of the globe. The offer of peace in Jesus is indeed an attractive one.

A State of Peace

Peace is more than just the absence of open conflict. Family members might not exchange cross words or come to blows, but that does not mean they are at peace. Nations might not be shooting at each other, but they still might not be at peace with each other. Individuals might seem calm on the outside but actually be churning with emotion on the inside.

Peace is a positive state of harmony and good will. This is illustrated by the peace offering that is described in the Law (Leviticus 7:11-38). The peace offering was a free-will celebration by the worshiper that was an expression of thanks for his relationship to God. It is the only one of the sacrifices of which the worshiper could partake himself, which made it in a sense a fellowship meal between that person and God. The peace offering was not a recognition of the mere absence of conflict with God. Instead, it was a statement of joy at a person's close and rich fellowship with the Lord.

After the atomic bomb was dropped on Hiroshima, Japan, an exhibition hall built in 1915 was the only building left standing in the targeted area of the city. The photo below shows the building in October of 1945. The 2008 photo above shows the structure in rebuilt Hiroshima. It is part of Hiroshima Peace Memorial Park, dedicated to the memory of those who died and to the promotion of world peace.

699

We can have peace with God because God is a God of peace (Romans 15:33). God sent Jesus "to guide our feet in the way of peace" (Luke 1:79) and to bring "on earth peace among men with whom He is pleased" (Luke 2:14). "Those who love Your law have great peace, and nothing causes them to stumble" (Psalm 119:165).

Inner Personal Peace

Peace among men must start with peace within oneself. "The wicked are like the tossing sea, for it cannot be quiet, and its waters toss up refuse and mud. 'There is no peace,' says my God, 'for the wicked'" (Isaiah 57:20-21). The illustration of a stormy sea tossing up mud is a vivid one to describe those who do not have inner peace.

People who are not at peace within cannot establish peace with others. "They have healed the brokenness of My people superficially, saying 'Peace, peace,' but there is no peace'" (Jeremiah 6:14). The best that can happen in a conflict between people who are not at peace within themselves is a superficial papering-over of differences, but this is not real peace.

The peace of God comes through Jesus. Isaiah described the Messiah as Prince of Peace (Isaiah 9:6). Jesus told His followers, "Peace I leave with you, My peace I give to you; not as the world gives do I give to you. Do not let your heart be troubled, nor let it be fearful" (John 14:27). He also said, "These things I have spoken to you, so that in Me you may have peace. In the world you have tribulation, but take courage; I have overcome the world"

Nichidatsu Fujii (1885-1985) was a Japanese Buddhist monk. After meeting Mahatma Gandhi in 1933, he became a committed pacifist. During World War II, he traveled throughout Japan encouraging his fellow citizens to resist participating in the war effort. After the war, he organized construction of Peace Pagodas in Hiroshima, Nagasaki, and other cities around the world. Pictured below (clockwise from top left) are those in Nepal, Sri Lanka, New York, India, England, and California.

Lesson 120 - Bible Study: Peace

(John 16:33). Peace comes by believing (Romans 15:13). Peace is part of the fruit of the Spirit who lives within Christians (Galatians 5:22). When we turn our worries over to God, "the peace of God, which surpasses all comprehension, will guard your hearts and your minds in Christ Jesus" (Philippians 4:7).

Peace Within the Fellowship

The Prince of Peace enables peace among believers. One remarkable aspect of peace among Christians is that it can happen even among people with great differences who had formerly been at odds with each other. When Peter spoke to the Gentile God-fearer Cornelius, he said that the word God sent consisted of "preaching peace through Jesus Christ" (Acts 10:36). Paul described how Jesus reconciled Jews and Gentiles to each other by reconciling them both to God in Himself. "For He Himself is our peace," Paul said, breaking down barriers and making one new kind of person: simply Christians (Ephesians 2:14-16).

Christians are to be "diligent to preserve the unity of the Spirit in the bond of peace" (Ephesians 4:3). When Paul discussed issues and attitudes that divide Christians, he said, "The kingdom of God is not eating and drinking, but righteousness and peace and joy in the Holy Spirit" (Romans 14:17). Thus, "we pursue the things which make for peace and the building up of one another" (Romans 14:19).

A common greeting that Paul used in his letters included his prayer for peace for his readers (for example, Romans 1:7 and Ephesians 1:2). He admonished the Colossians to "let the peace of Christ rule in your hearts" (Colossians 3:15). With this emphasis on peace, how sad it is that peace often does not reign within the fellowship of those who follow the Prince of Peace.

The United Nations deploys soldiers, police officers, and civilian personnel in an effort to promote and preserve peace. UN peacekeepers are generally not authorized to intervene to stop ongoing violence between opposing forces. This photo of shelling in Homs, Syria, was taken in 2012 by a UN worker shortly before the United Nations Supervision Mission in Syria ended because of escalating violence in that country's civil war.

Peacemakers

The Lord's people are to promote peace. "Depart from evil and do good," wrote the psalmist. "Seek peace and pursue it" (Psalm 34:14). "Blessed are the peacemakers," Jesus said. When they do so, they demonstrate the family characteristic: "for they shall be called sons of God" (Matthew 5:9). As we indicated earlier, this is more than just preventing people from exchanging blows. That is what a peace*keeper* does. A peace*maker* works to bring about genuine reconciliation and goodwill.

When Jesus sent the seventy out to preach, He told them, "Whatever house you enter, first say, 'Peace be to this house.' If a man of peace is there, your peace will rest on him; but if not, it will return to you" (Luke 10:5-6). Paul told the Christians at Rome, "If possible, so far as it depends on you, be at peace with all men" (Romans 12:18). Paul wanted all Christians to pray for rulers so that we might live peaceful lives (1 Timothy 2:1-2).

The message that Christians share is the same message Peter preached to Cornelius and that God communicated through Jesus: the message of peace. Paul encouraged Christians to have "shod your feet with the preparation of the gospel of peace" (Ephesians 6:15). When we have peace with God, peace with our fellow believers, and peace with others through the Lord Jesus Christ, we will know the true peace that God brings.

Not Peace, But a Sword

The pursuit of peace can sometimes bring about conflict. On one occasion Jesus said, "Do not think that I came to bring peace on the earth; I did not come to bring peace, but a sword" (Matthew 10:34). In the context, Jesus was talking about the division that must take place between those who follow Him and those who do not. Jesus is not willing to have peace at any price. Real peace demands making hard choices and casting your lot with Jesus when others oppose you.

Alfred Nobel (1833-1896) was the Swedish inventor of dynamite and a businessman involved in the manufacture of weapons. His will established a foundation to award annual prizes in Physics, Chemistry, Physiology or Medicine, and Literature. The Nobel Peace Prize was intended to honor those who have "done the most or the best work for fraternity between nations, for the abolition or reduction of standing armies and for the holding and promotion of peace congresses." The first Peace Prize was awarded in 1901 to Henry Dunant (1828-1910, shown at left), a Swiss businessman whose ideas were instrumental in establishing the International Red Cross and the Geneva Convention, and to Frédéric Passy (1822-1912), a French economist who promoted peace through international dialogue and arbitration.

Paul said, "The God of peace will soon crush Satan under your feet" (Romans 16:20). This crushing work might sometimes involve conflict and difficulty in the short term to accomplish the long-term result. This is what Jesus experienced. The writer of Ecclesiastes said there is "a time to love and a time to hate; a time for war and a time for peace" (Ecclesiastes 3:8). Sadly, conflict with those who would destroy peace is sometimes necessary in order to achieve peace.

The Way of Peace

The real answer to the world's problems is found in the peace of Christ. Peace through strength is found through the strength of Christ, not through worldly sources of strength. In Israel and Palestine, in northern Ireland, in terrorist training camps—anywhere that conflict exists, real peace can and will come when the peace of Christ is working in the hearts of men. "The Lord will give strength to His people; the Lord will bless His people with peace" (Psalm 29:11).

Peace and Conflict at the Modern Olympic Games

1. While recovering from World War II, London hosted the 1948 Summer Olympics. No new facilities were built, and attendees were asked to bring their own food because of shortages. Athletes from Germany and Japan were excluded, while the USSR declined to send any participants.

2. Melbourne, Australia, hosted the 1956 Summer Games, the first held outside Europe or North America. John Ian Wing, a seventeen-year-old Australian of Chinese ancestry, wrote a letter to the Olympic Committee suggesting that athletes should mingle together and wave to the crowd during the closing ceremonies, instead of marching in national groups. This tradition has been followed at each Olympics since.

3. The 1940 Olympics had been scheduled to occur in Japan, but Japanese aggression in the late 1930s led to their cancellation. Japan hosted the 1964 Summer Olympics in Tokyo and the 1972 Winter Olympics in Sapporo (Okurayama Ski Jump Stadium shown at right). Both Games were officially opened by Emperor Hirohito.

4. At the 1972 Summer Olympics in Munich, Germany, eight Palestinians took hostage eleven members of the Israeli Olympic team. During the ensuing standoff, all of the Israelis were killed. The Games continued, but the remaining Israelis and some other athletes left Munich.

5. Montreal, Canada, was the site of the 1976 Summer Games. Because of apartheid, South African athletes had been banned from the Olympics since 1964. Other African countries also wanted the Olympic Committee to ban New Zealand because their national (not Olympic) rugby team was touring South Africa. When this did not happen, twenty-six African countries, along with Iraq and Guyana, boycotted the games.

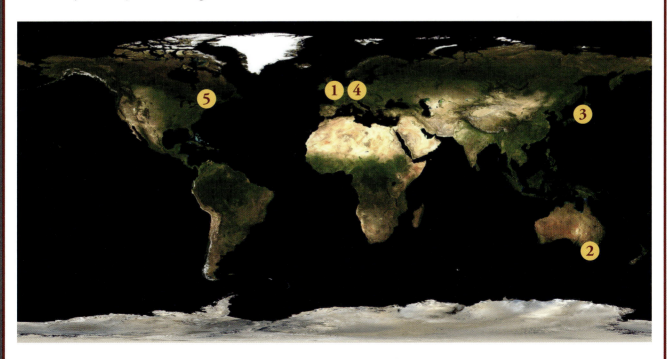

And He will judge between the nations,
And will render decisions for many peoples;
And they will hammer their swords into plowshares
and their spears into pruning hooks.
Nation will not lift up sword against nation,
And never again will they learn war.
Isaiah 2:4

Assignments for Lesson 120

Bible Recite or write Psalm 46:1-3 from memory.

In Their Words Read the excerpt from "Unity Between Nations" (pages 299-300).

Literature Finish reading *The Hiding Place*. Literary analysis available in *Student Review*.

Project Complete your project for the week.

Student Review Optional: Answer the questions for Lesson 120 and for *The Hiding Place*, and take the quiz for Unit 24.

25

The Cold War

Summary The United States and the Soviet Union engaged in a forty-five-year standoff called the Cold War. The space race was a highly visible part of the competition. The key person that we highlight is Ronald Reagan, who played an important role in ending the Cold War. We look at everyday life in the United States and in Communist Russia. The Bible study surveys what 1 Timothy says about fighting the good fight of faith.

Lessons
121 - Freedom vs. Communism
122 - Key Event: The Space Race
123 - Key Person: Ronald Reagan
124 - Everyday Life: The U.S. and the U.S.S.R.
125 - Bible Study: Fighting the Good Fight

U.S. President John F. Kennedy at the Berlin Wall, 1963

Memory Work

Learn Psalm 97:10-12 by the end of the unit.

Books Used

The Bible
In Their Words
Animal Farm

Project (choose one)

1) Write 300 to 500 words on one of the following topics:
   - Why do you think socialism and communism are attractive to people?
   - Do you think the efforts of the space race have proved as valuable as they seemed in the 1960s? What are your views on current efforts of the United States in space? See Lesson 122.
2) Prepare a traditional Russian meal for your family.
3) Make a poster with quotes from 20th century leaders that reveal their ideology. Use quotes that have sentiments you agree with and some that you don't. Represent the quotations and the leaders who said them on your poster in an interesting, artistic way. Use at least ten different leaders and quotations.

Literature

Animal Farm, published in 1945, is a brilliant satire on the failings of Communism. Interestingly, author George Orwell (pen name for Eric Blair, pictured at right) was a dedicated socialist. However, Orwell saw totalitarianism as an enemy of pure socialism. The book was a warning to the West about what was happening in the Soviet Union at a time when many in the West admired the Soviets for their brave stance against Hitler in World War II.

Animal Farm is an allegory. Mr. Jones is Czar Nicholas II, and Manor Farm is Russia. The song "Beasts of England" parallels "The Internationale," a Communist anthem. Napoleon is Stalin and Snowball is Trotsky (who fell out of favor with Stalin, went into exile, and was eventually murdered by agents of Stalin). The horses are the workers and the pigs are the Communist Party. Squealer is the Party's propaganda machine. Moses the raven is the Russian Orthodox Church. Foxwood is Britain, and Pinchfield is Nazi Germany. The adjustments made to the Seven Commandments are similar to the Communist rewriting of history. The book describes the hard, unrewarding work that characterized Communism and the failure of central planning. It also shows how people were willing to give in to Communist threats and to adjust their thinking to the Communist version of the truth.

Orwell was born in India in 1903, the son of a British foreign service officer. He was educated at Eton School in England, where he did not fit in with the wealthy students and became a confirmed socialist. He worked in the British foreign service in Burma for a while, then returned to England where he wrote for a living and worked with the socialist political movement. His other well-known book is *1984*, written in 1948. It is also a chilling denunciation of totalitarianism, though with a darker tone and descriptions of immorality. Orwell died in 1950.

Soviet Tu-95 Bear D (top) and U.S. F-4 Phantom II, 1974

Lesson 121

Freedom vs. Communism

World events that took place during the forty-five years that followed World War II were overshadowed by a single, huge issue: the rivalry and mutual suspicion that existed between the United States and the Soviet Union. The two countries never had a direct armed confrontation, which is why the uneasy period was called the Cold War, as opposed to a conflict that has heated up to the point of shooting.

To understand this conflict, we must recount the story of the Communist Revolution in Russia and bring events up to World War II.

The End of Imperial Russia

Russia in the early 20th century was a weakening giant. Its vast natural resources and huge population were governed by a powerful, absolutist czar who was resistant to change. Meanwhile, the new forces of liberalism and socialism were nipping at the czar's heels and wanting to bring about change.

After a confrontation between protesters and the czar's troops in 1905, Nicholas II promised a constitution, an elected legislature (the Duma), and other limited reforms. But opposition continued to build. The czar used secret police to spy on reformers, and revolutionaries resorted to terrorism against the government.

The coming of the Great War only made matters worse. The Russian army, poorly-led and badly equipped, suffered many casualties. In March 1917, food riots and labor strikes in St. Petersburg were followed by soldiers refusing to fight. Nicholas II abdicated, and Russia became a republic. Reform leaders in the Duma took control of the government.

Lenin and the Revolution

Another body, however, the Soviet of Workers' and Soldiers' Deputies, made up of radicals, challenged the Duma's leadership. In April 1917, Vladimir Lenin returned to Russia from exile and began orchestrating a Communist revolution. Germany assisted Lenin's return in the hope that he would help foment a revolution that would cause Russia to withdraw from the war.

Lenin was born into a middle-class Russian family. When his older brother was executed for plotting to assassinate the czar, Lenin devoted his life to the overthrow of the czar and the creation of a Marxist state in Russia. In 1903 his faction (the Bolsheviks, which means "majority") gained control of the Social Democratic Party. Their opponents within the party were the Mensheviks (minority). The Bolsheviks later formed a separate group that took the name of the Communist Party in 1918.

As the provisional republican government under Alexander Kerensky struggled with the war, the economy, and domestic security issues, Lenin's group prepared to move. On November 7, 1917, with the help of Russian soldiers, the revolutionaries took control of the public utilities of St. Petersburg. A naval cruiser pointed its guns at the government building. Kerensky escaped. That afternoon Lenin called a meeting of representatives from Soviets in other Russian cities, which he termed an "All-Russian Congress," and claimed to be in authority. A counterrevolution led by former czarist generals developed into a two-year civil war which the Communists won.

The Union of Soviet Socialist Republics (U.S.S.R., or the Soviet Union) was technically a collection of various individual states (Russia, Ukraine, Byelorussia, Siberia, etc.), but party headquarters in Moscow had all power and made all policy decisions.

The Collectivist State

Lenin began creating a Communist state according to his own vision of Marxism through increasing government control. Lenin died in 1924, and out of the power struggle that followed Josef Stalin emerged victorious. Stalin oversaw even greater economic planning by the central government and was merciless in wiping out any and all opponents to his authority.

This led to a decline in individual incentive, which contributed to an unproductive farm economy. During the 1930s, the Soviet Union did see rapid industrialization, though at what human cost this was accomplished we might never know. Despite Russia's progress, it is a valid question to ask whether the Soviet economic advances were any greater than what could have taken place under a democratic government.

Officially atheist in keeping with Marx's views, the Communist Party all but shut down the once-influential Orthodox Church and barely tolerated other expressions of faith. The Communists allowed no freedom of speech or of the press, no labor unions or assemblies. The government was subject to the party, which decided the candidates who would run for office (with no opposition, of course). Overseeing all activity was the secret police, and behind every government decree was the threat of prison camps and mass executions. Because the Soviets were masters at deception and double talk, the true nature of Stalin's repressive regime only came to light long after Stalin's death.

Communism in the World

Soviet economic growth, coupled with their stance against Germany and the need that Britain and the United States felt for Soviet assistance in the war, gave Stalin significant power in Allied deliberations about the post-war world. Stalin kept control of the Eastern European countries which the Soviets had taken over at the end of the war. In describing the Communist domination of Eastern Europe, Winston Churchill warned the world

This close-up of Stalin (left) and Lenin is cropped from a larger 1919 photo showing several early Communist leaders. The Communist Party often edited photos to remove people who had fallen out of favor.

Lesson 121 - Freedom vs. Communism

that an Iron Curtain had descended upon Europe, keeping freedom and the chance of prosperity away from millions of people.

Soviet Communists wanted to spread their revolution to other countries. Communist Parties were formed in most western nations, but they were never able to overthrow an existing government the way they had in Russia. Even when times were hard in the United States and other countries during the Great Depression, the example of Russian Communism scared the majority of people away from taking that route. The national Communist organizations, however, did serve to spread Marxist propaganda around the world.

Many in the West feared the potential of Communist expansion, and plenty of evidence supported this fear. Communists attempted to overthrow the government of Greece in 1947. The Soviets, who controlled East Germany and East Berlin, tried to stop supplies from getting into Allied-held West Berlin. The U.S.-sponsored Berlin Airlift overcame this roadblock in 1948-49 and was an embarrassing defeat for Stalin. Non-Communist countries created organizations such as NATO (North Atlantic Treaty Organization) to oppose any Russian aggression.

The Russians developed an atomic weapon in 1949, which heightened tensions in the Cold War. America and the Soviet Union began a massive arms race, building up stockpiles of conventional

This 1950 Chinese Stamp shows Stalin shaking hands with Mao Zedong, leader of the Chinese Communists.

and nuclear weapons to prevent an attack or to be able to retaliate if an attack came. Scientific advances by the Soviets, such as the launching of the first artificial satellite (*Sputnik*) in 1957, created further concerns in the West. Attempted uprisings in Hungary (1956) and Czechoslovakia (1968) were brutally crushed by Soviet troops. Hard-line Soviet leaders Nikita Khrushchev and Leonid Brezhnev in the 1950s through the 1970s gave Western leaders plenty of reasons to think that the Soviet threat to peace and freedom was real. Another reason for fearing Communist expansion emerged in 1949 with the Communist takeover of China. Russia and China were allies for a time, but they split in 1962 and became enemies within the Communist camp.

Korea and Vietnam

Although the United States and the Soviet Union did not fight each other directly during the Cold War, their competing interests were at stake in several incidents large and small around the world. The first major test was in Korea. The Soviet Union supported the invasion of North Korean troops into the South in 1950. The South was defended by a United Nations coalition of troops, the vast majority of whom were Americans.

The North Koreans, helped by Russian troops, pushed Allied troops far to the south. An Allied force swept around the Communists and cut off

U.S. Marines Capture Chinese Troops in Korea, 1951

Viet Cong soldiers carry a wounded American soldier to a prisoner exchange with U.S. Forces in (1973).

their supply lines. Allied troops were able to push the Communists back into North Korea almost to China. Then Chinese troops poured over the border and pushed the Allies back to about the middle of the country. A truce was declared in 1953, dividing Korea into a Communist North and a free South, a tenuous situation that has persisted to the present.

A similar scenario developed in the country of Vietnam in Southeast Asia, which had been a French colony. After nationalist Communists began undermining French control, France pulled out in 1954. Communists controlled the northern part of the country, and a U.S.-backed government held the South. Communist Vietcong guerrillas worked behind the scenes against the government in the South. China and Russia gave help to the Vietnamese Communists, and the United States sent advisers and special forces to support the South Vietnamese army. The view of the American government was that, if Vietnam fell to the Communists, other nations in Southeast Asia would fall like dominoes.

Beginning in 1965, the United States greatly escalated its involvement in Vietnam. The U.S. sent hundreds of thousands of troops to defend South Vietnam and initiated heavy bombing of the North. However, the Communist will to resist was strong. Meanwhile, the war became increasingly unpopular within the United States. Eventually the American government wound down its involvement in the war by giving more responsibility to the South Vietnamese army. After American troops pulled out following a truce, the Communists escalated their attacks and took over the South in 1975. Thousands of refugees escaped Vietnam, but the Communist government executed many opponents.

After South Vietnam fell, Communists also took over Cambodia and Laos. Communist leader Pol Pot oversaw about one million deaths in Cambodia (known as Kampuchea when led by the Communists). Laos is still Communist-led, but Cambodia has become a constitutional monarchy.

The Fall of Communism

The grip of Communism on the Soviet Union and Eastern Europe appeared firm. However, three major factors began to loosen this grip in the late 1980s.

First, increasing failures within the Communist economies showed that Marxist theories simply did not work. Communist nations lagged far behind the economic progress of the West. Hailed as a worker's paradise, they were anything but. The failure was made worse by heavy military spending by the Soviet

Lesson 121 - Freedom vs. Communism

Union to defend against a feared American attack. In addition, Communist suppression of freedom of thought stood in stark contrast to the intellectual and political freedoms that Westerners enjoyed.

Second, American President Ronald Reagan stood strongly against Communist tyranny and aggression. Reagan increased the external pressure on the Communist bloc. The standoff revealed that Communist foreign policy was a failure also.

Third, Soviet leader Mikhail Gorbachev, who took office in 1985, promoted more openness within Russia and announced that he would not automatically use troops to keep the Soviet Union together or to quell anti-Soviet activity in the satellite nations of Eastern Europe.

European Communism, which had been in place for seventy years, fell amazingly fast and with little violence. In August of 1991, the Soviet secret police, army officers, and Communist party conservatives attempted a coup to oust Gorbachev and restore a hard-line Communist government. The coup attempt only lasted about 72 hours and failed for lack of popular support. However, during

Russian President Boris Yeltsin (right) visits with U.S. President George H. W. Bush in 1992.

the uncertainty of the coup, Lithuania, Latvia, and Estonia, the Baltic republics that Stalin had seized at the end of World War II, declared their independence from the Soviet system.

When the Russian Republic, the Ukraine, and the other Soviet states also left, the Soviet Union was dead. Gorbachev resigned and the Soviet Parliament ceased to exist. Boris Yeltsin, a former Communist turned reformer, was elected president of the Russian Republic in 1991. He later became leader of the Russian federation, also known as the Commonwealth of Independent States, which includes most of the former Soviet Union.

Eastern Europe saw mostly nonviolent democratic revolutions take place between 1989 and 1992. In 1989 Poland elected as president Lech Walensa, a labor leader who had stood up to the Communist Polish authorities years earlier. The Berlin Wall was torn down in 1989 and Germany was reunited in 1990. Czechoslovakia, Hungary, Romania, and Bulgaria also saw the collapse of their Communist governments. Yugoslavia broke apart; and although Communist rule there ended, ethnic hatred in the Balkans erupted in new waves of violence and unrest.

The only remaining Communist countries in the world are China, Vietnam, Laos, and Cuba. As someone put it, the Cold War is over. We won.

During the fall of Communism, the Republic of Moldova declared its independence from the Soviet Union. Then the Pridnestrovian Moldavian Republic (or Transdniestria) declared its independence from Moldova. After a brief war, Transdniestria established itself as a separate, functioning presidential republic. A government building is pictured below. Symbols of Communism are still prominent in Transdniestria. Transdniestria is not recognized as a separate country by the international community.

Blessed are those who have been persecuted for the sake of righteousness, for theirs is the kingdom of heaven.
Matthew 5:10

Assignments for Lesson 121

Bible — The readings for this week are related to Lesson 125. Read 1 Timothy 1.

In Their Words — Read the excerpt from "The Sinews of Peace" (pages 301-305).

Literature — Begin reading *Animal Farm*. Plan to finish it by the end of this unit.

Student Review — Optional: Answer the questions for Lesson 121.

Robert Goddard Towing a Rocket in a Model A Truck, c. 1931

Lesson 122 - Key Event

The Space Race

Millions of people got up early in the morning and were glued to their television screens. It was an event of international—one might almost say cosmic—importance. National pride hung in the balance. It wasn't a sporting event, nor was it a state ceremony in Great Britain. It was a space launch.

Today space flights only make news when there is an accident or an interplanetary flight. During the 1960s, however, space was big news. It was not just the appeal of a new adventure or the wonder associated with seeing new gadgetry at work. Space flights were part of the Cold War. Every success and every failure was seen as saying something about America or the Soviet Union.

Background

Records from ancient China indicate that the Chinese sent small rockets into the air powered by gunpowder, perhaps as early as the third century BC. Arab traders brought knowledge of rockets to Europe in the late Middle Ages. These devices were used in military attacks.

In 1926 American scientist Robert Goddard (1882-1945) successfully launched a liquid-fuel propelled rocket on a brief flight. Meanwhile, German scientists were also studying rockets that could go higher than balloons or airplanes could. During World War II, the German military used unmanned rockets loaded with bombs to attack England. After the war, some German scientists came to the United States while other German scientists went to the Soviet Union. These men had a big impact on the space programs in each country.

Wernher von Braun (1912-1977), a leading German rocket scientist during World War II, became a leader at NASA in the United States after the war.

713

Sputnik: The Race Begins

On October 4, 1957, the Soviet Union successfully launched the first artificial satellite into earth orbit. *Sputnik* was small: 22 inches in diameter and about 184 pounds in weight. It transmitted data back to earth by radio signals.

The launch was a blow to American pride and raised serious questions among U.S. military personnel about what else the Soviets might be able to do, such as launching a nuclear missile toward the United States. The only use of atomic bombs in war had been by dropping them from airplanes.

The American space program went into high gear to launch its own satellite; but while its attempts were meeting with failure, the Russians launched Sputnik II on November 3, 1957. This satellite was much bigger, about 1,100 pounds, and carried a live dog to see how living things might fare in space.

Finally, the U.S. successfully launched the thirty-pound Explorer satellite on January 31, 1958. American rejoicing did not last long, however, because in 1959 the Russians hit the moon with an unmanned space craft. On April 12, 1961, Russian cosmonaut Yuri Gagarin became the first human to orbit the earth. The United States and the Soviet Union were in a race for space, and the Russians were winning.

Laika was the stray dog from Moscow that flew in the Sputnik 2 *capsule. This Romanian postage stamp honored her, the first animal to orbit the earth.*

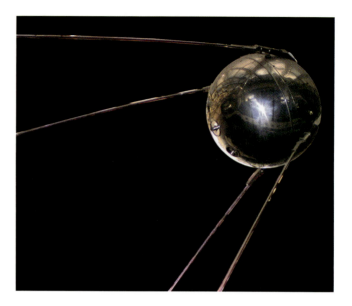

This is a reproduction of Sputnik, *a name which means "traveling companion".*

On May 5, 1961, Alan Shepard was the first American in space, taking a brief fifteen-minute flight and landing as scheduled in the Atlantic Ocean. John Glenn became the first American to orbit the earth, making three revolutions around the planet on February 20, 1962. American television networks covered every minute of the flight, from before liftoff to after splashdown.

The National Challenge

Just a few weeks after Shepard's flight, President John F. Kennedy issued a challenge to the American space program and the nation, saying, "I believe that this nation should commit itself to achieving the goal, before this decade is out, of landing a man on the moon and returning him safely to the earth." Expanding on this challenge, Kennedy cast the project in terms of American prestige:

> No single space project in this period will be more impressive to mankind, or more important for the long-range exploration of space; and none will be so difficult or expensive to accomplish. . . .

Lesson 122 - Key Event: The Space Race

> In a very real sense, it will not be one man going to the moon—if we make this judgment affirmatively, it will be an entire nation. For all of us must work to put him there.

Besides heightening the competition between the two nations, Kennedy's challenge also illustrated a basic difference between the American and Soviet societies: openness versus secrecy. The American space program was conducted almost completely in the open. Every failure, delay, and difficulty was public knowledge. When a flight had to be scrubbed at the last minute because of mechanical problems, it happened on nationwide television. The Soviets, on the other hand, conducted their program, like they conducted all of their government's operations, in strictest secrecy. The outside world usually didn't hear about the Soviet flights that failed in between the successful ones.

One side issue that came to the surface was the concern by American educators that public schools in the United States were lagging behind Russian schools in the study of science. Congress responded to the challenge early on, appropriating $900 million dollars in 1958 for math, science, and foreign language studies in public schools; loans to college students; and grants for graduate students. This was the first major Federal spending for education since 1862.

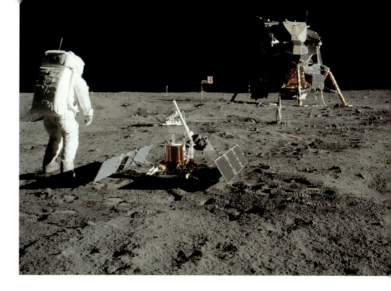

Neil Armstrong took this photo of Buzz Aldrin on the moon, with their Lunar Module in the background.

Competing Programs

During the 1960s, either an American or a Soviet space flight took place every few months. Each country tried to be the first to do something. The Soviets were the first to send a woman to space (1963) and the first to take a space walk outside of a capsule (1965). The Americans were the first to stay in space for 190 hours on a single flight (1965) and the first to send back live pictures from space and to accomplish a manned orbit of the moon (both 1968).

Spurred by Kennedy's challenge, two American astronauts landed on the moon on July 20, 1969. Other manned American moon missions followed. The United States remains the only country to land men on the moon (the last moon mission was in 1972). The Russians, meanwhile, took their space program in another direction and concentrated on building an orbiting space laboratory, a feat they completed in 1971. The first United States space station went into operation in 1973.

Neil Armstrong, Buzz Aldrin, Michael Collins, and their wives spent forty-five days visiting twenty-seven cities in twenty-four countries on a goodwill tour after their 1969 moon flight. Here they are in Mexico City dressed in sombreros and ponchos.

What Else Was Happening During the Cold War?

1. In the early 1960s, the Roman Catholic Church held a series of meetings in Rome called the Second Vatican Council (see photo at right). The Council encouraged positive interaction with other religious groups and ended the requirement to use Latin in the Catholic Mass.

2. The Beatles from Liverpool, England, became an international sensation in 1963. Their music has continued to be popular long after their 1970 breakup. The representation of the Beatles at right, made in 2007, is located in Kazakhstan, a former member of the Soviet Union.

3. After sorting through thousands of suggested designs, the government of Canada chose a new national flag. By proclamation of Queen Elizabeth II, the new Maple Leaf flag became official on February 15, 1965.

4. Representatives of Iran, Iraq, Kuwait, Saudi Arabia, and Venezuela formed the Organization of the Petroleum Exporting Countries (OPEC) in Baghdad in 1960. These and other member countries coordinate oil production for their mutual benefit. They have used their influence as a political weapon, especially after the 1973 Arab-Israeli War.

5. Communist leader Mao Zedong oversaw the Cultural Revolution against traditional values and practices in China from 1966 until his death in 1976. Approximately one billion copies of a book of quotations from Chairman Mao were distributed in China and around the world in 65 languages. Later Chinese leaders have distanced themselves from Mao's excesses, but his book is still available in China, as seen at right.

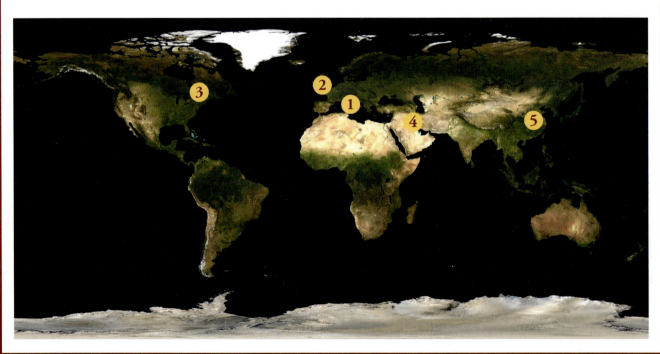

Lesson 122 - Key Event: The Space Race

An American crew and a Soviet crew launched separate space flights in July of 1975, and then the two spaceships docked together for the first joint U.S.-U.S.S.R. mission. They conducted experiments, shared meals, and held a joint news conference from space. The United States began emphasizing re-usable space vehicles in the Space Shuttle program, while the Russians concentrated on long-term flights in their orbiting labs.

The United States has received many benefits from its program of space exploration. Besides a greater knowledge of the universe, the space program has led to several practical developments in other areas such as improved medical technology, computer advances, and even cordless power tools.

A valid argument can be made that the United States won the space race. What Americans gained has benefited all mankind, and the U.S. program accomplished as much as or more than the Soviet efforts. Competition fueled rapid advances in space exploration; cooperation might prove to be more cost-effective in the long run as humans attempt to reach Mars and beyond.

The International Space Station began as a cooperative project between Russia and the United States. Construction started in 1998, and the first long-term crew arrived in 2000. Astronauts from twelve other countries have participated in missions, accompanied by a handful of space tourists. Mark Shuttleworth, an entrepreneur from South Africa, trained for a year and paid about $20 million to spend eight days on the ISS in 2002.

*Can you lead forth a constellation in its season,
And guide the Bear with her satellites?
Do you know the ordinances of the heavens,
Or fix their rule over the earth?
Job 38:32-33*

Assignments for Lesson 122

Bible Read 1 Timothy 2-3.

In Their Words Read the speech by Yuri Gagarin (pages 306-308).

Literature Continue reading *Animal Farm*.

Student Review Optional: Answer the questions for Lesson 122.

Lesson 123 - Key Person

Ronald Reagan (Left) Takes the Presidential Oath of Office with His Wife Nancy Beside Him, 1985

Ronald Reagan

Ronald Reagan was a key figure in the Cold War because, as much as anyone else, he helped to end it. His stance against Communism during his presidency was the right policy at the right time and helped bring down European Communism.

Reagan's Life

Ronald Wilson Reagan was born February 6, 1911, in tiny Tampico, Illinois. Nine years later, his family settled in Dixon, Illinois. After attending Eureka College, Reagan began a radio broadcasting career in Iowa.

In 1937 he was signed to appear in motion pictures and began his screen career in Hollywood. As an actor, Reagan appeared in over fifty films, including westerns, war movies, comedies, and tear-jerkers. He also worked in television, most notably as host of the series "General Electric Theater" and "Death Valley Days." Reagan married actress Jane Wyman in 1940; they were divorced in 1948. He married another actress, Nancy Davis, in 1952; and they were married for fifty-two years.

Reagan's first involvement in politics was as a Democrat. He supported Franklin Roosevelt and his liberal New Deal. Reagan campaigned for Richard Nixon's Democratic opponent when Nixon was running for the United States Senate in 1950. Reagan was president of a union, the Screen Actors Guild, on two different occasions. However, Reagan supported Republican Dwight Eisenhower in 1952 and 1956 and campaigned for Richard Nixon in 1960. Two years later Reagan officially became a Republican, even though Republican fortunes were on the decline.

Ronald Reagan (child on the right) with his parents Jack and Nelle and brother Neil (c. 1916).

Reagan campaigned for Republican presidential candidate Barry Goldwater in 1964. Then in 1966, Reagan was elected to the first of two terms as governor of California. He made a brief, last-minute attempt to win the Republican presidential nomination at the party's convention in 1968.

In the 1980 election Reagan defeated incumbent Jimmy Carter. At age sixty-nine, he was the oldest man ever elected president of the United States. He was re-elected in a landslide in 1984. After his second term in office, he retired from public life. Reagan disclosed in 1994 that he had Alzheimer's disease. He died on June 5, 2004, at the age of ninety-three.

Reagan's Faith

Early in his life, Reagan made a commitment to Christ and was baptized. He often spoke about his faith and how it guided his life. Reagan said that after he was wounded in an assassination attempt in 1981, as he was about to undergo surgery, he prayed for the man who had shot him.

In 1983 President Ronald Reagan delivered a wide-ranging speech to a meeting of the National Association of Evangelicals (NAE). The speech made a powerful case for Biblical stances on several issues. Many in the American media and many of Reagan's political opponents were appalled at this reference to the Soviet Union:

> I urge you to beware the temptation of pride—the temptation of blithely declaring yourselves above it all and label both sides equally at fault, to ignore the facts of history and the aggressive impulses of an evil empire, to simply call the arms race a giant misunderstanding and thereby remove yourself from the struggle between right and wrong and good and evil.

However, when imprisoned political dissidents in Russia heard about it, they were heartened that someone had finally told the truth about the system that had put them in prison for their thoughts.

Like all of us, however, Reagan's walk was not perfect. As governor of California, he signed a bill in 1967 liberalizing the state's abortion laws. This was a decision he later regretted. As president he was involved in a secret plan to sell military equipment to Iran (a violation of U.S. law) in an effort to free American hostages. He was also accused of a lack of oversight when information leaked that U.S. officials had used some of the money from the Iran weapons sale to support anti-Communist fighters in Nicaragua, another violation of U.S. law.

Reagan's Foreign Policy

Reagan's domestic policy was highlighted by significant tax cuts that stimulated the American economy but left ballooning federal deficits in the budgets passed by Congress. Although Reagan is best known for his stance against Communism, his entire foreign policy opposed oppression and favored freedom.

Reagan ordered U.S. Marines to Lebanon in 1982 to participate in a peace-keeping force there after a long war which involved domestic factions as well as involvement by Israel and nearby Arab countries. The president ordered an invasion of

Reagan met in 1983 with Afghan leaders who were fighting against the Soviets in their country.

Lesson 123 - Key Person: Ronald Reagan

British Prime Minister Margaret Thatcher was an ally of Ronald Reagan during the Cold War.

Ending the Cold War

Ronald Reagan believed in a few foundational principles that influenced his political life. He believed in the reality of right and wrong. Although he was a New Deal Democrat at one time, he saw the problems and failings of big government and liberal policies. His switch to the Republican Party was one of principle, not political opportunism. Reagan believed that his beliefs could be more effectively expressed in the Republican Party. In world affairs, he saw the wrongs that resulted from Communism and he was willing to speak out against them.

Reagan believed in the American dream—he had lived it—and in the great gift of freedom. He believed in the possibilities that people could accomplish when left to themselves without government interference. He believed this about the United States, and he also believed it about the millions of people whose lives and dreams Communism repressed. He was not satisfied with peaceful coexistence with Communism. He wanted to do what he could to end the wrong and usher in the right.

President Reagan was also willing to stand toe to toe with Communist leaders. He drew a line in the sand against the Soviet threat that in the 1980s was still quite real. He recognized that the Soviet

the small Caribbean country of Grenada in 1983 after a Marxist coup endangered American lives and threatened the political stability of the region. In a move designed to strike a blow at world terrorism, Reagan ordered the bombing of military installations in Libya in 1986 in response to terrorist attacks sponsored by the Libyan government. Reagan supported anti-Communist governments as well as groups that opposed Communism in Central America and elsewhere.

President Reagan held four summit meetings with Soviet President Mikhail Gorbachev. The two men developed a good working relationship despite (or perhaps because of) Reagan's forthright opposition to Communist expansion. The Reagan Administration implemented a major increase in defense spending and proposed a satellite-based defense system (the Strategic Defense Initiative, nicknamed the "Star Wars" system). Reagan and Gorbachev and their aides negotiated a treaty that led to sizable cutbacks in the nuclear weapons held by both sides. A significant percentage of existing weapons were actually destroyed.

Reagan had a cordial relationship with Soviet leader Mikhail Gorbachev.

leaders had a history of dishonesty, opposition to freedom, and suppression of religious expression. His strengthening of the American military and his proposal of the Strategic Defense Initiative signaled that Reagan was not going to back down from the Soviets. Reagan knew that peace comes only through strength. Those who are free must work on the basis of principle to defend freedom because opponents of freedom are willing to work without principle to tear freedom down.

As Soviet President Mikhail Gorbachev began talking about a new era of openness and reform, Reagan challenged Gorbachev in 1987 to give substance to his proposals by tearing down the Berlin Wall. The Wall, built by the Communists in 1961, separated East and West Berlin and was probably the best-known symbol of the Iron Curtain. Some Reagan advisers did not want the President to issue such a direct challenge, and pundits fretted about the possible impact of the speech. As usual, however, the hand-wringers were wrong and Reagan was right.

Reagan understood that basic values must undergird pragmatic attempts to carry out foreign policy. He once described the standoff between the United States and the Soviet Union this way: it was not that they each had strong armaments and therefore didn't trust each other; instead, they didn't trust each other and therefore they built up their armaments. If they could learn to trust each other, a better chance for peace would follow.

The man who once called the Soviet system an evil empire brought about peace, not war. A nuclear confrontation between the Russians and the Americans was less likely after Reagan's tenure than it had been before. He was not belligerent, but he was firm; and that firmness in what he believed to be right helped millions of people in the world to have a new day of freedom.

*Loyalty and truth preserve the king,
And he upholds his throne by righteousness.
Proverbs 20:28*

Assignments for Lesson 123

Bible Read 1 Timothy 4-5.

In Their Words Read "Mr. Gorbachev, Tear Down This Wall!" (pages 309-313).

Literature Continue reading *Animal Farm*.

Student Review Optional: Answer the questions for Lesson 123.

Kirov Stadium, St. Petersburg (2006)

Lesson 124 - Everyday Life

The U.S. and the U.S.S.R.

The United States and the Soviet Union were allies during World War II. After that war these two superpowers were on opposing sides in the Cold War. The author of this curriculum was born in 1952 to a U.S. Army veteran and his English bride. The author's wife, Charlene Boyd Notgrass, was born in 1953. In this lesson she tells the story of her childhood, showing what it was like to experience the Cold War on the American side. Following the story of her childhood in Tennessee, we tell about life in the Soviet Union.

Growing Up in America

While my parents were waiting for me to be born, Mother lived with her parents in Springfield, Tennessee, and Daddy finished his military service. He spent most of his two-year stint at Fort Campbell, near Clarksville, Tennessee. Daddy had been scheduled to go to Korea (a major battleground of the Cold War), but he was spared that duty when the Army discovered his teeth were bad. For years afterwards, Daddy loved to show children his false teeth. I appreciated those false teeth once I realized that his bad ones had kept him in the United States.

Every day Mother rode a Greyhound bus from Springfield to Nashville, and then she rode a city bus from the Greyhound station to the Aladdin factory. There she worked on an assembly line, putting tubes in oscillators for the Navy.

Daddy was discharged from the Army three days before I was born on December 2, 1953. American mothers in the 1950s kept their babies at home for several weeks before taking them out into the world of polio, whooping cough, and other childhood diseases. Mother and I spent about six weeks with her family; and then Daddy, Mother, and I moved to a little house in the country. It was owned by my paternal grandparents, Daddy Leland and Mama Sue Boyd, who lived next door.

My paternal grandfather was an entrepreneur. He ran his country store, raised tobacco on his farm, and owned commercial and residential rental properties. Daddy Leland's country store was in front of their house. It had an old-fashioned gasoline pump out front and a big red Coca-Cola cooler inside.

Soccer was popular in the Soviet Union in the 1950s, when many teams were formed. Kirov Stadium was completed in 1950 in Leningrad (now St. Petersburg). It could seat 100,000 fans, making it one of the largest facilities in the world. The stadium hosted soccer games until 2006, when it was demolished.

When a customer wanted to buy a "cold drink," he opened the silver top, got out a six-ounce green glass bottle, and paid a nickel. An opener was attached to the front of the cooler to remove the metal cap from the bottle. The customer put his empty bottle in a specially-made wooden case so it could be returned to the Coca-Cola bottling company where it was washed for reuse.

Our home in the country had electricity, a refrigerator, and an electric stove, but it had no running water. There was a cistern and a hand pump in the backyard. We had an outhouse and at night we kept a white enamel pot (otherwise known as a "slop jar") under the bed. Mother kept house, took care of me, and kept a small flock of chickens in the backyard. Three years after I was born, Mother gave birth to my brother Steve.

Every Sunday morning we went to a little country church a few miles away. The church was built on a hillside above the creek where Daddy had been baptized several years before. My great-great-grandparents and other relatives were buried on the hill above the church. The main floor had an auditorium with wooden theater seats that made a racket when people shifted in them or stood up to sing. I liked going to the basement for Sunday School. Once I got a little white King James New Testament for perfect attendance. On Sunday afternoons we went to see Mother's family about thirteen miles away. My parents didn't own any kind of vehicle, so we borrowed my grandfather's truck to make the visit.

After a year of farming his daddy's land, Daddy got a job at the Acme boot factory in Ashland City. Then he started working for the state highway department, clearing roadsides with a hand tool called a lively lead. He worked for his father on the weekends.

Daddy Leland built a supermarket in the county seat, and Daddy began to work there full-time. We still didn't own a car, so he rode into town with Daddy Leland.

Boyd's Market had a meat department with a butcher, a produce department (Daddy Leland went to Nashville four or five mornings a week to keep it supplied), and many shelves filled with groceries. The front doors were made of wood and were built at an angle into the front left corner. A little roof covered them. I remember the doors because we had a burglary one night. The burglar had carved out the wood around the lock so he could get inside.

When I was four years old, we moved into a big, old house my grandfather owned behind his supermarket. When built around 1900, it had been a grand home with a wraparound front porch, beautiful mantles with mirrors, hardwood floors, high ceilings, wide dark-stained woodwork, and a pair of beautiful wood and glass pocket doors. My mother was pleased that it also had running water.

My grandfather divided the house into a duplex. For a while my uncle and his new bride lived in the other side, but most of the time our near neighbor was a sweet, elderly lady, whom we loved dearly and whose grandchildren called her Little Mama. Mrs. Perry had a large living room/bedroom combination, a kitchen, and a bathroom downstairs.

The Soviet Union was officially atheist, but the United States had freedom of religion. This nativity scene was on display in Centennial Park in Nashville.

Lesson 124 - Everyday Life: The U.S. and the U.S.S.R.

Our family had four large rooms and a big hall with a staircase and bannister that my brother and I found irresistible. My mother certainly didn't have to dust the banister. We took care of that when we slid down it.

Mrs. Perry used one of the upstairs rooms for storage. Mother used the other two to store a few things, but they were mainly places where Steve and I and our cousins played. When another uncle was away in the military, my aunt and her two children lived in one of them.

When we first moved in, our heat came from one coal-burning stove in the middle of our side of the house and a little electric heater in the bathroom. Later, the coal-burning stove was replaced with a natural gas stove (Mrs. Perry had a gas stove on her side, too). I loved to put paper on top of the gas stove and color on it. I liked to see the wax melt as I colored. In the mornings, Mother would sometimes open the oven in the kitchen to warm things up a bit. In the winter, it was cold when you were away from the stove; but you could always go there to get warm. One winter night our goldfish bowl was sitting in the bay window about ten feet away from the stove. It got so cold the water froze!

For our large bay window, Mother made beautiful tie-back curtains out of muslin, trimmed with fringe. At Christmas we put a cedar tree in front of that window and decorated it with glass balls and silver icicles. Enjoyable pastimes for me were playing with my Betsy Wetsy doll and playing outside in our big tractor tire sandbox. When Steve and I got older, we enjoyed playing kickball and army in the backyard. Inside we liked to play Monopoly and listen to records. Sometimes we would dance to the tunes of the "Bunny Hop" and the "Mexican Hat Dance."

Mother washed our clothes on our screened-in back porch. She used a wringer washing machine and two big tubs that stood on legs. I loved to help. One day I got my hand caught in the wringer and Mother had to do first aid on my hand. After the Monday morning washing, she hung the clothes on

The Boyd family was free to travel around the country, unlike citizens in the Soviet Union.

two clotheslines in the back yard. When the clothes were dry, she sprinkled them with water before ironing them.

A year after we moved to town, we began to go to church in town, too. The big, new brick church building was across the street from our house. My brother and I always sat with our parents in the auditorium during church. My brother had to sit between them so they could both work to keep him quiet. The front of the auditorium had knotty-pine paneling—a common 1950s building material in the South. In the center was a beautiful pine arch that framed the waterfall scene that was painted on the back wall of the baptistery. The pulpit, the two podium chairs, and the communion table carved with "This do in remembrance of Me" were ornate and made from matching pine, as were the unpadded pews. Hardwood and a red carpet aisle runner covered the floor. Steve and I went to the basement for Sunday School. I liked the table sandbox with wooden clothespin Bible story characters. Vacation Bible School was always a special time at church. One week each summer, we had VBS on Monday through Friday mornings. I liked the daily refreshments, especially Popsicle day.

Mother made my clothes on her Singer sewing machine. She also made her clothes; and when Steve was little, she sewed for him, too. It was easy for her to get fabrics, thread, and buttons in our small town. When shopping for fabric, she went to the local department store or to the dime store (also called a five and dime or a five and ten cent store). Usually my clothes were made of cotton, but when I was a flower girl for my uncle's wedding, I had a dress of white satin. After we moved to town, my mother began a home business. She made dresses for women and girls and did clothing alterations for a men's clothing store.

We bought our first car around 1959, a big, green, used Plymouth. At first, Mother didn't drive. She really didn't need to drive. When we went shopping in town, we walked. We walked to church and Daddy walked to work. I could stand in my front yard and see my church and my elementary school. From my backyard, I could see the supermarket and the dime store. We used the car when we wanted to go to Nashville or to visit relatives in other towns.

In the fall of 1959, I started school in the first grade. Mother took me the first day and maybe for a few days after that, but then I walked by myself. I was just five years old. Like other children, I carried my books in a satchel (a satchel had a handle and was carried like a briefcase).

First, I would stop and see Daddy at the grocery store. Often he was squatting in one of the aisles marking prices with his metal pricing tool. Sometimes he was putting groceries on the shelves or checking out a customer. If I had a cold, I could buy a little white box of wild cherry cough drops to take to school with me.

After seeing Daddy, I crossed a street, walked in front of a car dealership, crossed a bridge, walked in front of another car dealership, and then passed a drug store and our town's other supermarket. I turned right and, after passing two small houses—one of which served as the offices for the board of education—I arrived at school. The school was so new that the cafeteria had not yet been built. The first year I had to take my lunch. After that I bought my lunch, which was 35 cents a day or $1.50 per week. The food was wonderful. We had freshly-made rolls, vegetables, meat, desserts, and milk. On Fridays we often had hamburgers with homemade buns. Girls always wore dresses to school. We were not allowed to wear pants to school until my senior year in 1970-71.

When I looked at the elementary school from our front yard, I could see the homes of a few African-American families between my house and the school, but those children couldn't go there because of segregation. They had to go to another school several blocks away, while African-American high school students had to go to a school in a different county. Some black women came to our home so my mother could sew for them, and several families shopped at Daddy Leland's store. My school wasn't integrated until I was in the seventh grade.

Paul Robeson (1898-1976), son of a former slave, was an African-American singer and actor. He sent his son, Paul Jr., to school in the Soviet Union because of racial prejudice in the United States. Robeson got into trouble with U.S. officials because he was critical of U.S. government policies and friendly toward the Soviet Union. This record is a collection of "negro songs," recorded by Robeson and published by the Soviet Ministry of Culture in the 1950s.

Lesson 124 - Everyday Life: The U.S. and the U.S.S.R.

The late 1950s saw a brief "thaw" in the Cold War. Vice President Richard Nixon visited the Soviet Union in 1959, and the Soviets returned the honor that same year. Soviet leader Nikita Khrushchev (second from right) and his wife, Nina (far left), visited President Eisenhower and his wife, Mamie, in Washington, D.C. The Khrushchevs spent two weeks touring the country. Unfortunately, hostility resumed in the 1960s.

I joined two clubs while I was in elementary school. In the second grade I became a Brownie Girl Scout, and in the fourth grade I joined 4-H. My favorite Girl Scout activities were meetings and camping. In 4-H I participated in sewing and cooking. Mother helped me make an apron when I was in the fourth grade. It was the first of many sewing projects I did for fun, for 4-H, and for the county fair.

One thing I especially enjoyed about my childhood was getting to visit Daddy at work. One of his jobs was delivering groceries to people's homes. A customer could call the store and place her order. After the items were gathered, Daddy took them to her house. Sometimes he would take me along. He enjoyed visiting with the elderly ladies, and they enjoyed him, too. Daddy would also pile grocery boxes into the back of Daddy Leland's pickup truck and take them across the Cumberland River to a hillside where the townspeople took their trash. Some days he would take me with him.

Our first television was a big wooden cabinet model. All the shows were in black and white. Before school, I loved to watch *Romper Room*. I cherished my letter I got from *Romper Room's* Miss Nancy and longed to be one of the children on her show. I also liked *Captain Kangaroo, Howdy Doody*, and *The Mickey Mouse Club*. Sometimes before school, we would watch the United States launch a spaceship at Cape Canaveral.

Dwight D. Eisenhower served as our President in the 1950s. The first election I remember was when John F. Kennedy defeated Richard Nixon. Our next door neighbor who lived across the alley was Miss Willie. The first political talk I remember overhearing was about John F. Kennedy. Miss Willie did not like him. When he was assassinated in 1963, I was almost ten years old and remember wondering what Miss Willie thought about it.

I felt safe in my world until the early 1960s. That was when I first remember hearing about the threat of nuclear war. We usually went to the Tennessee State Fair each year. One year a demonstration fallout shelter was displayed at the fair. Many people built fallout shelters to protect their families in case the Soviet Union (which we usually referred to as "Russia") ever dropped an atomic bomb on America.

Americans were told that if that happened, the land would be destroyed and radioactive nuclear fallout would be everywhere. We understood that, in the event of a nuclear attack, we could not live outside of a shelter. In the demonstration shelter, we learned about storing water, food, and medical supplies. It was scary to little children and to adults, too. One time a supersonic jet flew overhead while I was at school. The supersonic boom we heard was frightening to children who lived under the threat of an atomic bomb.

I usually didn't worry, even though we didn't build a shelter. I felt safe with my family. I was taught about our loving heavenly Father at home, at church, and at my public school, where we prayed and memorized Scripture. Since I believed in Him, I knew that there was hope whether or not a nuclear war ever happened.

Life in the Soviet Union

The Soviet Union was a Communist country. The Communist Party of the Soviet Union recognized three main groups within the country: the working class or proletariat, the peasants, and the white-collar intelligentsia. In theory, they worked together to create a Communist utopia. In actuality, the rulers of the Communist Party worked to maintain their power while oppressing the Soviet people. Elites in the Communist Party enjoyed better apartments, vacations, recreation, higher salaries, and luxury goods, while the general population lived a more austere existence.

The Soviet people could only join approved organizations. They were not allowed to set up their own businesses, except for a few small services like tutoring or babysitting. The Soviet police spied on their own people. Soviet citizens had to carry passports within their own country and get permission to move from one location to another within the country. They had to get special permission to travel outside the U.S.S.R.

When a Soviet citizen graduated from a university, the government dictated the job he or she had to take for the first few years after graduation. Most citizens had few material goods. Even in the late 1980s, most Soviet families lived in one- or two-room apartments. Sometimes they waited up to ten years for a government apartment.

Lesson of Music, *Taisia Afonina (Russian, 1950)*

This photo shows a 1950 performance at the Bolshoi Theatre in Moscow of the ballet Swan Lake, *composed by Peter Ilyich Tchaikovsky.*

Much of the clothing available in the U.S.S.R. was poorly made and unattractive. Many women made their own clothes, but they had a hard time finding sewing goods. Even needles and buttons were scarce sometimes.

The general population of the Soviet Union ate mostly bread, cabbage, and potatoes. Much of their meat was a sausage that could be kept at room temperature. Few families had refrigerators. Women often had to stand in line, sometimes for several hours, to get into a grocery store. Once inside, items customers wanted were often out of stock. Families hoarded goods when they believed a shortage was coming.

Many people in the Soviet Union worked on state-owned farms. Some were *kolkhozy* (collective farms) and the rest were *sovkhozy* (state farms). Collective farmers divided their profits while state farmers got wages and social benefits. State farmers were usually better off because they had better machinery and were able to specialize. Farmers were allowed to have a garden plot of their own to supplement their food and income. They had more incentive to work on their own plots and did not work as hard for the government. This contributed to the lack of food for the country.

Soviet believers suffered severe persecution in this officially atheist country. Churches were often controlled by the government and Bibles were hard

Lesson 124 - Everyday Life: The U.S. and the U.S.S.R.

Soviet chess players dominated international competition from the 1950s to the 1980s. Mikhail Botvinnik (1911-1995) was world champion for thirteen of the fifteen years between 1948 and 1963. He was an electrical engineer and computer scientist who worked on chess computer programs.

to find. The Council on Religious Affairs kept tabs on ministers and worked in conjunction with the Soviet secret police, the KGB. Still, by the time the U.S.S.R. disbanded in the late 1980s, about fifty million Soviets were Orthodox Christians, eight million were Catholics, one million were Protestants, one million were Jews, and 50 million were Muslims.

In 1917 the U.S.S.R. took over all private and Christian schools. All students had to go to public schools. Gifted children and children of the elite often went to schools specializing in art, ballet, foreign languages, or music. Soviet children were encouraged to join Communist-sanctioned youth organizations. They became Young Octobrists at age six, Pioneers at age ten, and members of the Communist Youth League from age fourteen through twenty-eight. Communists controlled newspapers, radio and television stations, and all magazine and book publishing. It was hard for Soviet citizens to know anything that the Communist Party did not want them to know.

Appraising the Differences

The contrasts between life in the United States and life in the Soviet Union during the 1950s and 1960s were many. The material differences were perhaps most noticeable: comfortable houses versus tiny apartments; well-stocked grocery shelves compared to almost bare shelves; plentiful clothing as opposed to scarce clothing. American capitalism worked well and Communism simply didn't.

The differences that ran deeper were not as noticeable but were even more important. Americans had freedom and the people of the Soviet Union did not. Americans could worship unmolested in little church buildings on hillsides while the Communists maintained a police check on all religious activities. Americans could travel freely while the authorities scrutinized all travel by Russians. Newspapers, magazines, radios, and televisions were plentiful in the United States; and ideas for and against the government were freely exchanged. In the Soviet Union, people who had a radio could only listen to state-approved broadcasts.

Life in America during this time was not perfect. Racial discrimination was wrong, and many people suffered unfairly because of it. Some in America did not share the economic prosperity that others enjoyed. The pull of materialism was strong, and many Americans still have not learned that stuff does not bring happiness. The threat of nuclear war seemed to be a real possibility. But America was and is free. Opportunities abound for the person who is willing to work. We can and should be thankful for the privilege to worship as we please.

Marx predicted that capitalism would soon fail and the Communist state would prevail. In the 20th century, we saw just the opposite happen. Communism failed and capitalist freedom prevailed. Let us cherish our freedoms and opportunities; and let us pray that soon all people will have the opportunity to think, work, and worship as they please. In 1985 it did not seem possible that within five years Russia and Eastern Europe would be as radically changed as they were.

To the only wise God, through Jesus Christ, be the glory forever. Amen.
Romans 16:27

Assignments for Lesson 124

Bible Read 1 Timothy 6.

Literature Continue reading *Animal Farm*.

Student Review Optional: Answer the questions for Lesson 124.

Detail from Saintly Rus, *Mikhail Nesterov (Russian, c. 1905)*

Lesson 125 - Bible Study

Fighting the Good Fight

Some causes are worth fighting for. Jesus "endured the cross, despising the shame" for the joy set before him (Hebrews 12:2). God told Joshua to "be strong and courageous" as he was about to lead the Israelites into the Promised Land (Joshua 1:6, 9). Paul said that for him, "to live is Christ and to die is gain" (Philippians 1:21). He was so focused on his goal that he could say, "One thing I do" (Philippians 3:13).

The United States has a worthy goal in opposing those who oppress others. Our country stands for freedom as enemies wage a war of terrorism and fear. Ronald Reagan dedicated himself to opposing the influence of an evil empire, and that empire crumbled.

All Christians all over the world have a common cause worth fighting for: the cause of Jesus Christ. "Let us run with endurance the race that is set before us" (Hebrews 12:1). Many Christians have shown that the cause of Christ is even worth dying for. You should not give your one life for a cause that is not worth fighting and dying for. Our battles in this cause might take different forms, but you can be assured that as a Christian you will be called upon to stand for your faith in one way or another.

Paul admonished the young evangelist Timothy to fight the good fight (1 Timothy 1:18, 6:12). The Greek phrase in 1 Timothy 1:18 is a military image: war the good warfare. Paul often used the idea of the Christian life as a battle (see, for example, Ephesians 6:10-17 and 2 Timothy 2:3-4). The Greek phrase in 1 Timothy 6:12 is an athletic image: agonize the good agony, or run the good race. Athletics was another favorite source of word pictures for Paul (see 1 Corinthians 9:24-27 and 2 Timothy 2:5). Both images convey the idea of total involvement in a cause with the goal of winning.

As Paul urged Timothy to fight the good fight, the apostle gave him specific instructions on how to do that. In this lesson we will consider how Paul told Timothy to engage in the greatest contest of his life.

In the Race by His Grace

Paul knew that he was in the Christian race because of God's grace toward him in Jesus Christ (1 Timothy 1:12-17). The Lord considered him faithful, strengthened him, and put him into service even though he had been living as an enemy of God. Paul knew that he had been shown mercy so that he could be an example of the Lord's mercy toward all those who would choose to believe. Paul saw himself as the chief sinner. He understood that if God could save him, God could save anyone.

After the Communist Revolution, hundreds of Russian Orthodox Church leaders were sent to labor camps or killed, and Church property was confiscated. Patriarch Vasily Bellavin (front center) spoke out against this persecution and was imprisoned for a time. He died in 1925 and is remembered in Russia as Saint Tikhon.

When a person is in sin, he is fighting as an enemy against God. The cross was an offer of truce by the winning side. When a person becomes a Christian, God plucks him from the losing side and enlists him in His army. God takes a jeering opponent and puts him on His team.

The Christian realizes that God has rescued him from defeat and made him a winner, not by any goodness or qualification of the person but because of God's goodness and mercy. Standing for the One who stood for you, even when you were His enemy, is a cause worth fighting for.

Fight for the Faith

Paul told Timothy to fight the good fight because some had not done so. Paul knew of those who had abandoned the faith and no longer followed what they knew to be right, which hardened their consciences (1 Timothy 1:19-20, 4:1-7). Some of these he knew by name because they had once been fellow soldiers in the cause.

Truth matters. If you do not stand for something, you will fall for anything. Timothy knew the truth, but false teachers were all around him. It was appealing to him, as it is attractive to us, to go along with what is popular or seems new and insightful. If it departs from the faith, however, it is not worth the effort. This does not mean that we have to fight within the faith—to be belligerent toward other believers. But truth is worth standing for. If we do not, it will be swept aside by relativism and the latest fad.

The Goal of Godliness

Paul gives specific ways in which we are to fight the good fight. Some of the tactics in this battle might surprise you.

First, we are to pray (1 Timothy 2:1-8). Paul wrote Timothy to explain to him how he ought to conduct himself in the household of God (1 Timothy 3:15). He instructed Timothy about how he was to instruct others. "First of all," he says (1 Timothy 2:1), the church is to be a praying people. This is a powerful weapon in the Christian's arsenal, and we need to take advantage of it. Prayer reminds us that it is not our battle but the Lord's (1 Samuel 17:47). You are not the commander, and victory does not depend on your strength.

Second, we are to live modestly (1 Timothy 2:9-15). The principle applies to all Christians, but the need Paul addresses here is for women to show godliness by how they live. This involves how a woman dresses, how she humbly receives instruction instead of trying to call the shots, and how she follows through on her domestic responsibilities.

Third, the church needs godly men as leaders (1 Timothy 3:1-13). Paul instructs Timothy about the kind of men that elders and deacons need to be. The leaders of the body of Christ must be men who are respected both in and out of the fellowship. Following Christ should make a difference in how

Lesson 125 - Bible Study: Fighting the Good Fight

a person lives, but not everyone can or should be a leader in the church. The church needs good examples of godliness more than it needs examples of good businessmen or debaters or intellectuals. Since we are in a fight, we want good soldiers on our side. Since we are in a contest, we want good players on our team.

Paul says that the mystery of godliness is great (1 Timothy 3:14-16). Notice how often Paul uses the word godliness in 1 Timothy (2:2, 2:10, 3:16, 4:7-8, 6:3, 6:6, 6:11). The way to fight the good fight is to be a godly person.

Always in Training

"Discipline yourself for the purpose of godliness," Paul told Timothy (1 Timothy 4:7-16). As important as physical discipline is, training in godliness is even more important because it is helpful both in this life and in the life to come. Godliness and its reward are the goal for which Paul labored and strove.

Timothy was not to make excuses because he was young. He was not to live in a hypocritical way that would let others point to his life as an excuse for not becoming a Christian. Instead, he needed to devote himself to what would strengthen his faith and strengthen his influence with others. This is how he could make a difference both in his life and in the lives of others. This is how he could fight the good fight.

Deal with People Properly

Paul instructed Timothy on how to relate to various kinds of people: older and younger men, older and younger women, widows, elders, slaves, and masters of slaves (1 Timothy 5:1-6:2). Handling your relationships well is an important part of fighting the good fight.

People are not the enemy. Some of them are on the enemy's side and might even be actively engaged in battling for the other side, but they are still not the enemy. Satan is the enemy. We are not called to fight people but to fight the snare into which they have fallen. We fight the good fight to help them, for what the good way can do for them, not to defeat them or to put them in their place.

God will hold you accountable for how you treat other people. This communicates a great deal about what Jesus really means to you. Some of the people with whom you engage in the good fight might become allies. You might spend time with others over and over, and they still might never change. All of them will one day stand before God, and how you deal with them could have an impact on what they hear on that last great day. Fighting the good fight includes how you treat others.

This Russian Orthodox icon commemorates priests who were killed at the Butovo firing range, a site of mass executions during the reign of Stalin. The icon is located at the Holy New Martyrs and Confessors of Russia Church in Brooklyn, New York. Russia sold the Butovo property to the Russian Orthodox Church in 1995, and a memorial chapel was built there.

Fight for the Right Things

Christians should have a clear idea of what they are fighting for. If they don't, their objectives might clash with the objective of the Commander (1 Timothy 6:3-21).

Money is not worth the fight. We didn't bring any into the world and we aren't going to take any with us. Fighting the good fight means being content with what we have. If we fight for money, we will look very much like people who are fighting the bad fight.

Talk is not worth the fight. Talk is cheap and won't get you anywhere. Talk can be easily confused for knowledge. Talkative people, however, are not necessarily godly; and godly people are not necessarily talkative. Paul said we need to avoid chatter and arguments, and he said it for good reason.

The One who stood for the good fight before Pilate is worth the fight. His coming glory is worth the fight. The calling that God gives us to reach the finish line is worth the fight.

"I have fought the good fight, I have finished the course, I have kept the faith" (2 Timothy 4:7). Surely Ronald Reagan felt a great deal of satisfaction when, two years after he challenged Mr. Gorbachev to tear down the Berlin Wall, the wall was torn down. The satisfaction was probably not for himself but for the victory of the cause for which he fought.

In the same way, the Christian's joy over the victory of the way of Christ will not be out of pridefulness for being right because he will know how often he had been wrong. Instead, the joy will come from the vindication of the cause to which he had devoted his life. The victory is not ours. The victory is Christ's, and His ultimate grace will be when He allows us to participate in it with Him. In the end, may we all be able to echo Paul's testimony that we have fought the good fight, finished the course, and kept the faith.

Fight the good fight of faith; take hold of the eternal life to which you were called, and you made the good confession in the presence of many witnesses.
1 Timothy 6:12

Assignments for Lesson 125

Bible — Recite or write Psalm 97:10-12 from memory.

Literature — Finish reading *Animal Farm*. Literary analysis available in *Student Review*.

Project — Complete your project for the unit.

Student Review — Optional: Answer the questions for Lesson 125 and for *Animal Farm*; take the quiz for Unit 25; and take the fifth history, English, and Bible exams.

26

The Making of Modern Asia

Summary In this unit we survey the stories of the larger Asian nations—China, India, Japan, and Korea—as well as Southeast Asia. We also look at the lives of three Christian missionaries who served in Asia. The Bible study examines what the Bible teaches about helping the poor.

Lessons
126 - China: From Dynasties to Communism
127 - India: A Clash of Cultures
128 - Japan, Korea, and Southeast Asia
129 - Christian Missionaries to Asia
130 - Bible Study: Helping the Poor

Singapore

Memory Work — Learn Zechariah 7:9-10 by the end of the unit.

Books Used

The Bible
In Their Words
Bridge to the Sun

Project (choose one)

1) Write 300 to 500 words on one of the following topics:

   - Write about the Olympic Games that were hosted in Beijing in 2008.
   - Research five Christian organizations that meet the needs of the poor. Write a basic description for each of how the organization started, where it is based, and what needs it addresses. (See Lesson 130.)

2) Create a beautiful Pachisi game for your family from wood, cloth, or specialty paper. Pachisi originated in ancient India. Research the history of the game before you begin your project.

3) Write a play based on the life or an incident in the life of a missionary to Asia. It can be one of the missionaries mentioned in Lesson 129, or another missionary. Your play should be at least seven pages long but can be as long as you like. Recruiting family and/or friends to perform your play might be fun, but is optional.

Literature

In 1930 Hidenari Terasaki was a Japanese diplomat serving in Washington, D.C. Gwen Harold of Johnson City, Tennessee, was visiting her aunt in Washington, and they attended a reception at the Japanese embassy. After getting to know each other over several months, Terasaki (or "Terry" as Gwen called him) and Gwen were married, despite their cultural differences.

Their diplomatic travels took them to China (where their daughter Mariko was born), Cuba, and back to Washington. Terry wanted Japan and the United States to be friends, and he strenuously opposed the attack on Pearl Harbor. After World War II, Terry served as a liaison between the Japanese Emperor and the Americans under General Douglas MacArthur.

Bridge to the Sun, published in 1957, is a moving story of love and commitment. It opens a window onto Japanese culture, and it shows how international events have real impact on individual lives. The book became a *New York Times* best seller, and the story was made into a major motion picture in 1961. Gwen Terasaki died in 1990.

Great Hall of the People, Beijing

Lesson 126

China: From Dynasties to Communism

The vast Middle Kingdom has been a prize sought by many strongmen for centuries. The pattern of politics in China has hardly ever involved democracy. Usually the powers of government have rested in the hands of an elite few. The Chinese have made many advances in technology and scholarship, often ahead of Europeans. However, these advances did little to help the millions of Chinese who worked hard to survive the best they could on farms and in cities while political battles swirled around them.

The Pattern of Dynasties

Ancient China was ruled by a series of dynasties. The most prominent of these were the Han, which governed until 220 AD; the Tang, from 618 to 907; and the Sung, in control from 960 to 1279. During the Tang dynasty, Chinese influence extended to the borders of India and Persia and into Korea, Japan, and Southeast Asia. The Sung leadership created a unified state centuries before similar nation-states were common in Europe. An efficient and well-trained civil service developed during the latter two dynasties, although access to government jobs was limited. Only children from wealthy families could afford the education required to study for the civil service examination. The dominant belief systems in China were Confucianism and, later, Buddhism.

Several important inventions appeared during the Tang and Sung periods. Printing began in the eighth century by Buddhist monks who carved wooden blocks to print sacred texts onto paper. The earliest known printed work is the Diamond Sutra from 868. Other Chinese inventions included the magnetic compass, maps, gunpowder, and the water wheel as a source of power. The Chinese also began making porcelain pottery during this period.

Mongols, Mings, and Manchus

Fierce Mongol invaders led by Genghis Khan attacked China during the 12th century. The Mongols captured Beijing in 1215. The grandson of Genghis, Kublai Khan, completed the Mongol conquest of China. Eventually, the Mongol Empire spread from the Pacific Ocean to the Danube River in Europe. A system of roads enabled the Mongols to establish regular contact with Arabs, Russians, and Europeans. Italian traders developed the most active trade with China.

Poor leadership by successors to Kublai Khan led to a weakening of their dynasty. A Buddhist monk organized opposition to the foreign Mongol rulers,

737

During the Sung dynasty, the practice of binding women's feet became common. It began among the royalty because they thought that tiny, delicate feet were beautiful. A girl's feet were tightly bound soon after birth to keep them from growing. Court dancers were probably the first to have it done, but it spread to all classes because it was thought that having large feet might keep a girl from finding a husband. The process was painful and limited women to taking tiny steps. This 1902 photo shows a woman with bound feet on the right and a woman with unbound feet on the left.

and in 1368 the Ming Dynasty began. It ruled China until 1644. The Mings restored Chinese culture and built a huge fleet of trading ships that traveled to India, Arabia, and East Africa. However, around 1433 the trading voyages ceased for reasons that are unclear to us. The Mings turned inward and limited their contact with outsiders. Foreign trade was only allowed in the city of Canton and then only under tightly controlled conditions.

Despite this inward orientation, China continued to be a highly prized target for aggression. Another wave of invaders, this time from Manchuria to the northeast of China, seized control in 1644. The Manchu established their capital at Beijing and ruled a strong and prosperous civilization until 1911. Foreign trade was once again encouraged, but only under strict guidelines.

European Influence

In the 1800s, internal problems led to external pressures on China. The country's rapidly growing population put pressure on its food supply; famines became frequent. In addition, the leaders became corrupt, as had often happened in China. To pay for the costs of this corruption, the Manchu increased taxes, which did not please the people.

Meanwhile, European nations began pressuring China to relax trade restrictions. Foreign trade and influence were not valued by the Chinese, since they saw themselves as the center of the world and thought they had all that they needed. The Chinese often saw Europeans as somewhat backward since they did not have Chinese technology and the fine products of China such as silk and spices. The Chinese did not see the need of exchanging diplomats with European nations, since the Europeans did not have much that the Chinese wanted.

A major exception to this general rule came when British merchants began selling opium from India and Turkey to the Chinese in the late 18th century. This made some Chinese merchants wealthy, but the Manchu leadership was concerned about the growth of the harmful practice and about the drain of silver from the country that the opium trade caused. In 1839 Chinese agents destroyed millions of dollars worth of British opium at Canton. In response, the British seized Canton and attacked the nearby area. Britain defeated China in this Opium War.

As a result of the war, China had to give Britain control of the port of Hong Kong (which was near Canton) and compensate the British for the lost opium. The Chinese also had to agree to loosen restrictions on trade with the British and to allow British subjects in China to be governed by British law, not Chinese law. This meant that the Chinese had little control over what the British did. Soon other European nations demanded similar arrangements in what were called unequal treaties.

Lesson 126 - China: From Dynasties to Communism

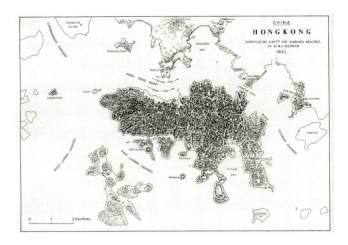

1841 British Map of Hong Kong

After centuries of influence flowing out of China into Europe, now the Europeans were beginning to influence the life, economy, and government of China.

An 1850 peasant uprising in China known as the Taiping Rebellion sought to restore Chinese traditions and to bring about reforms in land ownership and taxation. European countries helped the weak Manchu ruler to quell the rebellion since they had lucrative trade agreements in place and did not want to risk any changes. This enabled the Europeans to demand and receive even more concessions from the Manchu government, including reopening the opium trade and allowing foreign diplomats into Beijing.

Foreign domination of China continued to increase throughout the 19th century. Russia seized a portion of northern China in 1860 and built the port of Vladivostok on the Pacific Ocean. Japan defeated China in a war in 1894 and gained control of the Korean peninsula, which China had previously governed.

During the latter part of the 1800s, France, Germany, Russia, and Britain created what were called spheres of influence in different sections of China. Each country received trade concessions and recognition of their dominance in their particular area.

The Europeans were permitted to invest in mines, factories, and railways in their spheres of influence and could build military installations to protect their interests. The United States did not try to establish a sphere of influence. Instead, the U.S. pressured China and the European countries with interests there to follow what it called an Open Door Policy, giving all nations equal access to Chinese markets. The once proud and independent country of China was now the subject of foreign political and economic domination.

Regaining the Provincial Capital of Ruizhou *by Wu Youru (Chinese, 1886) depicts a scene of the Taiping Rebellion.*

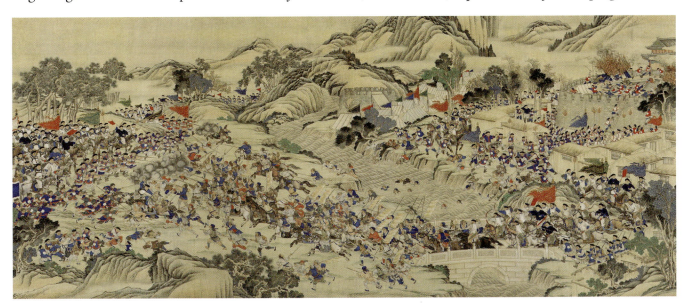

This 1898 French political cartoon by Henri Meyer portrays China as a pie being carved up by other nations, represented by Victoria (United Kingdom), Wilhelm II (Germany), Nicholas II (Russia), Marianne (a national emblem of France), and a samurai warrior (Japan). An ethnically-stereotypical Chinese official watches in horror.

Unrest and Rebellion

Around the beginning of the 20th century, some Chinese undertook movements to restore Chinese power and culture. The Fists of Righteous Harmony was a secret society formed in 1899. They came to be called the Boxers by Europeans. Their goal was to rid China of both the Manchu dynasty and the foreign traders and diplomats.

In 1900 the Boxers laid siege to a compound in Beijing that housed foreign representatives. A coalition of forces from the foreign countries represented in China defeated the Boxers and demanded from the Chinese government the right to maintain a military presence on Chinese soil and in Chinese rivers and coastal waters. To many Chinese, it appeared that they were hostages and victims in their own land.

Revolutionaries overthrew the Manchu dynasty in 1911 and proclaimed a republic. This move ushered in a period of intense turmoil and conflict within China. Not all of the fighting was directed against the Manchu or the foreigners. Powerful warlords in the provinces capitalized on the unrest as an opportunity to begin fighting each other and looting the people in the countryside.

A leading figure in the revolutionary movement was Dr. Sun Yat-sen, who had organized earlier uprisings against the Manchu but who was living outside of China when the 1911 revolt occurred. Sun quickly returned to China and was named president of the Chinese Republic. Sun was only president for a month before he was removed from office by an army general, but he continued to exert influence in the country.

Sun established a base of operations in Canton. He helped found the Kuomintang or Nationalist Party. Realizing that he would need an army to gain control of all of China, Sun designated Chiang Kai-shek to organize and lead the Kuomintang forces. After Sun died in 1925, Chiang led his forces on a march north from Canton, and in 1928 the Kuomintang established firm control over the Chinese Republic.

The Rise of the Communists

However, Chiang had to deal with another growing power, the Communist Party. Chinese Communists had organized in 1921 and joined the Kuomintang in hopes of gaining control of the Party. Chiang realized their hidden agenda and expelled them in 1927. The leader of the Communists, Mao Zedong, organized his forces in remote southeast China. The Nationalists battled the Communists in a civil war until 1934, when Chiang gained

Lesson 126 - China: From Dynasties to Communism

the upper hand. Then about 90,000 Communist soldiers began what was called the Long March to a far northwest province to reorganize. Only about 7,000 of the troops reached their destination, due to death and desertion.

During World War II, the Nationalists and the Communists stopped fighting each other to concentrate on the Japanese who had invaded the land. The United States gave assistance to Chiang, but Mao continued to build his army and to gain support among the people. By 1945 Mao controlled the north of China and Chiang controlled the south. The U.S. encouraged the two groups to form a single government, but neither side wanted to do this.

Civil war broke out again in 1945, and this time the Communists gained the upper hand. In 1949 the Communists under Mao finally defeated the Nationalist forces led by Chiang. The Nationalists retreated to the island of Taiwan off the coast of China; and Mao proclaimed the People's Republic of China on October 1, 1949.

Mao was devoted to what he understood to be the original Marxist-Leninist ideals. He introduced radical changes to Chinese politics, culture, and industry. After Stalin's death in 1953, the Soviet Union moved away from some of his policies. The Communists in China accused the Soviets of having lost the original socialist vision. This was part of a cooling of diplomatic relations between China and the Soviet Union.

This photo of Chairman Mao playing table tennis was included in the book of his quotations that was widely distributed in China.

China hosted the 2008 Summer Olympics in Beijing. This photo is from the Opening Ceremony.

When the United Nations was founded after World War II, the UN recognized the Nationalist government as the legitimate government of China. China received a permanent seat on the UN Security Council. After the Communist takeover of China, the Nationalist government based in Taiwan continued to control that seat in the United Nations. In 1971 the UN General Assembly voted to take representation away from Taiwan and give it to the People's Republic of China (the Communist government on the mainland). This move was supported by the other permanent members of the Security Council, except for the United States.

In 1972 U.S. President Richard Nixon, a strong anti-Communist, made a ground-breaking visit to China. The move opened the door to easing relations between the U.S. and the Communist Chinese government. Over the next several decades, China responded to its economic needs by aggressively seeking trade with the West and encouraging steps toward capitalism.

The Church in China

Tradition holds that Thomas, the disciple of Jesus, was the first person to preach the gospel in China. We have already studied about the Nestorian Stele, which describes Christianity in China from the 600s AD. Some Catholic missionaries went to China during and after the Middle Ages.

English Protestant missionary Hudson Taylor led a major effort to reach the Chinese people in the 1800s. The China Inland Mission (CIM) brought hundreds of missionaries into China, including single women. Gladys Aylward was rejected by CIM but managed to go to China on her own. Widespread Chinese skepticism of anything foreign, coupled with the chaos of civil war and the devastation of two world wars, hindered the further spread of the faith in the first half of the 20th century.

When China fell to the Communists after World War II, the government expelled all foreign missionaries. Officially atheist, the government sanctions the Three Self Patriotic Movement or Three Self Church. These churches are self-governing, self-supporting, and self-propagating (in other words, without any foreign involvement). They teach many standard Christian doctrines but are tightly controlled by the government. A person can purchase a Bible in China—but only at a Three Self Church bookstore. The Chinese Patriotic Catholic Association is also aligned with the Communist government. Its leadership does not recognize the authority of the pope.

The dynamic spiritual power in China is found in the thousands of house churches that are not recognized by the government and do not rely on foreign missionaries. The Communist government tolerates most house churches, but authorities sometimes break up house churches and persecute and imprison church leaders. The inconsistent policy is to some degree the result of how local government officials respond to the existence of house churches. Estimates of the number of believers in China vary widely, from about twenty million to over one hundred million.

After these things I looked, and behold, a great multitude which no one could count, from every nation and all tribes and peoples and tongues, standing before the throne and before the Lamb. . . .
Revelation 7:9

Assignments for Lesson 126

In Their Words Read the excerpt from *A Tour in Mongolia* (pages 314-316).

Literature Begin reading *Bridge to the Sun*. Plan to finish it by the end of Unit 27.

Student Review Optional: Answer the questions for Lesson 126.

Street Cricket in India

Lesson 127

India: A Clash of Cultures

During the Gupta empire in the first centuries AD, the Hindu faith spread throughout India. As we noted earlier, Hinduism had absorbed elements of Buddhism. Two other strong influences in India during this time were (1) the power of the Brahmans, the educated priestly class that preserved ancient traditions; and (2) the strict caste system in society, that dictated where people lived, what work they did, and whom they married. The lack of a single strong leader throughout all of India left it subject to foreign invaders. The Huns from central Asia, for example, invaded India in the fifth century AD.

Muslims and Mongols

In the tenth century, Islamic Turks and Afghans invaded and conquered the Indus River valley and eventually ruled most of India. Muslim rulers, called sultans, established their capital at Delhi in 1206. The Muslims were motivated by desires to spread the religion of Islam and to acquire wealth from the land and people. The sultans set up a provincial government system and lived in lavish style.

Mongols from central Asia invaded in 1398, led by Tamerlane. The Mongols showed no mercy to the inhabitants, completely wiping out the city of Delhi and killing or enslaving the entire population of the city. The only exceptions were artisans, who were sent to build Tamerlane's new capital at Samarkand (now in Uzbekistan). The Mongols did not stay in India long but left to pursue further conquests. Muslims returned to power, though now somewhat weaker because of the experience.

The followers of Islam did not allow their religion to be absorbed into Hinduism. The Muslims believed in one god, Allah; therefore, they abhorred the multiplicity of Hindu gods and often destroyed Hindu temples. Muslims valued the equality of believers while Hindus observed a regimented caste system. Muslims insisted on following the teachings of the Qur'an, while Hindus were tolerant of many different ideas. Muslims saw cows as merely a source of food while Hindus treated cows as sacred. Some Hindus in the north converted to Islam.

Another Mongol invasion, this one led by Babur, descended upon India in 1526. Babur claimed to be a descendant of Genghis Khan and Tamerlane. The Persian word for Mongol was Mogul, and Mogul was the word that became attached to this dynasty. The Moguls ruled India for about three hundred years.

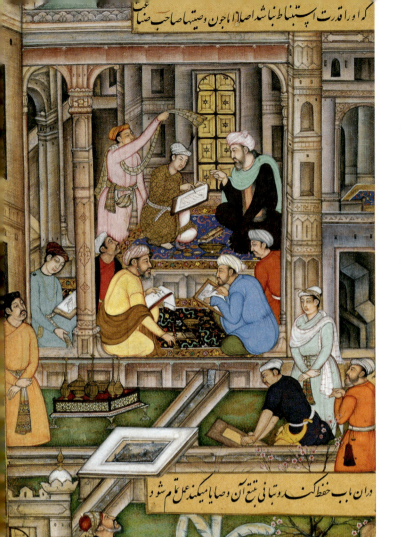

Unit 26 - The Making of Modern Asia

This is a late 16th-century Mogul illustration of Mogul artists and calligraphers.

Though they were Muslims, Babur and his immediate successors promoted toleration of Hinduism. Wealthy Moguls built elaborate palaces and manicured gardens. The Mogul Jahan had a beautiful tomb built in 1632 for his wife Mumtaz Mahal. The structure became known as the Taj Mahal. Later Mogul leaders returned to the policy of persecuting the Hindus, which prompted a strong Hindu reaction. In-fighting among Muslim princes also weakened Mogul authority.

During the Mogul ascendancy, traders from Europe arrived in India. Portugal opened the trade route, and other nations followed. Soon after the traders came Christian missionaries, but during the 1500s the Moguls strongly opposed Christian evangelistic work. In general, however, the Moguls did not feel threatened by the Europeans, who did not appear to live in the splendor and wealth that the Moguls enjoyed.

The Taj Mahal is part of a larger complex that includes a mosque (left), gardens, and other small tombs.

Lesson 127 - India: A Clash of Cultures

The British Come to India

In 1600 British merchants formed the East India Company to finance and promote trade between Britain and India. As trade with Europeans was increasing, the Mogul dynasty was weakening from poor leadership and fighting among provincial princes. The British East India Company took on military and political roles in India on behalf of Great Britain.

When the Seven Years' War erupted in Europe in 1756, Robert Clive of the East India Company organized a military force and ousted the French from their trading posts in India. The company also pressured provincial Indian governments to give it favorable treatment. Within a few years, the British East India Company was the strongest political and military force in India. It in effect ruled India unhindered until the mid-1800s. An 1857 uprising of Indian soldiers called sepoys who worked for the company drew the support of Hindu and Muslim princes and of many poor farmers, but the British prevailed. The incident led Parliament to assume oversight of India as a British colony, removing the East India Company from its position of power.

British rule brought technological advances to India in the form of better health care and improved travel and communication. Upper-caste Indian children attended British-run schools and became a new professional class in the country. Missionaries spread the gospel in India, and millions were converted there. However, the British policy of imposing their culture had some harmful effects. Britain sought to exploit India by extracting raw materials for use in manufacturing activity in Britain and by using it as a market for finished British goods. Indian artisans could not compete with lower-cost British goods. Indian farmers were encouraged to grow cotton for sale instead of food to feed their families. This led to occasional famines.

Rani Lakshmi Bai (1828-1858), queen of the Indian state of Jhansi, was a leader in the 1857 rebellion. She died in battle against the British. Equestrian statues of Lakshmi Bai, such as this one in Solapur, India, often portray her with her son on her back.

The Opposition Grows

Indigenous opposition to British rule increased the longer Britain remained in charge. This opposition was fed by a rising tide of nationalism among better-educated, middle-class Indians. This group formed the Indian National Congress Party in 1885. The goal of the Congress Party (as it was called) was merely home rule within the British Empire at first, but later the party advocated complete independence. Both Hindus and Muslims opposed British rule, but Britain depended on the division between those groups to weaken the effect of their opposition.

During World War I, Britain made vague promises about lessening its control over India at some point in the future. This did not satisfy the Congress Party or other nationalist leaders, and unrest grew among the Indians. The response by Parliament to jail protesters without a trial only increased native frustrations. Limited reforms enacted after World War I still did not mollify opposition to British rule.

The leader of the Congress party after the war was Mohandas Gandhi (1869-1948), an attorney who had been educated in Britain and had earlier worked for greater civil rights for Indians in South Africa. Gandhi's approach to the issue of British rule was to adopt an attitude of non-violent resistance. He urged a boycott of British business and encouraged a renewal of cottage industries.

Gandhi himself lived a simple life in voluntary poverty. He encouraged Indians to take pride in their culture, although he opposed the caste system. Indians recognized the power of his philosophy and gave him the title of Mahatma, "Great Soul." Britain extended more home rule powers to India in 1935, but by then the indigenous opposition would be satisfied with nothing less than complete independence.

Independence and Partition

By the end of World War II, the British government realized that it could no longer govern India. However, the Hindu-Muslim conflict threatened to destroy any advantages the country might gain by independence. Britain persuaded Gandhi and other Indian leaders to accept a plan

Rabindranath Tagore (1861-1941) was a Bengali author and poet, the first non-European to win the Nobel Prize in Literature (1913). He opposed the British occupation of India. Tagore (left) and Gandhi met in 1940.

for partitioning the country into a Hindu state and a Muslim state. In August of 1947, British rule ended and two new countries were created: India with a Hindu majority, and Pakistan with a Muslim majority.

The political boundaries did not reflect where all Muslims and Hindus lived, however. As a result, ten million people moved: Muslims in India moved to Pakistan, and Hindus in Pakistan moved to India. Violence and rioting erupted in several places. About a half-million people were killed, and millions were left homeless in the transition. Gandhi himself was assassinated in 1948 by a Hindu fanatic who did not like Gandhi's attempts to bring peace between Hindus and Muslims.

India under the leadership of Jawaharlal Nehru in the 1950s and 1960s was marked by the growth of industry, the modernizing of agriculture, and a greater sense of Indian unity. However, the mushrooming population strained the nation's resources. Opposition to the leadership of the Congress Party sometimes became violent. When Nehru's daughter, Indira Gandhi (her husband was no relation to Mohandas Gandhi), was prime minister, she declared a state of emergency in 1975 and jailed some of her critics. She was voted out in

Indira Gandhi met in 1969 with Nicolae Ceauşescu, Communist leader of Romania.

1977 but was elected again in 1980 by promising to avoid some of the unpopular policies of her earlier administration.

A major issue during her second tenure was an uprising of Sikh separatists. Indira Gandhi was assassinated in 1984 by two of her Sikh bodyguards. Her son replaced her as prime minister, but he was assassinated in 1991. Intense political and ethnic unrest have continued to result in violence from time to time.

Pakistan and Bangladesh

Pakistan initially functioned as a parliamentary democracy, but the system did not work well. A military dictatorship assumed power in 1958. Government corruption and extremely poor living conditions have led to continued civil and political unrest.

When it was formed, Pakistan consisted of two parts: the larger area to the northwest of India, and East Pakistan to the northeast of India, about 1,000 miles away. West Pakistan leaders dominated the Pakistani government from the beginning. Many in East Pakistan demanded self-rule. Flooding in East Pakistan in 1970 and a slow response by the national government led to stronger calls for separation. East Pakistanis won a majority of seats in the December 1970 election, but the military dictator threw out the results. Civil war erupted the next year.

Almost half of Bangladeshis work in agriculture. Rice is the most important crop.

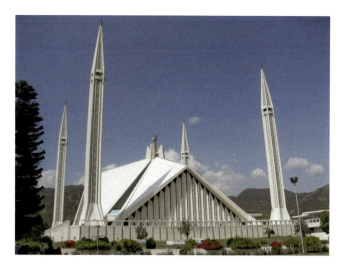

The Faisal Mosque was the largest in the world when it was completed in 1986. It is named after King Faisal of Saudi Arabia (1906-1975), who supported its construction. Located in Pakistan's capital of Islamabad, it is the national mosque of the country.

Millions of refugees tried to flee the fighting by crossing into India. India helped the East Pakistan rebels against the government of Pakistan. East Pakistan officially became the independent country of Bangladesh in December of 1971. Natural disasters, government corruption, and few opportunities for people to support themselves have combined to make life miserable for most people in Bangladesh.

To the Present

During the Cold War between the United States and the Soviet Union, Pakistan aligned itself with the U.S. while India remained officially neutral. Occasional issues, such as the Chinese invasion of Tibet in the early 1960s and the Soviet invasion of Afghanistan in 1979, have raised tensions in the region. Control of the Kashmir region has been a source of conflict ever since the end of British rule. Claimed by Pakistan and India, some local tribes favor independence for themselves. Since both India and Pakistan have developed nuclear weapons, the stakes of the confrontation between the two countries are high.

*Too long has my soul had its dwelling
With those who hate peace.
I am for peace, but when I speak,
They are for war.
Psalm 120:6-7*

Assignments for Lesson 127

In Their Words   Read "A Living Sacrifice" (pages 317-321).

Literature   Continue reading *Bridge to the Sun*.

Student Review   Optional: Answer the questions for Lesson 127.

Japanese Warriors (c. 1293)

Lesson 128

Japan, Korea, and Southeast Asia

Japan

About the third century AD, rulers from the Yamato plain on Japan's largest island began to lead a central government for the entire country. They claimed to be descendants from the sun goddess, whom they ranked first among the Shinto deities. Buddhism was introduced in the sixth century, but interference by Buddhist priests in government matters led emperors to avoid that religion. Later weak emperors led to the rise of local or tribal leaders who ruled smaller areas. Private armies of warriors called samurai developed to support these tribal leaders.

In 1180 the Minamoto family revolted against the ruling dynasty and established the first military government, with leaders called shoguns. Military governors and land supervisors oversaw civil officials. The shogun system resisted two attempted Mongol invasions in the 13th century. Fighting and feuding among rival families continued, and for about fifty years in the 14th century two rival dynasties ruled at the same time.

The first European traders that reached the country in the mid-1500s met a Japan characterized by local lords, vassals, and castle towns. The Catholic missionary Francis Xavier brought Christianity to the country in 1549. Shoguns did not like the fact that Catholics had to obey the pope, whom they saw as a foreign ruler. As a result, Christianity was banned in 1639. All Europeans except the Dutch were also excluded from the country.

Japan was re-unified in the late 1500s by strong military leaders. From the early 1600s until 1868, the Tokugawa dynasty ruled Japan from their castle town of Edo, which is modern Tokyo.

Shogun Tokugawa Hidetada (1579-1632)

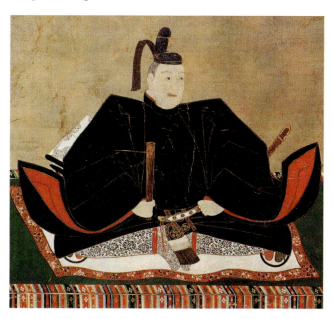

749

The isolationist policy that began in 1639 cut Japan off from almost all contact with the outside world. In the 19th century, Japanese society entered a period of turmoil. Peasant uprisings became common, the despised merchant class had gained economic power (the merchant class was considered to be below the peasants), and the shogun government was corrupt.

In 1854 U.S. Commodore Matthew Perry arrived leading an American fleet. Perry demanded that Japan open its ports to foreign trade. The increasingly discredited Tokugawa regime signed agreements with the U.S. and other foreign nations. Uprisings by local samurai led to the resignation of the shogun in 1867 and to the creation of an imperial government overseen by Emperor Meiji.

During the half-century of Meiji's reign, Japan was transformed into an industrialized world power. However, Japan did it their way instead of having it forced upon them as a colony of a foreign power. The emperor abolished feudalism, improved the efficiency of government, and replaced the samurai with an army of draftees, who were loyal to the emperor. Foreign industrial, scientific, and educational experts were recruited to come to Japan; and government missions went on study trips to other countries.

In 1889 domestic political pressure resulted in a constitutional government. Only one percent of the people could vote, however, and the emperor was still believed to be divine. Japan emerged as a world power after the 1894-95 war against China over control of Manchuria. Japan defeated China in the war and also gained control of Korea. Ten years later, Japan defeated Russia in the Russo-Japanese War and added Sakhalin Island and other territory to its empire.

As one of the Allies against the Central Powers in World War I, Japan seized German territories in Asia, including areas in the German sphere of influence in China. When the war ended, Japan demanded concessions from China that gave Japan power in Manchuria and Mongolia. Following the war, the Japanese government agreed to arms limitations as part of a world-wide effort to promote peace. The Japanese military, however, believed that the government was giving away the country's national security.

Promulgation of the Constitution, *Toyohara Chikanobu (Japanese, 1889)*

Lesson 128 - Japan, Korea, and Southeast Asia

The military led the people of Japan into the horrors of World War II. After Japan's defeat, the United States forced acceptance of a revised constitution. The emperor was allowed to remain as a ceremonial monarch, but a Western-style parliamentary system was created. Japan's military capabilities were severely restricted, and large numbers of American military personnel have been stationed in Japan ever since.

Japan prospered economically for many years after the war. Many Japanese companies that manufactured automobiles, motorcycles, and engines became international brands, including Honda, Isuzu, Kawasaki, Mazda, Mitsubishi, Nissan, Subaru, Suzuki, Toyota, and Yamaha. Other major Japanese companies have diverse operations in industries such as electronics and entertainment technology. These include Casio, Fujifilm, Fujitsu, Hitachi, Nintendo, Ricoh, and Sony.

Japan suffered a lengthy economic decline beginning in the 1990s. Though economic growth returned in the 2000s, the country had another major setback in 2011. A major earthquake off the Japanese coast produced tsunami waves that killed about 15,000 people and caused extensive damage. Equipment failures at the Fukushima Daiichi Nuclear Power Plant led to the release of radioactive material. It was the largest nuclear disaster since the 1986 disaster at the Chernobyl plant in Ukraine.

Korea

The people of the peninsula of Korea are ethnically related to both the Chinese and the Japanese. The first Koreans might have come from Mongolia. Because of Korea's many mountain ranges, small kingdoms and city-states were the norm on the peninsula. The Shilla Kingdom unified the country in 668. About three hundred years later, a powerful leader established the kingdom of Koryo. This is the origin of the name Korea. The Choson Dynasty ruled from 1392 until 1910.

Access to this area in Japan was restricted after the 2011 nuclear disaster.

Koreans fought against many invasions over this long period, usually by the Chinese or Mongols. The country resisted opening its ports to western traders in the 1800s. Korea became known as the Hermit Kingdom for its refusal to have contact with the West.

Around 1900 China, Japan, and Russia all wanted to expand the territories they controlled; and they all targeted Korea. Japan annexed Korea in 1910 and ruled with a firm hand until the end of World War II. The Japanese shipped many raw materials from Korea back to Japan and required that the Japanese language be used in schools and newspapers.

As the end of World War II neared, the United States agreed to let the Soviet Union take over the northern part of Korea in return for Soviet help against Japan. The U.S. administered the southern part of the peninsula. Each side hoped to unify the country on their own terms after the war. Elections were held in South Korea in 1948, but the Soviets resisted allowing elections in the North. In 1950 North Korean soldiers invaded the South to try to unify the country under Communism.

After the Korean War, the North and South took very different paths. South Korea, after some struggles with military dictators, became a modern democratic-republic with a prosperous economy.

Unit 26 - The Making of Modern Asia

This composite of multiple photos from space shows lights at night in and around the Korean peninsula. National boundaries have been outlined. China is on the left of the image, Japan on the right, and some ships at sea are scattered. South Korea is in the middle, with North Korea largely darkened above it. Electricity supply is not reliable in North Korea, and is generally shut off at night.

Christianity has grown significantly there, with a large percentage of the population professing faith in Christ. North Korea, by contrast, has endured harsh government control of the economy and society. North Korea boasts a large military, but political and religious persecution and shortages of food and medical care have killed hundreds of thousands of people.

North and South Korea never signed a peace treaty to end the Korean War, and tensions on the peninsula remain high. The so-called Demilitarized Zone (DMZ) between the two countries is actually one of the most heavily-fortified borders in the world. The two sides have taken cautious steps toward more open communication.

Southeast Asia

The region of Southeast Asia includes the area south of China and east of Bangladesh, as well as the Philippines, Indonesia, and other Pacific Islands. The region was strongly influenced by traders and explorers from China and India. Traders and Buddhist missionaries spread Chinese and Indian cultures and religions among the smaller people groups of Southeast Asia. Some parts of the region had powerful emperors while other places were ruled by local lords.

Significant western contact began when Europeans opened the spice trade in the 1500s. Spain conquered the Philippine Islands in 1571 as a bridge between the spice islands and Spain's American colonies. Otherwise, European countries only operated trading posts in the region and did not pursue colonization at that time.

During the 1700s, Europeans began to create plantations in Southeast Asia to grow crops such as rice, coffee, and sugar. The Industrial Revolution made Southeast Asian raw materials such as oil, rubber, and tin attractive to European nations. The Netherlands brought their trading posts under one colonial government as the Dutch East Indies in the 1800s. Also, Britain and France began a scramble to establish colonies in the region. Britain acquired Burma, Malaya, and Singapore, while France established French Indochina in what is now Vietnam. Both France and Britain hoped to use these colonies to move more easily into southern China.

Only Siam, now called Thailand, was not colonized by a European power. During the 1800s, Siamese rulers modernized their country and welcomed European trade. The country was a neutral buffer between the British in Burma and the French in Indochina.

A nationalist movement began in the Philippines in the late 1800s. These fighters helped the United States against Spain in the Spanish-

Lesson 128 - Japan, Korea, and Southeast Asia

The Malaysian capital of Kuala Lampur is home to the Petronas Towers. These twin office buildings are each 1,483 feet tall. Petronas is the national Malaysian oil and gas company.

American War. However, when the United States did not give the islands independence, the nationalists turned on the Americans and began fighting them. Their efforts were unsuccessful at the time. The United States only granted independence to the Philippines after World War II, in 1946.

European countries maintained a colonial presence in Southeast Asia until the Japanese took over most of the region before World War II. Countries in the region became independent after the war, but the area became a battleground in the Cold War between Communism and freedom, as we discussed in Unit 25.

Malaysia is divided into two sections, one on the southeast tip of Asia and one on the island of Borneo. After gaining independence from Britain, the modern country of Malaysia formed in 1963.

The British founded Singapore, on an island off the coast of Malaysia, as a trading outpost in 1819. It was briefly part of a federation with Malaysia, but it became independent in 1965. Singapore is one of the smallest countries in the world, and one of the most densely-populated.

Indonesia is an archipelago consisting of over 17,000 islands. A former Dutch colony, it gained independence in 1949. Indonesia is the fourth most-populous country in the world, and the country with the largest Muslim population.

Aung San Suu Kyi (b. 1945) opposed the military regime that took over Myanmar (Burma) in 1988. She spent almost fifteen years as a political prisoner under house arrest. As the military relaxed its control on the country, Suu Kyi was released in 2010 and was elected to the national parliament. She received the Nobel Peace Prize in 1991 and the Congressional Gold Medal in 2012.

Anna and the King

King Mongkut (or Rama IV) of Thailand reigned from 1851 to 1868. He invited Anna Leonowens, an Indian-born British woman, to teach his children and wives the English language and customs. Leonowens spent five years in Thailand. One of her pupils was Chulalongkorn, pictured below with his father the king in 1865. Leonowens composed two memoirs of her experiences. She eventually settled in Canada.

King Chulalongkorn (Rama V), who reigned from his father's death until 1910, oversaw the abolition of slavery and helped Thailand become a modern state. Leonowens' son, Louis, became an officer in the Thai army and founded a trading company there that still exists. Chulalongkorn met Anna Leonowens again in London in 1897.

American author Margaret Landon published an historical novel in 1944 called Anna and the King of Siam. *This novel became the basis for the greatly fictionalized (but highly enjoyable) Broadway musical and movie* The King and I. *The film was banned in Thailand (along with a 1999 remake), because it portrayed the king in a negative light. Showing disrespect toward the Thai monarch is still illegal.*

Those who go down to the sea in ships,
Who do business on great waters;
They have seen the works of the Lord,
And His wonders in the deep.
Psalm 107:23-24

Assignments for Lesson 128

In Their Words — Read King Mongkut's letter to the President of the United States and the President's reply (pages 322-326).

Literature — Continue reading *Bridge to the Sun*.

Student Review — Optional: Answer the questions for Lesson 128.

Missionaries Sent Out by China Inland Mission in 1887

Lesson 129

Christian Missionaries to Asia

Christian missionaries have gone by faith to remote parts of the globe, enduring difficult circumstances at great personal sacrifice, to share the message of Jesus with others. Those who have gone to Asia have loved and taught people who had an entirely different worldview. These snapshots of missionaries to Asia will help us appreciate what others have done in the name of Jesus.

Adoniram Judson

The son of a Congregationalist minister, Adoniram Judson was born in Massachusetts in 1788. He entered Andover Seminary in 1808 during what was known as the Second Great Awakening in the United States. He and other Andover students developed a deep desire to spread the gospel to other lands. In response to the interest of these students, the Congregationalist Association of Massachusetts formed the American Board of Commissioners for Foreign Missions, which was the first body to send foreign missionaries from the United States.

In 1812 Judson married Ann Hasseltine. Two weeks later, they left for India as Congregationalist missionaries. Judson had a desire to translate the Bible into the language of the people with whom he would be working. On the trip, he studied the Greek New Testament and became convinced that the Greek word for baptism means immersion. After landing in India, Judson and his wife were immersed by an English Baptist missionary.

Adoniram Judson (1788-1850)

Judson felt duty bound to inform the Congregationalist board of his change and to resign from their sponsorship. He also contacted Baptists in America to see if they wanted to support his mission work. Judson's interest (along with the encouragement of others) led to the formation of the General Convention of the Baptist Denomination in the United States for Foreign Missions, which sponsored Judson's work.

The Judsons had to leave India in 1813 because of pressure from the British East India Company, so they moved to Burma. There Judson translated the Bible into Burmese after first developing an alphabet, since Burmese was not a written language.

Ann, an active partner in the mission work, died in 1826. In 1835 Judson married Sarah Boardman, widow of another missionary. Sarah died in 1845, and shortly thereafter Judson returned to the United States for his only furlough. He was welcomed as a hero by Baptist churches, and his visit stimulated great interest in mission work. Judson married again in 1846, and he and his wife Emily left for Burma a few weeks later. He devoted much energy in his later years to a Burmese-English dictionary. However, Judson was plagued with poor health. He died in 1850 on an ocean voyage which had been prescribed as his only hope for getting better. He was buried at sea in the Bay of Bengal.

Amy Carmichael

Born in Belfast, Northern Ireland, in 1867, Amy Carmichael was the oldest of seven children. When she was seventeen, she and her family were returning home from church one wintry morning when she noticed an old woman, poorly dressed, laboring under a heavy burden. Amy and her two brothers helped the woman, despite the fact that this was not the kind of thing that respectable people did. That afternoon, Amy spent time in private reflection and prayer and was convicted that God wanted her to die to herself and serve other people.

Amy began reaching out to the shawlies. These were girls who worked in the textile mills and who were too poor to afford hats so they covered their heads with their shawls. Amy established a school for the girls and taught them about the Lord.

She was eventually sent by the Church of England as a missionary to Japan. Amy stayed there about two years, then returned to Britain because of her health. Someone suggested to her that traveling to India might improve her health. There she found her life's work. She helped to start the Dohnavur Mission to children. The children she is best known for helping were young girls who were sold by their parents to Buddhist temples at seven or eight years of age to be temple prostitutes. The Dohnavur Mission, still in operation, has helped thousands of children.

During her fifty-three years in India, Carmichael wrote many books and poems. Injured in a fall in 1931, she spent the last twenty years of her life as

Judson Church is located on the campus of Yangon University in Kamayut, Myanmar (Burma).

an invalid, but she continued to serve the needy children of the mission. She never married and was buried in an unmarked grave at Dohnavur.

Once a girl who was thinking about becoming a missionary wrote to Amy to ask what missionary life was like. Amy replied, "Missionary life is a chance to die."

Eric Liddell

The Flying Scotsman was born in 1902 to a Christian missionary family in China. He attended school in Scotland with his older brother while their parents served in China. Liddell grew up wanting to return to the mission field of China, but he was also an excellent runner. He attended Edinburgh University and studied science because he knew that the Chinese needed better science education.

Before his return to China, however, Liddell had the opportunity to compete in the 1924 Olympics.

Eric and Florence Liddell married in Tianjin, China.

Since many of the rescued children did not know their birthdays, the Dohnavur community celebrated Coming Day, as pictured above.

Liddell was scheduled to compete in the 100-meter dash, his best event; but his preliminary heat was scheduled for a Sunday. Liddell believed that the Lord's Day should be devoted to the Lord and not to games, so he refused to run and switched to the 400-meter race. This was all known and determined some months before the Olympics began. At the Olympics, on the day he could have been running for a chance at the gold, Liddell preached at an English-speaking church in Paris. In the 400-meter race (a difficult event for a sprinter) Liddell set a world record in winning the gold medal. He also won a bronze medal in the 200-meter race.

Liddell did not capitalize on his Olympic success for personal profit. After finishing his education two years later, Liddell went to China and taught science at an Anglo-Chinese school in Tientsin. He later went into full-time evangelistic work. Liddell was married in 1934 to a girl who had been one of his students, after she had completed nursing school in Canada. They had two daughters when the Japanese took control of China in 1937. Liddell insisted that his family go to Canada for safety, even though his wife was expecting their third child. He never saw his family again.

After Pearl Harbor, the situation in China worsened for foreign nationals; but Liddell refused to leave. The Japanese eventually imprisoned all foreigners in China, including Liddell. The Olympic champion spent the last two years of his life serving, teaching, and encouraging fellow prisoners. He developed terrible headaches but continued to smile and serve. He died in February of 1945 of a brain tumor and typhoid, just a few months before the end of World War II.

---

*Do you not know that those who run in a race all run,
but only one receives the prize?
Run in such a way that you may win.*
1 Corinthians 9:24

Assignments for Lesson 129

In Their Words — Read Adoniram Judson's Rules of Holy Living and the excerpt from *Things As They Are* (pages 327-330).

Literature — Continue reading *Bridge to the Sun*.

Student Review — Optional: Answer the questions for Lesson 129.

Street in the Philippines

Lesson 130 - Bible Study

Helping the Poor

Christians are called to help others with their physical needs. This is an important and often challenging responsibility. Christian missionaries around the world, including in Asia, have been confronted with widespread poverty among the people they seek to teach.

Old Testament Teaching

In the Law, God told the people of Israel to leave the gleanings in their fields for the needy and the stranger (Leviticus 19:9-10). The landowner did not need every last grape or stalk of grain. Instead, he was to remember that he (or his ancestor) was once a poor slave in Egypt. God promised that He would bless them in their work if they did this (Deuteronomy 24:19-22).

The Law also commanded the Israelites to treat the poor justly in legal matters. They were not to prefer the rich in order to win favors from them (Deuteronomy 24:17-18). Several of the prophets denounced Israel's failure to do this when they condemned Israel's sins (for example, Isaiah 1:17 and Amos 4:1).

Feed My Starving Children is a Christian organization that works with local partners to distribute food in many countries around the world, such as Tajikistan.

Starting in the 17th century, poor man statues (and an occasional poor woman) were placed outside churches in Sweden. Members could make donations to help the poor by placing coins in a slot in the chest. The statue at left is in Nurmo, Finland. (Finland was once controlled by Sweden but became an independent country in the 20th century.)

The Teaching of Jesus

Jesus had much to say about helping the needy. It is important to remember first of all that He Himself was poor. He had "nowhere to lay His head" (Luke 9:58). When you give to the poor, Jesus said, you are not to call attention to yourself for your good deed. Instead, your help should be so quiet and come so naturally from your heart that your left hand does not know what your right hand is doing. When we give secretly, God will reward us (Matthew 6:2-4).

Instead of judging others, we are to give to others. This giving we are to do generously, "for by your standard of measure it will be measured to you in return" (Luke 6:38). Jesus used the illustration of someone pouring into your cup so generously that the gift overflows into your lap. Such generosity from God will come to us when we are generous to others.

The dividing line between the sheep and the goats on the day of judgment, Jesus said, was that the sheep had helped people in need. In this way, they had served Jesus. The goats, on the other hand, had failed to help others and so had failed to serve Jesus (Matthew 25:31-46). Even a cup of cold water given in the name of Jesus will not go unnoticed (Matthew 10:42).

Shortly before Jesus was betrayed, arrested, and crucified, a woman anointed His head with expensive perfume. The disciples complained about her actions, saying that the perfume could have been sold and the money given to the poor rather than being wasted in this way. Jesus rebuked them for their thinking. She had done a beautiful deed for Him to prepare Him for burial. "You always have the poor with you," Jesus said. You will always have the opportunity to help the poor, if that is what you really want to do (and talking about it is much easier than actually doing it). But there should be no price ceiling on serving Jesus.

Serving the poor and serving Jesus are not mutually exclusive. Jesus said that the woman's loving, generous act would be told wherever the gospel is preached. The story of Jesus and the story of the woman's generosity to One who was poor Himself would go hand in hand (Matthew 26:6-13).

Helping the Poor in the Early Church

Almost immediately after the church was formed, Christians began helping those in need. Believers in Jerusalem sold property and gave the proceeds to the apostles, and the money was then "distributed to each as any had need" (Acts 4:35). As a result, "there was not a needy person among them" (4:34). The church undertook a daily distribution of food to widows (Acts 6:1). Dorcas was remembered for her "deeds of kindness and charity" (Acts 9:36). When Agabus the prophet predicted a famine, believers in Antioch sent help to Christians in Judea (Acts 11:27-30).

In the early part of Paul's ministry, the leaders of the church in Jerusalem encouraged him to remember the poor, something he was eagerly wanting to do anyway (Galatians 2:10). As an example of this, a major part of Paul's third missionary journey involved a collection he undertook among Gentile churches to help the poor saints from a Jewish background in Jerusalem (1 Corinthians 16:1-4, 2 Corinthians 8-9, Romans 15:25-26).

James said that pure and undefiled religion included giving assistance to widows and orphans in their difficulties (James 1:27). He rebuked those who discriminated against the poor in their assemblies (James 2:1-5). Those who are poor in things but rich in the Lord are in fact the rich in this life, but those who are materially wealthy are to be pitied if they are spiritually poor (James 2:5-7; see also Luke 6:20-21 and 24-25).

Apparently the need to help the poor was a major issue in the early church. Many of the first Christians were from the lower economic strata (see 1 Corinthians 1:26-29). It has often been the case that the wealthy believe that they have more to give up, and thus they are relatively more reluctant to become Christians. "How hard it will be for those who are wealthy to enter the kingdom of God!" Jesus said (Mark 10:23).

Our Calling Today

Since ancient times, some people have been wealthy and others poor. Some wealthy people inherit their riches or get them by unscrupulous means, while many who labor hard never seem to get ahead. Proverbs warns of the calamity that will come to the lazy person (Proverbs 24:30-34), but not all poverty is the result of laziness. Perhaps it will always be a mystery hidden in the justice of God why some are wealthy and some are poor. Our calling is not to wait until we figure it out but to do what we know we need to do according to God's Word.

In addition to meeting real needs of real people, helping the poor is a way to make the gospel attractive to outsiders. Sometimes we may be taken advantage of, but that is something the other person will have to explain to God. We don't want to miss serving Him by trying to judge the worthiness of someone who appears to need help.

Feed My Starving Children Effort in Kenya

Unit 26 - The Making of Modern Asia

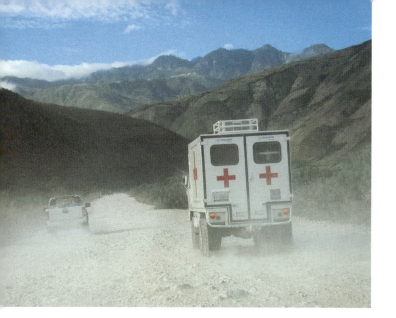

Love a Child is a ministry run by Christians that sends mobile medical clinics to remote villages in Haiti.

We should prayerfully look for thoughtful and imaginative ways to help others. Some churches, for instance, have an annual giveaway of things the members no longer need. Rather than having a garage sale, the church blesses many people in the community by simply giving the items away on a designated day. Or, churches that are near a major hospital sometimes sponsor a motel room or apartment for family members of patients who are from out of town. Individual families helping those in need often makes a profound impact on the person being helped. In other words, helping others does not have to be a church project. The best way to help others is always to do so from the heart.

For you know the grace of our Lord Jesus Christ, that though He was rich, yet for your sake He became poor, so that you through His poverty might become rich.
2 Corinthians 8:9

Assignments for Lesson 130

Bible — Recite or write Zechariah 7:9-10 from memory.

In Their Words — Read Recollections of Eric Liddell (pages 331-334).

Literature — Continue reading *Bridge to the Sun*.

Project — Complete your project for the unit.

Student Review — Optional: Answer the questions for Lesson 130 and take the quiz for Unit 26.

27

The Making of Modern Latin America

Summary The countries of South and Central America were formed in much the same way as the United States was. As colonies of European powers, they fought for independence and became New World republics. In this unit, we focus especially on Simón Bolívar and on Mexico. We also take a look at the indigenous peoples of Latin America. The Bible study will deal with the Biblical teachings on justice.

Lessons
131 - Many Countries, One Goal
132 - Mexico's Story
133 - Key Person: Simón Bolívar
134 - Everyday Life: Indigenous Peoples of Latin America
135 - Bible Study: Justice

Christ the Redeemer Statue, Rio de Janeiro, Brazil

Memory Work

Learn Proverbs 2:6-9 by the end of the unit.

Books Used

The Bible
In Their Words
Bridge to the Sun

Project (choose one)

1) Write 300 to 500 words on one of the following topics:

- Write an essay on the relationship between the United States and other countries in the Western Hemisphere. Discuss how it has been good, how it has been bad, and how it could be better.

- In Lesson 2, we described a boy named Pedro in the country of Honduras. Write a short story about him. Choose a particular incident or issue as your theme: growing up, coming to faith, making a living in a poor country, or some other topic.

2) Make a short video documentary about Latin American life, either in historic or current times. Your topic could be soccer, the preparation of traditional foods, the life of a well-known Latin American, an interview with someone you know from Latin America, or another topic of your own choosing. Your documentary should be at least five minutes long.

3) Sew a flag of one of the countries of Latin America. Learn how and when it was adopted and what the colors and/or symbols represent.

Mexico and Uruguay Prepare for a Match at the 2007 Copa América in Caracas, Venezuela

Lesson 131

Many Countries, One Goal

The ancient native tribes of Central and South America gave way to conquerors from Spain and other European countries in the 16th and 17th centuries. The American Revolution inspired many people to our south to rise up against European rulers just as the British colonies in America had done. By 1825 most Latin American countries had gained their freedom.

Factors to Overcome

The Spanish colonial system had a rigid social structure. At the top were the wealthy peninsulares, who came from the Iberian peninsula, on which Spain and Portugal are located. Only peninsulares could hold the highest political and Church offices, and many received huge land grants from the king. Below them were the creoles, who were ethnic Spanish born in America. They could not hold the highest offices, but they could gain wealth and power through business endeavors. The third class was made up of mestizos, or people of mixed European and South and Central American Indian descent. Mestizos held many different kinds of positions in the colonies, from laborers to lawyers. At the bottom of the social ladder were African slaves and the relatively few remaining indigenous peoples.

The peninsulares had the most interest in maintaining the status quo of the social structure in Latin America. Creoles, by contrast, were frustrated that they could never rise any higher in the power structure. In addition, some creoles were educated in Europe and learned about Enlightenment ideas of liberty and individual rights. Mestizos could only dream of holding any position of wealth or influence. Indians and slaves had nothing to lose in material terms through revolution.

Early Movements

Small, relatively weak attempts at revolution occurred in Peru and Colombia in the 1780s but were quickly crushed by the Spanish. The creole Francisco Miranda tried twice to take over Venezuela in the early 1800s, but neither attempt lasted long. Miranda was exiled to Spain and died in 1816.

The first successful revolution in the New World after the American Revolution was in Haiti, on the island of Hispaniola. About a half-million slaves worked on a few sugar plantations owned by the French. The 1789 revolution in France inspired the slaves to rise up against their masters. Toussaint L'Overture led a revolt that lasted about thirteen years.

Unit 27 - The Making of Modern Latin America

The Battle of Vertières, Part of the Haitian Revolution

The fighting took many lives and ended French control in Haiti. The rebels also seized the eastern half of the island, what is now the Dominican Republic. Napoleon sent his brother-in-law, Charles Leclerc, to Haiti to end the rebellion.

After more bitter fighting, Leclerc tricked Toussaint into being taken prisoner. Two other Haitian rebel leaders took up the cause. On January 1, 1804, the independent republic of Haiti was established. Most of the revolutionaries in Haiti were slaves. This frightened many Latin American landowners. The successful revolution encouraged those who wanted to see European rule end in the Western Hemisphere.

Revolutions Against Spain

Napoleon defeated Spain in 1808. He removed Ferdinand VII from the Spanish throne and replaced him with his brother, Joseph Bonaparte. Spain's Latin American colonies refused to recognize the change and began establishing new governments of their own. After Napoleon was defeated, the Congress of Vienna restored Ferdinand VII to the throne of Spain; but the tide of revolution in Latin America could not be turned back.

Simón Bolívar was the leading figure in the Latin American fight for freedom. We will examine his life in more detail later in this unit. José de San Martìn, a creole who had been educated in Europe, led Argentina to independence in 1816. San Martin and a Chilean general marched across the Andes into Chile, which became independent in 1818.

Brazil

Brazil gained its independence from Portugal without much of a struggle. The Portuguese royal family fled to Brazil during Napoleon's rule. Most family members later returned to Europe, but Prince Pedro remained to oversee the colony. Creoles in Brazil offered to make Pedro the ruler of Brazil in exchange for his helping Brazil become independent. The prince agreed in 1822 and became Pedro I, Emperor of Brazil. Pedro chose to rule as a constitutional monarch with an elected assembly.

The nation of Brazil covers almost half of the continent of South America, and its political and economic influence in the global community has become significant. Dilma Vana Rousseff (b. 1947) became the country's first female president in 2011. The 2016 Summer Olympics in Rio de Janeiro, Brazil, are the first hosted in South America. Two new sports are on the program, including golf (for the first time since 1904) and rugby (for the first time since 1924).

Lesson 131 - Many Countries, One Goal

San Martin worked with Bolívar to free Peru and Ecuador in the early 1820s.

Winning the Peace

Simón Bolívar and other freedom fighters dreamed of one nation made up of the former Spanish colonies. However, this did not happen for several reasons. Local groups that had banded together to oust the Spanish now began fighting each other. Power struggles among leaders of the groups led to several civil wars. In addition, the huge area and diverse geography would have been almost impossible to govern from one capital. Local interests and local leaders took precedence over any grand hypothetical scheme. The large colonies that gained independence eventually divided into eighteen South American countries. Even the Dominican Republic declared its independence from Haiti.

The difficulties for the new Latin American nations were many. They had created constitutional representative governments, but they had no real experience in running such governments. When problems arose, the military often took control and put dictators in place to run the country. The new nations had a new social structure, now headed by creoles who did not want to share power with mestizos. Slavery was abolished, but blacks and Indians had few rights and continued to live in poverty. The Catholic Church was still a powerful force and tended to support the status quo.

The new national economies had to struggle to climb up off the ground. Wealth was still largely held by only a few people. Latin American economies were tied to trade with European nations. Many countries were dependent on one or two products, such as sugar or copper. When world markets cooled for these items, the local economy lagged. Some nations were able to diversify their economies and introduce industry.

The Monroe Doctrine

As the revolutions of Latin America were running their course, Spain requested help from its allies in Europe to retake its Latin American colonies. Britain and the United States opposed such a move. Britain was hoping to develop trade relations with the new nations and wanted to have as little competition as possible. The U.S. also wanted to develop trade but tried to stand for the principle of freedom as well.

Britain asked the United States for a joint statement outlining their combined opposition to any attempt by European powers to intervene in Latin America. The U.S., however, acted on its own. Secretary of State John Quincy Adams wrote a section of President James Monroe's annual speech to Congress in 1823 which declared that European nations should no longer view the Western Hemisphere as a target for colonization. The Monroe Doctrine was given teeth by the power of the British Navy, and Europe kept its political hands off of the Western Hemisphere.

Construction began in 1784 on La Moneda Palace in Santiago, Chile, while it was still a Spanish colony. The building served as the national mint from 1814 to 1929, and also as the seat of government starting in 1845. This 1944 photo shows a military parade in front of the palace as part of Chile's celebration of its Independence Day (September 18th).

The USS Maine *Passes Morro Castle to Enter the Bay at Havana, Cuba (1898)*

However, Europe's deep financial pockets were welcome in Latin America. Britain, France, and Germany, as well as the United States, made significant investments in mines, railroads, industry, and other business ventures in the region. These arrangements led to European involvement in other ways. For example, the ruler of a Latin American country might arrange a loan from a European bank, pocket most of the money himself, and then default on the loan. This would cause the European nation involved to pressure the Latin American country to clean up its act or face serious consequences.

The U.S. Becomes a World Power

Through its contact with Latin America, the United States began to develop a world empire. In 1898 Cuba was still a colony of Spain; but rebels on the island were waging a war for independence. American newspapers supported the revolution, and the United States sent the battleship *Maine* to Havana to protect American interests there. However, the *Maine* was destroyed by a mysterious explosion; and many Americans demanded war with Spain.

The United States recognized the revolutionary government of Cuba, and Spain declared war on the United States in April of 1898. The U.S. won quick and decisive victories in the Spanish-American War in Cuba and in another Spanish possession, the Philippine Islands in the Pacific. Spain ended its war effort in December of that year and gave the Philippines, Cuba, Puerto Rico, and Guam to the United States.

Now the United States was a force to be reckoned with, especially in the Western Hemisphere. When the Cubans wrote a constitution for their new

Lesson 131 - Many Countries, One Goal

Hispanic Workers on the Panama Canal (c. 1910)

government in 1900, the United States insisted that a provision be included giving the United States permission to intervene in domestic Cuban affairs on behalf of American rights and citizens. A few years later, two Latin American countries defaulted on loans to European banks. Warships from those nations in Europe threatened the Latin American countries. President Theodore Roosevelt insisted that the Europeans withdraw their military presence. In what came to be known as the Roosevelt Corollary to the Monroe Doctrine, the United States claimed the exclusive right to exercise international police power in the Western Hemisphere. The policy was implemented several times by later American presidents.

As American foreign interests grew, Americans realized the importance of a canal through the isthmus of Panama (then a part of Colombia) so that the U.S. fleet could move quickly to either the Atlantic or the Pacific. The United States acquired the rights to the canal from the French company that had started the project but went bankrupt. When Colombia expressed a reluctance to allow the United States to control the canal, the U.S. encouraged the people of Panama to stage a revolution. This happened in 1903, and the United States recognized the new country of Panama. The two countries signed a treaty allowing the U.S. to dig the canal and hold the rights to it perpetually. The canal was completed in 1914.

In the 20th Century

The 20th century saw forward steps of economic progress and backward steps of political turmoil in Latin America. Economic uncertainty and a frequent lack of effective political leadership have led to a continued role by the military taking over the government in a *coup d'etat* (French for a blow of state). Often in such cases, a military strongman imposes strict limits on political freedom.

A threat to hemispheric peace emerged during the 1950s. After years of guerrilla fighting in Cuba, Fidel Castro ousted a corrupt dictator in 1959. He then proclaimed that he was a Communist and intended to make Cuba Communist.

Fidel Castro (far left) and Che Guevara (center), an Argentinian Marxist who supported the Cuban revolution, march in Cuba in 1960.

After the collapse of the Soviet Union, Fidel Castro recognized the need to make changes in Cuba. He relaxed restrictions on religion, even arranging for Pope John Paul II to visit Cuba in 1998. He also developed political and economic ties with other Latin American countries and Canada. In the photo at left, Castro (right) is shown visiting Brazilian President Lula de Silva. Because of health problems, Castro turned over control of the government to his brother Raúl in 2006.

Castro eliminated or exiled opponents, took over control of the land and businesses, and created an economic and military alliance with the Soviet Union. Castro encouraged Communist uprisings in other Latin American countries and appeared to pose a threat to the United States.

The southern tip of Florida is just ninety miles north of Cuba. When Castro assumed power, many Cubans fled to the United States. The U.S. government secretly assisted in a plan by some of these Cuban nationals to invade the island and oust Castro. In April 1961, about 2,000 Cubans who had been living in the U.S. made a landing by boat at the Bay of Pigs. The United States did not provide military air cover for the invasion, and the invaders were quickly defeated by Castro's forces. The invasion did not generate a Cuban uprising against Castro as planners had hoped. The incident was a disaster for United States foreign policy.

In response to the Bay of Pigs and continued U.S. opposition to Castro, the Soviet Union in 1962 began secretly installing long-range missiles in Cuba that could strike the United States. The Soviets denied that the buildup was taking place until U.S. spy planes flying over Cuba took pictures of the missile sites being constructed. President John F. Kennedy imposed a naval blockade against Cuba to keep further materials from arriving from the Soviet Union. After several weeks of heightening tensions, the Soviets backed down and removed the missile sites. In return, the United States promised not to assist any further invasion of the island to topple Castro.

Political unrest has flared from time to time in several countries. Cuba and Nicaragua gave assistance to a left-wing guerrilla group trying to overthrow the government in El Salvador. In the 1980s, the Communist Sandinistas led by Daniel Ortega kidnapped the ruling general in Nicaragua and seized power there. The Reagan administration supported the Contra ("against") rebels who opposed the Sandinistas. When Congress rejected Reagan's request for aid to the Contras, White House aides developed a scheme to give to the Contras some of the funds from a secret arms deal with Iran. The Iran-Contra Affair was seen as a major scandal during the Reagan Administration. Ortega lost a national election in 1990. Both left-wing and right-wing groups in several countries have committed human rights abuses against their enemies and suspected collaborators.

Lesson 131 - Many Countries, One Goal

The contrasts in Latin America are illustrated by comparing the huge profits Venezuela has enjoyed from its oil production to the huge profits that drug rings have garnered in neighboring Colombia. Natural disasters such as floods and hurricanes in several countries have cost many lives and set back economic progress.

Since the Franklin Roosevelt administration, the United States has tried to follow a good neighbor policy toward the Latin American countries. This has meant offering financial aid and other assistance instead of being a policeman and a dictator of terms. During the Jimmy Carter presidency, the United States signed a treaty giving control of the Panama Canal to the country of Panama. The Organization of American States, a hemispheric council of nations, has tried to promote economic progress and open communication among member nations.

Jorge Mario Bergoglio (b. 1936) became Pope Francis of the Roman Catholic Church in 2013. Born in Argentina, he is the first pope elected from Latin America, home to about 40% of the world's Roman Catholics. Here Francis meets with Cristina Fernández de Kirchner, President of Argentina.

You shall thus consecrate the fiftieth year and proclaim a release through the land to all its inhabitants. It shall be a jubilee for you, and each of you shall return to his own property, and each of you shall return to his family.
Leviticus 25:10

Assignments for Lesson 131

In Their Words — Read the excerpt from *Wonderful Adventures of Mrs. Seacole in Many Lands* (pages 335-337).

Literature — Continue reading *Bridge to the Sun*. Plan to finish it by the end of this unit.

Student Review — Optional: Answer the questions for Lesson 131.

Lesson 132

Mexico celebrated 200 years of independence in 2010, as seen at Federal buildings in Mexico City.

Mexico's Story

Through the 1700s, Mexico was generally prosperous for the ruling class; however, the system that favored the rich and abused the poor carried the seeds of its own destruction. The colonial social class pattern discussed in the previous lesson held true in Mexico. Spanish peninsulares ran the colony and held most of the money. Native-born creoles resented being dominated by the Spanish. Mestizos, slaves, and indigenous peoples shared little of the wealth.

Around 1800 Spanish power and prestige were in decline. Coupled with this, the colony of Mexico was simply too large to administer effectively. The jewel of the Spanish empire, Mexico extended from northern California to Panama and from Texas to the Pacific coast. Mexico had too few roads and soldiers to maintain order everywhere.

The Beginnings of Change

In 1810 a poor priest, Miguel Hidalgo, took a cue from the French Revolution and organized a force of Indians to create a new nation. Hidalgo marched toward Mexico City, captured a few provinces, and proclaimed a republic. He abolished slavery and redistributed land to the Indians. However, Hidalgo was captured by troops loyal to Spain and executed the following year. José Morelos then took up the banner of revolution and led a revolt further south. Morelos had some success at first, but he too was captured and was executed in 1815.

Memorial Statue of Miguel Hidalgo in Front of His Parish Church in Mexico

Lesson 132 - Mexico's Story

A few years later, a successful revolution came not as a move to gain freedom but as an attempt to protect the status quo. Creoles were fearful that the regime in Spain was getting too liberal and might endorse land redistribution. Under the leadership of Agustin de Iturbide, a group of creoles (with support from conservative Spanish) declared Mexico independent in 1821. The next year, troops who had gone unpaid overthrew the unpopular and fiscally unsound regime. A republican constitution was put in place in 1823, but chaos was the real ruler in Mexico for the next half-century.

The Age of Santa Anna

One of the leaders of the coup that ousted Iturbide was General Antonio Lopez de Santa Anna. Over the next thirty years, Santa Anna was in and out of power, sometimes siding with conservatives and sometimes playing the part of a liberal. Society and the economy were in disarray. The new country started out deep in debt from expenses incurred under Spain and Iturbide, and conservative and liberals vied for power.

It was during this time that settlers from the United States began moving into the Mexican province of Texas to settle a huge land grant that Mexico had given to the Austin family. The settlement of Texas was part of the movement in the U.S. called "manifest destiny," the belief that it was God's will for America to possess the continent from sea to sea. The Texans declared their independence from Mexico on March 2, 1836, with the goal of becoming another state in the American union. Santa Anna fought this move, but the Texans stood firm and the United States recognized the Republic of Texas in 1836.

Tensions continued to mount between the United States and Mexico. U.S. annexation of Texas in 1845 and conflict between American and Mexican troops in a disputed region of southwest Texas led to the Mexican War. The conflict was over almost before it began, with the disorganized Mexican army outmanned by the Americans.

At the 1847 Battle of Chapultepec in Mexico City, cadets from the Mexican military academy participated in the defense of the fortress against American troops. Six teenage boys who were among the last defenders to die during the battle are honored in Mexico City at the Niños Héroes (Boy Heroes) monument, the six columns shown below. One hundred years after the battle, U.S. President Harry Truman laid a wreath at the site and observed a moment of silence. He later told reporters, "Brave men don't belong to any one country. I respect bravery wherever I see it."

The treaty that ended the war gave the United States almost all of Mexico's territory north of the present U.S.-Mexican border (about half of the Mexican empire). Mexico was almost flattened with debt, destruction, and widespread banditry. Mexico sold another piece of property, the Gadsden Purchase, to the U.S. in 1853 for $10 million.

Juarez and Diaz

A group of liberals led by Benito Juarez came to power in 1855. They forced the Catholic Church to hand over some of its vast land holdings for poor people to buy. However, many of the poor were too poor to buy land. A new constitution went into effect in 1857. Civil war broke out in 1858 between liberals and conservatives. The conservatives turned to France for help. In 1862 the French Emperor Napoleon III attempted to establish Austrian prince Maximilian as Emperor of Mexico. Maximilian's government floundered, the French went home, and Maximilian was executed in 1867. Juarez died in 1872.

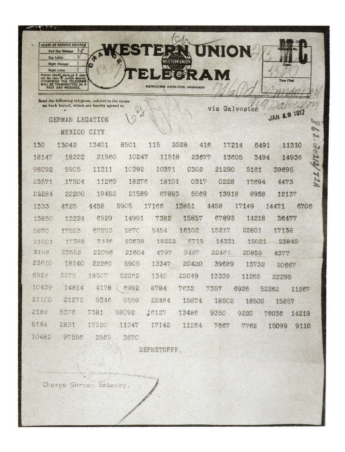

The Cinco de Mayo (Fifth of May) holiday celebrates a Mexican victory over French forces in 1862. It is more widely observed by Mexican-Americans in the U.S. than it is in Mexico. (The photo above was taken in Washington, D.C.) Independence Day in Mexico is September 16, the date in 1810 when Miguel Hidalgo rallied his troops to begin the fight for independence from Spain.

Porfirio Diaz came to power and ruled either as president or from behind the scenes until 1910. Order was returned to the provinces, the army was professionalized, and foreign investors helped to bring about marked economic growth. However, the only major economic change was that the rich tended to get richer. The poor generally still did not share in the economic bounty. Corrupt government officials took their share as well.

Mexico was involved in America's entry into World War I. The German foreign minister, Alfred Zimmerman, in 1917 sent a secret, encoded telegram (shown at left) to the Mexican government suggesting that they could recover what Zimmerman called "lost territory" in New Mexico, Texas, and Arizona if Mexico became an ally with Germany against the United States.

British agents intercepted the telegram; and when its contents were published in the United States, the outcry for war against Germany was loud and decisive. A declaration of war by the United States soon followed. Mexico rejected the German proposal.

Lesson 132 - Mexico's Story

Revolution of 1910 and Beyond

Diaz announced a free election for 1910. Opposition to Diaz began organizing. When the election took place, Diaz rigged the outcome so he would win. As a result, a revolt erupted and Diaz fled the country. A new government under Francisco Madero, a moderate, managed to anger both radicals and conservatives. With conservative support, General Victoriano Huerta overthrew Madero, who was put to death.

During Huerta's rule, Pancho Villa led a ragtag group of bandits in the north, Emiliano Zapata led a small army of farmers in the south, and other groups took up arms against Huerta. Powerless, Huerta fled. In August 1914 Venustiano Carranza, a rich landowner, seized power. The United States recognized the Carranza government in 1915, but it was only in 1917 that rebel forces ended their

Pancho Villa at a Camp in Mexico (c. 1911)

marauding attacks. Zapata was murdered in 1919, and Villa finally surrendered in 1920. A new, liberal, reform constitution went into effect in 1917.

The Mexican governments that followed Carranza beginning in 1921 tried to maintain order—by force when necessary—while developing the Mexican economy. Land reforms and higher wages helped the poorer classes. Catholic clergy, landowners, and the military generally opposed the reforms. Mining and industry increased, although the worldwide Great Depression brought economic growth to a halt for a time. In the 1930s, the Mexican government established state-run collective farms and nationalized foreign oil companies (meaning the government seized the oil companies' assets). The companies were eventually paid for their losses. Every president represented the Institutional Revolutionary Party (PRI). Opposition parties were eliminated in the 1920s, and others emerged only slowly in later times.

In Recent Years

Mexico has continued to experience periods of growth and periods of recession. Drug trafficking hurts individuals and society, but some government officials get money for turning their heads away from it. A major earthquake hit Mexico City in 1985, killing thousands.

Vicente Fox, President of Mexico from 2000 to 2006

Unit 27 - The Making of Modern Latin America

A large number of illegal aliens have entered the United States through Mexico (from Mexico and other Central American countries) looking for better economic opportunity. At the same time, after the 1994 passage of the North American Free Trade Agreement (NAFTA), which made Mexico, Canada, and the U.S. a free trade zone, many American companies closed their domestic installations and built factories in Mexico, where workers are generally paid less than workers in the United States.

Opposition to the political power structure grew for several years. In the 2000 national election, the PRI candidate lost for the first time in over seventy years. However, in the 2012 Presidential election, PRI candidate Enrique Peña Nieto won.

Tens of thousands of Mexicans have been killed in drug-related violence since 2006, when the Mexican military began participating in efforts to suppress the drug trade. A large peace march in 2011, pictured above, called for an end to the violence on both sides.

*The righteous is concerned for the rights of the poor,
The wicked does not understand such concern.
Proverbs 29:7*

Assignments for Lesson 132

Literature — Continue reading *Bridge to the Sun*.

Student Review — Optional: Answer the questions for Lesson 132.

Birthplace of Simón Bolívar Museum, Caracas, Venezuela

Lesson 133 - Key Person

Simón Bolívar

Known as the Liberator, Simón Bolívar helped five countries in South America gain their independence and was involved in governing several of them. He maintained a lifelong devotion to the cause of liberty. A man of intellect as well as a man of deed, Bolívar put his thoughts and words into action.

Simón Bolívar, 1819

Early Life and Background

Simón Bolívar was born in Caracas, Venezuela, in 1783 into a wealthy, slave-owning creole family (Spaniards born in America). Both of his parents died when Bolívar was a child. He was reared by relatives and educated by private tutors. One tutor, Simón Rodríguez, instilled in the young Bolívar the ideas of the Enlightenment which influenced his later political beliefs.

Bolívar went to Europe to complete his education. He was there during the waning days of the French Revolution and was moved by the struggle for liberty from oppression. Bolívar was married in 1802 to a fellow Venezuelan while they were in Spain, but after returning to Venezuela his wife died the next year and Bolívar never remarried. Bolívar then returned to Europe and saw the coronation of Napoleon I, which disgusted him.

In his travels, Bolívar also visited the United States and studied its republican form of government. He resolved to dedicate his life to liberating all of his fellow South Americans from control by Spain. Bolívar realized that if Spain retained a place of refuge on the continent, it might strike back against any former colony which gained its independence. Therefore, he resolved to do battle with the Spanish wherever he could.

The road to freedom was a difficult one for Bolívar. He fought in many battles, several of which he lost. Bolívar fought with Francisco Miranda in the latter's 1810 attempt to lead Venezuela to freedom. Bolívar was forced to leave the country but returned in 1812. The next year he led an army that captured the city of Caracas, but again the Spanish regained control of the city. He was an exile for a time in Jamaica and Haiti, hiding from the Spanish. While he was in Haiti, itself a relatively new republic, Bolívar gathered weapons and enlisted Haitians as freedom fighters. The president of Haiti gave Bolívar his blessing with one request: that he outlaw slavery wherever he was successful in fighting for liberty.

The Work of Liberation

In 1817 Bolívar once more returned to Venezuela. He gained the confidence and loyalty of local freedom fighters, and in early 1819 his forces captured the city of Angostura (now called Ciudad Bolívar, or Bolívar City). It became the capital for what was declared as the Republic of Grand Colombia, which included Venezuela, New Granada (Colombia and Panama), and Ecuador, although Spanish forces still held most of that territory. The Congress selected Bolívar as president.

Bolívar then led a daring expedition over the icy Andes Mountains into Colombia, where he won another brilliant victory over the Spanish. By the end of 1819, the new constitution was in place. Ecuador was liberated from Spanish control in 1822.

While Bolívar had been waging the war of independence in the north of the continent, José de San Martín had been leading similar efforts in the south. San Martín had already helped Argentina and Chile gain independence and had invaded Peru when he and Bolívar met in 1822.

This 1825 illustration commemorates the independence of Peru. It includes a poem that praises Bolívar as the Liberator of Peru in glowing terms.

San Martín turned the leadership of the forces of liberation over to Bolívar, who entered Lima, Peru, in 1823 and was named dictator and commander of the military. Forces of liberation defeated royalist armies in 1824 and 1825 to complete the battle for independence from Spain. The area of the last battle in southern Peru was formed into the country of Bolivia, named in the Liberator's honor. Bolívar helped to craft a new constitution for Bolivia.

Bolívar returned to Colombia to resume the presidency of the republic. In 1827 he proposed a new constitution that would give more power to the executive. When this idea was rejected, Bolívar assumed the role of dictator. His rule met with occasional outbreaks of resistance. Bolívar's power and influence were declining, and he was sick with tuberculosis. Venezuela and Ecuador broke away from the Grand Republic, and in 1830 Bolívar resigned. He died later that year at the age of forty-seven.

Lesson 133 - Key Person: Simón Bolívar

Bolívar has been commemorated with statues in places as diverse as San Francisco, California; New York, New York; Paris, France; Barcelona, Spain; Sofia, Bulgaria; Cairo, Egypt; and Tehran, Iran. Cities throughout Latin America have monuments also. This one in Colombia is dedicated to "Liberator of Colombia, Ecuador, Panama, Peru, and Venezuela, and Founder of Bolivia. A tribute from the government and people of Venezuela to the City of Santa Marta. 1953"

The Legacy of Simón Bolívar

Bolívar's reputation as the Liberator is justified for his role in doing more than any other single person to break Spain's hold over South America. He was an eloquent spokesman for freedom, national independence, and republican government. Bolívar came to oppose slavery and freed his own slaves in 1821.

Bolívar did not promote instant democracy. He thought that the best-educated and most-qualified people should run the government until the general populace was able to take part in it. He was primarily concerned with people like himself (the creoles) being able to assume positions of leadership in government. Bolívar held that a strong central government was the best way to run a country. Too much power in the hands of local leaders, he felt, weakened the progress and security that the central government could provide. He dreamed of building a federation of nations in Latin America to achieve economic success and greater security, but the idea never caught on with many people. In addition, Bolívar never held a position of leadership long enough to grasp the intricacies of running a republican government or to build popular support as a leader and not just a liberator.

Bolívar was discouraged near the end of his life at the political instability he saw in the countries he helped to found. Moreover, Bolívar's differences with other leaders as well as his own failings, coupled with the tendency of people to forget what had been done for them in the past, led to Bolívar becoming an unpopular figure in his last days. Venezuela did not allow his body to be returned there for burial until twelve years after his death. Today, however, many South Americans hold Bolívar in high regard as a hero of their independence. Venezuela and Bolivia observe his birthday as a national holiday.

For by wise guidance you will wage war,
And in abundance of counselors there is victory.
Proverbs 24:6

Assignments for Lesson 133

In Their Words Read the excerpts from Bolívar's "South American Independence Speech" (pages 338-340).

Literature Continue reading *Bridge to the Sun*.

Student Review Optional: Answer the questions for Lesson 133.

Guna Woman Selling Molas (Traditional Clothing) in Panama

Lesson 134 - Everyday Life

Indigenous Peoples of Latin America

Today Latin America is home to at least four hundred different indigenous people groups. Many of these groups maintain traditions of the past; but most have been influenced by European cultures, especially the Spanish. A few groups, such as those living in the Amazon River basin and in the remote interiors of French Guiana, live basically the same way they always have.

The indigenous people of Latin America are divided into two cultural groups, the highlanders and the lowlanders. Highlanders live in densely-populated villages in the highlands of Mexico and Central America and in the Andes of South America. Lowlanders live near the Amazon River and in the lowlands of Central America. Many other indigenous people live in cities in Central and South America while some have emigrated to North America and Europe.

Bolivia is the only Latin American country where indigenous people make up a majority of the population. Peru, Guatemala, and Ecuador also have large indigenous populations. In some countries the official counts of indigenous people is quite small. However, because of the stigma of being "Indian" or "indio," some might hide their true cultural heritage when census data is collected. Descendants of Europeans, Africans, Asian Indians, and other groups live in South America along with the indigenous peoples; and intermarriage has created a complex mix of cultural influences.

In 2006 Evo Morales, of the Aymara people, was the first member of an indigenous group to become president of Bolivia.

Languages and Literature

About four hundred indigenous languages are still spoken in Latin America. In some countries more than two hundred are spoken. The main indigenous language is Quechua (KEY-chwa), the official language of the Incas. Scholars believe that the Quechua language actually predates the Inca Empire by a thousand years. It was probably a trade language that spread on routes in the Andes Mountains.

About eight million people speak Quechua, but it is spoken in many dialects. Those who speak these different dialects sometimes have difficulty understanding each other. Quechua speakers live in rural areas, in cities in the Andes Mountains, in Amazon rain forests, and on ranches. Millions live in Lima, the capital of Peru, and Quito, the capital of Ecuador. Quechua communities are even found in Amsterdam, Madrid, and Washington, D.C.

About 1.5 million residents of Bolivia, Ecuador, and Peru speak Aymara. The Aymara people are concentrated around Lake Titicaca in Peru and Bolivia. Along with Spanish, Aymara is an official language of Peru. Guarani is spoken by natives in Brazil, Argentina, and Bolivia. A large majority of the residents of Paraguay speak Guarani, where it is an official language along with Spanish. Spanish and Guarani are also official languages of Paraguay. One million people speak Nahuatl, an Aztec language. Most speakers of the Nahuatl language live in Mexico. Several languages of the Maya are spoken by more than a half million people in Central America and in southern Mexico.

Traditionally, most stories, poems, and songs were passed down from generation to generation by professional reciters who spoke from memory. In the 1600s and 1700s the Quechua language was sometimes written down with the Roman alphabet that was used by the Spanish conquerors. A few Quechua wrote books.

Village Life

Indigenous groups have long histories of self-rule. Some villages in the Andes are led by camachios, which means "those who set things in order." In the Amazon, a village headman leads as the first among equals. He is expected to set an example of self-sacrifice for others in the village.

Many indigenous people continue their traditional farming lifestyles. In some villages, the

Felipe Guaman Poma de Ayala was a Quechua noble, born after the Spanish conquest of the Andes region of South America. In the early 1600s, Guaman Poma compiled a history of his region from before the Incas to the coming of the Spanish. He wrote in Spanish, but he used Quechua words. Guaman Poma sent his profusely-illustrated manuscript (cover page at left) to King Philip III of Spain with the hope that his descriptions of Spanish abuses would lead to reforms. The King likely never saw the book, and it was lost for centuries. The book was discovered in Denmark in 1908.

Lesson 134 - Everyday Life: Indigenous Peoples of Latin America

Textiles in Guatemala

land is owned communally. Highlanders grow crops using well-designed irrigation systems. Some people freeze-dry food in cold mountain air. Amazonian farmers cut and burn patches of the rain forest, creating temporary fields. They later leave the fields unused so the forest can regenerate.

Some indigenous peoples raise llamas and alpacas that are native to South America. The alpaca is smaller and has longer, softer wool than the llama. Male llamas have served as beasts of burden in the Andes Mountains for many centuries. Female llamas supply milk and meat. Wool from the alpaca and the llama is used for textiles. Llama skins are used for leather and their tallow (fat) for candles. Dried excrement is used for fuel, and rope is made by braiding the hair of the animals.

Some native peoples work in tourism. The selling of traditional crafts, such as woven goods and pottery, provides a source of income. Native Amazonians in Ecuador are developing ecotourism in their rainforests. In some places native peoples collect hardwood and other products of the forests for sale.

Clothing

At the time of European exploration, the typical garment for a man in Latin America was a short loincloth, a longer hip-cloth, a tunic, and a cape. A woman wore a loose blouse and wrapped a skirt around her waist. Over these she wore a cloak, called a poncho. It was made of one piece of fabric with a hole in the middle for the head.

Blue, brown, and black are traditional colors for highlanders. Weaving continues to be a common occupation of women living in the Andes. Most of their fabrics are made of cotton; but they also use wool from alpacas, llamas, and vicuñas. Weavers create patterns in the fabrics and also appliqué, embroider, paint, and stamp designs on them. In the Andean culture, clothing still indicates a person's regional identity and whether he or she is married.

In the southern highlands of Ecuador, traditional clothing for women includes straw hats and long shawls called serapes. Their long skirts are hand-woven in bright colors, such as red or orange, and are trimmed with embroidery. In Guatemala women wear the same style skirt with a loose blouse. They also wear sashes and scarves. Guatemalan women weave beautiful fabrics with designs unique to each village. A traditional outfit for a Guatemalan man is a pair of calf-length, loose, colorful trousers, a striped shirt, and an embroidered jacket. Native Bolivian women wear brightly colored clothes with derby or stovepipe hats. Some Latin American mestizos also wear traditional clothing.

Like several other indigenous groups, the Kayapo of Brazil wear headdresses. For centuries Indigenous peoples have worn these to show status, authority, or power. Materials used include feathers, glass, beads, and leather.

Kayapo Chiefs in Brazil (2005)

Food and Music

The tamale is a favorite food on special occasions in Central America. It is made of cornmeal, filled with various vegetables and meat, and then wrapped in a banana leaf. Dietary staples include corn, beans, chicken, rice, fruits, and vegetables.

Bolivia has a long tradition of ensemble music which accompanies dancers. The ensembles include panpipes of cane or bone, trumpets of conch shells, flutes, and drums. Other native Latin American instruments are rattles, shakers, whistles, and bells. After Spanish conquerors introduced stringed instruments, native Latin Americans began to make these as well. One is the armadillo-shell guitar, called a charango. The national instrument of Guatemala is the marimba. It is like a xylophone made of carved wooden bars. The marimba is also popular in Honduras.

Religion

The religion of many Latin Americans is a combination of Catholicism and native religion. The vast majority of people in Latin American countries

The oldest church in Montevideo, Uruguay, is the Montevideo Metropolitan Cathedral. Construction began in 1724.

Musicians in Umasbamba, Peru

are officially Catholic, but the influence of native religions is strong. In the Andes Mountains, villagers receive Catholic sacraments even though they still sacrifice to the mountains. In Peru the Starry Snow pilgrimage includes both a mass and a ritual climb, during which dancers in costume bring "sacred" ice from the mountains. In Guatemala villagers dressed in traditional Mayan costumes participate in an Easter procession in which they carry a statue of Jesus. Traditional musical instruments are used in both Catholic and indigenous festivals.

Protestant Churches, especially Evangelicals, Pentecostals, and Adventists, are growing rapidly among indigenous people and mestizos. The largest Protestant group in Paraguay is the Mennonites. In Nicaragua many people have joined the Moravian Church.

Migration of Indigenous People

When individuals can no longer earn a living by farming in the native village, they often migrate to Latin American cities. Upon arrival, they usually continue to associate with their fellow villagers. They often live close to one another but stop wearing traditional clothing and try to lose their accents.

Family elders stay in the village to farm the land. In some families, the women and children also stay in the village to farm while the men live and work in the cities. Some families survive on food produced in the village along with their income from work in cities. Some indigenous city dwellers go back to their villages for festivals. Sometimes their donations make traditional dances and rituals possible.

Many indigenous people from Latin America migrate to other continents either legally or illegally. They form small colonies in North America or Europe. In some cases, indigenous people who have moved to another country have begun charitable institutions that provide education and health care in their homelands.

Rights of Indigenous Peoples

During the 20th century, many Latin American countries excluded indigenous peoples from full citizenship unless they married non-natives or assimilated into the predominating culture. The political and social elites adopted a philosophy called *indigenismo*, which exalted native culture as a rich heritage but encouraged natives to assimilate. Brazil did not end its official policy of promoting assimilation into modern cultures until 1988.

*Each of them will sit under his vine and under his fig tree,
With no one to make them afraid,
For the mouth of the Lord of hosts has spoken.
Micah 4:4*

Assignments for Lesson 134

In Their Words   Read His Majesty's Speech at the Opening of the Legislature (pages 341-342).

Literature   Continue reading *Bridge to the Sun*.

Student Review   Optional: Answer the questions for Lesson 134.

Meeting of the Justice and Human Rights Commission in Peru

Lesson 135 - Bible Study

Justice

As you are working on your small farm, a political radical approaches you. He says that if his party gets in power, they will seize land from wealthy citizens and distribute it to poor people like you. Is his plan just?

Citing wrongs that were committed by the Catholic Church two hundred years ago, the government announces that it will impose stricter regulations on the Church. A limit will be placed on how much property the Church can own in a given diocese. Priests will be monitored so that they do not criticize the government. Church property will be taxed at one-half the usual property tax rate, with the money being earmarked for schools and roads. Is this program just?

An American company moves its plant to Mexico so that it can pay workers there thirty percent less. It will not have to provide employee benefits either, since Mexican workers do not expect them. Absolutely no law in the U.S. or Mexico is broken when they do this. Are the company's actions just?

We all want justice. We want to treat others justly and to be treated the same way. In Latin American history, justice has not always been done. Privileged classes got away with things for which working men would go to jail. Laws imposed segregation, and slaves had no rights at all. Military dictatorships have sometimes been corrupt and taken advantage of their power for personal gain.

The Bible has much to say about justice. As God's people who live in a world where injustice is common, Christians need to understand the Bible's teachings about justice.

God Is Just

In both Old Testament Hebrew and New Testament Greek, the word "just" is related to the word "righteous." Justice, then, is not so much about fair play and legal equity as it is about what is right, what ought to be.

"Truth and Justice" Graffiti in Montevideo, Uruguay

786

Lesson 135 - Bible Study: Justice

Between the 1960s and 1990s, Guatemala endured over thirty years of brutal conflict between groups seeking to control the country. Some members of the military seemed to target indigenous people for particular cruelty. In the 2000s, some of these leaders were brought to trial in Guatemala. These women from the Ixil tribe are waiting outside a courthouse in 2013. They were supported in their struggle for legal justice by Trócaire, an agency created by the Catholic Church in Ireland to work for long-term change in developing countries.

As with many traits discussed in the Bible, the standard is God:

The Rock! His work is perfect,
For all His ways are just;
A God of faithfulness and without injustice,
Righteous and upright is He.
(Deuteronomy 32:4)

In this passage, Moses contrasts the just God to the corrupt actions of Israel (see verses 5 and 6). God set the standard, but man did not measure up to it. God's actions are always just, in keeping with His character. "Your righteousness is like the mountains of God; Your judgments are like a great deep" (Psalm 36:6). The word translated righteousness here is actually more like reliability or dependability.

People Should Be Just

Men's actions are judged according to God, the perfect standard of righteousness. We should pursue the righteousness that is of God. God chose Abraham "so that he may command his children and his household after him to keep the way of the Lord by doing righteousness and justice" (Genesis 18:19). Solomon wrote Proverbs to teach his son "in wise behavior, righteousness, justice, and equity" (Proverbs 1:3).

Homeless Man in Costa Rica

Try to imagine this study of righteousness from the viewpoint of a peasant in a Latin American country. Is it right that one man inherits vast wealth while another works hard all his life and has almost nothing? Is it just that the Catholic Church has thousands of acres and does not need it, while a peasant would willingly work twenty more acres to support his family but cannot afford to own it?

Righteousness Given to Us

God always acts justly. We cannot be saved by our actions because we don't always act justly. God provided for our need by sending Jesus to take our punishment for us. As the thief on the cross pointed out to the other thief, the punishment they were receiving was just; but the punishment inflicted on Jesus was not (Luke 23:41). This is where God's justice blends into God's mercy. His standard is perfect justice; and He provided the just sacrifice so that He might declare us justified when we put our faith in Jesus (Romans 3:21-27).

As with so many traits that God's people are to possess and practice, Christians must not get their standard of right and wrong from the world. When Spanish explorers interacted with indigenous peoples, and when peninsulares dealt with other classes in colonial society, the rule they often followed was that might makes right. The powerful believed that they were right, but they were not always right by God's standards.

Isolated People Groups

Despite advances in communication and transportation, a small number of people in the world live with virtually no contact with the outside world. Some of these tribes live on islands between India and New Guinea, but the largest number are in the rainforests of South America.

Sometimes these people are isolated because they live in places that are still hard to reach. Other times it is because they actively resist attempts by outsiders to interact with them. The 2008 photo at right shows a group in Brazil aiming their bows and arrows at a helicopter flying over their village.

Loggers and ranchers often encounter these tribes as they expand into new land. Missionaries often attempt to make contact in an effort to help the tribes and share the gospel with them. When such isolated groups have finally had close contact with outsiders in the past, diseases have often killed many of them. Activists who support indigenous rights argue that the isolated groups should be able to decide if and when they make contact with outsiders.

Lesson 135 - Bible Study: Justice

As recipients of God's mercy, we are therefore to dispense God's mercy to others. At the very least, we should be just in our dealings with others, following the standard of what is right, not the standard of what is popular or easy or what seems fair to our fallible minds. What is just in some situations might not be clear; but if we follow God's principles of justice and mercy, we will not go wrong.

"The Just Shall Live by Faith"

The message of the prophet Habakkuk is that the just will live on the basis of faith when the world around them is falling apart. Habakkuk prophesied just before the Babylonian invasion of Judah. He agonized at the sin that he saw all around him in Judah. God assured him that those sinners will get their just desserts: He was sending the Chaldeans to punish Judah (Habakkuk 1:1-11).

God's reply, however, only begged another question. How could God use an unrighteous people to accomplish His righteous judgment (Habakkuk 1:12-2:3)? God's second reply assured Habakkuk that the Chaldeans would get their punishment one day as well (Habakkuk 2:4-20). The third chapter is a prayer by Habakkuk praising the Lord's justice and faithfulness. The closing verses (3:17-19) are a statement of trust in the Lord regardless of circumstances.

People who trust in God won't succeed in life by waiting for circumstances to be perfect or by having everything figured out. They will make it by faith in God even when circumstances are imperfect and when they don't have everything figured out. Justice involves faith: faith in a higher standard, faith in ultimate rewards and punishments, and faith in a just God who will act according to His just nature.

Óscar Romero, a Catholic archbishop in El Salvador, spoke out against the violation of human rights in his country. He said, "The church cannot be silent about injustice; if silent, it will become an accomplice." Romero was shot and killed in 1980 while celebrating Mass in a hospital chapel. No one was ever prosecuted for the crime. This wall of a community center in El Salvador is an example of how Romero is honored.

Righteousness is one of those big theological concepts that the Bible speaks of a great deal—but we don't. As a result, we often don't have a good idea of what God's righteousness involves, and we wind up getting from the world our definition of what is just. This is to our loss because righteousness is a basic and essential characteristic of God, an attribute given to us by God's love, and the standard we are to follow in our actions. We need a clear sense of what is just—what measures up to God's standard—as we live in a crooked and perverse generation (Philippians 2:15).

And they sang the song of Moses, the bond-servant of God, and the song of the Lamb, saying, "Great and marvelous are Your works, O Lord God, the Almighty; Righteous and true are Your ways, King of the nations!"
Revelation 15:3

Assignments for Lesson 135

Bible — Recite or write Proverbs 2:6-9 from memory.

Literature — Finish reading *Bridge to the Sun*. Literary analysis available in *Student Review*.

Project — Complete your project for the unit.

Student Review — Optional: Answer the questions for Lesson 135 and for *Bridge to the Sun*, and take the quiz for Unit 27.

28

The Making of Modern Africa

Summary The continent of Africa has many ethnic groups with distinct languages and cultural practices. Over the past few centuries, the presence of Islam has dominated the northern third of the African continent, the slave trade and European colonization have influenced central Africa, and Dutch and British rule have had the greatest impact on southern Africa. In this unit, we look at the countries of South Africa and Ethiopia, the Maasai tribe, and what the Bible says about Africa.

Lessons
136 - European Colonization
137 - Ethiopia
138 - Everyday Life: The Culture of the Maasai
139 - South Africa
140 - Bible Study: Africa in the Bible

Flags of the African Union, Addis Ababa, Ethiopia

Memory Work — Learn Philippians 2:3-4 by the end of the unit.

Books Used

The Bible
In Their Words
Cry, the Beloved Country

Project (choose one)

1) Write 300 to 500 words on one of the following topics:
   - Write about what the Bible teaches about relations between people from different ethnic groups. How can Christians be proactive about following Biblical principles in this area?
   - Choose one African nation and write about how the geography of the country impacts life there, both past and present.
2) Create a model of a central government building in an African nation. Locate one or more photos of the structure. Make your model as close to scale as you can and from the material of your choosing (wood, cardboard, clay, STYROFOAM™, LEGO® bricks, etc.).
3) Create a travel brochure for one African nation. Include drawings or photographs of attractions, both natural and man-made. Use both sides of a 8 1/2" x 11" sheet of paper for your brochure.

Literature

Cry, the Beloved Country is a story of redemption, of how good came about through what was seriously bad in attitudes, actions, social practices, and laws. The book describes much that is wrong, but you finish the story with a sense of hope.

The plot deals with real issues in South Africa at the time it was written, including the exploitation of cheap labor, the conflict between rural and urban life, and the hopelessness that many black South Africans felt. Relationships between different ethnic groups was much more complicated than simply whites versus blacks. Whites included the British and the Afrikaners (South Africans of Dutch descent). Afrikaners were a small percentage of the population but held almost complete political control from the mid-twentieth century until the early 1990s. You will read more about the history of South Africa in Lesson 139.

The narrative of the book sounds like the speech of black South Africans. The book mentions some hard, unpleasant things; but good triumphs in the end. Characters in the book who have faith in God act on that faith and do what is right.

Alan Paton was born in South Africa in 1903. His father was a Scottish immigrant and his mother was the daughter of English immigrants. Paton graduated from college in South Africa and taught for three years in an all-white school. He then served for twelve years as the principal of a reform school near Johannesburg for troubled black youths. He wrote *Cry, the Beloved Country* in 1946. It was published two years later and received world-wide acclaim. Paton then devoted himself to writing and involvement in South African politics. He died in 1988.

German Outpost in East Africa, c. 1910

Lesson 136

European Colonization

Europeans called it the "dark continent." The phrase had a double meaning. It referred to the darkness of Western ignorance about it and to the dark skin of its people. Although it lay just to the south of Europe, Africa was largely a mystery to Europeans before the mid-1800s. Most of the contact that whites had with Africans before that time took place at trading posts along the coast. With the rise of colonialism, European explorers plunged into the interior of Africa to find what riches they could and to claim lands for their home countries.

An amazing fact from the period of colonization is that, between 1870 and 1914, all of Africa came under European control except for Liberia and Ethiopia. Britain had an interest in Egypt for some time prior to this period and the Dutch had colonized southern Africa; but during this time of colonial expansion Belgium, France, Germany, Spain, Portugal, and Italy all vied for African territory. Not only did the Europeans fight the native Africans, but at times they also fought each other in Africa.

Europeans had several motives for exploring and colonizing Africa. Two major motives were national prestige and economic advantage. Establishing overseas colonies was something nations did in the late 1800s to enhance their status. Sometimes a European nation sought a particular territory in order to intimidate or limit the interests of another European nation. On a more practical level, colonizing nations hoped to find minerals and other resources that would increase their wealth.

- Belgium
- France
- Germany
- Great Britain
- Italy
- Portugal
- Spain
- Independent

EUROPEAN COLONIES IN AFRICA 1913

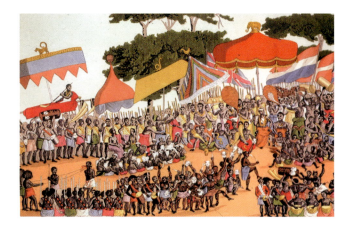

The Ashanti people of West Africa celebrate the first harvest of yams each autumn, as shown at left. The artist, English traveller Thomas E. Bowdich, published an account of his experiences in Africa in 1819.

They wanted to use colonies as outlets for goods manufactured in the homeland. A few individuals tried to build personal empires in Africa.

Spiritual and humanitarian concerns also played a role in European interest in Africa. Missionaries knew that Africans needed to know the gospel in order to be saved. These evangelists and other humanitarians wanted to improve the lives of Africans, who appeared to live much more primitively than Europeans did. An assumption held by many Europeans was that their culture was superior to African cultures and that it was the "white man's burden" to take the Christian faith and Western Civilization to the African people.

The first explorations of Africa moved up rivers from the coastlines. However, these trips were often costly in terms of sickness and death. When cures for malaria and yellow fever were discovered late in the 19th century, Europeans were able to move more confidently into the interior of the continent. Advanced weaponry gave the Europeans a decided advantage over tribal armies when confrontation occurred. This reality made European weapons a greatly-desired object of trade for African chieftains.

North Africa is largely desert. Occasional oases provide water and plants, such as the Gaberoun oasis in Libya that has date palm trees around a lake.

Lesson 136 - European Colonization

North Africa

The making of modern Africa is not just one story, any more than the making of modern Asia or Latin America is one story. Generally speaking, northern, central, and southern Africa each followed a different course.

Northern Africa, from the Mediterranean coast south through the Sahara Desert, was a prime area for Muslim conquest during the early Middle Ages. The Muslim presence profoundly influenced North African life and culture. The Ottoman Empire took control of North Africa in the early 1500s. As Ottoman control weakened in the late 1700s, Egypt and other North African countries were able to function as independent states.

Napoleon's invasion of Egypt in 1798 sparked a civil war there. Muhammad Ali, leader of Egyptian resistance to France, gained control in 1805. Ali sought to modernize Egyptian agriculture and education as well as the military. He also encouraged the development of textile, iron, and shipbuilding industries. Egyptian armies later took over areas of Sudan to the south of Egypt.

The modernization of Egypt by Ali and his successors was paid for by loans from European investors. These creditors pressured Egypt to pursue policies that they thought would insure repayment. A French company began building the Suez Canal in 1859. Britain gained a controlling interest in the project in the 1870s by buying shares from the indebted Egyptian government. The British used this financial interest to move troops into Egypt and take control of the country in 1882. Britain then ruled Egypt as a protectorate. Egypt continued to have a government but the British had significant influence over what happened. Egyptian debts were paid off and a dam was built on the Nile River at Aswan to provide water for farm irrigation, but many Egyptians resented the foreign domination.

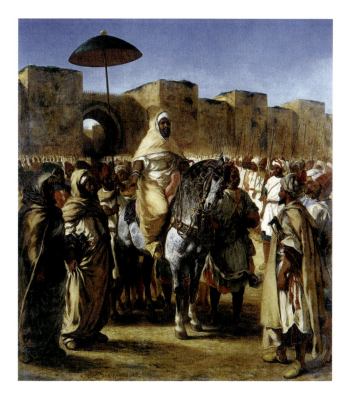

Moulay Abd-er-Rahman, Sultan of Morocco
Eugène Delacroix (French, 1845)

France conquered Algeria, Tunisia, and Morocco in western North Africa. Algerians resisted the French incursion, but they suffered great losses at the hands of the French. The French encouraged European settlement in Algeria, and over one million people from Europe emigrated to Algeria during the 1800s. France and Britain quarreled for many years over Egypt; but in a 1904 agreement, France recognized British control of Egypt and Britain recognized France's influence in Morocco. Germany later tried to bully its way into Morocco, but a 1906 international conference recognized the French sphere of influence there.

Italy tried to gain control of Ethiopia but was only able to take smaller areas in East Africa. The Italians also took over Libya in 1912 to prevent the French from spreading further eastward. The maneuverings in North Africa during the early 20th century were part of the competition for political advantage that led up to World War I.

Central Africa

The main European contact with the western coast of central Africa began with the slave trade in the mid-1400s. African societies already practiced slavery, so the selling of prisoners by tribal kings to Europeans was to the Africans just another business deal. Europeans often traded guns for slaves, and the Africans used these weapons to capture more slaves. The slave trade increased greatly when colonies in North America and the Caribbean Islands became dependent on slave labor for their plantations.

With the abolition of the slave trade in the early 1800s by Great Britain and the United States, this source of profit for African tribes disappeared. Some tribes turned to agriculture and began growing cotton and cacao beans to sell to the Europeans. A Muslim uprising in the early 1800s increased the influence of Islam in the region.

King Leopold II of Belgium took personal control of the area known as the Congo Free State in the late 1800s. Leopold sold the rights for the rubber and mineral resources in the Congo to European countries and made a handsome profit for himself. The companies exploited African workers mercilessly. Christian missionaries exposed these practices, and in 1906 the Belgian government took over the colony as the Belgian Congo. Spain, Germany, Portugal, and Britain claimed colonies in West Africa; but the largest part of the region was controlled by France.

Unit 28 - The Making of Modern Africa

Benin was a center of the African slave trade. This memorial in the coastal town of Ouidah is called Point of No Return. Hundreds of thousands of slaves were brought here from other parts of Africa, packed like cargo into slave ships, and taken away from their homes—forever.

In eastern Africa during the 1700s, Arab traders used African slaves to carry gold and ivory from the interior to coastal ports. Some African tribal leaders challenged the Arabs, and the disruption that resulted made it easier for Europeans to move in. African nations in the area became suspicious of each other, and many tribes looked to the Europeans for protection from their enemies. Britain and Germany were the chief European rivals for territories in East Africa.

A conference of European nations held in Berlin in 1884 and 1885 divided up Africa among the nations claiming to have interest there. The conference was planned to settle disputes and to help the colonial powers concentrate on controlling their assigned regions and gaining the economic benefits they believed awaited them.

This illustration is based on information from the journals of Scottish explorer and missionary David Livingstone. Arab traders took captured slaves across Central Africa to the east coast. They killed slaves who were unable to keep up, not wanting other traders to pick them up later.

Lesson 136 - European Colonization

Liberia

The American Colonization Society established Liberia in 1822 to encourage slaves in America to resettle in Africa. The society raised money to purchase the freedom of slaves and to pay for their passage to Liberia. The society promoted resettlement as a way to end slavery in the United States. However, only a few thousand slaves moved to Liberia through this effort. By the 1830s and 1840s, most slaves in America had been born in the U.S. and considered themselves Americans, not Africans.

The Republic of Liberia was established in 1847 with Monrovia at its capital (shown above in 2009). After World War II, Liberia became a founding member of the United Nations and the United States supported modern development there. Political turmoil and civil war plagued the country from the 1980s to the early 2000s. A peace treaty led to new elections in 2005, and the country has been slowly recovering since that time. Ellen Johnson Sirleaf (b. 1938 and pictured at left) became president of Liberia in 2006, the first elected female head of state in Africa.

From Colonies to Countries

In general, European nations ruled their colonies with little input from or involvement of the native population. The British, who controlled one-third of the continent by the late 1800s, did in some cases utilize local leaders who reported to British colonial governors. European governments and businesses sought to extract all of the wealth that they could from the colonies. This meant that most of the profits went to Europe and did not return to Africa. Some railroads and factories were built in Africa.

The Europeans brought—and often imposed—their culture, business practices, and educational systems. The whites provided some jobs and other economic opportunities for Africans. However, during this time, many Africans lost elements of their native cultures.

Christian missionaries brought the gospel to Africa, and many natives were converted. Often the new believers had a hard time giving up all of their former beliefs and practices that were part of their culture. Churches in Sub-Saharan Africa have continued to see significant growth, and the gospel has made inroads even in Muslim areas of North Africa. The continent does still have largely unevangelized areas.

As a result of colonization, a few Africans began receiving an education in Europe (and were shocked there to see Europeans holding menial jobs—all of the Europeans they had known in Africa were people of power and influence!). In Europe they gained a new vision for what their homelands could become, and they wanted to secure freedom for their people. At the same time, some Europeans argued for an end to colonialism. During the 20th century, all African colonial nations became independent. Some countries formed through violence against their colonial overlords, while others gained independence more peacefully.

Unit 28 - The Making of Modern Africa

Since gaining independence from Britain in 1956, Sudan was controlled by members of the Muslim majority in the northern part of the country. After decades of political and military conflict, South Sudan achieved independence as a new country in 2011. This photo shows an elderly man walking to his polling place to vote in the referendum on independence.

Independence has not brought an end to problems for Africans. The continent has seen its share of dictators who exploit their own people for personal gain. Inefficient governments have contributed to famine conditions in various African nations. Some African nations have become harbors for terrorists. Economic development is a major issue for many nations in Africa. The spread of AIDS has also been explosive.

Christianity has had a major impact on Africa. Less than 10% of the population was estimated to have been Christians in 1900. By 2000 the percentage had grown to almost 50%, and the percentage is even higher in many Sub-Saharan countries.

The people of Africa have suffered in part because a large portion of their population was stolen into slavery and because European colonizers exploited and repressed the remaining population. However, as the influence of Christianity declines in Europe and America, Christians in Africa can play an important role in promoting truth, justice, and righteousness in their native countries and around the world.

Envoys will come out of Egypt;
Ethiopia will quickly stretch out her hands to God.
Sing to God, O kingdoms of the earth,
Sing praises to the Lord.
Psalm 68:31-32

Assignments for Lesson 136

In Their Words   Read the excerpt from *Memoirs of an Arabian Princess* (pages 343-346).

Literature   Begin reading *Cry, the Beloved Country*. Finish it by the end of Unit 29.

Student Review   Optional: Answer the questions for Lesson 136.

Camel Train in Ethiopia

Lesson 137

Ethiopia

As the oldest independent nation in Africa, Ethiopia has held a significant role in the making of modern Africa. A large plateau covers over half of the country. Rivers and valleys cut through this plateau, which is bordered by mountains and deserts. Ethiopia, formerly known as Abyssinia, is the large gray area in East Africa in the map on page 793.

Axum

In the centuries before Christ, people from the kingdom of Sheba in the southern Arabian Peninsula likely migrated across the Red Sea to the area of modern Ethiopia. They had established the kingdom of Axum by the 100s AD. The Solomonid rulers of this kingdom claimed to be descendants of a union between King Solomon and the Queen of Sheba.

An ancient Greek book on shipping mentions Axum, which was a significant trading center. Their coins provide tidbits of historical information from the third century to the seventh. Axumite kings also spread their influence around the Red Sea into Arabia.

The gospel came to this region of Africa early with the conversion of the Ethiopian eunuch (Acts 8:26-40). King Ezana of Axum accepted the Christian religion about 333 AD, twenty years after Constantine had recognized it in the Roman Empire. According to the traditional story, a Syrian believer named Frumentius became an adviser to Ezana when he came to the throne as a boy. The leader of the Coptic Church in Egypt, Athanasius of Alexandria, appointed Frumentius as bishop in Axum, initiating a long connection between the churches in Egypt and Ethiopia.

Pictured below is one of eleven 12th-century churches carved out of rock in Laibela, Ethiopia. This one, Biete Ghiorgis (Church of St. George), was created in the shape of a cross.

Semien Mountains

The Abyssinian Church, or the Ethiopian Orthodox Union Church, was the official state church of Ethiopia until 1974. Some of its churches and monasteries built many centuries ago are still in use. The Axumite language of Ge'ez is no longer a commonly-spoken language, but it is used in the liturgy of the Ethiopian Church and in the Abyssinian Bible. Jewish influences remain in Abyssinian Church practices. They utilize images of the Ark of the Covenant, they observe Saturday and Sunday as special days, and they include ritual dancing in their meetings.

Changes and Confusion

After the rise of Islam in the 600s, Muslims began to surround and eventually capture portions of the Axumite kingdom. The Zagwe dynasty removed the Solomonids from power in the 1100s, but Solomonids began to regain control in the next century. Muslims maintained authority in some areas, especially in the southeast.

The Portuguese began exploring the coast of Africa in the 1400s. The Ethiopian emperor invited the Portuguese to help resist a Muslim invasion in the first half of the 1500s. Together they defeated the Muslim attackers in 1543. Catholic missionaries came to Ethiopia, but most Ethiopians maintained attachment to their Abyssinian heritage as a vital part of their independent culture.

Unit 28 - The Making of Modern Africa

The 1600s brought a period of artistic expression to Ethiopia with European and Islamic influences. The emperors Fasiladas, his son, Johannes I, and his son, Iyasus I, ruled from 1632-1706. Regional leaders divided the country after the death of Iyasus.

Stronger European influence came to Ethiopia in the mid-1800s with British and later Italian presence. After internal conflicts and war with the Egyptians and the Sudanese, Ethiopia began to reunite under Menelik II in 1889.

The Modern Nation

Menelik and the Italians signed a treaty of friendship. Interpretation of the two translations of the treaty differed, however, and the two nations warred between 1895 and 1896. Ethiopian forces prevailed at the decisive Battle of Adwa, and Menelik confirmed the independence of his country. He made Addis Ababa his capital.

Emperor Lij Iyasu had a brief reign around the beginning of World War I, but Tafari Makonnen deposed him and set up his aunt as Empress Zauditu. Makonnen came to power as Haile Selassie I after Zauditu died in 1930.

The Battle of Adwa (Ethiopian, c. 1970)

Lesson 137 - Key Country: Ethiopia

Benito Mussolini, dictator of Italy, brought conflict back to Ethiopia when he invaded in 1935. Haile Selassie called for help from the League of Nations, but this time the Italians defeated the Ethiopians. British and Ethiopians cooperated to restore Haile Selassie to his throne in 1941.

Haile Selassie made moderate changes to Ethiopian government, but he spent much time on foreign affairs. After strikes and demonstrations against Haile Selassie's government, Mengistu Haile Hariam and other military leaders removed him from power in 1974. They established a socialist republic that eventually turned into a Communist state with Soviet and Cuban support. Civil war among rival groups continued in the 1970s and 1980s. Droughts struck the country during the same period. Starvation killed an estimated one million Ethiopians during the 1980s.

By 1991 military forces opposed to Mengistu had driven him from power. Meles Zenawi led efforts to establish a new government in Addis Ababa. The United Nations General Assembly had merged Eritrea with Ethiopia after World War II, but Eritreans had long sought independence, which they declared in 1993. A border dispute between Ethiopia and Eritrea led to war in the late 1990s.

Market in Harar, Ethiopia

Haile Selassie helped to form the Organization of African Unity (OAU) in 1963. It was headquartered in Addis Ababa. The OAU disbanded in 2002 and was replaced with the African Union. The African Union Conference Center and Office Complex, pictured above, was opened in Addis Ababa in 2012. The government of China sponsored construction.

Ethiopia Today

The people of Ethiopia have had much in common with others on the African continent: conflict between Muslims and Christians, conflict between different ethnic groups, European colonialism, Communist expansion, and economic difficulties. The current government, which still exercises a significant amount of control over the economy, is seeking to offer new opportunities for the people. Nearly half of the population of ninety-three million is under fifteen, so the country has much potential for growth.

Under the 1995 constitution, Ethiopia is a federation of nine regions, each of which is home to one of the major ethnic groups in the country. A president serves as chief of state and a prime minister as the head of government, with a council of ministers selected by the prime minister and confirmed by the lower house of parliament. The parliament has two houses, the House of Federation and the House of People's Representatives.

The green, gold, and red of the Ethiopian flag were first used in 1897 under Emperor Menelik. The current flag was adopted in 1996. Because of Ethiopia's resistance to the colonial powers, many other African nations have used these colors when designing their national flags.

After its separation from Eritrea, Ethiopia is landlocked. Most of the people work in agriculture, with coffee being a major commodity. Ethiopia is seeking to boost prosperity by increasing its industrial sector. Business ties between China and Africa have grown significantly since the early 2000s, and Ethiopia illustrates this. For example, a Chinese car company builds vehicles in Ethiopian factories for sale in the country. Other Chinese factories are opening in Ethiopia, which has a good supply of natural resources and where labor costs are even lower than in China.

And he ordered the chariot to stop;
and they both went down into the water,
Philip as well as the [Ethiopian] eunuch,
and he baptized him. When they came up out of the water,
the Spirit of the Lord snatched Philip away;
and the eunuch no longer saw him,
but went on his way rejoicing.
Acts 8:38-39

Assignments for Lesson 137

In Their Words Read the Prayer from an Ethiopian Anaphora (page 347).

Literature Continue reading *Cry, the Beloved Country*.

Student Review Optional: Answer the questions for Lesson 137.

A Group of Maasai Welcome Tourists to Their Village

Lesson 138 - Everyday Life

The Culture of the Maasai

The Maasai are an East African tribe that has held on to long-standing traditions in the face of modern changes. They are probably descendants of the Nilotic people who once lived in Sudan and the Cushite people of Ethiopia. The name Cushite is derived from Cush, the son of Ham, the son of Noah (Genesis 10:6-8).

Historically, the Maasai were a united and powerful people with fierce warriors. Over the centuries, the Maasai spread into the grasslands of the Great Rift Valley. Archaeology and their own oral history indicate that they lived near Lake Turkana in north central Kenya at one time.

The Maasai live in what they call Maasailand, which extends across southern Kenya and north central Tanzania. They are one of forty ethnic groups within Kenya and one of 120 in Tanzania. Since the Maasai live dispersed in numerous small settlements, population figures are hard to determine. Estimates range from half a million to one million.

A Semi-Nomadic People

According to traditional Maasai belief, their god Enkai gave all cattle to them. As a result, in times past, they frequently sent groups of young men on raiding parties to steal cattle from others. They also demanded tribute from trade caravans.

Today the Maasai live a semi-nomadic lifestyle pasturing their herds. In a constant quest for water and grazing land, they move their great livestock herds seasonally across the open savannah. The Maasai often travel hundreds of miles to find fresh pasture. Though the governments of Kenya and Tanzania have tried to make them live in permanent settlements, the Maasai have resisted. They ignore international boundaries and demand the use of national parks for grazing land.

Aerial View of Maasai Settlements in Tanzania

The Social Order of the Maasai

The Maasai have sixteen sub-tribes (*iloshom* in their language). The basic social and economic unit of the Maasai is the village, or manyatta. Since they are semi-nomadic, the villages are semi-permanent settlements. Several families live near each other, pasturing their flocks of cattle, goats, and sheep together. Huts are made of sticks and cow dung. The community has a fenced area into which they herd their livestock at night. Each clan has characteristic cattle brands.

The Maasai have initiation rites for both males and females. Males are divided into five clearly defined age groups: child, junior warrior, senior warrior, junior elder, and senior elder. Men do not marry before they are thirty years old because they must have served as a warrior and they must have the ability to support a family. A girl can be married when she reaches puberty.

Young warriors use blunt arrows to hunt small birds. The birds are stuffed, tied to a frame, and worn as a headdress. The Maasai are renowned for their beautiful beadwork, which is used as body ornamentation. Beading patterns identify an individual's place in the social order. Young men often paint their bodies with ochre for decoration. A young man might spend days creating an ornate hairstyle, which is shaved off by his mother during his initiation into adulthood.

When something bad happens to a Maasai, he seeks out a diviner or laibon. A laibon performs rituals for social or moral transgressions and also

Maasai Women Building a House

works as a medicine man. In Tanzania in recent years, the Maasai laibons have gained a reputation as the best healers. A laibon is respected for his knowledge of traditional healing. They might earn extra income with their knowledge and herbs in urban centers in Tanzania and Kenya.

Food and Language

The basic food of the Maasai is fresh or curdled milk. They decorate long gourds and use them to store and carry the milk. On special occasions, they drink blood drawn from the jugular vein of a bull or cow (without killing the animal). Their meat usually comes from goats and sheep.

The Maasai rarely slaughter a cow except for ceremonial purposes. When they do slaughter a cow, they use every part for clothing, bedding, food, and containers.

Lenana was a leading Maasai medicine man who cooperated with the British, as seen in this photo from about 1890. Mission workers from various denominations have worked among the Maasai, but they remain largely unreached with the gospel. A New Testament in the Maasai language was published in London in 1923 by the British and Foreign Bible Society, and the Jesus *film has been translated into the Maasai language.*

Lesson 138 - Everyday Life: The Culture of the Maasai

Scholars estimate that Africa has over a thousand languages. Only about fifty languages are spoken by more than 500,000 people each. Most are spoken by relatively few people. The Maasai speak Maa, a language they share with the Samburu and Ilchamus tribes of Kenya and the Arusha and Baraguyu tribes of Tanzania.

The Maasai Today

Some Maasai wear sneakers. Some have cell phones. But they are one of the few indigenous peoples who have largely retained their traditional way of life. This makes the Maasai an attraction for tourists, much like the Amish are in the United

Maasai Feet (Notice Sneakers at Left)

States. Many Maasai live on a limited income, and they are using creative means to capitalize on their widely-recognized cultural identity.

Some companies have used "Maasai" (or the older spelling "Masai" as a brand name). The Maasai Intellectual Property Initiative seeks to earn income for the betterment of their tribe from companies who use their name. They also want to restrict uses of their cultural brand that are offensive to them.

Maasai Mara National Reserve is a wildlife park in southern Kenya, established in 1961 and named after the Maasai people. It is home to a wide variety of animals, including cheetahs, elephants, wildebeest, zebras, and giraffes. A herd of wildebeest are following a few zebras in the aerial photo at right. Maasai Mara is part of a larger region known as the Serengeti, a name meaning "Endless Plains" in the Maasai language.

Unit 28 - The Making of Modern Africa

Maasai School

Other Maasai such as Salaton Ole Ntutu have created innovative businesses. In addition to selling traditional crafts, his Maji Moto Maasai Cultural Camp provides day outings and overnight encampments. Visitors can practice warrior training skills, participate in daily chores, listen to songs and stories, and walk across the plains with Maasai guides. Part of the proceeds support a school, a health clinic, a village for widows and women with AIDS, and conservation efforts.

For every beast of the forest is Mine,
The cattle on a thousand hills.
I know every bird of the mountains,
And everything that moves in the field is Mine.
Psalm 50:10-11

Assignments for Lesson 138

Literature — Continue reading *Cry, the Beloved Country*.

Student Review — Optional: Answer the questions for Lesson 138.

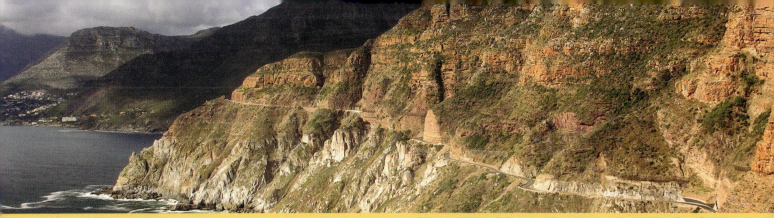

Chapman's Peak Drive Near Cape Town, South Africa

Lesson 139

South Africa

South Africa has seen it all: ancient peoples, European exploration and settlement, colonization, development and exploitation of its abundant natural resources, ethnic divisions and conflict, politically-charged turmoil in the late 20th century, world-recognized figures, and finally (at least outward) resolution of long-standing problems. In the story of South Africa we see the results of foreign influence and the struggles of native peoples to live successfully in the 21st century. History bears upon the present everywhere, but it is especially obvious in South Africa.

From Ancient Times

Anthropologists believe that groups of Africans migrated into the region of South Africa over 1,000 years ago. These are known as Bantu people, for the Bantu language they spoke.

Portuguese explorers sailed around the tip of South Africa in the late 15th century. In 1652 the Dutch founded the colony of Cape Town as a rest stop for Dutch trading ships on their way to the East Indies. The Dutch came to dominate the region, enslaving some Africans while pushing others into the more barren lands to the north.

The early 1800s were a time of transition and conflict in South Africa. Great Britain seized the colony from the Dutch during the Napoleonic Wars to protect their sea trading routes to the East. Meanwhile, the Zulus, one of the Bantu groups that had migrated there, developed a strong empire in the northeastern part of South Africa. Other African tribes that the Zulus defeated moved into central Africa.

The Boers, South African Dutch who were descendants of the original European settlers, resented British rule. Britain imposed the English language and abolished slavery, which the Dutch

Jumping is a common element of African dances, including those of the Zulu. These modern Zulu men, wearing traditional clothing, are dancing in front of traditional Zulu homes.

Cecil Rhodes

Cecil John Rhodes (1853-1902) was an Englishman who went to South Africa at seventeen to join his brother on a cotton farm. He got involved in diamond mining and became very wealthy. Rhodes formed the DeBeers Mining Company and at one point controlled 90% of the world's diamond production. He was appointed prime minister of the Cape Colony in 1890, a year after receiving a charter to form the British South Africa Company.

The company acted as both a business and a government. It took control of the area north of South Africa that was named North and South Rhodesia (now known, respectively, as Zambia and Zimbabwe). Rhodes wanted to expand the areas under British control on the Cape to secure its trade route to India and to build a "Cape to Cairo" empire that included a transcontinental railroad and telegraph. The caricature above was published in Punch *magazine in 1892 as "The Rhodes Colossus." Rhodes was ousted as South African prime minister in 1896 but continued to exercise power in the Rhodesias. In his will, Rhodes designated some of his fortune to be used for Rhodes Scholarships to Oxford University.*

had used as a labor force. In the 1830s, about 10,000 Boers undertook a migration to the northeast of the Cape Colony, settling in what became the Orange Free State and the Transvaal. This exodus was called the Great Trek. However, the area into which they moved was claimed by the Zulus. The Boers and the Zulus fought for years, but neither side was able to gain a complete victory. Britain recognized the Boer republics in 1852, and in 1879 British forces helped the Boers deliver the final blow to the Zulus.

British Expansion

Despite the assistance that the Boers had received from the British, the Boers came to feel threatened by the British for two main reasons. First, when gold and diamonds were discovered in Boer lands in the 1880s, hundreds of British miners and speculators flooded into the territory to seek their fortune. Second, Cecil Rhodes' vision for connecting northern and southern Africa included taking over the Boer-controlled lands.

Tensions finally exploded into the Boer War in 1899, which lasted for three years. The British defeated the Boers. Coupled with the harsh treatment that Boers endured in British concentration camps, this defeat left deep bitterness among the Boers toward the British. The British promised self-rule for the Boer states; but in 1910 they were folded into the Union of South Africa, which combined all of Britain's colonies in the region into a single unit as part of the British

The British held Boer women and children in concentration camps to discourage their fighting men. Twenty thousand inmates died from hunger and disease.

Lesson 139 - Key Country: South Africa

Empire. In 1931 the Union of South Africa became a member of the British Commonwealth.

Black South Africans were generally relegated to low-paying jobs. They were also subject to strict social segregation. Blacks had to carry passes even to travel in certain urban areas. In the Union of South Africa, only whites could vote. British whites and Boer whites (who came to be called Afrikaners and their language Afrikaans [af-rih-KAHNS]) competed for control of the land and of the country's vast mineral wealth. Both white groups had strong prejudice against the blacks.

Afrikaners and Apartheid

Between 1910 and 1948, Afrikaner political leaders developed their ethnic identity and political power and portrayed black Africans as a dangerous group. As the larger white group, Afrikaners won control of the whites-only government in 1948. They formalized a strict policy of apartheid (apartness or segregation) among the races that was already largely in place by custom. Complicating the issue was Afrikaner recognition of two other racial groups: Asians, who were mostly from India, and "coloureds," or mixed-race people. These latter two groups were also subject to apartheid laws.

ANC cultural ambassadors, such as this group performing in East Germany in 1986, raised awareness of apartheid.

Sign at a Beach in Cape Town, South Africa (1985)

South Africa is over twice as large as France. It is blessed with abundant fertile lands and natural resources. South African mines have yielded gold, diamonds, and other valuable minerals. The country is one of the most industrialized nations in the world. However, white-controlled governments oversaw this economic development and non-white South Africans did not generally benefit from this prosperity. Discrimination against them included their being forced to live in segregated areas that had inferior housing. Blacks could not even attend church services with whites. Almost 80% of South Africans are black. Whites and "coloureds" each comprise about 9%.

The enforced poverty and segregation that non-white South Africans endured hurt the country's domestic economy and made it a subject of harsh criticism from many other nations. Demonstrations against apartheid that began around 1960 were brutally suppressed by South African officials. The African National Congress (ANC) was a group that worked for black equality, sometimes by the

Zimbabwe

Like South Africa, (Southern) Rhodesia also went through a transition from white minority rule to majority black rule in the 20th century. Still a British colony in 1965, the British government required a change to allow blacks to participate fully in government before it would grant independence. To avoid this, the white Rhodesian government declared its independence from Britain, the first time this had been done since the American colonies had done it in 1776. Opposition from the world community and a long civil war eventually led to full independence as a black-ruled nation in 1980. Robert Mugabe, pictured at right, served as first prime minister of Zimbabwe until 1987, when he became president. Under his administration, white citizens in Zimbabwe have been subjected to discrimination by black citizens.

use of violence. The government of South Africa occasionally sent military raids into neighboring countries where ANC terrorists were thought to be hiding. ANC leader Nelson Mandela was sent to prison in the early 1960s for his part in the violence.

One proposed solution to the racial question was the formation of areas within South Africa where blacks could live. In 1959 the government began creating several regions for Bantus to live. Once again, three hundred years after the practice began, white South Africans were telling Bantus where they could not live and began pushing them into other areas. South Africa withdrew from the British Commonwealth in 1961 and became the Republic of South Africa.

Changes to the System

During the 1980s, international pressure on South Africa was matched by increasing domestic violence. South Africa had been banned from the Olympics since 1964, and many nations refused to do business with the country. Black South African Anglican Bishop Desmond Tutu was awarded the Nobel Peace Prize in 1984 (after an ANC leader had won it in 1961). A general strike by some two million black South African workers largely paralyzed the country in June of 1988.

Joseph Shabalala founded a male choral group in South Africa in 1960. Known as Ladysmith Black Mambazo since 1964, the group has toured internationally and released numerous best-selling recordings. Shabalala became a Christian in the 1970s, and gospel music has been an important part of their message ever since.

Lesson 139 - Key Country: South Africa

Not all of the violence was black versus white. The ANC and the Inkatha Freedom Party, two black African groups, fought each other for years primarily over control of a mainly Zulu province. The conflict cost an estimated 10,000 lives or more.

A new constitution in 1983 gave blacks the right to vote in parliamentary elections. The law against interracial marriage was repealed in 1985. In 1990 the white government lifted its ban on the ANC; and Nelson Mandela was freed from prison. The next year, President F. W. de Klerk announced his intention to end apartheid. In negotiations for a new system of government, the black homelands were dissolved and became part of a system of provinces.

F. W. de Klerk and Nelson Mandela visited the United States in 1993 to receive America's Liberty Medal for their work to end apartheid.

South Africa hosted the finals of the 2010 FIFA World Cup, the first African nation to do so. Thirty-two teams competed at ten stadiums around the country. This photo of a match between Portugal and Ivory Coast was taken at Nelson Mandela Bay Stadium in Port Elizabeth.

De Klerk and Mandela jointly received the Nobel Peace Prize in 1993. Elections in 1994 gave ANC candidates over 62% of the vote. Nelson Mandela served as president from 1994 to 1999. He remained a prominent figure in South Africa until his death in 2013.

In 1995 the new South African government established the Truth and Reconciliation Commission (TRC) to help the country recover from the effects of human rights abuses during apartheid. Many citizens gave input on what they thought the commission should do before the law setting it up was enacted. The commission sought to hear from former government officials and from members of groups that had fought the apartheid government, but primarily it heard from victims who suffered during apartheid.

The commission's emphasis was on letting people tell their stories so that the truth could be known. The commission had authority to grant amnesty to perpetrators of abuse if they requested it. The commission received over 7,000 requests for amnesty and granted about 1,500. Some people received prison sentences for their wrongs. The TRC, which issued its final report in 2003, is widely seen as having contributed to South Africa being able to recover from its difficult past.

In 1990 less than 1% of South African adults were estimated to have HIV/AIDS. By the late 2000s, almost 20% of South African adults were infected with HIV/AIDS, giving South Africa the largest infected population of any country in the world.

Racial division and exploitation. Violence and warfare. Long-standing issues and current problems. Scars from the past and hope for tomorrow. These are all part of the story of South Africa.

---

*Let the mountains bring peace to the people,
and the hills, in righteousness.
Psalm 72:3*

Assignments for Lesson 139

In Their Words   Read Desmond Tutu's Nobel Peace Prize Lecture (pages 348-354).

Literature   Continue reading *Cry, the Beloved Country*.

Student Review   Optional: Answer the questions for Lesson 139.

Ancient Egyptian Crocodile Statue

Lesson 140 - Bible Study

Africa in the Bible

We usually think of the Bible as focusing on the Middle East. The emphasis in the Old Testament is from Israel east to Babylon and Persia, while the New Testament story moves from Israel west through southern Europe to Rome. However, the Bible has a considerable number of references to places in Africa. Most of these relate to Egypt, but the Bible mentions other areas.

It is generally believed that the descendants of Ham populated the continent of Africa. Genesis 10:6 refers to two sons of Ham as Cush and Put, which are early names for what were later called Ethiopia and Libya, respectively.

Egypt in the Old Testament

Abram went to Egypt when a famine struck Canaan (Genesis 12:10-20). Egypt played a prominent role in the story of Joseph. Joseph was sold to Potiphar as a slave but rose to be second only to Pharaoh over the whole land. The family of Israel moved en masse to Egypt to find relief from the famine and settled in the land of Goshen.

The story of the Israelites resumes in Exodus with a different emphasis. In Exodus, Egypt is not a place of refuge but of misery. Moses was born and reared in Egypt, fled when he feared that Pharaoh was after him, but returned to lead Israel out of bondage in the Exodus. During the Israelites' time in the wilderness, some of the complaining people occasionally expressed a desire to go back to Egypt (as in Numbers 14:4).

As the kingdom of Israel grew in importance during the united monarchy, Solomon cemented an alliance with Egypt by marrying a daughter of Pharaoh (1 Kings 3:1). He built a beautiful home for her (1 Kings 9:24), but she and Solomon's other foreign wives led him into idolatry (1 Kings 11:1-8).

Hadad was an Edomite who fled to Egypt as a child when the Israelite army had raided Edom. Hadad gained favor in Egypt and married into the royal family. When David died, Hadad returned to Edom and became an adversary to Solomon (1 Kings 11:14-22).

Jeroboam was an opponent of Solomon who fled to Egypt. After Solomon's death, Jeroboam returned to Israel and led the division of the ten northern tribes against the Davidic dynasty. To make a separate place of worship for the North, he made two golden calves and presented them to Israel as the gods that had brought them out of Egypt (1 Kings 12:2-13:33). He probably learned about calf-worship while he was in Egypt. During Rehoboam's reign in Judah, the Egyptian king Shishak raided Jerusalem and carried off the treasures of the house of the Lord and other spoil (1 Kings 14:25-26).

In later years, both Hoshea of the Northern Kingdom and Hezekiah of Judah tried to strengthen their position against Assyria by making an alliance with Egypt (2 Kings 17:4, 18:21). Nahum predicted the downfall of Nineveh, the capital of Assyria, and said it would be similar to the destruction that the Assyrians wrought on No-amon, another name for the Egyptian city of Thebes (Nahum 3:8-10).

Egypt and Babylon clashed repeatedly for control of the Middle East, and Israel was sometimes dragged into this conflict. Jeremiah prophesied that Egypt would be defeated by the Babylonians at the battle of Carchemish on the Euphrates River, which took place in 605 BC (Jeremiah 46:2). On his way there, Pharaoh Neco killed Josiah, king of Judah, at Megiddo (2 Kings 23:29). Jeremiah warned Judah against relying on Egypt to keep from falling to the Babylonians. Jeremiah's fate is not clear in the Bible, but some Bible scholars believe that he was taken to Egypt with people from Judah who wanted to flee the Babylonians.

Other Old Testament References

Cush (Ethiopia). The people of Israel grumbled against Moses because he married a Cushite woman (Numbers 12:1). Students of the Bible differ on the meaning of this. It could refer to a second wife after Zipporah died, or it could be a belated criticism of Zipporah herself. Some people who lived in the Sinai region came there from Cush, so Jethro's family might have been Cushites.

Tirhakah, a Cushite king of Egypt, attempted to fight the Assyrians; but his army was no match for them (2 Kings 19:9). The Persian empire was said to extend to Ethiopia (Esther 1:1). When Zephaniah described the restoration of Judah to their land, he said that worshipers would come "from beyond the rivers of Ethiopia" (Zephaniah 3:10); in other words, from a long way off.

Put (Libya or Lubim). Invaders from Put entered Egypt between the twelfth and eighth centuries BC. Lubim and Ethiopia helped Shishak in his invasion of Judah (2 Chronicles 12:2-3). Nahum said that Put tried to help Egypt withstand the assault by the Assyrians (Nahum 3:9).

The pyramids of Meroe were built in the Kingdom of Cush, modern Sudan.

Lesson 140 - Bible Study: Africa in the Bible

Cyrene, originally a Greek settlement in North Africa, was taken over by the Romans, who remodeled the existing Greek theater into this amphitheater.

New Testament References

Joseph and Mary took Jesus to Egypt as a child to escape the murderous wrath of Herod when the wise men did not return to him after visiting the home where Jesus was (Matthew 2:13-15). Simon of Cyrene (a city in Libya) carried Jesus' cross when He was on His way to be crucified (Mark 15:21).

On the Day of Pentecost in Acts 2, some who were present were Jews from "Egypt and the districts of Libya around Cyrene" (Acts 2:10). In Acts 8, an angel led Philip to the chariot of the court treasurer of Candace, queen of the Ethiopians. Archaeological records indicate that the king of Ethiopia at the time was considered too sacred to carry out any royal business. Official duties were performed by the queen mother, whose title was Candace. The treasurer might have been a God-fearer, but the emphasis placed on Cornelius as a Gentile in Acts 10 suggests that the treasurer was Jewish. He had been to Jerusalem to worship, and he was wealthy enough to have his own copy of the scroll of Isaiah.

Acts 13:1 describes prophets and teachers in the church in Antioch. Among these were Lucius of Cyrene and Simeon, called the Niger (or black man). This raises an interesting possibility that could be nothing more than speculation. Mark 15:21 refers to Simon of Cyrene as "the father of Alexander and Rufus," as though people in the early church knew who Alexander and Rufus were. Paul greets Rufus as "a choice man in the Lord," along with his mother, in Romans 16:13.

Based on the tidbits of information given in the Bible, here is a possible scenario showing how these facts might fit together. Simon of Cyrene became a follower of Jesus at some point, either at the time of the crucifixion, as a result of his experience in carrying the cross of Jesus, or at the preaching of Peter on the

Day of Pentecost. His wife was converted also, and their sons Alexander and Rufus became Christians as well. Simon (also called Simeon) became a prophet or teacher in the church in Antioch. Paul would have known the family in Antioch, and Rufus might have become an evangelist who was in Rome when Paul wrote the letter to the church there.

God has used people and nations in Africa to accomplish his purposes since early in human history. The gospel spread to Africa soon after the time of Christ, and African Christians have been faithful to the Lord ever since, often in the face of intimidation and persecution. Let us learn from their example.

Whom the Lord of hosts has blessed, saying, "Blessed is Egypt My people, and Assyria the work of My hands, and Israel My inheritance."
Isaiah 19:25

Assignments for Lesson 140

Bible — Recite or write Philippians 2:3-4 from memory.

In Their Words — Read the excerpt from *The Last Journals of David Livingstone* (pages 355-358).

Literature — Continue reading *Cry, the Beloved Country*.

Project — Complete your project for the unit.

Student Review — Optional: Answer the questions for Lesson 140 and take the quiz for Unit 28.

29

Summary

Into the 21st Century

As we close our chronological study of world history, we look at two key issues in our world: technology and global trade. We examine the modern Middle East, a region of conflict and transition. The key persons we feature are the homeschooling family. We also present a fascinating history of time-keeping. The Bible study surveys church history in recent centuries.

Lessons

141 - Technology and Trade
142 - The Making of the Modern Middle East
143 - Key Persons: The Homeschooling Family
144 - Everyday Life: A History of Keeping Time
145 - Bible Study: Modern Church History

A woman is rescued from debris six days after the 2010 earthquake in Haiti.

Memory Work — Learn Proverbs 23:24-25 by the end of the unit.

Books Used — The Bible
In Their Words
Cry, the Beloved Country

Project (choose one)

1) Write 300 to 500 words on one of the following topics:

   - How has homeschooling impacted your life? How do you imagine it could impact your future life?

   - Discuss the wise use of modern technology and how it can be abused.

2) Interview someone who works in technology and/or trade. See Lesson 141. Compose at least ten questions ahead of time. You can conduct your interview by phone or in person. Be respectful of your interviewee's time and keep the interview within an hour. If possible, make an audio recording of the interview.

3) Write a play about a homeschooling family. Your play should be at least seven pages long, but can be as long as you like. Recruiting family and/or friends to perform your play might be fun, but is optional.

Children Using Computers in Ghana

Lesson 141

Technology and Trade

Advances in technology affect people around the world every day. These technologies are tools that can be used for good or evil. We usually do not hear the idea, common in previous generations, that scientific advancements will lead to the end of war and the elimination of poverty and disease. We know better than that now. People generally understand that technology itself is neutral and can be used to help or to harm depending on the motives of the human beings using it.

Book Production

Charles Dickens wrote all of his novels in long hand. The text was then set by hand, individual letter by individual letter. One galley proof copy of a novel was printed so that Dickens could note any corrections that were needed before the book was published. C. S. Lewis could have used a typewriter, as many writers did in the 20th century; but since he never learned to type, he also wrote all of his books by hand. The text was then set up on a linotype machine, a galley proof was printed for the author and publisher to make corrections, and then the book was printed and bound.

Would the quality of writing by Dickens and Lewis be different if they had access to modern technology? It is hard to imagine their writing being any better, and much that is produced using the latest technology is not as good as what they did. Advanced technology does not necessarily produce better writing.

To create *Exploring World History*, we used multiple computers to type, edit, and lay out the lessons. We used the Internet to aid our research and to share ideas among ourselves. We used machines in our office to print color pages for preview and proofreading. When the books were finished, we sent them over the Internet to a printing company in another city. Workers there used large printing presses to produce the pages and covers, and an assembly line to bind them all into the book you are holding.

Computers

Over the centuries, people envisioned machines that could perform mathematical calculations quickly. Before the advent of electricity, however, they could only be conceived of as using mechanical power. The French mathematician Blaise Pascal built about fifty adding and subtracting machines in the 1640s. Another Frenchman, Joseph Marie Jacquard, used pre-punched paper cards to program the operation of a weaving loom in 1790. Charles Babbage in England proposed what he called an analytical machine around 1833, which would have involved a complicated set of punched cards and interlocking gears to perform calculations. Only part of the machine was ever built.

ENIAC (Electrical Numerical Integrator And Calculator) was the first general purpose electronic computer, built around the end of World War II. ENIAC covered about 1,800 square feet, about the size of a moderate three-bedroom home, weighed thirty tons, and used over 17,000 vacuum tubes (devices that amplify electronic signals). Further research and development during the second half of the 20th century led to transistors, integrated circuits, and microprocessors that cut the size and increased the capabilities of computers.

While the hardware side of computing developed, programmers also worked on software, the program of functions that a computer performs to accomplish a given task. As computers have been made with greater memory capacity, larger programs have been written that can perform more complicated functions.

The Internet

Computers are connected through networks that share information through digital data transmission lines. The first network involved four computers in the U.S. Defense Department in 1969. Universities soon developed computer networks also. The Internet is a huge network of networks spread across the world.

Developments in computers and the Internet have changed the way people around the world teach and learn, do research, communicate, conduct business, work, shop, and advertise. These changes have also begun affecting politics, as information (and sometimes propaganda) is made available and, in some cases, voting is taking place online.

The ease of Internet access and desktop publishing means that ideas can be distributed more widely and more easily, even those ideas that are not picked up by major media and publishing companies. Ideas that are outside of the mainstream can now receive wide circulation through the Internet and by new methods of printing. The process of on-demand publishing, for example, can print one copy of a book in a matter of minutes from files stored on a computer. Major publishers usually commit to printing a book only if they believe they can sell a large number of copies. Ebooks and on-demand printing have made more books available.

Some information that is available on the Internet is not good. Some is inaccurate, and inaccurate information can be circulated just as quickly as accurate information. Other material on the Internet is not morally wholesome, and those whose minds are turned against the Lord's way of holiness use the Internet to circulate their degrading material. This has sparked a debate between those who advocate absolute freedom of speech and those who see a need to regulate what material is available to Internet users.

The Apple iPad launched in 2010. This photo shows a man looking at a display at an Apple Store in Tokyo. At 1.5 pounds, the iPad was a tiny fraction of ENIAC's weight and cost about .01% as much ($600 versus $6,000,000 in today's dollars for ENIAC). ENIAC could perform a few hundred calculations per second, while the iPad is capable of performing billions of calculations per second, and of accessing the Internet.

Lesson 141 - Technology and Trade

In 1990 only twelve million people had mobile phone subscriptions, and almost half of those were in the United States. By 2013 the number of mobile subscriptions was almost the same as the number of people alive (about seven billion, though some people have more than one device). The top row shows users in Egypt, Italy, and Oman, while the bottom row shows users in South Africa, India, and Argentina. In the middle is the entrance to a church in Hong Kong with a sign asking visitors to be quiet and turn off their mobile phones.

Medical Technology

The field of medicine is one that has several moral issues related to the application of modern research and technology. Amazing medical advances have been made. For example, doctors can perform surgery on infants who are still in the womb. Transplant surgeries for major organs, as well as knee and hip replacements, have become almost commonplace. Diagnostic tests can identify cancer and other abnormalities much sooner than in previous years, which often means that treatment can be more effective.

Greater options for treatment, however, can make for difficult decisions for those who are ill and for their families. For instance, medication that alleviates the pain of a suffering person can also slow the body's functioning, which can hasten death.

In another example, when the author's father-in-law suffered a heart attack in December of 2003, he suffered brain damage because his brain did not get oxygen for a certain period of time; but he was kept alive by a respirator. Then his family had to make the agonizing decision of whether or not to remove the respirator. This was done, and he died within a short time.

Health care is not a right that someone should expect to receive at no charge. Much health care around the world is provided for free, and Christians are at the forefront of this noble effort to serve fellow human beings. However, like other goods and services in the economy, health care is a service that professionals are best able to provide when they are compensated for their training, knowledge, and time. When government officials attempt to manage the delivery of health care, prices go up and quality and availability go down.

Global Trade

Specialization and trade among individuals make them all better off. In a similar way, specialization and trade among nations make them all better off. Natural resources, workforce training, and access to capital combine to give different countries advantages relative to other countries in terms of producing certain goods and services. Allowing the free movement of people and goods among nations enables businesses and individuals to prosper because they can do what they do best and buy from others what others do best.

International trade grew by 50% between 2000 and 2010. This gives consumers around the world

Global Terrorism

Terrorism is the use of violence to make a political point. Throughout history, a wide variety of individuals and groups have used terrorism to bring attention to their demands. Modern technology has allowed terrorist groups to coordinate and execute more complex and deadly attacks.

One prominent terrorist group is al-Qaeda, a loose network spread across the world that coordinates planning, funding, and training for attacks. Organized by Osama bin Laden, a wealthy Saudi Arabian, its stated goal was to fight those who support Israel and the presence of Western soldiers in Islamic countries. Terrorists associated with the network have been tied to attacks in many countries, including Indonesia, Iraq, Pakistan, Saudi Arabia, Turkey, the United Kingdom, and Yemen. Al-Qaeda attacked the World Trade Center in 1993, three U.S. embassies in Africa in 1998, and the USS Cole, stationed in the Middle East, in 2000.

The most destructive attacks connected to al-Qaeda took place on September 11, 2001. Hijackers took control of four airplanes in the United States. Two of the planes crashed into the main World Trade Center towers in New York City (see destroyed towers above), one crashed into the Pentagon, and one crashed in a field in Pennsylvania when passengers attempted to overpower the hijackers. About 3,000 people were killed. The United States government quickly targeted al-Qaeda, and many al-Qaeda operatives were captured or killed over the next several years. Osama bin Laden himself was killed by U.S. forces in Pakistan in 2011.

Lesson 141 - Technology and Trade

access to a wider variety of products at a lower cost. Changes in the economy and competition from others do cause disruptions: people lose jobs, businesses close. But in the long run, trade makes life better for everyone.

When new technologies emerge, often only the wealthy can afford to use them. But as a technology matures and competition increases, the price goes down and more people are able to use it. The world saw this pattern over and over in the 20th century with cars, telephones, and air travel, for example.

An open exchange of goods and services naturally leads to an exchange of ideas. Learning about other cultures helps us understand how to relate to them. Christians in many countries have faced extreme persecution in recent decades, but the number of Christians has also grown rapidly. As the world continues to get smaller through technology and trade, Christians can take advantage of opportunities to share the most important information available—the good news that God loves people and wants fellowship with them.

The vast majority of international trade is carried on ships during part of its journey from one country to another. This photo shows a container ship passing through the Panama Canal.

Come now, you who say, "Today or tomorrow we will go to such and such a city, and spend a year there and engage in business and make a profit." Yet you do not know what your life will be like tomorrow. You are just a vapor that appears for a little while and then vanishes away. Instead, you ought to say, "If the Lord wills, we will live and also do this or that."
James 4:13-15

Assignments for Lesson 141

In Their Words — Read "The Great Outsourcing Scare" (pages 359-362).

Literature — Continue reading *Cry, the Beloved Country*. Finish it by the end of this unit.

Student Review — Optional: Answer the questions for Lesson 141.

Syrian Billboard Showing President Bashar al-Assad, 2008

Lesson 142

The Making of the Modern Middle East

The Middle East stretches from Turkey to Iran and from the former Soviet republic of Georgia to Yemen on the Arabian Peninsula. A popular uprising known as the Arab Spring began in late 2010 in Tunisia in North Africa and spread to many Arab countries in the Middle East. Protestors used modern technology to bring their demonstrations and appeals for freedom to a worldwide audience. Several countries have seen changes in government as long-serving strongmen have fallen from power.

Some citizens want to establish modern democratic governments in these countries. Others see democracy as a weak form of government and want to enforce strict Islamic principles. Regardless of the outcome in each country, the Middle East will continue to be in the news, as it was for much of the 20th century.

A Land of Promise and Conflict

Israel is a small area between the Mediterranean Sea to the west and the Jordan River to the east, and between Lebanon to the north and the Sinai Peninsula to the south. Its location on major trade and travel routes gives the region military and economic importance. Its major role in the Biblical story gives Israel spiritual significance for Jews and Christians.

This land has repeatedly been the subject of conflict between nations that wanted to control it. Through the centuries, this territory has been in the possession of many nations, including Canaanite tribes, Old Testament Israel, Assyria, Babylon, Greece, the Seleucid dynasty, Rome, Byzantium, Muslim Caliphs, European Crusaders, the Ottoman Empire, Great Britain, and modern Israel.

God promised to make a great nation of Ishmael, Abraham's son by Hagar (Genesis 16:10 and 21:13, 18). *The Book of Jubilees*, an ancient Jewish work, includes this passage:

> And Ishmael and his sons, and the sons of Keturah and their sons, went together and dwelt from Paran to the entering in of Babylon in all the land which is toward the east facing the desert. And these mingled with each other, and their name was called Arabs, and Ishmaelites (Keturah was Abraham's wife after Sarah died, see Genesis 25:1-4).

God promised to give the land of Canaan to Abraham and his descendants forever (Genesis

17:8). However, that promise was conditioned upon Israel's faithfulness to God (Deuteronomy 28:58-67). Israel was not always faithful, so God sometimes gave control of the land to other nations, as recorded in the Old Testament and in the history of the period between the Old and New Testaments.

At the time of Christ, Palestine (a Greek name for the region) was part of the Roman Empire. The people who lived there included Jews, Samaritans, and some Gentiles. Rome continued to control the area until the empire divided between east and west. Palestine became part of the Eastern Roman (or Byzantine) Empire. The Eastern capital of Byzantium was later renamed Constantinople.

Muslims took control of Palestine in 634. Except for brief periods of control by Crusaders from Europe and later Mongol invaders, it remained in Muslim hands until the early 1900s.

The Jewish Desire for a Homeland

During and after the Middle Ages, Jews in Europe and Russia were often treated with prejudice and contempt. In the late 1800s, persecutions against Jews became more widespread. Many Jews came to believe that the only answer to these attacks was for Jews to have their own homeland, where they could live in peace and security. This growing desire developed into the Zionist Movement. Zion was another name for the homeland of Old Testament Israel, from Mount Zion, the location of the temple in Jerusalem.

The Zionist Movement's leading spokesman was Theodor Herzl, a Jewish journalist born in Hungary in 1860. Herzl published the 1896 book *The Jewish State* and organized several Zionist conferences or congresses in Europe beginning in 1897. People proposed various places where a Jewish homeland might be located, but European Jews became focused on creating a Jewish homeland in the historic land of Israel.

However, this idea met opposition for two main reasons. First, Palestine was part of the Ottoman

Young Women in Nazareth, c. 1910

Empire, and the Ottomans did not want to give it up. Second, Palestine already had people living there: Arabs. The majority of Muslims in the Middle East are also Arabs, but "Arab" and "Muslim" are not synonymous. Some Arab Christians lived in Palestine, along with Jews. The people of Palestine had been living together with relatively little conflict.

European Jews began buying land in Palestine to enable Jews from Europe and Russia to settle there. The Arabs in Palestine at first welcomed this development because it brought in much-needed economic activity. As Jews prospered there, some Arabs moved in from other countries to find work. However, the Arab population in Palestine began to feel threatened by the increased presence of Jews and started opposing the Jewish influx.

Effects of World War I

During World War I, the Ottoman Empire sided with Germany and the Central Powers. In 1916 two of the Allied Powers, Great Britain and France, made a secret agreement in which they divided up much of the Ottoman Empire should the Allies prove victorious. Britain would establish new governments in what was known as southern Syria and Mesopotamia (what became modern

Israel, Jordan, and Iraq); while France would establish new governments in northern Syria (what became modern Lebanon and Syria).

The agreement said nothing about a Jewish state. In the spring of 1917, Britain invaded and seized Palestine. Later that year, British Foreign Secretary Arthur Balfour announced that Britain endorsed the idea of a Jewish homeland in Palestine. This was the first declaration by a major world power in favor of the idea.

Following the war, both Arab and Zionist delegations made appeals to the delegates at the Paris Peace Conference, asking them to consider their desires in the post-war world. In 1922 the weak and defeated Ottoman government crumbled, and the modern nation of Turkey came into existence. Turkey agreed to the division of Syria that Britain and France had worked out. This arrangement was endorsed by the League of Nations in what was called a mandate system: France had the League's mandate to oversee Syria, and Great Britain had the League's mandate to oversee Palestine.

The mandate period in Palestine was extremely unstable. Thousands of Jews moved into the area, trusting British protection and anticipating the establishment of a Jewish homeland. The Jewish population of Palestine rose from less than 84,000 in 1922 to 608,000 in 1948. At the same time, non-Jewish residents in Palestine began actively protesting and resisting the rapid in-migration of Jews. Then Jewish nationalists, who wanted complete independence, began resisting the British presence in the hope of driving the British out and gaining control of the region.

In 1946 a bomb blast destroyed part of the King David Hotel in Jerusalem where British mandate offices were located. The group that planned the attack gave warnings by telephone, but British officials decided not to take any action. Ninety-one people of various nationalities were killed. The leader of the group responsible for the bombing was Menachem Begin, a future prime minister of Israel.

Modern Israel

Britain announced in 1947 that it would no longer be able to govern the region. The United Nations (UN) endorsed dividing Palestine into a Jewish state and an Arab state with Jerusalem as an international city administered by the UN. Jews accepted this endorsement of a state; and on May 14, 1948, the state of Israel was proclaimed. The United States was the first nation to recognize the new country, followed by the Soviet Union.

To the Arabs of Palestine and the surrounding area, the formation of a Jewish state was an insult and amounted to the taking of their land. The event fueled a growing distrust between Jews and Arabs. Thousands of Palestinian Arabs fled from their homes in the newly-formed country of Israel and became refugees in surrounding countries.

A civil war between Jews and Arabs in Palestine began even before the official declaration of independence. The day after the declaration, May 15, 1948, soldiers from Egypt, Jordan, Iraq, and Syria launched the first of several wars against Israel. Their stated goal was to drive Israel into the sea. However, Israel defeated the Arab armies and captured additional territory. Jordan meanwhile captured the area west of the Jordan River called the West Bank, including East Jerusalem; and Egypt took control of the Gaza territory or Gaza Strip, in the area once inhabited by Philistines.

In the 1967 Six Day War, Egypt, Syria, and Jordan again attacked Israel; but Israel again

Israeli Soldiers with Captured Arab Soldiers in Ramla, Israel, 1948

Lesson 142 - The Making of the Modern Middle East

> ## The Palestinians
>
> *Before the establishment of modern Israel, the term "Palestinian" was used to refer to people who lived in Palestine, whether they were Arabs or Jews. Since then it has come to be used almost exclusively to refer to the Arab residents of Israel, the West Bank, and the Gaza Strip.*
>
> *The Palestinian Liberation Organization (PLO) formed in 1964 with the goal of creating an independent State of Palestine. After years of tension and outbreaks of violence, in 1993 the State of Israel and the PLO each recognized the right of the other to exist. This led to the creation of the Palestinian National Authority.*
>
>
>
> *Yasser Arafat (1929-2004, shown at left in photo) was the first president of the Palestinian National Authority. In recognition of their combined efforts, Arafat along with Israeli Foreign Minister Shimon Peres (b. 1923, center) and Israeli President Yitzak Rabin (1922-1995, right) received the 1994 Nobel Peace Prize. Rabin was assassinated the next year by a fellow Israeli.*
>
> *In November 2012, the United Nations General Assembly voted to recognize the Palestinian National Authority as a non-member observer state (the same status given to Vatican City), and Palestinian leaders began to use State of Palestine as an official name.*

defeated its enemies. Israel captured the Gaza Strip from Egypt, the West Bank including East Jerusalem from Jordan, and the Golan Heights from Syria. The Israeli government began building settlements for Israelis in these areas. Israel annexed the Golan Heights in 1981, but the international community did not recognize this action. In later years Jewish settlements were built around East Jerusalem.

Egypt and Syria again attacked Israel on Yom Kippur (the Jewish Day of Atonement, the holiest day in the Jewish calendar) in 1973. Again Israeli forces pushed back the attackers. A cease-fire was declared after about three weeks of fighting. Many in the region began to long for peace. Israel and Egypt concluded a peace treaty in 1979, ending hostilities between the two countries. Israel and Jordan signed a peace agreement in 1994.

Since 1987 Palestinian Arabs have protested Israeli control over the West Bank and Gaza. Terrorists have attacked Israel and Israeli forces have entered the West Bank and Gaza. In 1988 Palestinian Arabs declared that a separate Arab state of Palestine existed, consisting of the West Bank and Gaza. About 120 nations have extended diplomatic recognition to Palestine, but at this point the United Nations has only given it observer status. Israel continues to restrict movement in the West Bank and Gaza.

Modern Israel is a religiously complex society with a secular government which does not attempt to follow the Old Testament laws. Some Jews in Israel observe few or none of the Jewish laws and festivals. Others attend synagogue and observe traditional rituals and customs. Israel's Orthodox Jews follow even stricter observances. Some Jews are Christians, believing in Jesus as God's promised Messiah. Most Arabs in Israel are Muslim, though a small minority are Christians.

Jerusalem

Jerusalem is important to Jews because King David established it as the capital of Israel (2 Samuel 5:5-9), and the Lord designated Jerusalem as the place where His temple was to be built (1 Kings 8:1-11). Jerusalem is important to Muslims because the Qur'an says that Muhammad ascended into heaven from the temple mount in Jerusalem for one night in 621. Muslims consider Jerusalem the third most sacred city in Islam, behind Mecca and Medina in Saudi Arabia. Muslims completed the Dome of the Rock in 691 and the Al-Aqsa Mosque a few years later, both on the site of the Jewish temple in Jerusalem. The photo above shows a Jordanian soldier on the left with Israeli policemen talking across a barbed wire fence in Jerusalem.

Today West Jerusalem is mostly Jewish, while East Jerusalem is mostly Arab Muslim. The UN resolution that called for statehood recognized and accepted this division. When the state of Israel was declared in 1948, the new country announced its capital to be Jerusalem. However, the Israeli government temporary located at Tel Aviv on the Mediterranean coast until the following year. Since the Israeli claim of Jerusalem as its capital goes against the international recognition of it as a neutral city, all foreign embassies to Israel are located in Tel Aviv. Palestinian Arabs, meanwhile, believe that Jerusalem should be the capital of their state. In other words, both Jews and Palestinians believe that Jerusalem is the capital of their respective homelands.

Israel has multiple political parties that span the political spectrum. The Palestinians also have several groups that have competed for leadership.

A key question in the Israeli-Palestinian conflict is, "Whose land is it?" Does the land belong to Israel because God gave it to His people centuries ago or because Israeli statehood was endorsed by the UN? Does the land belong to the Palestinians because Israel lost control of the land, because the Palestinians were living there when Israel was formed, or because the UN also endorsed Palestinian statehood?

Other Countries in the Region

Egypt

Though Egypt is geographically in Africa, it has close political and cultural ties to the Middle East. After the Suez Canal was completed in 1869, Great Britain seized control of Egypt's government in 1882. Egypt finally gained full independence in 1952. Egypt's third president, Anwar Sadat, concluded a peace treaty with Israel in 1979. He was assassinated in 1981 by people who opposed his peace efforts. Popular unrest in the Arab Spring movement led to the ouster of President Hosni Mubarak in 2011. Though Mohammed Morsi was elected president in 2012, the military removed him from office the next year and an interim government was put in place.

Iran

This country was known as Persia until 1935. In 1979 Islamist militants overthrew the ruling shah (or king) and established an Islamist theocracy led by a religious scholar and an elected council. Iranian students seized the American embassy in Tehran in November 1979 and held Americans as hostages until January 1981.

Iran has been developing nuclear technology, which it claims is only for peaceful purposes. The country is under strict economic sanctions set by the United Nations, the European Union, and

Lesson 142 - The Making of the Modern Middle East

the United States. Iran now holds elections for president and a consultative assembly as its national government, although a supreme theocratic leader is still chief of state. A relatively more moderate president, Hassan Rouhani, was elected in 2013.

Jordan

The area east of the Jordan River was part of the British mandate during the transition from the Ottoman Empire, hence it was called Transjordan. In 1946 the country gained independence from Britain as the Hashemite Kingdom of Jordan. Jordan gave up all claims to the West Bank region in 1988. King Hussein ruled from 1953 until his death in 1999. His son, Abdallah II, has instituted some democratic reforms.

Lebanon

After World War I, France defined the borders of Lebanon as a separate country from Syria. Lebanon, home to many political and religious groups, has seen significant instability since it gained independence in 1943. Lebanon is almost 40% Christian, the largest percentage of Christians among Middle Eastern countries. A civil war from 1975 to 1990 cost about 120,000 lives and caused extensive destruction. Syrian forces occupied some of the southern area of Lebanon from 1976 to 2005. Hezbollah, a militant Muslim group based in southern Lebanon, has had frequent clashes with Israeli troops.

Libya

This North African country has also played a part in issues in the Middle East. Italy ruled Libya from 1911 until the Italians surrendered in 1943 during World War II. Libya passed to UN oversight and gained independence in 1951. A military coup in 1969 brought Muammar al-Gaddafi to power as dictator. The Gaddafi government supported terrorist activities in what is called state-sponsored terrorism. In 2003 Libya admitted to this involvement and agreed to end the development of weapons of mass destruction.

In 2011 the Gaddafi government responded harshly to reform demonstrations and protests. This led to a civil war, which in turn resulted in UN-sponsored air and naval intervention against the government. Gadaffi was removed from power in August of 2011 when rebel forces captured the capital city of Tripoli.

The League of Arab States was founded in Cairo in 1945. It has twenty-two members. All are shown on this map except the island nation of Cormoros far to the south between the east coast of Africa and Madagascar.

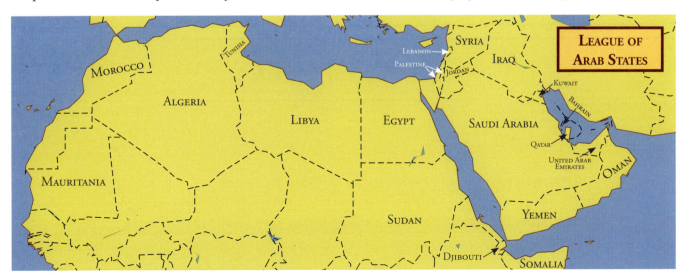

Gadaffi continued to be protected by loyal soldiers, but he was killed in a battle a few weeks later between his loyalists and soldiers of the transitional government. A new parliament and prime minister were elected in 2012. During a violent protest in the city of Benghazi on September 11, 2012, Islamist militants killed U.S. Ambassador Chris Stephens and three other Americans.

Saudi Arabia

In 1932 after thirty years of work, a member of the Saud family unified the lands of several local leaders on the Arabian peninsula into a single Kingdom of Saudi Arabia. The Saud family still rules the country, which is a leading producer of oil for world consumption. Saudi Arabia, birthplace of Islam, enforces a strict interpretation of Islamic Sharia law.

Syria

Syria was under French mandate until independence came in 1946. A series of political coups resulted in years of instability. From 1958 until 1961, it joined with Egypt in the United Arab Republic. In 1970 Hafiz al-Assad seized power in another coup. Following his death, his son Bashar al-Assad was affirmed as the country's ruler in a 2000 referendum. Anti-government protests erupted in 2011 as a growing number of Syrians demanded reforms. The protests grew into a civil war that claimed over 100,000 lives. The government was found to have used poison gas on rebels in 2013. In the face of a threatened attack by the United States, Syria agreed to hand over its supply of weapons of mass destruction to UN officials.

Conclusion

Christians face official and unofficial persecution in most Arab countries. However, the church continues to grow in small, underground communities of faith. The peace of Christ is the only solution that can heal deep-seated and long-term divisions between people.

Seek peace and pursue it.
Psalm 34:14

Assignments for Lesson 142

In Their Words — Read the Declaration of Establishment of State of Israel (pages 363-365).

Literature — Continue reading *Cry, the Beloved Country*.

Student Review — Optional: Answer the questions for Lesson 142.

Homeschooling in South Korea

Lesson 143 - Key Persons

The Homeschooling Family

An estimated one to two million children are homeschooled each year in the United States. The number is growing in the U.S. and in other countries around the world. A commitment by parents to train their children in the ways of the Lord is a crucial decision for the family. The decision to homeschool affects the family involved, and that family can have an impact on the society around them. Homeschooling families are key persons in the 21st century.

Who Are Homeschoolers?

Just as each person is unique, each family is unique. Each homeschooling family has its own particular setting, experiences, strengths, and weaknesses. Homeschoolers range from fervent disciples of Christ to fervent secularists and from strict conformists to social rebels.

Christian parents who homeschool are willing to take a bold step on the basis of their faith. Homeschooling requires considerable time and effort. Parents who homeschool risk suspicion and condemnation by others in the community. They take a risk by not training their children according to the typical method. They take this step and this risk because their faith leads them to do it. They accept God's admonition to train their children in His ways. Homeschooling parents are not the only people who take training their children for the Lord seriously, but this commitment is a strong motivation for many of those who homeschool.

Parents who homeschool are trying to put their child rearing and family responsibilities first. They want to make sure that they reach these goals, whatever else in life they might miss. Again, many non-homeschooling families make their home a high priority also, but homeschooling is how many families choose to live out their commitment to this priority.

Homeschoolers want to guide what their children learn. They choose not to leave the content of their children's education to the public school system, society, the media, or any other source. Christian homeschooling parents want good, uplifting, true, and godly perspectives to fill their children's minds and hearts.

This means protecting their children from harmful influences that can lead them away from the Lord. These parents know the value of their children, the potential for negative influences, and the relatively limited time they have to be

Homeschooling in South Africa

Does Homeschooling Work?

To answer the question of whether homeschooling works, we have to determine what goals homeschooling parents are trying to accomplish. The most commonly perceived goal for any kind of schooling is successful training in academic subjects. Statistics indicate that homeschooled students tend to score above the national average on standardized achievement tests and at or above the national average on college entrance exams. Evidence indicates that homeschoolers tend to get above average grades in their college coursework. Colleges, which once were skeptical about homeschoolers, now actively recruit them. Homeschooling, as a whole, works with regard to academics.

the primary influence on their children, so they seek to mold a child's heart and mind in the ways of God.

Some families homeschool to help their child accomplish more academically. A child may have special needs or particular interests that a public school cannot address. The motivation to homeschool can be not so much a reaction to public schools as it is a proactive decision by parents to do the best they can for their children.

A majority of the families who started homeschooling in the United States in the 1980s and 1990s did so with a desire to help their children grow up to be Christians. The influence of Christians in the homeschool movement is still significant, but parents who are not Christians also choose homeschooling to impart to their children their philosophical or religious framework.

Homeschooling families use a wide range of approaches to learning, including unit studies, traditional school textbooks, specialized curriculum (typical courses of study but with materials designed for homeschoolers), online courses, and video classes. Homeschooling families often organize cooperatives where parents or other adults teach art, music, science, and other subjects.

Parents also want their children to be able to relate well to others. One benefit of homeschooling is that children can spend time with people who are both older and younger, not just those of the same age level. This helps make children less dependent on peers and able to interact in a wide variety of social settings.

From God's perspective, whether homeschooling works involves how closely a homeschooled student walks with the Lord, how well he or she is a light for

Homeschooling in Guatemala

Lesson 143 - Key Persons: The Homeschooling Family

Homeschooling in Germany

the Way, and whether the student bears good fruit or bad fruit. These traits are difficult to quantify, but homeschooling families have every opportunity to give spiritual training top priority. They can also avoid some negative influences that pull people away from the Lord.

Homeschooling does not guarantee that a child will be adequately trained academically, successful in college, able to function well in society, spiritually mature, and happy and secure in his or her own home as an adult. These traits are developed in the home environment, and the success of homeschooling or any educational approach will largely depend on how strong the home is. Ultimately, no matter how good or bad his home environment is, each person must decide for himself whether or not he is going to work hard, be responsible, build good relationships, and honor the Lord with his life, both as a young person and as an adult.

Homeschooling in Uganda

Why Are Homeschooling Families Key Persons?

Homeschoolers who are able to communicate intelligently, work independently, and get along well with others serve as leaven in society. With a knowledge of history, they ask more questions and challenge previously unchallenged assumptions so they can make life better in our country and our world. With a strong moral foundation, they are an influence for godliness in the midst of a culture of ungodliness.

Our world faces many problems because of weak families, a lack of spiritual commitment, worldliness, and wasted lives. Many homeschooling families have dedicated themselves to doing better than what they see in the world around them. They encourage people to walk with the Lord, use their talents well, build strong homes, and contribute to society. This makes homeschooling families key persons.

*Give me your heart, my son,
And let your eyes delight in my ways.
Proverbs 23:26*

Assignments for Lesson 143

Literature — Continue reading *Cry, the Beloved Country*.

Student Review — Optional: Answer the questions for Lesson 143.

Bláa Kannan Café in Akureyri, Iceland

Lesson 144 - Everyday Life

A History of Keeping Time

The Bible has much to say about time. On the fourth day, God created lights in the expanse of the heavens. He declared them to be for signs and for seasons and for days and years. Amos 5:8 teaches that God changes deep darkness into morning and darkens day into night. The righteous meditate on the law of the Lord day and night (Psalm 1:1-2).

Jewish time gave twelve hours to every day from sunrise to sunset (John 11:9). Midday was whenever the sun was highest in the sky. The Lord taught that our worry cannot add one hour to our lives (Matthew 6:27) and that we must not worry about tomorrow (Matthew 6:34). Jesus told a parable about a wedding where the bridegroom came at midnight (Matthew 25:1-13). He taught about being ready at the second watch or the third (Luke 12:38).

In the early morning when it was still dark, Jesus went away to pray (Mark 1:35). When evening came, Jesus' disciples went down to the sea (John 6:16). During the fourth watch of the night, Jesus walked on the water (Matthew 14:25). People would get up early in the morning to listen to Jesus at the temple (Luke 21:38). Jesus was crucified at the third hour (Mark 15:25). Jesus appeared to Saul (Paul) about noon (Acts 22:6-8).

When Jesus was on the cross, darkness fell upon all the land from the sixth hour until the ninth hour (Matthew 27:45). About the ninth hour, Jesus cried out (Matthew 27:46).

God sent Jesus at just the right time—when the time was fulfilled (Mark 1:15), when the fullness of the time came (Galatians 4:4). The prophets had wondered when the time of the coming of the Messiah would be (1 Peter 1:10-12). We must make the most of our time (Ephesians 5:16). God will exalt the humble at the proper time (1 Peter 5:6). We do not know the time that Jesus will return (Mark 13:33-37). He does not know either, but our Father does (Matthew 24:36).

Since the beginning, people have been using the lights of the heavens to determine times, days, seasons, and years. Some people groups in history, including the Jews, have used cycles of the moon to measure time; but most people today measure time using the cycles of the sun. Our day is based on the rotation of the earth, and our week has seven of these days. Our year is approximately 365 ¼ days long because that is how long it takes the earth to orbit the sun. People have invented instruments to measure the passage of time during the day and calendars to measure the years.

Ancient Clocks

Ancient Egyptians, Greeks, and Romans used water clocks or clepsydra (from the Greek *kleptein* meaning "to steal" and *hydor* meaning "water"). They were in use by 1400 BC in Alexandria, Egypt. Water flowed from one container to another through a small opening. Hours were marked on either the receiving container or the one from which the water came. In ancient Athens the length of orations and speeches were timed by a clepsydra. Around 270 BC Ctesibius of Alexandria invented a water clock with gears.

The gnomon, or shadow clock, was another ancient time keeper. It is a stick or obelisk stuck vertically in the ground. An eighth century BC shadow clock from Egypt is still in existence. By around 700 BC, Egyptians had sundials. Anaximander, who lived around 600 BC, is credited with introducing the sundial to Greece. Chaldean astronomer Berossus described a sundial about the third century BC. Ptolemy, who lived in the second century AD, applied his knowledge of trigonometry to sundials.

The Chinese measured time by burning a knotted rope and watching how long it took the fire to go from knot to knot. Notched candles were also used in this way. An hourglass has two glass containers connected by a narrow neck and filled with a liquid or grainy substance, usually sand. When the device is turned upright, the sand flows from one container into the other in one hour.

Al-Jazari (1136-1206) was a Middle Eastern scholar. He left instructions and drawings for a variety of mechanical devices, including the elephant clock, shown at left, that featured a chirping bird and a human figure striking a cymbal every half hour. A modern replica of the clock, shown below, is on display at the Ibn Battuta Mall in Dubai, United Arab Emirates.

Lesson 144 - Everyday Life: A History of Keeping Time

At right above is an opening from Christiaan Huygens' 1673 book Horologium Oscillatorium *showing his design for a pendulum clock. At left above is a clock built using his design.*

Mechanical Clocks

Around 1300 Europeans began to develop mechanical clocks that had to be reset using a sundial. They kept only hours and therefore had only one hand. In the late 1300s, German clockmakers began to experiment with alarm clocks. A monastery clock from a Nuremberg monastery dates from around 1380. It has raised knobs on its dials. Using the raised knobs, monks could read the time with their fingers in the dark and use the bell alarm to rise in time for morning prayers.

Early mechanical clocks were heavy. Henry De Vick, a German, built a clock for the Palais de Justice in Paris during the 1300s. The clock was powered by a 500-pound weight that fell 32 feet. The word clock originally meant bell and was used for time-measuring devices placed in the bell towers of churches.

In the late 1500s, Galileo described the property of the pendulum that makes its swing constant, called isochronism. In 1656 Christiaan Huygens, a Dutch scientist, designed the first practical pendulum clock using the principle described by Galileo (see photo above). It was accurate to within five minutes a day. The pendulum clock was improved by three Britons: physicist Robert Hooke, clockmaker George Graham, and carpenter John Harrison.

Many early clocks were highly decorative. Cuckoo clocks have been made in Germany's Black Forest since the 1730s. Some early English clocks were shaped like lanterns or birdcages. In America in the 1800s, cabinetmakers made the wooden housing for clock mechanisms purchased from clockmakers. In the early 1900s, ornate wooden shelf clocks called kitchen clocks were popular.

Longcase clocks that stood on the floor were introduced by Englishman William Clement in the 1670s. After Henry Clay Work wrote the song "Grandfather's Clock" in 1875, people began to refer to a tall wooden cabinet clock with a long pendulum as a grandfather clock.

American Henry E. Warren invented the electric clock in the early 1900s. The quartz clock, using vibrating quartz crystals, was invented in the 1920s. The cesium atomic clock was developed in 1955 in England.

This cuckoo clock, built in 1997 in Triberg, Germany, claims to be the world's largest. Visitors can go inside the clock to see the inner workings.

Unit 29 - Into the 21st Century

Relojes Centenario, a company founded by Alberto Olvera Hernández, in Zacatlán, Mexico, has been building large clocks for churches and commercial facilities since the 1910s. A museum at the company headquarters has original and replica examples of historical timepieces. The universal clock created by Centenario, pictured at left, displays the time in major cities around the world simultaneously.

Watches

German Peter Henlein (c. 1485-1542) was a locksmith and clockmaker. After experimenting for ten years, in 1510 he made one of the first portable clocks. It used the coiled spring which had been invented in Italy about 1450. In 1675 Christiaan Huygens improved the watch. Using a balance wheel, his was accurate to within two minutes per day.

Watches were usually shaped like balls or drums. They were kept in a pocket or hung from a belt. In the

As long-distance travel and communication increased in the 19th-century, time zones were introduced to coordinate timekeeping in different places.

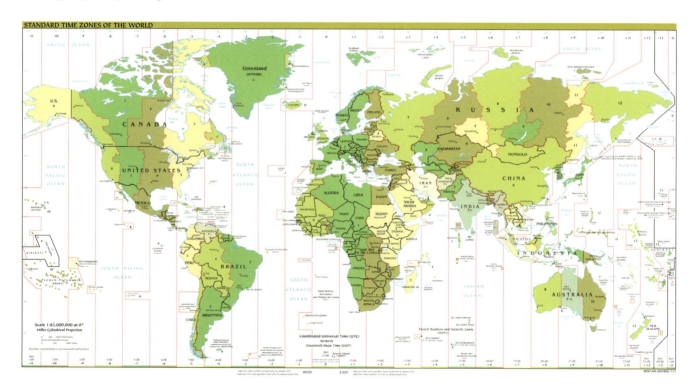

Lesson 144 - Everyday Life: A History of Keeping Time

This timekeeping device from about 1510 is attributed to Peter Henlein.

1700s, villages in the Jura Mountains of Switzerland became the center of watchmaking. Families made watch parts at home. They were then assembled and sold by master watchmakers.

Pocket watches were the most common portable clock until wristwatches became popular after World War I. The first electronic watch with a digital display went on sale in 1972. The gold-cased watch had a price tag of $2,100. Within a few years, electronic watches were available for less than $10.

Calendars

Ancient Babylonians used a lunisolar calendar. It had twelve months of thirty days each. When needed, they added extra months to keep the seasons and years in line. The Egyptians used a solar calendar of twelve months with thirty days each and five extra days at the end of the year. King Ptolemy III made a decree in 238 BC that an extra day be added every fourth year. The Greek calendar had 354 days. They made scientific calculations to determine when they should add months to stay on the solar year cycle.

When Julius Caesar came to power, the Romans had used a 365-day calendar for so long that the seasons did not come at their proper times. Caesar reformed the calendar by adding eighty days to one year to make up the error and a leap day every four years to keep the calendar regular. The seventh month was named July for Julius Caesar in 44 BC. The eighth month was named August for Augustus Caesar in 8 BC. September, October, November, and December, the seventh, eighth, ninth, and tenth months in the old Roman calendar, are now the ninth through twelfth months.

The Julian calendar served Europe until the 1500s, when Pope Gregory made another change. The Julian year was eleven minutes and fourteen seconds too long. By 1582 the vernal equinox was off by ten days. Roman Catholic Church holidays were not occurring in the right seasons. Pope Gregory XIII decreed that ten days be dropped from the calendar one year.

To avoid giving special recognition to Sunday, from 1929 to 1940 the Soviet Union experimented with continuous cycles of five- and six-day work weeks. However, the Soviets continued to use the Gregorian calendar, and they retained the traditional Russian names for the days of the week: "Resurrection" for the first day and "Sabbath" for the last day. In 1940 the Soviets returned to a seven-day cycle, with Sunday as the common day off.

Y2K

In the 20th century, computer programs were generally designed to use two digits to designate a year instead of four (75 instead of 1975, for example). As the year 2000 approached, people thought that some computers might read the year 00 as 1900. Because computers control much modern technology, concerns were expressed about power grids malfunctioning, transportation systems shutting down, and other potential disasters. Fortunes were made off of people's fears. Many Americans moved from cities to the country, installed wood stoves, stockpiled food, and stored water. Corporations and governments spent billions of dollars to fix Y2K (Year 2000) computer problems. For the most part, the expensive computer fixes worked; and the change from 1999 to 2000 went smoothly. (The photo above of a French sign was taken on January 3, 2000.) The transition from 2009 to 2010 caused a few glitches, but the world should be safe from major computer date crises until the year has five digits—the year 10,000.

European countries began to adopt the Gregorian calendar. Riots occurred in England and America when the British adopted it in 1752. Some people thought that eleven days of their lives were being stolen. Many countries associated with the Eastern Orthodox Church still use the Julian calendar for Church feasts. The Gregorian calendar is sometimes called the Christian calendar because it begins with the traditional year of the birth of Jesus.

The Aztecs used two calendar systems, one with 260 days and one with 365. January 1, 2000 began the year 4697 in the Chinese calendar. The Jewish calendar has remained constant since about 900. The beginning date is 3761 BC, which is considered to be the year the world was created. The Jewish calendar is the official calendar of Israel. The Islamic calendar begins with the year 622 AD, when Muhammad migrated from Mecca to Medina.

He has made everything appropriate in its time.
Ecclesiastes 3:11

Assignments for Lesson 144

Literature — Continue reading *Cry, the Beloved Country*.

Student Review — Optional: Answer the questions for Lesson 144.

Farming Workshop in Kenya for Methodist and Presbyterian Church Members

Lesson 145 - Bible Study

Modern Church History

In this lesson we survey some of the major developments in church history during recent centuries: the rise of evangelicals, mission work around the world, and trends in the 21st century.

The Wesleys and Evangelicalism

While Charles Wesley was at Oxford University in the early 1700s, he started the Holy Club to encourage greater devotion to God. Members committed themselves to regular personal devotions and met for Bible study and prayer. Jeering students called the group Methodists for their strict method of spiritual discipline. John, Charles' older brother, returned to Oxford as a fellow at Lincoln College and assumed leadership of the club.

John and Charles Wesley were ordained as ministers of the Church of England. In 1737 they went to the British colony of Georgia in America. While on that trip they met a group of Moravians, whose deep and simple devotion to God impressed them. Upon their return to England, the Wesley brothers experienced a conviction of the need to spread the gospel in Britain. Sometimes they preached in church buildings, but more often they preached in market places or in open-air settings.

This was a shocking departure from normal Anglican practice, but the Wesleys drew large crowds of people from all walks of life, including the growing numbers of factory workers. To help converts mature in their faith, John organized small groups or societies that met regularly for Bible study and prayer. John practiced and taught others to practice circuit-riding, by which evangelists traveled thousands of miles on horseback to preach. Charles became one of the world's great hymn writers. He is credited with writing over 7,000 hymns, many of which are still widely used today.

The Wesleys intended for their work to remain within the Church of England. However, the growth of the movement, especially in revolutionary America where the Church of England was not highly valued, led to an eventual separation from Anglicanism. The Methodist Church was formed, which eventually spread around the world.

The work of John and Charles Wesley is widely regarded as the beginning of Evangelicalism. The First and Second Great Awakenings (mid-1700s and early 1800s, respectively) in the United States were also key developments in this movement.

841

Evangelicals emphasize evangelistic preaching and teaching to encourage people to be converted to Jesus Christ as Savior and Lord. They strongly believe in the authority of the Bible, the centrality of Jesus and the cross to the Christian faith, and the need for Christians to live transformed lives. These emphases are different from churches that focus on ritual over preaching in their services and that are generally not as evangelistic but depend on the children of members growing up to become members themselves. The United States and Brazil are two countries that have the highest number of Evangelicals.

Missions and Societies

European believers took the message of Christ to parts of the world in which the gospel was not known during and after the Age of Exploration. For example, Spanish Catholics established missions in Central and South America, what became the western United States, and the Philippines. French Catholics established missions in Canada, Louisiana, and Southeast Asia. Dutch Protestants took the message of Christ to South Africa and Sri Lanka.

Christians from Great Britain played a major role in 19th-century world missions. Anglicans

Orthodox Churches

After Constantinople became the second capital of the Roman Empire, the Bishop of Constantinople became the leader of a fellowship that grew increasingly distinct from the Roman Catholic Church. This fellowship came to be known as the Orthodox Church or the Eastern Orthodox Church. Its leader came to be called the patriarch.

Over time, many Orthodox Churches were established in Eastern Europe, often identified with particular nations. Among these are Greek Orthodox, Ukrainian Orthodox, Romanian Orthodox, and several others. Orthodox Churches generally recognize the current Ecumenical Patriarch of Constantinople as the first among equals of Orthodox bishops, but he does not exercise the same authority over Orthodox Churches that the pope does over the Roman Catholic Church.

Prince Vladimir of Russia converted to the Christian faith in 988, and Orthodoxy became Russia's established Church. As Russia grew in power and influence, Russians began to see the capital of Moscow as the third Rome, after Rome itself and Constantinople. Russians believed that they deserved a patriarch to head their Church. In 1589 the head of the Russian Orthodox Church was declared a patriarch.

The Russian Orthodox patriarch was intimately involved with the Russian czar in the political life of the nation; in other words, church and state were strongly united. During the years of Soviet Communism, the Orthodox Church was a special target of hatred, and many Orthodox Church buildings were closed, turned into museums, or used for other secular purposes. After the fall of Communism in the late 20th century, the Russian Orthodox Church reclaimed what it saw as its proper role in Russian society, although it does not have the same intimacy with the current government of Russia as it did in czarist days.

Shown above is a Bulgarian Orthodox Church in Sofia, Bulgaria (c. 16th century).

Erik Jansson (1845-1931, left) was a Swedish Baptist who went to Brazil as a missionary in 1912.

had formed the Society for the Propagation of the Gospel in 1701. Other denominations also formed missionary societies, which became the most common model for carrying out mission work. People who wanted to become missionaries applied to a society. When they were accepted, the society provided financial support and oversaw the work of the missionaries. In the 19th and 20th centuries, thousands of Americans also devoted themselves to mission work.

Christians sought to make Bibles and other printed teaching materials available to believers around the world. The British and Foreign Bible Society was begun in 1804 to print and distribute materials. The American Bible Society began in 1816, with the goal of distributing Scriptures to pioneers in the American West, immigrants, and Native American tribes. Bible societies formed in other countries as well. In 1946 representatives from several of these organizations formed a cooperative group, United Bible Societies (UBS). One accomplishment of the UBS is the publication of a standard text of the Greek New Testament that is widely used by students and translators.

At the beginning of the 1800s, the Scriptures had been translated into sixty-eight languages. According to 2012 statistics from the Wycliffe Global Alliance, the complete Bible is now available in 518 languages. The New Testament has been published in 1,275 additional languages, and speakers of 1,005 other languages have access to at least one book of the Bible. About 700 languages, spoken by a total of almost one hundred million people, do not have any known translation of the Scriptures. Wycliffe Global Alliance is a network of organizations that make new translations of the Bible available in print, audio, and video formats for people in isolated language groups.

This photo from Wycliffe Global Alliance shows a translation team in the Democratic Republic of Congo.

Into the 21st Century

The 19th century saw a remarkable expansion of the Christian faith. In addition to the mission work mentioned earlier, this period saw the ministries of such powerful preachers as British Baptist Charles H. Spurgeon in England and such effective evangelists as Charles Finney and Dwight Moody in the United States. This century was also the time of a number of well-known hymn writers, such as Frances Ridley Havergal in Britain and Fanny J. Crosby in the U.S. Campaigns to abolish slavery in the British Empire and the United States were led by believers, including William Wilberforce in Britain and Frederick Douglass in the U.S.

In the 20th century, two world wars, the rise of Communism and Naziism, and the growing acceptance of secular and relativistic thought brought new challenges to the Christian faith. Active church membership in Western countries generally declined during the century. And yet, as in every century since the time of Christ, God's people showed remarkable faith in the face of difficult times.

The 20th century saw the rise of large Christian publishing, Christian music, and Christian broadcasting industries in the United States. The writings of C. S. Lewis alone sold millions of copies. Through live crusades, TV, and radio, American evangelist Billy Graham might have preached Christ to more people than any other person in history.

As the 21st century began, about 2.2 billion people in the world considered themselves Christians. Roman Catholicism was the largest branch of Christendom, with an estimated 1.2 billion adherents. Some 1.6 billion people were Muslims.

For many generations, denominational loyalty was a major factor in Christian life. Most people who were reared in a particular denomination remained members of that denomination as adults. However, in more recent years many Christians have left the denominations of their youth and joined other churches. The number of non-denominational, independent, community, and Bible churches, as well as house churches, has increased.

The world has entered what many call the post-modern or post-Christian era. Many people question long-accepted truths and traditional teachings and are skeptical of the benefits of the modern age. Many see truth as being relative for each individual.

In some ways, the 21st century bears striking similarities to the first century AD. Christianity is not the dominant worldview in western society.

Pentecostalism developed in the late 1800s and early 1900s. It emphasized a belief in the active work of the Holy Spirit, including the manifestation of miraculous signs such as healings and speaking in tongues (other languages). Pentecostal denominations include the Assemblies of God, the International Circle of Faith, and the United Pentecostal Church International. Pentecostal churches have seen significant growth in China, Africa, and Latin America (see photo below). Charismatic is a term for Christians in other denominations who hold beliefs similar to Pentecostals. By the early 2000s, the number of Pentecostals and charismatics around the world was estimated to be over 500 million.

Lesson 145 - Bible Study: Modern Church History

Sharon Pastre, a woman from Singapore, worked in Hong Kong. After visiting the Philippines and seeing the extreme poverty there, she founded International Care Ministries in 1992. ICM provides ongoing humanitarian services. In partnership with Feed My Starving Children, ICM was in a position to distribute food within days of the 2013 typhoon in the Philippines.

Immorality has become more acceptable. Just as unwanted babies were cast out by first-century parents, today in countries such as Germany and South Korea, baby boxes are placed outside of hospitals and clinics for parents to place children they do not want to parent.

Despite the discouraging news, God is still on the throne. He is in charge, He knows what He is doing, and His timing is perfect. Jesus is still Lord. Christians are still doing remarkable things by their faith in God. When calamity strikes, Christians are generous with their time and money. People are being brought to Christ, and families are living faithfully, some in very difficult circumstances. From the time of Adam and Eve's sin, the world has been less than what Christians would like it to be. This is because God's people do not in the final analysis belong here. Christians are committed to and bound for a better place.

As we feel concern about the negative influences on Christians, the church, and the world in general during the last two hundred years, we need to remember that human beings have the ability to choose. No one forces people to believe evolution, higher critical thinking, or atheism. Just because a book is published does not mean that people have to believe what it says. A world characterized by paganism and anti-Christian bias did not kill the church in the first century AD. Instead, Christians convinced people of the truth of their message.

Christian Unity

Since the Protestant Reformation, the number of Christian denominations has grown exponentially. Christians have often tended to focus on their differences rather than on what they have in common. Recent decades have seen the rise of parachurch organizations such as Campus Crusade for Christ, Prison Fellowship, and Teen Challenge. These ministries are separate from any one particular church or denomination, and they are often supported by believers from many different denominations. Christians from various backgrounds also work together through disaster relief organizations, agencies that serve families and children, and medical mission groups.

These are positive examples of how Christians work together for the cause of Christ. Those of us who are Christians in the 21st century should continue to evaluate ourselves to ensure that we are sharing the gospel in effective ways and backing up our message with holy lives. We do not want the world to see the church as a dysfunctional group of jealous and critical busybodies. Instead we want to show a united group of people who want to communicate and demonstrate the love of God.

I do not ask on behalf of these alone, but for those also who believe in Me through their word; that they may all be one; even as You, Father, are in Me and I in You, that they also may be in Us, so that the world may believe that You sent Me.
John 17:20-21

Assignments for Lesson 145

- **Bible** — Recite or write Proverbs 23:24-25 from memory.
- **In Their Words** — Read the hymns by Charles Wesley (pages 366-367).
- **Literature** — Finish reading *Cry, the Beloved Country*. Literary analysis available in *Student Review*.
- **Project** — Complete your project for the unit.
- **Student Review** — Optional: Answer the questions for Lesson 145 and for *Cry, the Beloved Country*, and take the quiz for Unit 29.

30

Looking Backward, Looking Forward

Summary In this closing unit we look at several issues related to history, faith, and today's world. After reviewing the impact of Christianity, we consider lessons that we can learn from world history. We discuss the challenge of living as a Christian in today's world and being aware of the world's continuing need for Christ. Finally, the Bible study reminds us that this world will not last forever. A better world is coming.

Lessons
Lesson 146 - How Christianity Changed the World
Lesson 147 - Lessons from World History
Lesson 148 - Living in the Modern World
Lesson 149 - Becoming a World Christian
Lesson 150 - Bible Study: Eternity After This World

Old and New in Sarajevo, Bosnia and Herzegovina

Memory Work Learn Isaiah 40:29-31 by the end of the unit.

Books Used The Bible
In Their Words
The Abolition of Man

Project (choose one)

1) Write 300 to 500 words on one of the following topics:
   - Write about some lessons you have learned from this study of world history and what you would like to study further.
   - Write an essay in response to *The Abolition of Man* about the need to recognize absolutes and how modern education and other institutions are tearing away at the acceptance of those absolutes.
2) Take a family field trip to an organization in your community that exists to serve people in the name of Christ. Take a tour of their facility and find out how your family can get involved.
3) Create a collection of photos showing evidence of worldview, both Christian and non-Christian, around your community. See Lesson 148. Compose your photos intentionally and artistically. Your finished project should be in the form of a slideshow on an electronic device, prints of the photographs displayed on a poster, or photos in book form. Include a minimum of fifteen photos.

Literature

Clive Staples Lewis was born in 1898 in Northern Ireland. His family were nominal members of the Church of England, but Lewis abandoned his faith as a young man. He was wounded in World War I and attended Oxford University. Lewis later accepted a teaching position in Medieval Literature at Oxford and became widely respected for his academic ability. He taught at Cambridge University later in life.

Lewis became friends with several believers at Oxford, including J. R. R. Tolkien (of *The Lord of the Rings* fame), who helped him regain his faith. In the 1930s, Lewis began writing and speaking in defense of the Christian faith. Lewis wrote many books and essays before his death in 1963. Children (and adults) enjoy the seven books in the *Chronicles of Narnia* series. *The Screwtape Letters* portray a man's struggle with temptation and sin from the point of view of Satan's agents who do the tempting. Lewis also wrote a science fiction trilogy that presents Christian truths in that literary genre. Many of Lewis' letters have been published, and a host of books have been written about him.

The Abolition of Man is based on a series of lectures Lewis gave in 1943 on a subject he believed to be of great importance. Lewis was responding to the modern trend of denying the reality of absolutes, such as good and bad, right and wrong. He points out that such absolutes are part of the fabric of our world. Denying them is (1) impossible, since the critics are only setting up another set of absolutes, and (2) harmful, since it leads to people making decisions that are not grounded in a sense of right and wrong.

Inuit Christian Cemetery in Greenland

Lesson 146

How Christianity Changed the World

When Augustus Caesar died in 14 AD, there were no Christians in the world. On the whole, the world was pagan. Pagan temples were the norm in cities throughout the Roman Empire. The people who lived in Europe, Asia, Africa, and the Americas were also almost all pagans.

The thought world was pagan. Most people lived by the belief that many gods populated the heavens. In this view, humans were the pawns of gods that for the most part cared little about mere mortals. People were only a by-product or an afterthought of the actions of the deities. Immorality was not only tolerated but was even encouraged by some belief systems.

One nation, Israel, had been given a detailed knowledge of God and had a relationship with Him. But relatively few people living at that time had a concept of the one true God.

The Teacher

Less than twenty years after Augustus died, a disturbance took place in a corner of the Roman Empire called Judea. A teacher arose among the Jews and said some amazing things. For instance, He told His followers:

> *You are the salt of the earth; but if the salt has become tasteless, how can it be made salty again? It is no longer good for anything, except to be thrown out and trampled under foot by men. You are the light of the world. A city set on a hill cannot be hidden; nor does anyone light a lamp and put it under a basket, but on the lampstand, and it gives light to all who are in the house. Let your light shine before men in such a way that they may see your good works, and glorify your Father who is in heaven. (Matthew 5:13-16)*

Think about His amazing perspective that this little group of people in this far-off corner of the Empire was the salt of the earth and the light of the world!

The Followers

After this teacher, Jesus, had been crucified and raised from the dead, He commissioned His

849

disciples to go into all the world and proclaim the good news that He had provided a way for the world to be reconciled to God (Matthew 28:19-20). While thousands of people accepted this life-changing message of love, service, and self-sacrifice, the existing power structures in Israel and later in the Roman Empire felt threatened by it and tried to destroy it. The small band of believers was attacked time after time throughout the Empire. Emperor Nero blamed Christians for starting a huge fire in Rome, and the persecution of this group began on a large scale. Roman authorities regularly demanded that Christians recant their faith; if the Christians refused, they were sometimes thrown to the lions in the Colosseum. Persecutions in the Roman Empire continued in varying degrees of intensity for almost three hundred years.

It would have been easy for the members of this group to scatter and give up. But they didn't give up. Christians took their role as the salt of the earth and the light of the world seriously. They were the leaven of positive influence. People saw something in the Way of Jesus that was worth living for and worth dying for. The gospel created a transformed people. Those people were empowered by God, and within a generation they began to change the world. The church grew quickly, and it has not stopped.

The Impact

History shows us many ways in which the influence of Christianity changed how people around the world lived and thought.

The Value of Children. In Greek and Roman cultures, which are often held up today as great civilizations, infanticide was commonplace. If a father did not want a child that had been born to him, whether the child was handicapped, female, or simply unwanted, the child was often either put to death or abandoned in the streets. Abandoned children many times were picked up and sold into slavery. In some pagan cultures, children were offered as human sacrifices to the gods. Germanic tribes also routinely rid themselves of unwanted children. Abortion was common in the Roman Empire.

Christians, however, had a different view of children because Jesus had taught them the value of children (Mark 10:13-16). Believers rescued and reared children who had been abandoned. Early Christians wrote in opposition to abortion. As Christianity spread and people were converted to Jesus, the world became a safer place for children.

The Value of Adults. As bad as our culture is, we have not yet stooped to the level of thousands of people attending the battle of two men who fight each other to the death. This kind of gladiatorial combat was common in the Roman Empire. Sometimes men fought each other, and sometimes a man was pitted against a wild animal. Our shock at this practice is an indication of the influence of Christianity on our thinking.

Slavery was commonplace in the Roman Empire. The influence of Christianity led to the gradual ending of slavery in Europe in the centuries

Joni Eareckson Tada became a quadriplegic confined to a wheelchair as a seventeen-year-old. She leads the Joni and Friends International Disability Center. One of their ministries is providing wheelchairs for disabled children and adults around the world.

Lesson 146 - How Christianity Changed the World

following Christ. Slavery entered the West again centuries later, and in the 1800s Christians again led the fight to have it abolished. Slavery has never completely gone away, however; the fight against forced labor and human trafficking continues today.

Prisoners had no rights in the ancient world. If a prisoner received any food or care, friends or relatives had to provide it for him from outside of the prison. The practice of crucifixion is evidence enough that Rome cared nothing about the rights of prisoners. The humane treatment of prisoners was another result of the growing influence of the Christian view of the worth of human beings, even people who had been convicted of crimes.

The Value of Women. In Jesus' day, women had few legal rights. They usually could not own property in their names. A woman's testimony was not admitted in a court of law. A wife had no rights if a man wanted to divorce her. Women were rarely even seen in public in Rome or Athens.

Jesus treated women differently. He dealt with them with respect and honor, treating them as fellow humans when many men considered them little more than property. The church continued to treat women with respect. The large number of women named in the New Testament is an indication of the important role that women played in the early church.

In India a standard practice of the Hindus was suttee, in which a widow was expected to throw herself onto the funeral pyre of her dead husband. If she showed any reluctance to do this, others took it upon themselves to throw her onto the pyre. The influence of Christians in India significantly lessened this practice. Christian influence in China also ended the painful practice of binding the feet of girls.

Morality and Marriage. In pagan cultures, immorality was rampant. In Greece and Rome, homosexuality was openly practiced and accepted.

The Christian Care Centre in the Solomon Islands, run by Anglican nuns, provides a refuge for victims of domestic violence and other abuse.

Marriage was seen as being of little value beyond the procreation of the next generation. Jesus brought a profound revolution in sexual morality and in the honor given to marriage. When Jesus said that looking at a woman lustfully was the same as adultery, when He said unfaithfulness was the only valid reason for a divorce, and when, through Paul's letters, He told husbands to love their wives, these were startling teachings that seriously challenged the accepted practices of the day.

Care for the Sick. In the ancient world, the poor were overlooked and the handicapped were rejected. Medical care, such as it existed, was usually available only for the wealthy. No government programs provided assistance to those who could not provide for themselves. Jesus' encounters with blind and lame beggars indicate how they were consigned to the lowest and least respected places in society.

Once again the influence of Christianity changed the way people responded to those in need. We read in Acts how the first Christians provided for widows and took up collections for the poor. History tells us that the church in later times cared for the sick, fed the hungry, helped widows and orphans, clothed the poor, and provided hospitality to strangers. During times of plague, when those who could do so usually fled from towns that were

Watoto is a community in Uganda founded to serve children who have lost one or both parents to AIDS or war. Children from the community have toured the world as part of the Watoto Children's Choir. Their stories, songs, and dances raise awareness of the needs of African children.

struck by a plague, Christians were known to be the people who stayed and cared for the victims.

The founder of the International Red Cross, Jean Henry Dunant of Switzerland, was a devout believer who witnessed extreme suffering on a battlefield. He resolved to do something to help wounded soldiers. In 1863 Dunant and others founded the organization that became the International Red Cross. The symbol for the organization was the Swiss flag in reverse, a red cross on a white background. The use of the cross was significant because the cross of Christ was significant to Dunant.

Education, Work, and Art. Christianity transformed education. Schools existed for the privileged few in the ancient world, but the first modern universities were founded for the purpose of theological training. Reformation leaders Martin Luther and John Calvin encouraged the establishment of public schools to teach children how to read, so that people could read the Bible. Christians in England began Sunday Schools to teach children who worked in factories six days per week. These first Sunday Schools taught academic subjects as well as the Bible.

The impetus for the Scientific Revolution was the belief that God is rational, that His universe is orderly, and that His works can be known. Seeking to understand the science of the universe was seen as a way to give glory to God.

The Christian belief in the worth of the individual influenced several areas of life. In economics, the result of this belief was free enterprise capitalism, a marketplace where individuals and businesses competed with each other without interference from the government. People came to believe that society and the economy did not have to be top-down operations, controlled by those with power. Martin Luther encouraged the idea that anyone's work—not just service within the church—is a calling and should be performed to honor God. The concepts of political freedom and the legitimacy of democracy were the result of Christianity's belief in the value of the individual.

Much medieval art and architecture, and much classical music, were created for the glory of God. The English language has been profoundly influenced by the words and phrases that were used in the King James Bible.

Christians have not done everything right. Christian people re-introduced slavery into the West around 1600. For many years European and American Christians refused to give women and people of other ethnic groups equal rights. The record of Western (Christian) nations administering colonies included the exploitation of people and natural resources. Overall, however, the long-term story has been that Christians have changed the world for the better because Christ gave people a transformed view of themselves, others, and the world around them. As Christians have acted on these beliefs, the world has been changed.

Lesson 146 - How Christianity Changed the World

Jesus did not come with a primary motive of making changes in health care, the economic system, the political system, education, or any other given field of human endeavor. He called people to become His disciples. As people became His disciples, however, their changed hearts led them to make changes for the better for themselves and in the lives of those around them. The vast majority of positive changes in the social, economic, and political realms in the last two thousand years have come about not because of Buddhism, Islam, Taoism, paganism, or secularism but because of Christianity.

Role Reversal

After Jesus returned to the Father, Rome was the great world power. Christianity was a tiny band of peace-loving people who claimed allegiance to One who had been executed by the Romans as a criminal. For years the movement of Christ-followers was technically illegal and was the target of numerous periods of persecution. The mighty Roman Empire fell a few centuries later, but the little band survived and grew. The Roman Empire is now consigned to history, but that little group is now a world-wide movement. The church is an eternal kingdom that survives today and will last into eternity. Few would have thought this possible in Jesus' day.

This reversal is illustrated by the 2008 concert of the European singing group Il Divo at a coliseum in Croatia that was built by Romans. During the concert, the group sang "Amazing Grace." Centuries before, Christians were put to death in the Colosseum in Rome. Yet in 2008 a Christian song was sung in the ruins of another Roman coliseum.

Tristan da Cunha is the most remote inhabited island in the world. It has two churches—St. Mary's Anglican Church and St. Joseph's Catholic Church, pictured below. Members have an annual unity service which alternates from year to year between the two buildings. The motto of the island is "Our faith is our strength."

What This Means for Us

The impact of Christianity on the world is relevant to our situation today. We live in a world in which human life is cheap. Innocent people are blown up to make political statements; abortion has become accepted; homosexuality is increasingly not just accepted but openly promoted. Marriage and Biblical morality are ridiculed. The Christian consensus that our society once accepted is now largely abandoned. Even paganism is becoming more accepted. We are told that believing one religion is right and others are wrong is intolerant. Christians are facing active, physical persecution in some parts of the world; and we even see increasing opposition to the practice of Christianity in the nation whose motto is "In God We Trust."

The response that Christians make to our situation today can be guided by our first century spiritual forefathers. The first century world was not transformed by Christians sponsoring voter registration drives, forming political action groups, or lobbying the Roman Senate. Some Christians today have the opportunity to serve in public office, and Christians should certainly use their freedoms and the opportunities God gives them to work for good and the honor of God. However, the overall response by the church to our cultural situation today should be the same as those early Christians: living our lives as salt, light, and leaven. This is how the first century world was changed, and it is how the world will be changed today. Jesus is still the Savior. He is still worth living for, and He is still worth dying for.

So then, while we have opportunity, let us do good to all people, and especially to those who are of the household of the faith.
Galatians 6:10

Assignments for Lesson 146

In Their Words   Read the selected Canaan Hymns (page 368).

Literature   Begin reading *The Abolition of Man*. Plan to finish it by the end of this unit.

Student Review   Optional: Answer the questions for Lesson 146.

An especially helpful source for this lesson was *How Christianity Changed the World* by Alvin Schmidt (Grand Rapids: Zondervan, 2001, 2004). It was formerly published as *Under the Influence*.

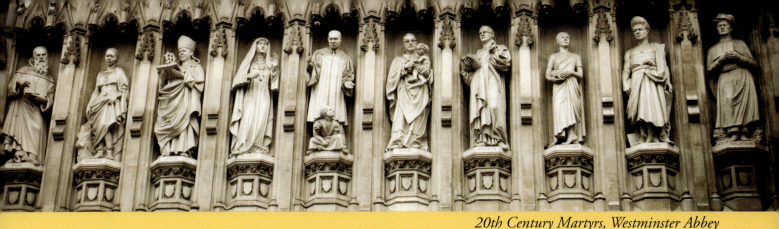

20th Century Martyrs, Westminster Abbey

Lesson 147

Lessons from World History

You have covered much ground in this study of world history—learning about key people, events, and ideas; reading literature from various times and places; and considering the message of the Bible as it relates to the story of mankind. As you read the following points, think of some things that have been particularly eye-opening or significant in your mind.

The Main Issues Do Not Change

The issues in world history have been largely the same regardless of time or place. The builders of the tower of Babel wanted to make a name for themselves. So did Alexander, Julius Caesar, Napoleon, and Adolf Hitler. Ancient kings believed that controlling vast amounts of land gave them power and significance. So did the Mongols, the colonizing nations of Europe, and Josef Stalin. The few often acquire great wealth for themselves by the labor of the poor. This was true in ancient Egypt, in medieval Europe, and in the Industrial Revolution. It is true today.

God gives mankind tremendous talents, resources, and opportunities. What we do with them determines whether we bless or burden other people. It also determines the kind of legacy we leave behind us. This applied to the ancient Sumerians and to the scholars of the Renaissance and it applies to 21st-century Americans.

The statues above, unveiled in 1998, represent followers of Christ who died violent deaths during a century that was filled with intense persecution against believers in many parts of the world. From left to right are Maximilian Kolbe (see page 685); Manche Masemola, of the South African Pedi tribe, killed by her parents for wanting to be a Christian; Janani Luwum, an Anglican leader in Uganda, killed for criticizing Uganda's dictator Idi Amin; Grand Duchess Elizabeth of Russia, murdered by Bolsheviks during the Russian Revolution; Martin Luther King Jr., American minister and civil rights leader; Óscar Romero (see page 789); Dietrich Bonhoeffer (see page 685); Esther John, a Pakistani convert from Islam who became a nurse and missionary; Lucian Tapiedi, a native of Papua New Guinea, killed with other Christian ministers and teachers during World War II; and Wang Zhiming, a Chinese pastor killed during the Cultural Revolution. The power of a martyr's influence is seen in the stories of Manche Masemola's mother, and Hivijapa, the man who killed Lucian Tapiedi. Both of them later became Christians.

Some people dedicate themselves to righteous causes and are executed, like William Tyndale. Others dedicate themselves to acquiring power and pleasure, like Louis XIV of France. Both Tyndale and Louis XIV died, but the legacy each left is quite different because of how they used their talents, resources, and opportunities.

Conflict Between Good and Evil

Former British Prime Minister Margaret Thatcher (1925-2013) said, "I am in politics because of the struggle between good and evil. I believe in the end good will triumph." When we look at the world and its history, we can easily see that evil is real; but we can also see that good is real.

The brutality of the Roman Colosseum and the brutality of Muslim terrorists are examples of evil. However, the same world has also given us Mother Teresa in India and George Müller in England. The conflict began for humans in the Garden of Eden. We play it out generation after generation in every nation of the world.

Mother Teresa (1910-1997, center) was born to Albanian parents in a region of the Ottoman Empire that is now Macedonia. She spent most of her life in India. There Teresa founded the Missionaries of Charity to serve the needs of the poor, sick, and other outcasts. Kay Kelly (1944-2010, right), who was healed of cancer in 1978, worked to improve life in her hometown of Liverpool, England. She also raised money to support Mother Teresa's work. They met in 1980.

Lesson 147 - Lessons from World History

Some say that we cannot know good and evil, that these are relative, not absolute, terms. People like this are a minority in the history of the world. King David of Israel believed in good and evil. The apostle Paul believed in good and evil. Augustine believed in good and evil. People will differ on the specifics. Absolute monarchs believed that their system was good, while revolutionaries saw it as evil. Osama bin Laden saw the terrorism he organized as good, even though most of the rest of the world saw it as evil. The fact that the moral vision of some people is clouded does not mean that the realities are not out there to be seen.

Noble People Are Still Fallible

People, events, and institutions are a mixture of good and bad. We like stories that have clear villains and heroes so that we can know whom to cheer and whom to boo. We would like history to tell us, "This leader was good because . . . ." and "This event was bad because . . . ." Real life, however, is not that way. We are not that way. The poet Robert Browning wrote that in this sense we are like neither God nor the beasts. "God is, they are/Man partly is and wholly hopes to be." This does not negate the second point above, that good and evil are real; but it is rare for an individual and rarer still for a society or culture to see with single vision. Our selfish motives and agendas mix in with the good we know and want to accomplish, as Paul describes in Romans 7.

David was a man after God's own heart, but he sinned miserably. The Roman Empire accomplished amazing feats, but they did not recognize the value of human life. The Catholic Church was a voice of Christianity in the Middle Ages, but the corruption of some leaders was shocking. The technological progress of the 19th and 20th centuries made the world better in many ways, but this progress at times was accompanied by the abuse of workers and the environment.

Illustration of King David (Portuguese, 1509)

If the history you read portrays everything in black and white, then (1) it is not the history of people who are anything like you and me and (2) someone else has done your thinking for you. Our challenge and our opportunity is to develop the discernment to be able to differentiate between the good and the bad. We might want simplistic answers, especially in this day of ten-second sound bites that try to address complicated issues. You should seek to be knowledgeable and eloquent enough to give good, well-rounded answers to such questions as, "Was the French Revolution good or bad?" We need to be wise about whom we hold up as heroes, learning from their strengths but not denying their weaknesses. This is not to say that everything is 50-50. Some people, events, and trends are much more good than bad; some are the opposite. We need to be willing to recognize this.

During World War II, Japanese Americans were forced to leave their homes and live in camps such as the Gila River Relocation Center in Arizona. This photo shows Christian residents there celebrating Thanksgiving Day with a sunrise service.

The reality of our humanity is one reason why God, Jesus, the Bible, and God's plan for the church stand out so sharply against the darkness of the world. They are completely good. "God is Light, and in Him there is no darkness at all" (1 John 1:5). Jesus was "tempted in all things as we are, yet without sin" (Hebrews 4:15). God's Word is truth (John 17:17). The church was part of God's eternal purpose which He accomplished in Christ (Ephesians 3:10-11). How people do church is not always good, but God's concept of the church is wonderful.

The Answers Are in the Bible

Mankind has tried just about everything else. The religions and philosophies of the world have provided ideas and perspectives that could fill a library of their own. Emperors have thought that their power would solve the problems of the world. People have looked to science, reason, medicine, technology, education, government funding, government control, a state-established church, and a host of other means as the way to provide the answers that people need; but at some point all of these attempted answers have failed.

The Bible has the answers because the Bible is true, a fact that has been confirmed to this author through six decades of experience. God made us, and He gave us the instruction manual to follow so that our lives will function well. When we don't do as we should, it is because we have not consulted the manual. If Christianity were just another man-made religion, it could not offer the hope that it does. When the practice of Christianity has departed from God's Word and followed the ways of men, it has offered turmoil and oppression instead of hope. Buddhism does not offer hope. Islam cannot change us on the inside. Reason does not satisfy when the World Trade Center crumbles or armies destroy each other. The continued difficulties in the world are not evidence that Christianity does not have answers. As G. K. Chesterton wrote, "The Christian ideal has not been tried and found wanting; it has been found difficult and left untried."

Lesson 147 - Lessons from World History

Good Is Real and Will Triumph

Christians believe that the world is headed somewhere, that it is not simply spinning in an endless cycle of reincarnation and repetition. The destiny to which the world is headed is the last day, when God will recognize and reward His people and punish for eternity those who have chosen not to follow Him. This final day of reckoning, along with the teaching and example of Jesus and the Scriptures, have been motivations for Christian people to do good. Flawed as we are, humans have within them the capacity to choose what is right. Whatever the situation, people have chosen to do what is right and noble even at the cost of their own lives.

Joseph did what was right when he could have become bitter and vindictive. The martyrs of the early church remained true to Jesus when it would have been easy to deny Him. Corrie ten Boom kept her faith and helped others under the trying circumstances of a German concentration camp. When war and famine have brought disaster, people have responded with assistance. People around the world, in villages and cities, have been willing to love their neighbors as themselves. Good is real, and it is worth believing in and living for.

George and Louisa MacDonald celebrated their 50th anniversary in 1901.

The Scottish writer George MacDonald wrote, "I know that good is coming to me—that good is always coming, though few have at all times the simplicity and the courage to believe it." If we believe in the ultimate triumph of God and in His ability to bring good out of bad, we can trust that good will win.

Developing a Sense of History

Much more has taken place in our world than what we have outlined in this curriculum. Billions of people have lived, many of whom were well-known in their day and who are still remembered by others. Much good has been accomplished that has blessed the lives of millions. Many people have had an impact on their country, their community, and their family. All of that is significant and worthwhile. However, in this curriculum, we have focused on a limited number of events, people, and ideas. How do we decide what is "historic"?

Trends and events that are historic have an impact on many people, whether in one country or around the world. Sometimes the effect on people takes a long time to develop fully. The Scientific Revolution discussed in Unit 19 changed the outlook of many people around the world, but that change was not immediate or obvious. The same was true with the higher criticism of the Bible that developed in the late 19th century, which we discussed in Unit 23. These new ideas trickled down from scholars, who taught teachers and ministers, who then taught the general public. These are subtle changes, ones that rarely make a splash but that do affect many people.

Truly historic events are worth remembering in this generation and in the future. We can learn valuable lessons, be inspired to continue the good, and be alert to prevent the re-occurrence of evil. God instituted the yearly festival of the Passover so that every generation of Israelites would remember what He had done for them. The memorials and patriotic holidays in our country are designed to

Unit 30: Looking Backward, Looking Forward

In 1994 in the African country of Rwanda, ethnic Hutus, with the support of the government, killed between 500,000 and 1,000,000 ethnic Tutsis. Paul Rusesabagina, son of a Hutu father and Tutsi mother, used his position as manager of the Hôtel des Mille Collines in Kigali, Rwanda, to protect 1,200 Tutsi refugees in the hotel during three months of violence.

help us remember the price that was paid for our freedom because we tend to forget and to take our freedom for granted. Other countries have similar holidays and memorials.

Much of the information published in news media from day to day is not worth remembering. The winner of a sports championship, the outcome of a sensational criminal trial, and the latest gossip out of Hollywood are not historic events that need to be passed down from one generation to another. However, other events that happened many years ago do need to be remembered: the courage of reformers who answered to God and not to men; the sacrifices of missionaries who went to other countries so that more people might know the Lord; and the attitudes that led to genocide in countries such as Turkey, Germany, and Rwanda.

A sense of history gives us a good filter to sift through the mountains of information placed before us every day. Since we all have a limited amount of time and energy, we need to concentrate on the things that matter most. The things that have eternal value and consequences should be at the top of our list.

Yet those who wait for the Lord will gain new strength;
they will mount up with wings like eagles, they will run and not get tired,
they will walk and not become weary.
Isaiah 40:31

Assignments for Lesson 147

Literature — Continue reading *The Abolition of Man*.

Student Review — Optional: Answer the questions for Lesson 147.

Nidaros Cathedral, Trondheim, Norway

Lesson 148

Living in the Modern World

Elijah was in despair. The nation of Israel, which had once committed itself to following God, was now given over to the worship of a pagan deity. The king and queen of Israel, Ahab and Jezebel, were themselves pagans. These rulers were Elijah's avowed enemies and were out to get him. Elijah had just seen the unmistakable hand of God achieve a stunning victory in a dramatic showdown between himself and 450 prophets of the pagan deity Ba'al, but even that had not turned the tide of unbelief in Israel.

So Elijah was in despair. Where was the prophet of the eternal God of Israel? Hiding in a cave. The Lord asked him, "What are you doing here, Elijah?"

Elijah answered, "I have been very zealous for the Lord, the God of hosts, for the sons of Israel have forsaken Your covenant, torn down Your altars, and killed Your prophets with the sword. And I alone am left, and they seek my life, to take it away" (1 Kings 19:14).

Elijah had taken his eyes off of God; and God had caught him looking instead at all of the negative things around him, all of the apparently valid reasons for being in despair. Focused on what he did, Elijah understandably hid in a cave.

God told Elijah to get up and be about what He had for him to do. In other words, God told Elijah to quit fretting and to get to work. God also told him that he was mistaken in thinking that he was the only one who was faithful. God said, "I will leave 7,000 in Israel, all the knees that have not bowed to Ba'al" (verse 18). God had thousands who were still faithful to Him in that unfaithful country. Elijah couldn't see them because he was afraid, discouraged, and hiding in a cave. When Elijah left the cave and started serving God again, he began to see again how God was working.

"They Have Forsaken Your Covenant"

Evolution.
    Existentialism.
        Immorality.
           Post-modernism.
               Relativistic thinking.
                  War.
                     Terrorism.
                       Corruption.

Sin is real. The failings of mankind are real. Sin is costly to people in many ways: ruined lives, fractured families, devastated battlefronts, and much more.

Albert Camus (1913-1960) was born in French Algeria. He participated in the resistance against German occupation of France during World War II and published several books and plays. Camus saw life as an absurd paradox, and he thought that religion represented an illogical attempt to escape from reality. Since he did not want to believe that life was completely meaningless, Camus argued that people had to create their own meaning. He received the Nobel Prize for Literature in 1957. He died in an automobile accident.

Evil is all around us. A Christian family can hardly sit down to watch a television program or movie together for all of the bad language used and all of the suggestive situations portrayed. Immorality and ungodliness appear to have won the day.

One reason for our discomfort with much of what we see around us is that many people—and it seems as though many in the media—do not share the same basic assumptions that Christians hold. They have a different worldview. The assumptions of Freud, Darwin, and Dewey that we discussed in earlier lessons appear to be the assumptions of our world. Many people do not accept the idea that Jesus is the one way to God. They do not accept the inspiration and authority of the Bible. They do not accept the Biblical definition of morality. They do not accept the definition of truth that conservative Christians hold. They come at life with different assumptions, and as a result they arrive at different conclusions. What they say and do is at odds with our worldview, and this frustrates us. Christians feel constantly under attack because the assumptions we hold are constantly under attack.

Make no mistake about it. Evil is real. The battle is on.

Corinth with Cell Phones

The skeptics, the cynics, and the unbelievers will point out how much is wrong in our world. Even believers can all too easily camp on the reality of evil. That is not difficult to do. It does not take great intelligence or profound awareness to point out evil because evil is everywhere.

But think about the world into which the gospel was first preached, that crooked and perverse generation (Philippians 2:15). They had serious problems also. As bad as it was, that was the age that Paul called "the fullness of the time" (Galatians 4:4). In other words, it was just the right time for Jesus to come.

When we look around us, we can see much that is wrong and ungodly. Sometimes it seems as though we live in Corinth but with cell phones. But do we stop there and go hide in a cave in despair, or can God give us a different perspective the way He did with Elijah?

Looking at Our World

My eyes shed streams of water,
  Because they do not keep Your law.
    (Psalm 119:136)

Lesson 148 - Living in the Modern World

We feel anger. We sometimes feel afraid. We want to run away and hide. The cave seems very attractive. However, when the psalmist looked around him and saw disobedience to God's Word, he felt grief and sadness for those who were missing the joy of living for God. He hurt for the effect that their assumptions and decisions had on their lives and on the lives of those whom they influenced. Most of all, he hurt for the way God was being dishonored.

What should we do? It is the fullness of time for us, the time when we are alive and can make a difference. Instead of stopping at anger, fear, and frustration, we can feel a burning conviction to help people see the truth that will set them free. We can refuse to let what is around us dampen the joy we have at knowing Christ and His way.

Faith, Hope, and Love

For now we see in a mirror dimly, but then face to face; now I know in part, but then I will know fully just as I also have been fully known. But now faith, hope, love, abide these three; but the greatest of these is love.
(1 Corinthians 13:12-13)

Better times are coming. What will endure until the end is not cynicism, fear, and negativity. What will bring about the victory is faith, hope, and love.

Now, will not God bring about justice for His elect who cry to Him day and night, and will He delay long over them? I tell you that He will bring about justice for them quickly. However, when the Son of Man comes, will He find faith on the earth? (Luke 18:7-8)

If the Son of Man were to come to Europe today, He would find many cathedrals that are largely empty except for tourists. If he were to come to the United States, He would find little faith expressed in the popular media. He might find His Father's name chiseled on marble walls but not much faith exercised within those walls.

However, if He comes to China, He will find millions of believers in house churches despite the official godlessness of the government. If he comes to Africa and South America, he will find growing numbers of people who live by a vibrant faith. And if He comes to millions of homes in the United States, He will find people who gratefully, joyfully live by faith.

There are still many who have not bowed the knee to the gods of this age. Many are faithful in the midst of difficult circumstances. You know some of them. There are many more whom you will never know in this life. They are serving, loving, pushing back the darkness, and making a difference for good in a crooked and perverse generation.

The question is, will He find faith in you? You can find plenty to do, plenty to read, and plenty to watch that will build up your faith and not tear it down. Don't let Him find you in a cave.

Music has long had a powerful cultural influence. Sadly many popular artists sing about inappropriate topics or throw away their lives through substance abuse and immorality. The Irish rock band U2, formed in 1976, became one of the most popular musical groups worldwide. Their lyrics contain spiritual themes, but the message is not always clear. The band members have been involved in various charitable works. They met Brazilian President Dilma Rousseff in 2011.

Hope does not disappoint. (Romans 5:5)

The word for hope in the New Testament does not mean a wish, as in, "I hope I get an iPod for Christmas." Hope in the Bible is a confident expectation. Christians have hope that Christ will return and set things right, a confident expectation that He will reward the faithful and punish evildoers.

When Jesus was reviled and faced the suffering of the cross, "He kept entrusting Himself to Him who judges righteously" (1 Peter 2:23). We can do the same. God is not going to miss a thing. He knows exactly what His people are doing, He knows exactly what the enemies of the cross are doing, and He will bring all to rights at just the right time.

One of the scribes came and heard them arguing, and recognizing that He had answered them well, asked Him, "What commandment is the foremost of all?" Jesus answered, "The foremost is, 'Hear, O Israel! The Lord our God is one Lord; and you shall love the Lord your God with all your heart, and with all your soul, and with all your mind, and with all your strength.' The second is this, 'You shall love your neighbor as yourself.' There is no other commandment greater than these." (Mark 12:28-31)

Love is the unfailing motivation for doing good. We need never fail to love because of the lack of love around us. This is how we can live effectively in the modern world.

Living in the Present

Historian David McCullough has said that no one lives in the past. Julius Caesar, Charlemagne, and Queen Victoria didn't walk around saying, "Isn't this interesting? Here we are living in the past!" Everyone who has ever lived has lived in the present—his or her present, in what to them was the modern world.

When did Elijah live? He lived in the present, in his modern world. He could have wished for the good old days, when the people of his nation confessed faith in God and could clearly see Him working powerfully. However, even though things were different all around him from what they had been, Elijah could still serve God. He could still know the hand of God, and he could still find thousands of people who followed God, if he would only look beyond his immediate circumstances to see it.

When do we live? We live in the modern world, of course. But one hundred years from now, this will be the past. This might be some of the good old days that people of the future look back to and long for.

After joining the staff at Sherwood Baptist Church in Albany, Georgia, brothers Alex (left) and Stephen Kendrick began to fulfill their dream of making wholesome feature films. In 2002 they worked with volunteers from their church to produce a movie shown in a local theater. This 2004 photo shows them during filming for their second movie, Facing the Giants. Their films have received worldwide attention, and the success of the movies has enabled Sherwood Baptist Church greatly to expand its ministries.

Lesson 148 - Living in the Modern World

So how should we live in this modern world? The way God told Elijah to live in his modern world. We should live not in despair, even with the very real negative things around us, but with faith in the even more real and even more powerful living God who loves us.

Does it seem to you that there are 450 prophets of Ba'al out there, each one with a blog, a book, a movie, or a podcast? People who oppose God's way and who try to turn others against Him might seem to have a great deal of influence. In the overall scheme of things, that doesn't really matter. God is still there, and He is still in charge. As you live in this modern world, get out of your cave and do with confidence the work that God has for you to do.

For as he thinks within himself, so he is.
Proverbs 23:7

Assignments for Lesson 148

Literature — Continue reading *The Abolition of Man*.

Student Review — Optional: Answer the questions for Lesson 148.

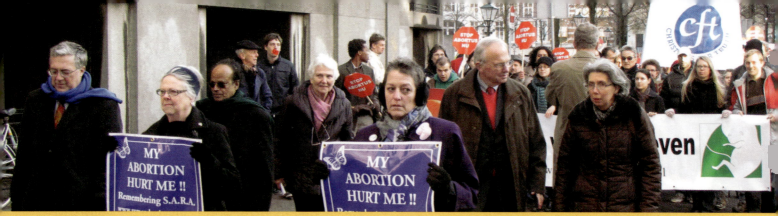

March for Life in the Netherlands (2011)

Lesson 149

Becoming a World Christian

A new Christian from Hong Kong asked what he should do when he visited his non-Christian family, whom he wanted to influence for Christ, and they had a ceremony in which they worshiped their ancestors.

A Christian from Nigeria wondered how to explain to others in his country why the church shared in the Lord's Supper in the morning. Why didn't we do it at supper time?

During the civil unrest in South Africa in the 1980s over the policy of apartheid, a black South African studying the Bible by mail with an American teacher asked that teacher, "What causes misunderstandings and riots in the world?"

A Christian from India, living in America, was very excited about the young woman in India that his parents had selected for him to marry. He had a picture of her, but he had never met her.

Christians from the United States were visiting a church in Mexico. Some of the Americans went to visit the home of one of the church members. She and her children were living in a house with walls made of flattened cardboard boxes. It had a wood burning stove inside it that the woman used for cooking.

Life outside of the United States can be quite different from what we are used to. Life for Christians outside of the United States can be quite different from what Christians in the United States have become accustomed to. People in other parts of the world have different questions, operate under different assumptions, and live (often happily) under conditions American Christians would find hard to tolerate. As Christians, we have a responsibility to be aware of how other people in the world live and think, so that we can learn and so that we can teach.

We Have Been Entrusted with Much

Americans are richly blessed. We rarely have to be concerned about having enough food or making sure the water we drink is not contaminated. We have closets full of clothes for all kinds of weather. Most American Christian families have several copies of the Bible. Our Sunday assemblies are never raided by policemen who haul people off to jail just for being at a church meeting. We have almost instantaneous communication with just about every

Lesson 149 - Becoming a World Christian

place in the world. A world of information is at our fingertips.

Jesus said, "From everyone who has been given much, much will be required; and to whom they entrusted much, of him they will ask all the more" (Luke 12:48). God will require more giving from us than He expects from the poor laborer in Africa. He will expect more from us than He will from the girl in a village in India who never got an education. Paul traveled widely and preached to many people in the first-century Mediterranean world using ships and foot power. How can we use air travel, printing presses, and electronic communication effectively to reach our world today?

Our study of world history has not been intended to be just an academic exercise to fulfill a school requirement. We want you to love God more and to love people more as a result of having gone through this material. We want you to be a better person and a better Christian. You have been given much, so much will be expected of you. One way that you can accomplish this is to become keenly aware of the vastness and complexity of the world in which we live, and to appreciate the fact that God rules it all. You can make a difference in the lives of others who live far away from you, perhaps whom

Church on Easter Island

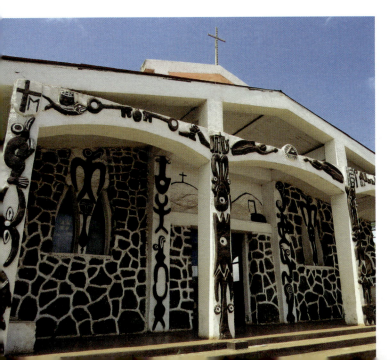

Meeting Times for a Church in China

you will never even meet this side of heaven, by lifting up your eyes to look at our world from God's point of view.

How to Become a World Christian

First, you can pray. Paul wanted Christians to pray for "all men, for kings and all who are in authority, so that we may lead a tranquil and quiet life in all godliness and dignity" (1 Timothy 2:1-2). This is not so that we can be comfortable, but because God wants all men to be saved (1 Timothy 2:4). The gospel has a better chance of being spread and being heard when there is peace as opposed to war.

Second, you can be aware of life in other countries. Perhaps you have lived in another country or know someone who has. You will have a more mature understanding of the gospel if you see how it speaks to people whose lives are very different from yours. Ignorance generates fear, while knowledge brings people closer together.

Part of this awareness involves trying to resist being ethnocentric, which means seeing everything about one's own culture as the best, right, and only way to do things. For one thing, it isn't true. For another, it will make you critical of other cultures just because they are different. In addition, if you ever go to another country, you will have a hard time adjusting because everything will not be like it is in America.

In England cars travel on the left side of the road. It is not better or worse than the American way of driving on the right side; it is just different. If you drive in England, you will have to adjust quickly whether you like it or not. English drivers are not tolerant of Americans who drive on the wrong side of the road!

Third, you can learn to love people from other countries. God does (John 3:16). This should not be a condescending love that feels pity for the poor people who do not have computers and DVD players. Instead, try to empathize with someone whose father spent several years in prison for believing in Jesus. Appreciate what it means to have one meal per day, and that meal always be beans and rice. Think about what it is like to walk past Buddhist temples or Islamic mosques every day. Imagine trying to live for Jesus in a society where billboards and television present images that we would consider pornographic and where about as many couples live together as get married. People in those countries do not need your pity; they need Jesus.

Church in Kenya

Church in Fiji

Lesson 149 - Becoming a World Christian

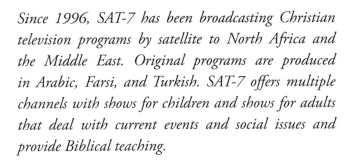

Since 1996, SAT-7 has been broadcasting Christian television programs by satellite to North Africa and the Middle East. Original programs are produced in Arabic, Farsi, and Turkish. SAT-7 offers multiple channels with shows for children and shows for adults that deal with current events and social issues and provide Biblical teaching.

Fourth, you might be called to go to another country and share the good news of Jesus. Your father might have an opportunity to work in another country and take your family to live there also. Your parents might want to be missionaries and work full-time building up the church and reaching out to others. A door might open for you later in your life to live outside of the United States, either as a self-supporting, vocational "tent-making" missionary or as someone supported financially by other Christians. This is how the gospel has always been spread: by people who believe going out to teach people who need to believe.

If you are not able to go yourself, you can still be involved in mission work. Paul considered the Christians in Philippi to be participants in the gospel with him, even though most of them had never left Philippi (Philippians 1:5). Missionaries need willing financial supporters. They love to communicate with friends in America. You can help supply them with teaching materials that are expensive or impossible to obtain where they are.

Vessels Used by the Master

"If anyone cleanses himself from these things [such as empty chatter, ungodliness, and other dishonorable practices], he will be a vessel for honor, sanctified, useful to the Master, prepared for every good work" (2 Timothy 2:21).

The Lord has good things planned for your life. You cannot know exactly what shape that good will take or how it will come about, but you can be prepared for whatever God will do and however He wants you to serve Him. He has placed you where you are, in your family, community, nation, and world, for a purpose. Part of your preparation can be to have a grasp of what it means to be a Christian in our world today, a world shaped by what has happened in world history.

"For I know the plans that I have for you," declares the Lord,
"plans for welfare and not for calamity to give you a future and a hope."
Jeremiah 29:11

Assignments for Lesson 149

In Their Words Read "Righteousness Exalteth a Nation" (pages 369-372).

Literature Continue reading *The Abolition of Man*.

Student Review Optional: Answer the questions for Lesson 149.

Alpha and Omega Stained Glass Window, Hiefenech, Luxembourg

Lesson 150 - Bible Study

Eternity After This World

"The world is passing away" (1 John 2:17). You have devoted a considerable amount of time studying what is no longer the case about something that is not always going to be around. Your efforts have not been wasted, however, because what we do in this finite, temporary world makes a difference in the world that awaits us.

As we said in the first unit, eternity existed before this world came into existence. After this world ends, eternity will continue. Eternity is going on right now, in fact. We can connect with it by having eternal life in Jesus (1 John 5:13). We can live on a higher plane in this life by living in Jesus. This is also the way we can prepare for the world to come.

Be Ready

"What I say to you I say to all, 'Be on the alert'" (Mark 13:37).

The end is coming. All that we do or make or accomplish will one day be gone. Until the Lord returns, no one who lives on this earth gets out of here alive. The testimony of Scripture and our experience tell us that our lives will end one day. Either we will depart this life with the world still here, or we will live to see the end of this world and the coming of Christ. Either way, the end is coming.

When we know that a particular event is coming, we have the responsibility to be ready for it. When April 15 rolls around, for instance, we should be ready to pay our taxes. We know that the eternal day of reckoning is ahead of us, so we have a responsibility to be ready. The way to be ready is to become a Christian and to live faithfully for Him (Acts 2:38, 2 Corinthians 5:9-10).

Don't Try to Predict

"But of that day and hour no one knows, not even the angels of heaven, nor the Son, but the Father alone" (Matthew 24:36).

A great many people who claim to believe the Bible apparently do not believe in this verse because they keep trying to predict when Jesus will come. Hal Lindsey did it in the 1970s with his book, *The Late Great Planet Earth*. The predictions he made did not come to pass. A pamphlet made the rounds of churches in 1988 proclaiming, "88 Reasons Why the Lord May Come Back in 1988." He didn't. When the Persian Gulf War erupted in 1990-91, the speculators had another field day.

Illustrations of the Book of Revelation in a Church in Macedonia

They were convinced that this was the great war in the Middle East that they expected to usher in the end of the world. It wasn't. As we approached the year 2000, discussion of the Y2K computer bug and the possibility of "the end of civilization as we know it" brought another round of books and videos predicting the end. It didn't happen. The premise behind the entire *Left Behind* book series (which began to appear in 1995) was the speculation that became to many the expectation that Jesus was coming soon, somehow in connection with the year 2000.

Hal Lindsey wasn't the first and the Y2K fervor won't be the last in the great rage to determine when Jesus will return. The Christian centuries are full of failed predictions about the return of Christ. Apparently it began with Christians in Thessalonica, who were so convinced that the Lord was coming soon that they quit work and just waited—and then started to mooch off of those who were still working (2 Thessalonians 3:6-12). Jesus said, "The Son of Man is coming at an hour that you do not expect" (Luke 12:40). Only God knows when Jesus is coming, and it appears that He will not come when speculation is highest and when many people expect Him to come. Speculations and predictions sell books and videos, but they do not honor the truth of God's Word.

The World's Last Day

Several passages in the Bible describe the end of this world and the beginning of eternity. We can put these verses together to get an idea of what will happen. The world's last day apparently will look like many other days. Life's activities will be going on as usual (Matthew 24:36-44). Suddenly, the Lord will appear in the sky with the voice of an archangel and the sound of a trumpet. The dead in Christ will rise and those who are alive will meet Jesus in the air (1 Thessalonians 4:13-5:3). This world will pass away, and a new heaven and a new earth will appear—not a different physical realm, but an entirely new spiritual realm (2 Peter 3:11-13, Revelation 21:1). The judgment before God's throne will take place (Revelation 20:11-14). Those whom the Lord welcomes to Himself will enjoy the new heaven and earth forever, while those who did not live for God will suffer for eternity (Matthew 25:31-46, Revelation 21:2-8).

The ways and woes of this life will be gone. There will be no more tears, no more death, no more pain (Revelation 21:4). We will see what is truly eternal and what really matters. As C. S. Lewis has pointed out, civilizations last only a relatively few years or centuries; but a person's soul lasts forever. The Lord and His awesome, glorious presence will be there, the souls of men and women will be there, and the truth of His Word will last forever. We will bask in eternal light provided by the glory of the Lord and the Lamb (Revelation 21:10-22:5).

Our existence there will be far better than anything ever known on this earth. We will understand what is true far better than we ever will here. We still won't know everything, but we will understand with greater depth than ever before. We will see the faithful of all the ages in the presence of God. I believe that we will know each other in heaven, but we will not be troubled by those who are not there because we will know no more pain or tears. We will have come to where we belong. We were made to praise the Lord, and we will do that for all eternity.

We will see that the sacrifices we made for the Lord while on the earth were worth it. Paul says that our momentary, light afflictions here are producing for us an eternal weight of glory. We will finally be able to see what now we can only perceive by faith (2 Corinthians 4:17-18). As much as we enjoy life here, I don't think we will miss it.

What We Do Now Affects What We Will Do Then

We are to live every day of our brief lives on this temporary planet with the permanence of eternity in mind. We have many things to do that, in the eternal scheme, are more important than studying world history. However, history has its proper place. God inspired the Bible so that we could know the history of how He worked with Israel, how He brought Christ into the world, and how He established the church.

God wanted His people to know His history. God reminded Israel of their history. Moses,

The Last Judgment, *John Martin (English, 1853)*

Joshua, and Stephen were just some of the people who recalled history for their listeners. The Passover and the other feasts were reminders about Israel's past. The Lord's Supper reminds Christians of the historical event in which Jesus bore our sins on the cross.

Knowing God's story and the story of mankind is one way of loving and honoring God with our minds (Matthew 22:37). Knowing your past will help you live better in the future. This is why you have been studying world history.

You might forget a point about the feudalism of the Middle Ages or about the development of modern India, but make sure you do not miss your appointment with eternity. Live every day with the past in mind and eternity in view.

Behold, I am coming quickly, and My reward is with Me, to render to every man according to what he has done. I am the Alpha and the Omega, the first and the last, the beginning and the end.
Revelation 22:12-13

Assignments for Lesson 150

Bible — Recite or write Isaiah 40:29-31 from memory.

Literature — Finish reading *The Abolition of Man*. Literary analysis available in *Student Review*.

Project — Complete your project for the unit.

Student Review — Optional: Answer the questions for Lesson 150 and for *The Abolition of Man*; take the quiz for Unit 30; and take the sixth history, English, and Bible exams.

Celebrate — Thank God for making you a part of world history by putting you in this time and place.

Detail from Tahitian Women on the Beach, *Paul Gauguin (French, 1891)*

Credits

Images

Images marked with one of these codes are used with the permission of a Creative Commons Attribution or Attribution-Share Alike License. See the websites listed for details.

CC-BY-1.0	creativecommons.org/licenses/by/1.0/
CC-BY-2.0	creativecommons.org/licenses/by/2.0/
CC-BY-2.5	creativecommons.org/licenses/by/2.5/
CC-BY-3.0	creativecommons.org/licenses/by/3.0/
CC-BY-3.0 DE	creativecommons.org/licenses/by/3.0/de/
CC-BY-SA-2.0	creativecommons.org/licenses/by-sa/2.0/
CC-BY-SA-2.0 DE	creativecommons.org/licenses/by-sa/2.0/de/
CC-BY-SA-2.5	creativecommons.org/licenses/by-sa/2.5/
CC-BY-SA-2.5 BR	creativecommons.org/licenses/by-sa/2.5/br/
CC-BY-SA-3.0	creativecommons.org/licenses/by-sa/3.0/
CC-BY-SA-3.0 BR	creativecommons.org/licenses/by-sa/3.0/br/
CC-BY-SA-3.0 DE	creativecommons.org/licenses/by-sa/3.0/de/
CC-BY-SA-3.0 LU	creativecommons.org/licenses/by-sa/3.0/lu/
CC-BY-SA-3.0 NL	creativecommons.org/licenses/by-sa/3.0/nl/

The World Map used in the "What Else Was Happening?" sections is from the NASA Visible Earth Project / NASA Goddard Space Flight Center Image by Reto Stöckli (land surface, shallow water, clouds). Enhancements by Robert Simmon (ocean color, compositing, 3D globes, animation). Data and technical support: MODIS Land Group; MODIS Science Data Support Team; MODIS Atmosphere Group; MODIS Ocean Group Additional data: USGS EROS Data Center (topography); USGS Terrestrial Remote Sensing Flagstaff Field Center (Antarctica); Defense Meteorological Satellite Program (city lights).

Uncredited images are in the public domain in the United States, taken from Wikimedia Commons and other sources.

i	Emmanuel Dyan / Flickr / CC-BY-2.0
v	José Porras / Wikimedia Commons / CC-BY-3.0
vi	USAID Africa Bureau
437	Qypchak / Wikimedia Commons / CC-BY-SA-3.0
440	Sébastien Bertrand (tiseb) / Flickr / CC-BY-2.0
441	Quistnix / Wikimedia Commons / CC-BY-1.0
443t	Library of Congress
444	hr.icio tomasz przechlewski / Wikimedia Commons
445	Beinecke Rare Book and Manuscript Library, Yale University
446t	Willi Heidelbach / Wikimedia Commons / CC-BY-SA-3.0
446b	Notgrass Family Collection
447	Aodhdubh / Wikimedia Commons / CC-BY-SA-3.0
448	Ms. Tharpe / Flickr / CC-BY-2.0
451t	John Allen (jalodrome) / Flickr / CC-BY-2.0
452	Cross: Brooklyn Museum / Wikimedia Commons / CC-BY-3.0
452	Easter Island: Arian Zwegers / Flickr / CC-BY-2.0
452	Porcelain: World Imaging / Wikimedia Commons / CC-BY-SA-3.0
459	Library of Congress
460	Wasforgas / Wikimedia Commons / CC-BY-SA-3.0
463	Atlas of Italian Art
473	GFreihalter / Wikimedia Commons / CC-BY-SA-3.0
474	Nilington / Wikimedia Commons
477	Rebecca Wilson (Saucy Salad) / Flickr / CC-BY-2.0
478	tomasz przechlewski (hr.icio) / Flickr / CC-BY-2.0
479	mahalie stackpole / Flickr / CC-BY-SA-2.0

Page	Credit
481	Earl McGehee (ejmc) / Flickr / CC-BY-2.0
483	Hi540 / Wikimedia Commons / CC-BY-SA-3.0
485	Paul Keller / Flickr / CC-BY-2.0
488t	Ralf Kayser (ralky) / Flickr / CC-BY-2.0
491	Bundesarchiv (Bild 183-R0211-316) / CC-BY-SA-3.0 DE
493	Library of Congress
497	Magallanes1 / Wikimedia Commons
499t	AlejandroLinaresGarcia / Wikimedia Commons / CC-BY-SA-3.0
502t	ClarkSui / Wikimedia Commons / CC-BY-SA-3.0
504	Michael L. Baird (Mike) / Flickr / CC-BY-2.0
509t	Tony in Devon / Wikimedia Commons / CC-BY-3.0
509b	Library of Congress
511	rockriver / Flickr / CC-BY-2.0
512t	Dmitry Denisenkov (ddenisen) / Flickr / CC-BY-SA-2.0
513	Igloo: Clayoquot / Wikimedia Commons / CC-BY-SA-3.0
513	Cliff Dwelling: (Luis sierra) / Wikimedia Commons / CC-BY-SA-3.0
513	Stilt Houses: 3coma14 / Wikimedia Commons / CC-BY-SA-3.0
515	Matthewjparker] / Wikimedia Commons / CC-BY-SA-3.0
517	James Emery (hoyasmeg) / Flickr / CC-BY-2.0
519	Racklever / Wikimedia Commons / CC-BY-SA-3.0 See the map on page 793. Ethiopia, formerly known as Abyssinia, is the large gray area in East Africa. A large plateau covers over half of the country. Rivers and valleys cut through this plateau, which is bordered by mountains and deserts.
520	Library of Congress
523	National Library of Medicine
527t	NASA/SDO, AIA
528t	Jim & Rhoda Morris, http://www.scitechantiques.com / Wikimedia Commons
530	NASA / JPL-DLR
531t	Paul Hermans / Wikimedia Commons / CC-BY-SA-3.0
531b	Hel-hama / Wikimedia Commons / CC-BY-SA-3.0
532t	Spigget / Wikimedia Commons / CC-BY-SA-3.0
534	Herry Lawford / Flickr / CC-BY-2.0
539t	Australian Museum / Wikimedia Commons / CC-BY-SA-3.0
539b	Henry Rzepa / Wikimedia Commons / CC-BY-SA-2.5
541	Notgrass Family
547	Steinsky / Wikimedia Commons / CC-BY-SA-3.0
561l	Mark Fosh (foshie) / Flickr / CC-BY-2.0
561r	Philip Halling / Wikimedia Commons / CC-BY-SA-2.0
562t	Bappah / Wikimedia Commons / CC-BY-SA-3.0
563	Library of Congress
564t	Dbown100 / Wikimedia Commons / CC-BY-3.0
564b	Nathanael Shelley (nathanaels) / Flickr / CC-BY-2.0
566	Bjørn Christian Tørrissen / Wikimedia Commons / CC-BY-SA-3.0
567	Pistachios: Paolo Galli / Wikimedia Commons / CC-BY-SA-3.0
567	Leeks: Björn König / Wikimedia Commons
567	Triclinium: Walters Art Gallery / Wikimedia Commons / CC-BY-SA-3.0
568t	Takeaway / Wikimedia Commons / CC-BY-SA-3.0
568b	Jean-Paul Barbier / Wikimedia Commons / CC-BY-SA-3.0
569b	Acroterion / Wikimedia Commons / CC-BY-SA-3.0
570	Hajime NAKANO (jetalone) / Flickr / CC-BY-2.0
571t	Bryan Allison bryangeek / Wikimedia Commons / CC-BY-SA-3.0
571b	USAID / Cafe Bom Dia
581	Library of Congress
585	Marc Ryckaert (MJJR) / Wikimedia Commons / CC-BY-3.0
586	Library of Congress
588	Bibliothèque Nationale de France
591	I, Sailko / Wikimedia Commons / CC-BY-SA-3.0
593	User:Mattes / Wikimedia Commons / CC-BY-SA-3.0
594b	Webster / Wikimedia Commons / CC-BY-SA-3.0
597	Library of Congress
599b	Hahaha / Wikimedia Commons / CC-BY-SA-2.5
600	Hans Bernhard (Schnobby) / Wikimedia Commons / CC-BY-SA-3.0
602	Gilbert G. Groud / Wikimedia Commons / CC-BY-SA-2.0 DE
603	Jastrow / Wikimedia Commons
604	Horta-Guinardó District Administration / Wikimedia Commons / CC-BY-SA-3.0
605	Library of Congress
606	Stacey Cavanagh, blogsession.co.uk / Flickr / CC-BY-2.0
607t	Jialiang Gao (peace-on-earth.org) / Wikimedia Commons / CC-BY-SA-3.0
611	Nikonic (Lantro Photography) / Flickr / CC-BY-2.0
613	Athena Flickr - Athena's Pix / Flickr / CC-BY-2.0
615	Quist / Wikimedia Commons / CC-BY-SA-3.0

Credits

619	CHeitz / Flickr / CC-BY-2.0
620	AlanMc / Wikimedia Commons
621	Library of Congress
623	Robert Cutts (pandrcutts) / Flickr / CC-BY-2.0
624	*George Müller of Bristol* / Kregel Publications
625t	*George Müller of Bristol* / Kregel Publications
626b	*George Müller of Bristol* / Kregel Publications
628	*George Müller of Bristol* / Kregel Publications
629	taylorandayumi / Flickr / CC-BY-2.0
630	Sarah777 / Wikimedia Commons
631t	Daikrieg el Jevi / Flickr / CC-BY-2.0
631b	Vmenkov / Wikimedia Commons / CC-BY-SA-3.0
632t	Photograph © Andrew Dunn, 5 November 2004. Website: http://www.andrewdunnphoto.com/
632b	Colin Smith / Wikimedia Commons / CC-BY-SA-2.0
633b	galio / Flickr / CC-BY-SA-2.0
634b	Marcin Cieślak (Saper) cc-by-25.jpg / Wikimedia Commons / CC-BY-2.5
635b	Christian Kath / Wikimedia Commons / CC-BY-SA-3.0
637	National Library of Ireland
638	Compassion International
642	The Corrie ten Boom Fellowship
643t	Bryce Edwards / Flickr / CC-BY-2.0
645	Adam Carr / Wikimedia Commons
646b	Mohan / Wikimedia Commons
649	Paul Krawczuk (p.j.k.) / Flickr / CC-BY-2.0
650b	Tedgrant / Wikimedia Commons
653	H. Raab (User:Vesta) / Wikimedia Commons / CC-BY-SA-3.0
656t	Prince Roy / Flickr / CC-BY-2.0
658t	historicair / Wikimedia Commons
659	Mike Peel (www.mikepeel.net) / Wikimedia Commons / CC-BY-SA-2.5
661	Dmitry A. Mottl / Wikimedia Commons / CC-BY-SA-3.0
662	Txo / Wikimedia Commons
669	Yogibear / Wikimedia Commons
671	Toni Frissell / Library of Congress
672	Kahjo-TZ / Wikimedia Commons
673	U.S. Department of Defense
676b	British Library
677t	Library of Congress
677b	Bibliothèque Nationale de France (four small images)
678	Library of Congress
679	Jean-Pol GRANDMONT / Wikimedia Commons / CC-BY-SA-3.0
680	Library of Congress
681t	U.S. Army Signal Corps
681b	National Archives (U.S.)
682r	Daniel Ullrich, Threedots / Wikimedia Commons / CC-BY-SA-3.0
683	Imperial Household Agency
684	Polish Institute and Sikorski Museum London
685	National Archives (U.S.)
686t	Imperial War Museums
687	Finland: Seppo Palander / Wikimedia Commons
687	Аркадий Зарубин / Wikimedia Commons / CC-BY-SA-3.0
687	Singapore: Schristia / Flickr / CC-BY-2.0
687	Egypt: Farawayman / Wikimedia Commons / CC-BY-3.0
687	Japan: Chris Gladis (MShades) / Wikimedia Commons / CC-BY-2.0
688	U.S. Army
689t	Library of Congress
689b	Poul-Werner Dam / Flickr / CC-BY-2.0
690t	Imperial War Museums
690b	Library of Congress
691	National Archives (U.S.)
693	663highland / Wikimedia Commons / CC-BY-SA-3.0
694	I, PHGCOM / Wikimedia Commons / CC-BY-SA-3.0
695	Leidenaartje / Wikimedia Commons
696b	Joi Ito / Flickr / CC-BY-2.0
697	Joe Mabel / Wikimedia Commons / CC-BY-SA-3.0
698	mrhayata / Flickr / CC-BY-SA-2.0
699t	liddybits / Flickr / CC-BY-2.0
699b	Shigeo Hayashi / Wikimedia Commons
700	Nepal: Prakaz wiki / Wikimedia Commons
700	Sri Lanka: Anton 17 / Wikimedia Commons / CC-BY-SA-3.0
700	New York: Oosoom / Wikimedia Commons / CC-BY-SA-3.0
700	India: Christopher Beland / Wikimedia Commons
700	England: Oosoom / Wikimedia Commons / CC-BY-SA-3.0
700	California: Debashis Pradhan / Wikimedia Commons / CC-BY-SA-3.0
701	David Manyua / United Nations
702	Library of Congress
703	Eckhard Pecher / Wikimedia Commons / CC-BY-2.5
705	Robert Knudsen / John F. Kennedy Library

707	U.S. Navy Lt. Morris	751	Abasaa / Wikimedia Commons
709b	National Archives (U.S.)	752	NASA
710	U.S. Air Force SSGT Herman Kokojan	753t	Shiva Kumar Khanal / Wikimedia Commons / CC-BY-SA-3.0
711t	RIA Novosti Archive, Image #859348 / Dmitryi Donskoy / CC-BY-SA-3.0	753b	Htoo Tay Zar / Wikimedia Commons / CC-BY-SA-3.0
711b	Richardfabi / Wikimedia Commons	755b	Library of Congress
713	NASA	756	Wagaung / Wikimedia Commons / CC-BY-SA-3.0
714t	NSSDC, NASA	757t	Dohnavur Fellowship
715	NASA	759t	Compassion International
716	Vatican: Lothar Wolleh / Wikimedia Commons / CC-BY-SA-3.0	759b	Feed My Starving Children (FMSC) / Flickr / CC-BY-2.0
716	Beatles: Ken & Nyetta / Flickr / CC-BY-2.0	760	Honka-Ossi / Wikimedia Commons / CC-BY-SA-3.0
716	Flag: Makaristos / Wikimedia Commons	761	Feed My Starving Children (FMSC) / Flickr / CC-BY-2.0
716	Books: McKay Savage / Flickr / CC-BY-2.0	762	Feed My Starving Children (FMSC) / Flickr / CC-BY-2.0
717	NASA STS-132	763	Artyominc / Wikimedia Commons / CC-BY-SA-3.0
719	Reagan Library	765	Liliana Amundaraín (arepa182) / Flickr / CC-BY-2.0
720	Reagan Library	766b	Agência Brasil / CC-BY-SA-3.0 BR
721	Reagan Library	767	National Archives (U.S.)
723	User:Conscious / Wikimedia Commons / CC-BY-SA-3.0	768	U.S. Department of Defense
724	Notgrass Family Collection	769t	National Museum of Health and Medicine / Flickr / CC-BY-2.0
725	Notgrass Family Collection	769b	Museo Che Guevara
726	Jarekt / Wikimedia Commons	770	Agência Brasil / CC-BY-SA-3.0
727	National Archives (U.S.)	771	presidencia.gov.ar / CC-BY-2.0
728t	RIA Novosti Archive, Image #854874 / Anatoliy Garanin / CC-BY-SA-3.0	772t	Uwebart / Wikimedia Commons / CC-BY-SA-3.0
728b	www.leningradschool.com / Leningradartist / CC-BY-SA-3.0	772b	Paige Morrison / Wikimedia Commons / CC-BY-SA-2.5
729	Dutch National Archives / Harry Pot / CC-BY-SA-3.0 NL	773	Enrique Dans (edans) / Flickr / CC-BY-2.0
733	Brooklyn Church	774t	Nestor Lacle (Nestor's Blurrylife) / Flickr / CC-BY-2.0
735	Jesse (jjcb) / Flickr / CC-BY-2.0	774b	National Archives (U.S.)
737	Thomas.fanghaenel / Wikimedia Commons / CC-BY-SA-3.0	775t	Library of Congress
738	Library of Congress	775b	Gustavo Benítez / Presidencia de la República (Mexico)
741t	People's Republic of China	776	Zapata / Wikimedia Commons / CC-BY-SA-3.0
741b	U.S. Army (Tim Hipps, FMWRC) / Flickr / CC-BY-2.0	777t	Erik Cleves Kristensen / Flickr / CC-BY-2.0
743	© Jorge Royan http://www.royan.com.ar / Wikimedia Commons / CC-BY-SA-3.0	779	KANDU / Wikimedia Commons / CC-BY-SA-3.0
744b	David Castor / Wikimedia Commons	781t	Markus Leupold-Löwenthal / Wikimedia Commons / CC-BY-SA-3.0
745	Dharmadhyaksha / Wikimedia Commons / CC-BY-SA-3.0	781b	Agência Brasil / CC-BY-SA-3.0 BR
746b	Romanian Communism Online Photo Collection	783t	Francisco Anzola / Flickr / CC-BY-2.0
747t	Fraz.khalid1 / Wikimedia Commons	783b	Valter Campanato, Agência Brasil / CC-BY-SA-3.0 BR
747b	Balaram Mahalder / Wikimedia Commons / CC-BY-SA-3.0	784t	David Stanley (D-Stanley) / Flickr / CC-BY-2.0
		784b	John Walker (j.o.h.n. walker) / Flickr / CC-BY-2.0
		786t	Congreso de la Republica del Perú / Flickr / CC-BY-2.0
		786b	John Seb Barber / Flickr / CC-BY-2.0

Credits

787	Elena Hermosa, Trocaire / Flickr / CC-BY-2.0
788t	Richie Diesterheft (puroticorico) / Flickr / CC-BY-2.0
788b	Gleilson Miranda, Secretaria de Comunicação do Estado do Acre FUNAI / CC-BY-SA-2.5 BR
789	Alison McKellar / Flickr / CC-BY-2.0
791	Radio Okapi / Flickr / CC-BY-2.0
793t	Koloniales Bildarchiv
793b	Eric Gaba / Wikimedia Commons / CC-BY-SA-3.0
794b	Franzfoto / Wikimedia Commons / CC-BY-SA-3.0
796t	Dominik Schwarz / Wikimedia Commons / CC-BY-SA-3.0
797r	Erik (HASH) Hersman (whiteafrican) / Flickr / CC-BY-2.0
797l	Shealah Craighead / White House
798	Oxfam East Africa / Flickr / CC-BY-2.0
799t	Achilli Family [Journeys / Flickr / CC-BY-2.0
799b	Alan (A.Davey) / Flickr / CC-BY-2.0
800t	Hulivili / Wikimedia Commons / CC-BY-2.0
800b	Tropenmuseum of the Royal Tropical Institute (KIT) / CC-BY-SA-3.0
801t	Maria Dyveke Styve / Wikimedia Commons / CC-BY-SA-3.0
801b	Ahron de Leeuw / Flickr / CC-BY-2.0
802	SKopp / Wikimedia Commons
803t	William Warby (wwarby) / Flickr / CC-BY-2.0
803b	Ganesh Raghunathan / Flickr / CC-BY-2.0
804t	Jerzy Strzelecki / Wikimedia Commons / CC-BY-SA-3.0
805	Feet: Paul Shaffner / Flickr / CC-BY-2.0
805	Cheetahs: Siddharth Maheshwari / Wikimedia Commons / CC-BY-SA-3.0
805	Elephants: Sumit.pamnani / Wikimedia Commons
805	Wildebeest: T. R. Shankar Raman / Wikimedia Commons / CC-BY-SA-3.0
805	Giraffes: Maureen Didde (maureen lunn) / Flickr / CC-BY-2.0
806	N. Feans / Flickr / CC-BY-2.0
807t	Simisa / Wikimedia Commons / CC-BY-SA-3.0
807b	Hein waschefort / Wikimedia Commons / CC-BY-SA-3.0
808b	National Army Museum (UK)
809t	Ullischnulli at the German language Wikipedia / Wikimedia Commons / CC-BY-SA-3.0
809b	Bundesarchiv (Bild 183-1986-0920-016) / CC-BY-SA-3.0 DE
810t	U.S. Navy Photo by Mass Communication Specialist 2nd Class Jesse B. Awalt
810b	Stephen Neilson / Wikimedia Commons / CC-BY-SA-2.0
811t	Carol M. Highsmith Archive / Library of Congress
811b	Meraj Chhaya / Flickr / CC-BY-2.0
813	Einsamer Schütze / Wikimedia Commons / CC-BY-SA-3.0
814	walter callens retlaw (Snellac Photography) / Flickr / CC-BY-2.0
815	Travcoa Travel / Flickr / CC-BY-2.0
817	U.S. Navy Photo by Mass Communication Specialist 2nd Class Justin Stumberg
819	IICD / Flickr / CC-BY-2.0
820	Yosomono preetamrai / Flickr / CC-BY-2.0
821tl	Al Jazeera English / Flickr / CC-BY-SA-2.0
821tm	High Contrast / Wikimedia Commons / CC-BY-3.0 DE
821tr	Arian Zwegers / Flickr / CC-BY-2.0
821m	Ewloskalw / Wikimedia Commons / CC-BY-SA-3.0
821bl	Omaranabulsi / Wikimedia Commons / CC-BY-SA-3.0
821bm	Victorgrigas / Wikimedia Commons / CC-BY-SA-3.0
821br	Evelyn Proimos / Flickr / CC-BY-2.0
822	U.S. Navy / Chief Photographer's Mate Eric J. Tilford
823	Biberbaer / Wikimedia Commons / CC-BY-SA-3.0
824	James Gordon (james_gordon_losangeles) / Flickr / CC-BY-2.0
825	Oregon State University Special Collections & Archives
826	Photography Department, Government Press Office, State of Israel
827	SAAR YAACOV GPO israel / Wikimedia Commons / CC-BY-SA-3.0
829	U.S. Geological Survey / Map-It http://woodshole.er.usgs.gov/mapit/
831	Brad Voeller
832t	Micklyn Le Feuvre http://www.redbubble.com/people/micklyn
832b	Hebron Ministries / Juan Carlos Barahona
833t	Mary Evelyn McCurdy
833b	Godfrey and Olga Kyazze
835	Andrea Schaffer / Flickr / CC-BY-2.0
836r	Jonathan Bowen / Wikimedia Commons / CC-BY-SA-3.0
837t	rob koopman (koopmanrob) / Flickr / CC-BY-SA-2.0
837b	Abhijeet Rane / Flickr / CC-BY-2.0
838t	AlejandroLinaresGarcia / Wikimedia Commons / CC-BY-SA-3.0
838b	Central Intelligence Agency / Modifications by TimeZonesBoy / Wikimedia Commons

839t	Pirkheimer / Wikimedia Commons / CC-BY-SA-3.0
840	Bug de l'an 2000 / Wikimedia Commons / CC-BY-SA-3.0
841	ARC - The Alliance of Religions and Conservation / Flickr / CC-BY-2.0
842	Ann Wuyts (vintagedept) / Flickr / CC-BY-2.0
843b	Wycliffe Global Alliance / Heather Pubols
844	Alan (A.Davey) / Flickr / CC-BY-2.0
845	International Care Ministries / Feed My Starving Children (FMSC) / Flickr / CC-BY-2.0
847	Jennifer Boyer (Anosmia) / Flickr / CC-BY-2.0
849	P. León / Flickr / CC-BY-2.0
850	Joni and Friends International Disability Center
851	Dept of Foreign Affairs and Trade (DFAT photo library) / Flickr / CC-BY-2.0
852	Laura Dye / Flickr / CC-BY-2.0
853	Brian Gratwicke / Flickr / CC-BY-2.0
855	gadgetdude / Flickr / CC-BY-2.0
856	Noble36 / Wikimedia Commons
858	National Archives (U.S.)
860	SteveRwanda / Wikimedia Commons / CC-BY-SA-3.0
861	Christian Haugen / Flickr / CC-BY-2.0
862	Library of Congress
863	Dilma Rousseff (Roberto Stuckert Filho / PR) / Flickr / CC-BY-SA-2.0
864	Sherwood Pictures
866	Apdency / Wikimedia Commons
867t	User:Vmenkov / Wikimedia Commons / CC-BY-SA-3.0
867b	(cc) David Berkowitz - www.about.me/dberkowitz / www.marketersstudio.com / Flickr / CC-BY-2.0
868t	Andrew Turner / Flickr / CC-BY-2.0
868b	Kay Adams (kayadams.com) / Flickr / CC-BY-2.0
869	SAT-7 (http://www.sat7usa.org)
871	Jwh / Wikimedia Commons / CC-BY-SA-3.0 LU
872	Edal Anton Lefterov / Wikimedia Commons / CC-BY-SA-3.0
881	Josep Renalias / Wikimedia Commons / CC-BY-SA-3.0

Bible Quotations in Lessons 84-85

Scripture quotations marked TLB are taken from *The Living Bible* copyright © 1971. Used by permission of Tyndale House Publishers, Inc., Carol Stream, Illinois 60188. All rights reserved.

Scripture quotations marked Amplified Bible are taken from the Amplified® Bible, Copyright © 1954, 1958, 1962, 1964, 1965, 1987 by The Lockman Foundation. Used by permission. (www.Lockman.org)

Scripture quotations marked NIV are from THE HOLY BIBLE, NEW INTERNATIONAL VERSION®, NIV® Copyright © 1973, 1978, 1984, 2011 by Biblica, Inc.® Used by permission. All rights reserved worldwide.

Scripture quotations marked (NLT) are taken from the Holy Bible, New Living Translation, copyright © 1996, 2004, 2007 by Tyndale House Foundation. Used by permission of Tyndale House Publishers, Inc., Carol Stream, Illinois 60188. All rights reserved.

Scripture taken from The Message. Copyright © 1993, 1994, 1995, 1996, 2000, 2001, 2002. Used by permission of NavPress Publishing Group.

The Hawai'i Pidgin translation is Copyright 2000, Wycliffe Bible Translators. All rights reserved.

Joanina Library, University of Coimbra, Portugal (18th Century)

Index

Pages 1-434 are in Part 1. Pages 435-874 are in Part 2.

Abraham (Abram), 28, 35, 38-39, 55, 69, 75-91, 143, 281, 284, 290, 303, 383-384, 455, 511, 566, 574, 603, 629, 661, 788, 813, 824-825
Adam and Eve, 28, 31-32, 42, 89, 535, 652, 654, 845
Afghanistan, 33, 240, 261, 720, 743, 747
Africa, 15, 37-38, 205-206, 261, 383-384, 401, 457, 486, 496-497, 502-503, 512, 538, 562, 602, 611, 649, 673, 682, 684, 687, 703, 791-816, 829, 832-833, 852, 855, 860, 869
Agriculture (and Farming), 7, 12, 37, 53, 56, 61, 148, 164, 193-194, 197, 201, 205, 207, 209, 220, 232, 237-239, 249-250, 367, 396-397, 437, 478, 568, 571, 588, 591, 611-613, 620, 635, 673, 708, 723-724, 728, 745-747, 775, 782-785, 795-796, 802, 841
Aircraft, 71, 583, 634-635, 674, 684, 706
Alaska, 207, 589, 607, 694
Alexander (the Great), 160, 162-163, 172, 191, 222-223, 230, 240, 253, 261, 279, 282, 495, 570, 632, 855
Alfred (King), 389-390, 392
Al-Qaeda, 822, *see also* September 11, 2001, Attacks
Algeria, 261, 795, 829, 862
Ambassadors, *see* Diplomacy
America, United States of, *see* United States of America
Americas, The, 207-208, 270, 493, 496-497, 503, 607, *see also* North America *and* South America
Anabaptists, 477-480
Anglican, see Church of England
Antarctica, 276, 607, 674
Apartheid, 703, 809-812, 866
Aqueducts, 247, 265

Argentina/Argentinian, iii, 208, 240, 617, 806, 769, 778, 782, 821
Aristotle, 222, 228-229, 386, 425-427, 521-523, 525, 632, 662, 665
Armada, see Spanish Armada
Armenia, 174, 401, 481
Arms and armor, 52, 160, 200, 240, 332, 349, 397, 408, 420, 422, 545, 577, 592, 596, 673, 676-678, 681, 709, 749, 775, 826, 828, 857, *see also* Battles in art
Art and architecture
    African, 205-207, 261, 423, 452, 602, *see also* Ethiopian
    Bulgarian, 99, 285, 842
    Byzantine, 222, 295, 380, 389
    Chinese, 166, 185, 190, 193-203, 298, 452, 739
    Czech, 76, 403, 430
    Danish, xvi, 103, 303, 396
    Dutch, 83, 96-97, 102, 106-107, 109-110, 116-117, 142, 173, 179, 181-182, 300, 320, 324, 328, 333, 371, 400, 441, 462, 475, 500, 508, 527, 550, 555, 573
    Egyptian, 34, 49, 57-61, 63, 422, 455
    English, 111, 177, 311, 392, 432, 439, 499, 507, 533-534, 542, 548, 561, 564, 649, 659, 794, 872
    Ethiopian, 31, 82, 799-800
    European (ancient), 34, 36, 171, 209-210
    Flemish, 89, 96, 354, 601
    Frankish, 113, 145, 377

Art and architecture *(continued)*
    French, 140, 210, 213, 215, 228, 252, 257, 327, 353, 370, 379, 421, 456, 458, 528, 543, 548, 556-558, 579, 601-603, 635, 657, 740
    German, 95, 127, 130, 141, 147, 153, 169, 174, 227, 282, 296, 299, 302, 321, 347, 399, 425, 436, 459, 465, 473, 516, 594-595, 600-603, 645, 663, 669
    Greek, 217, 219-220, 226, 232-233, 237, 242, 244-245, 317, 599-601, 603
    Hungarian, 75, 347
    Indian, iv, 32, 188-189, 486, 744-745
    Irish, v, 619-620
    Islamic, 15, 31, 33, 70, 207, 230, 836, 380, 382-388, 744, 747
    Italian, 44-45, 77-79, 81-82, 129, 139, 163, 166, 178, 214, 225, 229, 243, 258, 269, 287, 291, 315, 326, 334, 357, 362-363, 366, 402, 435, 437, 438, 445, 449-451, 453-454, 461, 463, 527, 532, 582, 591, 600-601, 603-604, 633, 639
    Japanese, 171, 290, 423, 495, 562, 693-697
    Jewish, 80, 127, 132, 149, 282, 307, 352 (temple treasures), 517
    Korean, 148, 367
    Macedonian, 275, 380, 872
    Native American, 34, 92, 120, 148, 171, 207-208, 391, 423, 452, 781-783
    Pacific Islands, 34, 208, 452, 539, 867
    Persian, 31, 95, 157, 159-160, 164, 167, 180, 383-384, 386, 632
    Polish, 351, 359
    Roman, 165, 247, 249, 253, 255-256, 259, 264, 266-267, 271, 320, 322, 346, 348-349, 352, 354, 364, 567
    Russian/Soviet, 18, 70, 179, 281, 284, 319, 336, 337, 378, 410, 486, 577, 589, 602, 607, 641, 647, 664, 687, 728, 731, 733, 839
    Southeast Asian, 295, 309, 452
    Spanish, 105, 134, 250, 306, 329, 410, 433, 445, 475, 505, 601-602, 662
    Swiss, 432, 602, 663
    Viking, 393-396
    Other, 47, 92, 134-137, 174, 214, 289, 314, 486
    see also Cathedrals and Church Buildings
Arthur, King, 210
Aryans, 187-190
Ashoka, 187, 191
Assyria/Assyrian, 16, 55, 58, 68-69, 131, 134, 137-138, 156, 159, 213-216, 292, 603, 814, 816, 824
Astronomy, 41, 62, 194, 196, 203, 261, 279, 289, 386, 455, 521-522, 527-530, 533, 631, 662-663, 836-837
Athens, 218-219, 221-229, 232-239, 241-244

Atlantic Ocean, 136, 251, 396, 495-497, 499, 502-504, 510, 582, 611, 617, 674, 677, 709, 714, 769, 853
Atomic bomb, *see* Nuclear weapons
Australia, 71, 92, 209, 479, 611, 617, 649, 684, 687, 703
Austria, 132, 171, 213, 283, 458, 475, 507, 547, 558, 568, 579, 581-585, 587, 591-595, 605, 656-658, 674-678, 683, 685, 774
Austria-Hungary, *see* Austria and Hungary
Aztecs, 207, 209, 423, 498, 782, 840
Banking, 417, 438-439, 497, 500, 555, 581, 768
Baptists, 474, 479-480, 755-756, 843-844, 864
Battles in art, 16, 70, 160, 222, 232-233, 240, 252, 347, 363, 405, 475, 499, 507-508, 548, 550, 557, 577, 579, 605, 739, 766, 800, *see also* Arms and armor
Beatles, The, 8, 716
Bede (English historian), 41, 211
Bedouins, 86, 401
Belgium, 426, 449, 475, 508, 582, 585, 600, 613, 676, 684, 793, 796
Ben-Gurion, David, 282
Berlin Wall, 705, 711, 722, 734
Bermuda, 447
Bethlehem, 115-119, 139, 257, 281, 366
Bible manuscripts, 21, 155, 177, 223, 277, 294-295, 300, 311, 441, 447, 481, 575, 667
Bible translation, 112, 179, 211, 290, 339, 359, 371, 401, 431-432, 441, 447, 454, 470, 481-485, 498, 607, 663, 755-756, 804, 843
Bismarck, Otto von, 591, 595-597, 605, 674, 678
Boats, *see* Ships
Boer War, 689, 808
Boers, 689, 807-809
Bohemia, *see* Czech
Bolivia, 778-784
Bonhoeffer, Dietrich, 491, 685, 855
Brahe, Tycho, 521-522
Brazil/Brazilian, iii, 385, 486, 496, 504, 537, 571, 635, 763, 806, 770, 782-783, 785, 788, 842-843, 863
Britain/British, *see* Great Britain
British East India Company, 499, 745, 756
Buddhism, 189-192, 196, 198, 240, 367, 452, 486, 695-697, 700, 737-738, 743, 749, 752, 756, 868
Bulgaria, 711, 779, 842
Burma (also Myanmar), 513, 611, 706, 752-753, 756
Byzantine Empire, 375, 379-381, 387, 405, 411, 419-420, 437, 440, 502, 570, 631, 825
Calvin, John, 471, 473-479, 852
Calvinists (Reformed), 479, 483, 508, 553
Cambodia, 452, 710
Canada, 11, 391, 397, 479, 498-499, 562, 611, 615, 617, 674, 687, 695, 703, 716, 754, 757, 770, 776, 842

Index

Canary Islands, 289, 504
Caribbean, 503-505, 611, 633, 721, 765-766, 768-770, 796
Carmichael, Amy, 756-757
Carthage (city/empire), 137, 148, 240, 251, 304, 347
Castles, 408, 414-415, 419, 437, 469, 554, 594, 697, 749
Castro, Fidel, 769-770
Catacombs, 271, 317, 360, 456, 600
Cathedrals, 31, 63, 267, 297, 346, 377, 403, 406, 410, 426, 428, 474, 580, 600, 690, 784, 861
Catholic Church, see Roman Catholic Church
Ceaușescu, Nicolae, 5, 746
Celts/Celtic, 210, 406, 481
Central America, 7, 101, 209, 367, 391, 497-498, 631, 646, 721, 776, 781-782
Cervantes, Miguel de, 445
Ceylon, see Sri Lanka
Chile, 240, 497, 537, 766-767, 778
China/Chinese, 13-14, 58, 92, 101, 120, 132, 166, 185, 190-204, 206, 240, 261, 298, 346, 367, 385-386, 391, 400, 401, 422, 424, 443-444, 452, 495-496, 500, 503-504, 514, 538-539, 568, 570-571, 573, 607, 629-631, 633-634, 647-648, 664, 683-684, 688, 693, 695, 703, 709-710, 713, 716, 737-742, 750-752, 755, 757-758, 801-802, 844, 851, 867
Church buildings, 31, 237, 267, 275-276, 278, 296, 313, 330, 354, 356, 358, 360, 366-367, 369, 371, 373, 380, 391, 395, 397-399, 431, 441, 444, 473, 564, 619, 638, 756, 761, 772, 799, 821, 842, 844, 847, 853, 855, 858, 867, 868, 871, 872, see also Cathedrals
Church of England/Anglican, 17, 40, 472, 475, 482, 484, 548, 550-551, 619-620, 649, 756, 810, 841, 843, 851, 853, 855
Churchill, Winston, 684, 689-692, 708
Cicero, 258, 441, 445, 662
Clothing, 92, 202, 238, 262, 264, 376, 393, 438, 535-539, 562, 696-697, 781, 783-784, 803-804, 807
Coins, 159, 161, 192, 198-199, 206, 237, 257, 271, 279, 303, 316, 364, 366, 390, 417, 533, 799
Cold War, 705-730, 747, 753
Colombia, 765, 769, 771, 778-779
Columbus, Christopher, 410, 496-497, 502-506, 515, 568
Communism, 16, 18, 594, 606, 643-648, 677, 679, 681-683, 685, 688, 706-716, 720-722, 728-730, 732, 740-742, 751, 753, 769-770, 801, 842
Computers, 446-447, 688, 729, 819-820, 840, 843
Concentration camps, 491, 642, 685, 808, 858-859
Confucius/Confucianism, 195-197, 664, 737

Congo (also Kongo), 38, 452, 796, 843
Copernicus, Nicolaus, 522-523, 528
Cranach, Lucas (the Elder), 31, 141, 282, 470, 663
Creation, 22-23, 27-30, 40-41, 44, 47, 653-654, 660
Crete, 120, 218-219, 243, 601
Croatia, 22, 346, 853
Cromwell, Oliver, 548-549
Cuneiform writing, 53-54, 62
Cyprus, 136, 321, 323, 331-334
Cyrus (the Great), 128, 132, 159-160, 162, 169-170, 172, 177, 240
Czech (also Bohemia and Czechoslovakia) people and nation, 403, 430, 432, 459, 587, 593, 650, 656, 663, 683-684, 709, 711
Da Vinci, Leonardo, see Leonardo
Dance, 32, 99, 207, 225, 454-455, 571, 665, 696, 725, 738, 784-785, 800, 807, 852
Daniel, 69, 128, 162, 172-176
Dante Alighieri, 416
Danube River, 219, 737
David, King, 42, 46, 79, 115, 119, 128, 130-131, 134-135, 139-145, 156, 281, 283-284, 297, 303-304, 384, 450-451, 454, 668, 682, 828, 857
Dead Sea, 91, 280, 352, 358
Democracy, 223, 233-234, 298, 552, 560, 681, 686, 708, 711, 737, 747, 751, 780, 824, 829, 852
Denmark/Danish, vi, 212, 389-397, 522, 551, 595, 684, 782
Devil, see Satan
Dickens, Charles, 297, 520, 615, 626, 819
Diplomacy (also Ambassadors), 12, 71, 132, 222-223, 282, 333, 367, 424, 524, 555, 584, 592, 595, 736, 738-741, 827, 830
Dreyfuss Affair, 588
Dunant, Henry, 702, 851
Dutch, see Netherlands, The
Easter Island, 452, 867
Eastern Orthodox, see Orthodox Churches
Ecuador, 766, 778-779, 781-783, 844
Egypt/Egyptians, 4, 15, 34-35, 47, 49, 53, 56-64, 86, 91, 94-98, 101-103, 105-113, 120, 122-123, 134, 137, 146-147, 160, 166, 171, 187-188, 222, 224, 226, 245, 251, 253, 256, 275, 300, 358, 360, 364, 379, 386, 387, 401, 422, 443, 455, 512, 516, 533, 535, 538, 570, 579-580, 600, 603, 611, 618, 629, 631-632, 664, 687, 779, 793, 795, 798-800, 813-816, 821, 826-830, 836, 839
Einstein, Albert, 658
El Salvador, 770, 789
Elizabeth I, 483, 508-510
Elizabeth II, 692, 716

England/English, 5, 9, 13, 17, 40, 101, 136, 209-212, 248, 267, 377, 389-392, 397, 399-400, 405-408, 412-416, 422-423, 425, 427, 430, 432, 436-438, 441, 445, 457-458, 471-472, 474, 479, 481-484, 497-500, 502-503, 507-510, 519-520, 522-525, 531-534, 538-539, 547-554, 556, 561-564, 569-571, 581, 586, 592, 600, 611-630, 632-633, 635, 644, 649-650, 657, 663, 665, 676-677, 684, 689-690, 700, 706, 713, 716, 723, 742, 755, 808, 820, 837, 839, 841, 844, 852, 856, 867-868, *see also* Great Britain *and* United Kingdom

English Channel, 408, 509, 684

English Language, 12-13, 211, 223, 248, 259, 277, 386-387, 390, 402, 406, 416-417, 420, 432, 454, 481-485, 533, 587, 644, 691, 754, 756-757, 807, 852

Ethiopia, 206, 315, 340, 571, 683, 791, 793, 795, 798-802, 814-815

Evangelicalism, 485, 720, 784, 841-842

Evolutionary Theory, 38, 41-42, 47, 52, 535, 649-655

Exodus, The, 62, 69, 98, 105-108, 114, 287, 813

Falkland Islands, 617

Farming, *see* Agriculture

Ferdinand of Aragon, 409-410, 496, 503-505, 507

Feudalism, 375, 379, 405, 407, 411-418, 420, 442, 548, 556, 580, 587

Film, *see* Movies

Finland, 687, 761

Flags, 594, 682, 711, 716, 791, 802

Formosa, *see* Taiwan

France/French, 8, 12, 18, 31, 34, 36, 209-211, 247, 266, 347, 353, 354, 376, 378-379, 386, 397, 405-408, 412-414, 416-417, 421-422, 425, 428, 430-432, 437, 441, 444-445, 450, 453, 471, 473, 475, 483, 485, 497, 498-499, 502, 508, 510, 523, 526, 536-537, 539, 547, 549-550, 552-562, 564, 566, 568-571, 579-588, 592-597, 601, 612-613, 618, 627, 630, 632, 634-635, 665, 674-681, 683-684, 689-691, 702, 710, 739-740, 745, 752, 765, 767, 769, 774, 779, 793, 795-796, 819-820, 825-826, 829-830, 840, 842, 862

French and Indian War, 499, 551, 555

French Revolution, 347, 354, 520, 523, 526, 545, 553-560, 591, 614, 772, 777

Galileo Galilei, 522-523, 527-530, 837

Gandhi, Indira, 746-747

Gandhi, Mohandas (Mahatma), 700, 746

Garden of Eden, 3, 28-29, 52, 535, 599, 661, 856

Garibaldi, Giuseppe, 592-593

Gautama Buddha, *see* Buddhism

Geneva Bible, 483, 490

Germanic tribes, 210, 212, 346-347, 375, 412

Germany, 142, 188, 220, 344, 376-378, 386, 393, 395, 399, 408-409, 411, 414, 417, 422, 431-432, 438, 444, 456, 458-460, 467-472, 475, 477, 479, 482, 491, 497, 507, 522, 525, 532, 537, 551, 568, 585, 587-588, 591, 593-597, 600-601, 612-613, 627, 630, 634-635, 643-646, 652, 658, 663, 665, 668-669, 673-688, 690-691, 703

Ghana, 206, 513, 819

Gorbachev, Mikhail, 711, 721-722

Great Britain/British, 8, 12, 50, 70-71, 210-211, 363, 378, 389-390, 395, 397, 399, 407, 457, 475, 479, 499-500, 510, 520, 524, 548, 550-551, 558, 561, 571, 579, 581-582, 584-585, 587, 597, 600, 607, 609-639, 674-692, 706, 708, 720, 738-739, 745-747, 752-757, 767, 774, 793-801, 804, 807-810, 824-829, 837, 839, 841, 843-844, 851, 856, *see also* England *and* United Kingdom

Great War, The, *see* World War I

Greece/Greeks, 52, 58, 101, 134, 148, 161-162, 169, 172, 191, 209-210, 215, 217-246, 250, 261, 263, 267, 317, 324, 328-329, 338, 341, 380, 401, 437, 455-456, 500, 512, 521, 535, 568, 570, 585, 630-631, 664, 678, 709, 799, 815, 824, 839, 842

Greek language, 22-23, 59, 78, 112, 123, 132, 136-137, 160, 163, 166, 202, 211, 261, 272, 277, 279, 287, 314, 319, 353, 356, 358, 361, 363, 365, 377, 381, 406, 419, 440-441, 445, 477, 481-484, 489, 523, 665, 755, 787, 836, 843

Greek philosophy, 228-231, 242-246, 267, 386, 662

Greenland, 378, 391, 394, 396-397, 849

Guatemala, 34, 208, 781, 783-784, 787, 832

Guevera, Che, 769

Gutenberg, Johann, 443-444

Hagar, 76, 83, 384, 824

Hagia Sophia, 330, 366, 373, 380, 438, 586

Haiti, 17, 369, 765-767, 778, 817, 822

Hannibal, 240, 251

Hawaii, 539, 589, 684, 833

Hebrew language, 2, 34, 40-41, 58, 112, 115, 123, 125, 128, 154, 170, 173, 177-178, 182-183, 211, 304, 359, 386, 447, 481-485, 509, 651, 664, 787

Henry of Portugal, Prince, 496

Henry VIII, 471-472, 482-483, 503, 508, 619

Herodotus, 161, 226, 235

Herzl, Theodor, 675, 682, 825

Hieroglyphics, 58-59, 208

Hinduism, 32, 101, 120, 188-192, 664, 743-746, 851

Hirohito, Emperor of Japan, 683, 703

Hiroshima, 685, 699-700

Hitler, Adolf, 188, 594, 681-685, 689-690, 855

Hittites, 55, 77, 87, 120, 122, 135, 138, 150, 187

Holland, *see* Netherlands, The

Index

Holy Roman Empire, 377-378, 409, 432, 439, 471, 503, 507, 594
Homer, 220, 225, 249, 445
Honduras, 7, 784
Hong Kong, 611, 738-739, 821, 845, 866
Houses, 51, 95, 185, 394, 414-415, 462, 511-514, 589, 623-626, 637, 656, 804
Hungary/Hungarians, 206, 378, 385, 459, 587, 593, 636, 674-676, 678, 709, 711, 825
Hus, Jan, 430, 432-434, 469, 482
Iceland, vii, 378, 394, 397, 502, 835
India/Indians (Asian), iv, 8, 12-13, 15, 41, 53, 101, 160, 166-167, 187-192, 209, 215, 222, 240, 367, 382, 385-387, 401, 422, 475, 495-496, 498-499, 505, 536, 538, 570-571, 611, 618, 630, 632, 643, 664, 676, 687, 689, 700, 706, 737-738, 743-747, 752, 754-757, 788, 808-809, 821, 851, 856, 866-867
Indian Ocean, 25, 423, 495-496, 631, 649
Indians (American), 7, 68, 85, 499, 504-506, 569, 607, 620, 695, 765, 767, 772, 781-785, 787-788, 843
Indonesia, 34, 209, 367, 385, 387, 530, 607, 752-753
Indulgences, 432, 467-469, 475
Indus River Civilization, 92, 187
Inquisition, 410, 427, 430, 432-433, 440, 475, 503, 509, 528-529
International expositions, 38, 614
Iran, 34, 69-70, 157, 163, 167, 170, 260, 630, 689, 716, 720, 770, 779, 828-829, *see also* Persia
Iraq/Iraqi, 28, 52, 68-71, 341, 455, 680, 703, 716, 826, 829
Ireland/Irish, 210, 304, 389, 395, 398, 549-550, 600, 612, 619-622, 630, 637, 787
Isaac, 69, 76-79, 82-83, 86-88, 303, 603
Isabella of Castille, 409-410, 496, 503-507
Ishmael, 76-77, 83 (image), 384, 824
Islam/Muslims, 5, 9, 14-17, 70, 77, 170, 202, 206-207, 241, 304, 308, 375-376, 378, 380, 382-388, 391, 401, 405, 409-410, 412, 419-423, 425-426, 437-438, 440, 486, 496, 502, 509, 521, 562, 571, 674, 729, 743-747, 753, 795-796, 798, 800-801, 824-825, 828-830, 832, 840, 844, 852, 855-856, 858, 868
Israel (ancient/medieval), 8-9, 13, 15, 66, 75, 78-79, 84, 99-156, 169-170, 261, 278-337, 352, 358, 366, 401, 419-422, 454, 511, 515-518, 567, 599, 629, 662, 760, 787, 813-816
Israel (modern), 14, 52, 91, 118, 135, 154, 177, 273, 282, 288, 292, 515, 517, 589, 675, 682, 702, 716, 720, 824-829, 840
Italy/Italian, 8, 45, 210, 240, 249-252, 255-258, 335, 337, 346-349, 358, 363, 375-376, 378, 380, 383, 386, 409, 412, 414, 416-417, 421-422, 426, 431, 438-441, 445, 449, 453, 456-458, 469, 471, 475, 496-497, 500, 502-503, 507, 522, 570-571, 579, 586, 591-593, 595, 600, 630, 633, 662, 665, 674, 676, 679, 681, 683-686, 738, 793, 795, 800-801, 821, 829, 838
Jacob, 42, 69, 73, 76-79, 87-88, 94-98, 101, 105, 172, 280, 303, 454, 629
Japan, 8, 13-16, 171, 240, 290, 423, 447, 479, 495, 503, 511, 536, 562, 570-571, 589, 607, 614, 630-631, 676, 683-687, 693-700, 703, 736, 739-741, 749-752, 756-758, 858
Jefferson, Thomas, 17, 551, 557, 564
Jerusalem, 15, 69, 80, 126, 130-132, 141-143, 145, 149, 162, 169-170, 176, 239, 252, 282, 284, 287, 292, 297, 299, 303-308, 313, 315-316, 318, 321-326, 329-333, 336, 351-352, 366, 377, 381, 383, 391, 419, 421-422, 485, 573-574, 629, 675, 678, 690, 761, 814-815, 825-828
Jews, 66, 70, 76-77, 108, 112, 126, 128, 132, 137, 162, 164, 170, 175, 177-184, 188, 245, 252, 260-261, 267, 279-283, 289, 292-293, 304-308, 313-337, 351-354, 358, 382, 384, 410, 421, 426, 470, 496, 588-589, 617, 624, 642-643, 656, 658, 664, 675, 682, 685-686, 729, 800, 815, 824-828, 835, 840
Joan of Arc, 408
John the Baptist, 281, 287, 289, 292, 296, 298, 316, 384, 456
Jordan River, 90, 102, 108, 110, 149, 291, 824, 829
Jordan, 52, 71, 332, 345, 826-829
Joseph (husband of Mary), 257, 281, 284, 305, 360, 815
Joseph (son of Jacob), 56, 60, 62, 87, 94-98, 101, 384, 813, 859
Joséphine (wife of Napoleon), 580-582
Josephus, 41, 252, 278
Judson, Adoniram, 755-756
Julius Caesar, 210, 252-253, 255-256, 345, 839, 855
Justinian, 259, 380
Kant, Immanuel, 525
Kenya, 803-805, 841, 868
Kongo, *see* Congo
Koran, *see* Qur'an
Korea (North and South), 13, 148, 171, 367, [Part 2] i, 443-444, 570, 688, 694, 709-710, 737, 739, 750-752, 831, 845
Korean War, 709-710, 723, 751-752
Latin America, 585, 763-790, 844, *see also* Mexico, South America, *and* Caribbean
Latin language, 21, 54, 142, 211, 249, 251, 259, 261, 268, 272, 333, 344, 358-359, 377, 386, 390, 406, 416-417, 419, 428, 431-432, 440-441, 444-445, 456, 470, 481-484, 509, 533, 567, 652, 663-665, 716
League of Nations, 679-680, 683, 801, 826

Lebanon, 71, 136, 147, 149-150, 266, 631, 720, 824, 826, 829
Lenin, Vladimir, 647, 707-708, 711
Leonardo, 449-453, 601, 634
Liberation theology, 646
Liberia, 793, 797
Libya, 160, 322, 349, 721, 794-795, 814-815, 829-830
Liddell, Eric, 757-758
Literature, 54, 59, 128, 133, 188, 211, 224-226, 243, 257, 359, 377, 380, 386-387, 399, 416, 423, 445, 520, 611, 644, 746, 754, 782, 862
Livingstone, David, 796
London, 9, 210, 248, 268, 297, 405, 417, 479, 483, 548, 561, 571, 611, 614-615, 624, 633, 636, 644, 659, 671, 692, 703, 754
Louis Philippe, King of France, 583, 586-588
Louis XIII, 553-554
Louis XIV, 547, 554-555, 584, 856
Louis XVI, 555-557
Luther, Martin, 41, 434, 436, 441, 465-472, 477-478, 482, 488, 594, 663, 852
Lutheran Church, 456, 475, 479, 593, 623, 643, 685
Maasai, 803-806
Macedonia/Macedonians, 218, 222-223, 242, 275, 328-329, 341, 380, 856, 872
Magellan, Ferdinand, 497
Malaysia, 566, 753
Mali, 15
Mandela, Nelson, 809, 811
Maori, 29, 339, 513
Maps (historic), vi, 37, 199, 215, 227, 240, 305, 394, 483, 493, 496, 502, 581, 584, 609, 621, 739
Maps (illustrations), 68, 138, 161, 191, 254, 383, 503, 672, 793, 829
Marco Polo, 424, 495, 503
Marie Antoinette, 557-559
Martyrs, 276, 353-354, 362, 408, 432, 480, 482, 733, 855, 859
Marx, Karl, 643-646, 657, 730
Marxism, 643, 646-648, 707-710, 721, 741, 769
Mary (mother of Jesus), 256, 281, 284, 289, 297-299, 305, 354, 358, 360, 365, 371, 384, 486, 505, 600, 815
Mayan Civilization, 101, 208-209, 391, 782, 784
Mecca, 304, 382-386, 828, 840
Medici Family, 438-439, 497, 530
Medicine, 15-16, 31, 45, 62-63, 120, 191, 202-203, 208, 227-228, 384, 386, 417, 523-524, 561, 649, 657, 717, 727, 752, 821-822, 851
Mediterranean Sea (and area), 54, 56, 75, 101, 136, 148, 165, 168, 211, 213, 220, 223, 239, 251, 269, 279, 320, 331, 334, 337, 348, 380-381, 397, 422, 438, 496, 502, 538, 579, 631, 633, 795, 828

Mesopotamia, 32, 52-55, 62, 65, 68-71, 75, 77, 103, 135, 137, 187, 194, 222-223, 603, 631, 826
Methodism, 841
Mexican War (with United States), 773-774
Mexico/Mexicans, 120, 208-209, 261, 367, 486, 498-499, 513, 571, 581, 587, 630, 677, 715, 765, 772-776, 781-782, 786, 838, 866
Michelangelo, 44, 119, 451
Middle East, 34, 37, 51, 76, 85-87, 119, 160-161, 168, 202, 223, 230, 269, 282, 308, 375, 383, 386, 419-422, 452, 502, 580, 586, 631, 680, 682, 813-814, 824-830, 836, 869, 872
Military, *see* Arms and armor *and* Battles in art
Mining, 211, 438, 775, 808
Missionaries, 316, 323-324, 326, 333-334, 377, 381, 395, 398-402, 447, 475, 498, 501, 507, 607, 617, 624, 627, 686, 742, 744-745, 749, 755-759, 788, 794, 796-797, 800, 804, 841-845, 855, 869
Moguls, 743-745
Monarchy, 65, 223, 407, 549-550, 553, 556-558, 560, 586, 588, 644, 710
Monasticism (also monasteries and monks), 72, 190, 211, 279, 344, 358-359, 360, 369-371, 377, 379, 389, 399, 405, 415, 430-432, 437, 441, 445, 468, 470, 472, 475, 481-482, 503, 507, 567, 571, 600, 664, 800, 837
Mongols/Mongolia, 70, 87-88, 194, 387, 411, 424, 486, 737-738, 743, 749-751, 825, 855, *see also* Mogul
Monks, *see* Monasticism
Morocco, 85, 136, 261, 795, 829
Moses, 37-41, 47, 64, 91, 101-102, 105-107, 109-114, 122-123, 287, 306, 383-384, 454, 515-517, 599, 629, 654, 668, 813-814, 873
Mosques, 15, 77, 207, 237, 380, 385-386, 388, 744, 747, 828, 868
Mother Teresa, 856
Movies, 253, 719, 754, 804, 864
Muhammad (founder of Islam), 382-385, 828
Music, 36, 86, 92, 139-140, 175, 207, 225, 349, 360, 393, 449, 454-460, 588, 665, 695-696, 716, 726, 728-729, 754, 784, 810, 844, 852, 863
Muslims, *see* Islam
Mussolini, Benito, 593, 681-685, 801
Myanmar, *see* Burma
Nagasaki, 685, 687, 700
Napoleon Bonaparte, 59, 410, 526, 553, 559-560, 579-584, 594, 766, 777, 795, 855
Napoleon III, 586-587, 592, 596, 774
Native Americans, *see* Indians (American)
Naval history, *see* Ships
Nepal, 661, 700
Netherlands, The (also Dutch and Holland), 344, 371, 375, 378, 400, 412, 415, 438, 441, 462, 471, 475,

Index

478-480, 498-500, 507-509, 514, 537-538, 550, 554-555, 558, 561-562, 568, 582, 585, 602, 632-633, 642, 663, 674, 677, 684, 687, 695, 749, 752-753, 793, 807, 837, 842, 866

New Zealand, 29, 339, 513, 569, 611, 617, 649, 684, 687, 703

Newton, Isaac, 58, 149, 523, 531-534, 564

Nile River, 15, 56-57, 59, 62, 101, 105-106, 110, 171, 358, 795

Nineveh, 69, 137, 213-215, 814

Noah, i, 32-34, 37, 40, 51, 58, 66, 75, 111, 384, 652

Nobel Prizes, 702, 746, 753, 810-811, 827, 862

Nobel, Alfred, 702

Nomads, 36, 51-52, 85-88, 207, 210, 240, 382-383, 803-804

Normans, 210, 212, 378, 395, 405-406, 414, 619

North America, 92, 120, 148, 261, 367, 391, 423, 457, 486, 495-499, 513, 562, *see also* Canada, Greenland, Mexico, *and* United States of America

North Korea, *see* Korea

Northern Ireland, 5, 611-612, 619-622, 756

Norway, 87, 212, 389, 393-397, 405, 607, 631, 674, 684, 861

Nuclear weapons (atomic weapons), 71, 658, 685, 688, 699, 709, 714, 721-722, 727, 729, 747, 829

Nuremberg Chronicle, 28, 90, 131, 211

Olmecs, 120, 208-209

Olympic Games, 148, 233, 455, 562, 604, 703, 741, 757, 767, 810

Orthodox Churches, 276, 380-381, 410-411, 419, 438, 588-589, 607, 706, 708, 729, 732-733, 840, 842

Ottoman Empire, 70, 380, 387, 437-438, 486, 502, 537, 579-580, 585-586, 592, 617, 620, 674-676, 678, 795, 824-826, 829, 856

Pacific Islands, 171, 452, 496, 535, 562, 631, 649, 686, 752, 851

Pacific Ocean, 497, 581, 588-589, 633, 649, 674, 684-685, 693, 739, 768, 772

Pakistan, 92, 387, 629, 746-747, 855

Palestine, *see* Israel

Palestinians, 154, 308, 827-829

Panama Canal, 633, 769-770, 822

Panama, 769, 772, 778-779, 781, 783

Parliament (development), 407, 550

Pascal, Blaise, 819-820

Pax Romana, 253, 263

Pearl Harbor, 15-16, 684, 736, 758

Peloponnesian War, 226, 229, 232-236

Pentecostalism, 784, 844

Pericles, 234-237

Persia, 31, 68-70, 72, 131, 157-184, 190, 206, 215, 222-223, 226, 233-234, 282, 386-387, 401, 424, 452, 500, 536, 568, 630, 632, 743, 814, 828, *see also* Iran

Persian Gulf, 52, 136, 871

Peru, 92, 171, 209, 423, 452, 538, 631, 646, 765-766, 778-779, 781-782, 784, 786

Petrarch, 445

Philip II, King of Spain, 507-510

Philippines, 15, 124, 148, 391, 497, 607, 686, 752-753, 759, 768, 842, 844

Philistines, 103, 134-135, 137-140, 143, 146, 154, 317, 826

Phoenecians, 9, 101, 136-138, 148, 223, 251, 570, 631

Pilate, Pontius, 260, 269, 271, 310, 336, 358, 365, 734

Planes, *see* Aircraft

Plato, 228-229, 386, 440-441, 662

Poland/Poles, 12, 23, 71, 142, 459, 478, 522, 562, 650, 678, 683-684, 685, 711

Pompeii, 160, 263, 265

Portugal/Portuguese, 452, 486, 495-498, 500, 502-505, 562, 581, 584, 744, 765-766, 793, 796, 800, 807, 811, 857

Post-modernism, 844, 861

Printing, 443-447, 456-457, 468, 481, 484, 538, 697, 737, 819-820

Protestant Reformation, *see* Reformation, Protestant

Prussia, 537, 547, 558, 582, 584, 587, 591, 593-596, 605, 623-624, 643, 663, 674

Psalms, 128, 141-142, 360, 444, 454-455, 498, 625, 668

Ptolemy, 163, 455, 521-522, 836

Punic Wars, 240, 251

Pyramids, 4, 15, 34, 58, 61-64, 92, 208, 391, 579, 814

Qur'an, 382, 384, 743, 828

Railroads (and Trains), 601, 611, 629-630, 633, 636, 675, 739, 767, 797, 808

Raphael, 163, 225, 243, 315, 334, 450, 601

Reagan, Ronald, 711, 719-722, 731, 734, 770

Red Cross, International, 682, 702, 851

Reformation, Protestant, 395, 401, 430-432, 441-442, 467-480, 486, 507, 593, 665, 845, 852

Rembrandt, 97, 173, 328, 573, 601

Renaissance, 375, 435-442, 445, 449-453, 456-458, 462-463, 467-468, 495, 591, 600-601, 604, 630, 665, 855

Rhodes, Cecil, 808

Rhodesia, *see* Zimbabwe

Roman Catholic Church, 5, 7, 16-17, 168, 297, 357-360, 375, 379, 401, 406, 409-410, 414, 419, 422, 425-434, 440-442, 456, 467-468, 470-472, 475, 477-478, 481-482, 484, 488, 508, 521-522, 527-529, 550, 553, 557, 559, 581, 585-588, 593, 619, 646, 656, 664, 681, 685, 695, 716, 729, 742, 746, 749, 767, 774-775, 784, 786-789, 800, 839, 842, 844, 853, 856-857

Roman Empire (and Republic), 70, 165, 191, 210-211, 223, 240, 242, 247-272, 279-280, 282-283, 292-293, 314, 316, 320, 325-327, 329-337, 343-356, 363-366, 375, 412, 456, 481, 500, 512, 535, 567, 599-600, 603, 630-631, 664, 681, 815, 824-825, 836, 839, 842, 844, 849-854

Roman roads, 263, 265, 325, 334, 337

Romania, 5, 356, 711, 714, 746, 842

Romanov Dynasty (Russia), 547, 588-589

Rome, City of, 70, 249, 256-257, 259, 263-264, 266-269, 271, 303, 314, 329-330, 347-348, 351-352, 357, 361, 371, 376-377, 389, 394, 398, 409, 411, 440, 468, 528, 580, 592-593, 681, 684, *see also* Roman Empire

Romero, Óscar, 789, 855

Roosevelt, Franklin, 689-691, 719, 770

Rosetta Stone, 59

Russia/Russians, 132, 276, 338, 378, 380-381, 384, 389, 397-398, 401, 410-412, 421, 459-460, 486, 536, 538, 547, 581-582, 584, 587, 588-589, 592, 594-595, 597, 607, 617-618, 647, 650, 664, 674-679, 684, 687, 693-694, 706-708, 717, 732-733, 737, 739-740, 750-751, 825, 839, 842, 855, *see also* Soviet Union

Rwanda, 860

Saddam Hussein, 70-71

Sahara Desert, 86, 495, 795

Saladin, 77, 421-422

Samaritans, 287, 292, 294-295, 306, 315, 570, 825

Sami people, 87, 536

Sarah (Abraham's wife), 55, 75-77, 79, 81, 83, 87, 89

Sarajevo, 675, 847

Satan (and Devil), 20-21, 32, 137, 143, 241, 295, 309, 334, 432, 461-464, 489, 605, 608, 702, 733

Saudi Arabia, 17, 369, 383, 716, 747, 828-830

Saxons, 210, 212, 389-390, 392, 395, 399-400, 405-406, 481

Scandinavia, 87, 378, 394-395, 402, 471, 475, 536, *see also* Denmark, Finland, Norway, *and* Sweden

Scotland/Scottish, 106, 210, 267, 400, 406, 423, 457, 471, 475, 483, 485, 508-509, 537, 548-549, 568, 612-613, 619, 630, 633, 636, 757-758, 796, 859

September 11, 2001, Attacks, 9, 14, 71, 89, 822

Shakespeare, William, 248, 445, 587

Ships, 33, 136, 147, 192, 201, 213, 234, 334, 396, 422, 438, 475, 495, 497, 499-500, 504-505, 507-510, 569, 607, 614, 631-633, 649, 674, 677, 738, 752, 768, 796, 807, 822

Siam, see Thailand

Sicily, v, 234, 251, 376, 591-592

Sikhism, 486, 747

Simón Bolívar, 766-767, 777-780

Singapore, 123, 611, 687, 735, 752-753, 845

Sistine Chapel, 119, 437, 451

Slavery, 17, 38, 52, 95, 97, 101, 118, 150, 199, 230, 238-239, 250-252, 262-263, 315, 328, 345, 348-349, 393, 399, 422, 486, 497-499, 501, 506, 539, 552, 562, 612, 616, 726, 733, 754, 765-767, 772, 777-778, 780, 796-798, 807, 813, 844, 850, 852

Socrates, 228-230, 235, 441, 662

Sodom and Gomorrah, 82, 89-93

Somalia, 423, 829

South Africa, 89, 208, 485, 611, 684, 687, 689, 703, 717, 746, 807-812, 821, 832, 842, 855, 866

South America, 36, 171, 209, 240, 423, 486, 495-499, 504-505, 611, 633, 649, 765-771, 777-785, 788, 842, *see also* Argentina, Brazil, Chile, Colombia, Ecuador, Uruguay, *and* Venezuela

South Korea, *see* Korea

South Sudan, [Part 2] iv, 798

Soviet Union (also U.S.S.R.), 16, 18, 89, 538, 594, 635, 641, 648, 680-684, 688, 690-691, 706-717, 720-730, 741, 747, 751, 769-770, 801, 824, 826, 839, 842, *see also* Russia

Space Exploration, 1, 20, 46, 530, 635, 713-717

Spain/Spanish, 7-9, 16, 37, 202, 208-210, 240, 251-252, 266, 346-347, 376, 380, 383, 386-387, 391, 397, 407, 409-410, 421-422, 431, 433, 441, 445, 471, 475, 496-499, 502-510, 538, 552, 555, 558, 571, 581, 584-585, 587, 595, 601, 607, 630, 632, 650, 662, 683, 752, 765-768, 772-774, 777-782, 784, 788, 793, 842, 796

Spanish Armada, 507-510, 617

Spanish-American War, 768-769

Sparta, 218, 221, 223, 232-235, 664

Sports, 148, 233, 367, 697, 703, 741, 743, 757, 765-766, 811

Sputnik, 709, 714

Sri Lanka, 240, 500, 687, 700, 760, 842

St. Peter's Basilica, 268, 371, 377, 440, 451, 467-468

Stalin, Josef, 689-691, 706, 708-709, 711, 733, 741, 855

Stamps, 396, 530, 709, 714

Subways, 615, 636

Sudan, 611, 689, 795, 798, 800, 803, 814, 829

Sumer/Sumerians, 51-55, 57, 61-62, 68, 71, 122, 187, 443, 599, 855

Sweden/Swedes, 278, 389, 393-395, 397, 588, 663, 761

Switzerland/Swiss, 130, 385, 471, 473-475, 477, 479, 483, 523, 538, 553, 585, 623, 630, 663, 681, 702, 839, 851

Syria/Syrians, 47, 52, 68, 71, 137, 222, 316, 318, 322, 331, 353, 358-359, 367, 379, 384, 419, 421, 454, 481, 512, 580, 600, 701, 799, 824, 826-827, 829-830

Taiwan, 148, 171, 340, 741

Tanzania, 803-805

Index

Taoism, 196, 697
Tasmania, 607
Temple (Jerusalem), 105, 125-127, 132, 143, 145, 147, 149-150, 162, 170, 252, 280, 282-284, 293, 299, 304-308, 314, 326, 330-331, 352, 661, 675, 825, 828
Temples, 53-54, 63, 135, 163, 170-171, 196, 209, 221, 227, 237, 244, 256, 265, 267, 330, 354, 561, 603, 664, 695, 697, 743, 756, 849, 868
Terrorism, 5, 9, 16, 71, 526, 620, 675, 702-703, 707, 721, 731, 838, 809, 822, 827, 829, 856-857
Thailand (and Siam), 568, 752, 754
Thatcher, Margaret, 721, 856
Thomas à Kempis, 344
Thomas Aquinas, 44-45, 425-429, 440, 662, 665
Torah, 23, 122, 123, 664
Tower of Babel, 34, 38, 68, 75, 89, 215, 314
Trade, 9, 51, 53, 56, 60-61, 75, 87, 92, 95, 131, 136-137, 148, 171, 187, 191-192, 194, 198, 206, 220, 223, 233, 250-251, 257, 265, 269, 325, 348, 384, 387, 393, 405, 408, 415-418, 422, 424, 437-438, 441-442, 444, 452, 495-498, 500, 505, 507-508, 551, 554-555, 561-562, 613, 618, 675, 738-739, 741, 744-745, 749-752, 768, 776, 803, 808, 822
Trains, *see* Railroads
Transdniestria, 711
Tristan da Cunha, 853
Trojan War/Troy, 101, 218-220, 225, 249
Tunisia, 86, 148, 207, 251, 401, 795, 824, 829
Turkey (modern), 55, 69-70, 85, 188, 219, 325, 330, 332, 334, 367, 373, 380, 386, 599, 676, 678, 826, 869
Turks, 87, 230, 419-421, 437-438, 502, 537, 743
Tyndale, William, 482, 484-485, 490
U.S.S.R., *see* Soviet Union
Uganda, 638, 833, 852, 855
Ukraine/Ukranians, 289, 292, 708, 711, 751
United Arab Emirates, 571, 829-830, 836
United Nations, 71, 688, 701, 709, 741, 797, 801, 826-827, 829-830
United States of America, 8-9, 12-13, 17-18, 38, 52, 70-71, 207-208, 238, 259, 267, 282, 341, 457, 459-460, 471, 474, 479, 484-485, 500, 509-510, 520, 537, 539, 550-555, 560-562, 564, 568-569, 581, 587, 589, 597, 599, 601-602, 604, 607, 611-613, 617, 619-620, 630, 663, 665-666, 670, 673-674, 677, 679-681, 683-686, 688-691, 707-711, 713-715, 717, 719-727, 729, 736, 739, 741, 747, 750-753, 754-756, 767-770, 773-777, 796-797, 811, 820-821, 826, 828-833, 837, 839-844, 852, 855, 858, 866-868
Uruguay, 765, 784, 786
Ussher, James, 40, 58
Vatican City, 425, 450, 528-529, 593, 716, 827
Vedas, The, 120, 189
Venezuela, 505, 716, 765, 771, 777-780
Victoria, Queen, 50, 616, 740
Vietnam, 4, 148, 423, 570, 710-711, 752
Vietnam War, 709-710
Volcanoes (eruptions), 40, 261, 264, 562, 607, 693
Waldensians, 431-432, 469
Wales/Welsh, 209-210, 358, 406, 612-613, 630, 650
Weapons, *see* Arms and armor
Wesley, Charles, 841
Wesley, John, 615, 841
Westminster Abbey, 405, 483, 534, 548, 855
Wilberforce, William, 616, 844
World Trade Center, 9, 822
World War I (Great War), 38, 70, 210, 380, 551, 590, 597, 621, 659, 673-682, 707, 745, 750, 774, 825-826, 829, 839
World War II, 8-9, 450, 491, 594, 681-692, 699-700, 703, 713, 736, 741, 746, 751, 753, 757-758, 829, 855, 858
World's Fair, *see* International expositions
Wycliffe, John, 432-434, 469, 482, 484, 490, 843, 856, 860
Zarathustra, *see* Zoroastrianism
Zedong, Mao, 647, 709, 716, 740-741
Ziggurats, 34, 53, 62
Zimbabwe (and Rhodesia), 206, 611, 808, 810
Zionist Movement, 675, 682, 825-826
Zoroastrianism, 163-168
Zulus, 807-808, 810

Also Available from Notgrass Company

Exploring America by Ray Notgrass

Your child can earn one year of credit in American history, English (literature and composition), and Bible. Engaging history lessons, combined with primary sources, provide a rich understanding of our nation's past. High school.

Exploring Government by Ray Notgrass

With a special emphasis on the U.S. Constitution, lessons cover Federal, state, and local government and also contemporary issues in American government. This one-semester course provides a half-year credit. High school.

Exploring Economics by Ray Notgrass

This one-semester course provides a half-year credit. It gives a practical and thorough overview of economic terms and concepts to help the student understand how our economy works and grasp contemporary economic issues from a free market perspective. High school.

America the Beautiful by Charlene Notgrass

This one-year American history, geography, and literature course combines the flexibility and richness of a unit study with the simplicity of a textbook-based approach to history. Ages 10-14.

Uncle Sam and You by Ray and Charlene Notgrass

This one-year civics and government course has daily lessons that teach your child about the foundations of American government, the elections process, and how Federal, state, and local governments work. Ages 10-14.

For more information about our homeschool curriculum and resources, call 1-800-211-8793 or visit www.notgrass.com.